EXPOSITORY STUDIES IN 1 CORINTHIANS

Titles by Ray C. Stedman in the "Discovery Books" Series:

Authentic Christianity (2 Corinthians 2:14–6:13)
Behind History (Parables of Matthew 13)
Death of a Nation (Book of Jeremiah)
Jesus Teaches on Prayer
The Queen and I (Book of Esther)
Riches in Christ (Ephesians 1–3)
The Servant Who Rules (Mark 1–8)
The Ruler Who Serves (Mark 9–16)
Spiritual Warfare (Ephesians 6:10–18)
Understanding Man (Genesis 2–3)
From Guilt to Glory (Romans) Vols. 1 and 2
Expository Studies in 1 John
Expository Studies in Job

A DISCOVERY BIBLE STUDY BOOK

EXPOSITORY STUDIES IN 1 CORINTHIANS

THE DEEP THINGS OF GOD

RAY C. STEDMAN

WORD BOOKS
PUBLISHER
4800 WEST WACO DRIVE
WACO, TEXAS
76703

Discovery Books are published by Word Books, Publisher, in cooperation with Discovery Foundation, Palo Alto, California.

ISBN 0-8499-2937-7
Library of Congress Catalog Card No. 81-51005

Printed in the United States of America

84760

Contents

5

6

EXPOSITORY STUDIES IN 1 CORINTHIANS

1
—
The Corinthian Crisis

Some years ago on a Sunday morning I was preaching on a section from the sixth chapter of 1 Corinthians. I was commenting on verse 9 where the apostle says,

> Do you not know that the unrighteous will not inherit the kingdom of God? Do not be deceived; neither the immoral, nor the idolators, nor adulterers, nor homosexuals, nor thieves, nor the greedy, nor drunkards, nor revilers, nor robbers will inherit the kingdom of God. And such were some of you.

I remember I was so struck by those words, "such were some of you," that I stopped and said to the congregation, "This was the make-up of the church at Corinth. These people had come out of this sordid background. Many of them, perhaps, still were struggling with much of the aftermath in their lives of these evil things. I am curious as to how many of you here have some of these things in your background." I then did a rather bold thing. I said, "If any of you have anything like this in your background I'd like to ask you to stand where you are quietly for a moment that we might know how much we're like the church at Corinth."

I did not know it, but a young man was present with us that morning who had never been in church before. He told me afterward that he had been converted at a recent Billy Graham Crusade, and he came to church with fear and trembling, not knowing what he was getting into. He said he heard me make that announcement, and he looked around to see if anyone would stand. At first no one did, but then a little old lady right on the aisle got up. Others then began to stand, and soon two-thirds of the congregation was standing. This young man said he looked around at that crowd and said to himself, "These are my kind of people!"

That story highlights a feeling I often have when reading these Corinthian letters. There is no church in the New Testament more like the churches of San Francisco, or New York, or Chicago than this Corinthian church. Corinth was a city of wealth and culture, at the crossroads of the Roman Empire, through which all the trade and commerce of the Empire passed. It was a city of beauty, a resort city, but it was also a city of prostitution and passion. It was devoted to trade and commerce, but also the worship of the goddess of sex.

On the little hill that rises behind the ancient city there was a temple to Aphrodite, and every evening the priests and priestesses—male and female prostitutes—would come down from the temple into the streets to ply their trade. Corinth was known throughout the length and breadth of the ancient world as a city of great and widespread immorality. It was in some ways, therefore, what we could call the San Francisco of the ancient world. The letter might well be titled, "First Californians." Here are the opening words:

> Paul, called by the will of God to be an apostle of Christ Jesus, and our brother Sosthenes,

(If you have read the Book of Acts lately you will know that Sosthenes was at one time the ruler of the synagogue in Corinth. He had been converted, evidently, after a difficult time in that city and now is with Paul in Ephesus.)

> To the church of God which is at Corinth, to those sanctified in Christ Jesus, called to be saints together with all those who in every place call on the name of our Lord Jesus Christ, both their Lord and ours: Grace to you and peace from God our Father and the Lord Jesus Christ.

Paul is writing this letter from Ephesus in about A.D. 56 or 57. He had founded the church in Corinth about five years earlier when he had come alone, driven out of Macedonia by the persecution there. He had left Timothy and Luke behind and had come to Athens, and from there to Corinth. After the founding of the church (which took about two years) he left and went on other journeys. Now he is in Ephesus, and word has come to him that there is difficulty in the church at Corinth.

Troubles and Questions

Paul wrote a letter to the Corinthians (referred to in the ninth verse of the fifth chapter) which has been lost to us. All we know of it is what the apostle says there, that he wrote the letter to the Corinthians telling them that they should not keep company with those who had fallen into immorality. Subsequently, a group of men had come from Corinth to visit him in Ephesus (their names are given in the final chapter of this letter: Fortunatus, Stephanas, and Achaicus), and they had brought word, evidently, of further troubles there. With them they also brought a letter from this church asking the apostle to answer certain questions that they had. First Corinthians is his answer to that letter and the reports that he had received from the Corinthian church.

In some ways, most remarkably, this letter is different from the other letters the apostle wrote. His letters usually began with a rather lengthy doctrinal section and closed with a practical section in which he applied what he is teaching. But here, right from the very beginning, he plunges into the problems of the church, and intersperses a practicality of doctrine with revelations of truth throughout the letter.

This is certainly the most practical of all Paul's letters. Even in this opening greeting, his concern for the church in its various problems is clearly reflected. It begins with an emphasis upon his apostleship. "Paul, called by the will of God to be an apostle." That affirmation was necessary because certain ones in Corinth were ready to challenge that fact on the grounds that Paul had not been one of the original twelve disciples. Some were wondering if he were not even a false apostle; therefore, he puts his apostleship first as he writes.

Then in verse 2 he describes the Corinthians as "sanctified in Christ Jesus." Now, in almost all the other letters, Paul's greeting to people is based not upon sanctification, but justification. But here he refers to this group as having been sanctified. These two words are theological terms. Justification is the description of the change God makes within an individual when he comes to Christ. It is what we also call being "born again," an experience that we are hearing much of today. It means an inward change of nature, and therefore a fundamental difference in outlook and attitude because of a deep change within. Now sanctification is the visible result of that in the behavior of individuals. It is all that inner change working out in terms of practice so that you see that someone is different. Paul refers to this with the Corinthians because their behavior was what was in question.

At the close of that same verse he stresses the Lordship of Jesus. He sends the letter to all those "who in every place call on the name of our Lord Jesus Christ," and that would surely include us. Then he adds, "both their Lord and ours." This was because in this Corinthian church there were people who were turning away from the authority of Jesus, and following after men. Divisions had come into the church, and early in the letter the apostle reflects his concern over their departure from the centrality of Christ.

Bad News and Good News

In verses 4 through 8 the apostle starts with the good news for these people. He has both bad news and good news for them in this letter, but as he always does, he starts with the good news: that which is true of them because they are Christians, regardless of how they are behaving. He lists some of the fullness of provision that they enjoyed because they were Christians.

> I give thanks to God always for you because of the grace of God which was given you in Christ Jesus, that in every way you were enriched in him with all speech and all knowledge—even as the testimony to Christ was confirmed among you—so that you are not lacking in any spiritual gift, as you wait for the revealing of our Lord Jesus Christ; who will sustain you to the end, guiltless in the day of our Lord Jesus Christ.

Paul takes note of several things that were true of the Corinthians, and they form the foundation of his approach to them. Freely he admits there were blessings and possibilities and provisions God had given them that they fully and freely shared. First of all, notice that their entrance into the Christian faith was orthodox, i.e., they were saved by grace: "I give thanks to God always for you because of the grace of God which was given you in Christ Jesus." These people had been pagans, and now they are born again by having received the grace of God.

In this letter there is no problem or wrestling with the matter of legalism. These people were not caught up with wrong rituals (you have that in the letter to the Colossians); they were not involved with disputes over circumcision (you get that in Galatians); and there was no resting upon dead works (you get that in Philippians). Here in Corinthians the problem was license. They had accepted the grace of God in such a way that they did not think it made any difference how they behaved, and that is what was causing the problem.

didn't understand dif. between freedom + license

Now, the apostle admits that they understood the grace of God. There are no questions raised in this letter on the deity of Christ or the virgin birth, or the substitutionary atonement, or the incarnation of Jesus. They all understood that they were set free from their sins by the gift of God through Jesus Christ. Their entrance, therefore, is clearly based upon God's grace.

Furthermore, Paul says, their equipment, having become Christians, is superb: "in every way you were enriched by him with all speech and all knowledge" (v. 5); "so that you are not lacking in any spiritual gift as you wait for the revealing of our Lord Jesus Christ" (v. 7). "In every way," he says, "you were enriched."

The word for "enriched" is the word from which we get our word plutocrat. They were rendered plutocrats, spiritually. They had a wealth of enrichment, and Paul points out that it was in two particular areas, in the word and in knowledge. The word for "speech" here is really the word logos, the word of God. This is his admission to them that they were avid Bible students. They did not have the New Testament as we have it—it was not written yet—but they had among them New Testament prophets who were preaching and teaching the same truth that we have in the New Testament. Therefore, they had all the truth available to them that is available to us.

The Corinthians were theologians, very likely, and, as was often true in Greek cities, they loved to get together to discuss philosophies and doctrine and to probe various problems. They were, therefore, able to answer some of the deep and heavy questions with which we still wrestle today. I am sure they could have told you where Cain got his wife. They could have told you what happens to those in other lands who never hear the gospel. They could have told you when the Antichrist would appear. They were Bible students, and Paul recognizes that and commends them for it. They were theologians; they were Trinitarian, supralapsarian trichotomists! (You may not know what that means, but they did!)

Now, more than that, Paul says, they were not lacking in any spiritual gift. In my book, Body Life, I have listed at least 21 different spiritual gifts that are referred to, and, according to Paul, there in Corinth every one of them was manifested. They had gifts of miracles, healings, teachings, tongues and interpretation of tongues, knowledge, and leadership. There was not a single one of the gifts of the Spirit lacking in this church. Can you imagine what kind of fascinating meetings they must have had when they all got together? No one wanted to miss church in Corinth! They never knew whether somebody would be healed, or some miracle would be demonstrated, or some remarkable prophetic utterance would come forth, or somebody would speak in a language they had never learned and someone else would interpret. But that is still not all. Not only was their entrance orthodox and their equipment superb, but their expectation was right. They were waiting for the revealing of our Lord Jesus Christ; they understood that when he appeared he would set things right on earth. They were not given to naïve and liberal delusions that they would, by their own efforts, handle all the problems of the world and correct all the evil in life and so bring in the kingdom. They were not propounding self-reliant schemes for earning status and a position of blessing with God. They understood that it was Christ who would sustain them to the end. It was he who would present them blameless before the Father. Paul acknowledges that all this is true of them.

Failure in the Church

But then in verse 9 the apostle seems suddenly to change the subject, and he introduces rather abruptly a description of the fellowship that they needed among them

God is faithful, by whom you were called into the fellowship of his Son, Jesus Christ our Lord

This is the key verse of 1 Corinthians. God had called them to a very important relationship. By implication, here at the very beginning of this letter we learn the reason for all of the problems in the Corinthian church. They had not understood the implications of their calling, and the relationship they personally and individually had with Jesus Christ himself. Instead (as we see beginning with the very next verse), the apostle has to deal with divisions, scandals, lawsuits, immorality, drunkenness, quarreling, and with much misunderstanding of the truth about idols and demons and various other matters. It is clear that despite this full provision which they had received, they were experiencing a great failure in the church. They had the ability to do all these mighty things in the Spirit, but not much was happening out in the city. Instead of making an impact on Corinth, Corinth was making an impact on the church. All these ugly attitudes and actions going on every day and night out in the city were beginning to infiltrate the church. Despite all their mighty provision, there was little manifestation of the power of God. It reminds me of Peter Marshall's vivid description of contemporary Christians: "Christians are like deep-sea divers, encased in suits designed for many fathoms deep, marching bravely forth to pull plugs out of bathtubs!"

What was wrong? Well, what was wrong was the Corinthians' lack of understanding of what it meant to have Jesus Christ living within them. I have traveled widely in the course of my work, and almost everywhere I have gone I have found that the major struggle of churches is right at this point. They have lost the sense that Jesus is among them, that they have an individual relationship to the Lord of glory himself. They no longer live their lives in the awareness and the excitement that they are partners with Christ in everything they do. When that begins to fade from Christian consciousness all these troubles that the Corinthians were experiencing begin to crowd in upon us. Therefore, this letter is written to call these people back, as it is written to call us back as well, to an awareness of what it means to have fellowship with Christ.

Fellowship with Christ is the work of the Holy Spirit. It is his task to take the things of Christ and make them known to us, to make the person of Jesus vivid and real in our daily experience. That is what Paul is talking about here—Christ made real to the heart, enabling him to satisfy the thirsts of the soul; Christ providing the power it takes to meet the demands of both the law and the love of God. Fellowship with Christ is not only direction in what to do, it is also dynamic—it is how to do it. Oftentimes churches fall into the habit of trying to draw direction from the Lord with no awareness of the great provision of the dynamic. It is not only guidance he gives us, but resource as well. It is not only an understanding of life, but an undergirding, in order that we might perform it. It is not only a program that he sets before the church, but the power to carry it out.

When any one of us forgets this, we drift into the terrible syndrome of recognizing the Lord on Sunday, and from Monday through Saturday living our life on our own without any recognition of his presence with us. He is no longer Lord of all our life, but only a part of it. If he is not Lord through our life all day long then he is Lord only of the margins, only of the left-overs, only of the weekends. The church is called to an understanding of the presence of Christ in the human heart to supply to it the dynamic, the sense of adventure, the innovative spirit that opens doors in unusual and unanticipated ways, lending adventure and color to life.

Now this was what was missing in Corinth, and as we open this letter and go on into it further, we will see how in every case the apostle calls them back to that. They were suffering divisions because they had lost sight of the Lordship of Jesus. They were immoral because they had forgotten that the members of their bodies were the members of Christ. They were in lawsuits with one another because they had failed to see that Jesus was judge of the innermost motives of the heart. They were quarreling because they had forgotten that others were members of Christ's body and, therefore, they were members one of another. All that the apostle does to heal the hurts at Corinth is to call them back to an awareness of fellowship with the Lord Jesus Christ.

Appeal for Unity

Now the apostle Paul begins dealing with incipient division in the church at Corinth, in a powerful appeal for unity, verse 10:

> I appeal to you, brethren, by the name of our Lord Jesus Christ, that all of you agree and there be no dissensions among you, but that you be united in the same mind and the same judgment.

Paul always expresses great concern about the possibility of a split in the church. You may be reminded by his words in verse 10 of the similar passage in his letter to the Philippians where, in chapter 2, he says to that church (vv. 1, 2),

> So if there be any encouragement in Christ, any incentive of love, any participation in the Spirit, any affection and sympathy, complete my joy by being of the same mind, having the same love, being in full accord, and of one mind.

You may recall also that in writing to the church at Ephesus he exhorted the elders there to be careful to "maintain the unity of the Spirit in the bond of peace" (Eph. 4:3).

Church unity is a very important matter, and because of its significance Paul puts it first in the list of problems he has to deal with here at Corinth. Many of the other problems were flowing out of this division within the congregation. Here in verse 10 he briefly shows us the ground of unity, and the nature of unity in a church. The ground, of course, is the name of our Lord Jesus Christ. "I appeal to you," he says, "by the name of our Lord Jesus Christ." Their relationship to Christ was the only unifying factor of the church. There is no other name big enough, great enough, glorious enough and powerful enough to gather everybody together, despite the diversity of viewpoints and the differences of background or status in life, than the name of Jesus. That is why the apostle appeals to it. He recognizes that we share a common life if we have come to Christ; we are brothers and sisters because we have his life in us. He is the ground, always, of unity. And more than that, we have a responsibility to obey him, to follow his Lordship. Therefore, the only basis upon which you can get Christians to agree is by setting before them the Person of the Lord Jesus, and calling them back to that fundamental base. This is what Paul does here.

He describes the nature of unity in this way, "that you be united in the same mind and the same judgment." That does not mean that everybody has to think alike. With all the differences among people it is impossible to get them to think alike. But yet the apostle says they are to be "of the same mind." Now how could that be? I think the letter to the Philippians helps us here, because in the passage just quoted Paul goes on to say, "Let this mind be in you which was also in Christ Jesus." He then describes for us the mind of Christ as a willingness to give up rights and personal privileges and take a lower place. Then comes that great Christological passage where he describes Jesus

> . . . who, though he was in the form of God, did not count equality with God a thing to be grasped, but emptied himself, taking the form of a servant, being born in the likeness of men. And being found in human form he humbled himself and became obedient unto death, even death on a cross (Phil. 2:6–8).

That is the mind Paul is talking about. When everybody decides to put the things of Christ first, and is willing to suffer personal loss that the honor and glory of Christ might be advanced, this is what brings harmony to a congregation. That is always the unifying factor in a church, and that is the mind that is to be among us, the mind that does not consider itself the most important thing.

I remember a few years ago being at a Family Congress in St. Louis, Missouri. One of the evening speakers was Dr. Oswald Hoffman, the very capable and powerful preacher on the Lutheran Hour radio program. He was introduced in a rather extended and flowery way, but he came on and in his great booming voice said, "I'm not Dr. Oswald Hoffman, the great preacher of the Lutheran Hour. I'm a nobody— just like you!" I've not forgotten that incident because it seems to me to capture the very attitude Paul is describing here. Who are we, that we should put our interests and our desires ahead of those of the Lord for his church? The church never belongs to anybody but the Lord. This is what Paul uses as the basis for unity in this church— not only the attitude of selflessness, which is the mind of Christ, but the responsibility to submit to his Lordship, the common responsibility that we have together.

Paul goes right on in verse 12 to describe the forms that these divisions were taking in the church of Corinth:

> What I mean is that each one of you says, "I belong to Paul," "I belong to Apollos," or "I belong to Cephas," [another name for Peter] or "I belong to Christ."

There was the real trouble at Corinth. These were not full-blown schisms yet; they had not split off into other congregations, but there were four cliques, or factions, within the congregation. There were, first of all, the loyalists who said, "We are of Paul. He started this church. We came to life in Christ by Paul, and Paul is the one we're going to listen to above all others." Undoubtedly there was a big group that followed Paul. Then there were the stylists, those who were attracted by different styles of preaching, and they had especially been drawn to Apollos. From the Book of Acts we learn that Apollos was an outstanding orator in a world that loved and appreciated oratory. He was a rhetorician who was especially capable in the allegorical style of teaching of the Old Testament. I am sure there were many in Corinth who were saying, "Oh, I love to hear Apollos! He's a great preacher, a warm, capable, eloquent man, who can make Scripture come alive!"

Then there were the traditionalists (there always are), those who say, "Well, I don't know about Paul or Apollos. Let's get back to the beginnings. Let's go back to Jerusalem. We are of Peter." (Peter, evidently, had been through Corinth and had preached there.) So they said, "When Peter came, we really felt that we were on solid ground. After all, he was one of the first apostles that Jesus himself called." So they were quarreling over the relative merit and authority of these various teachers.

There was still a fourth group, and in some ways I think they were probably the worst. They were drawing themselves up and saying, "Well, you may be of Paul or of Peter or of Apollos, but we are of Christ! We go back to the Lord alone. What he says we'll listen to, not Paul or Peter or anyone else—it makes no difference to us." With that spirit of self-righteous smugness they were separating from the rest, dividing up the congregation and quarreling with one another over these things.

Now, you do not have to be very old to recognize that this is still a problem in the church. The same viewpoints are still dividing people. There are those who are emotionally attached to some great Christian leader who has helped them, and they will only listen to him. They read only his books or listen only to his tapes. And there are others who are drawn to some speaking style that has attracted them. They love to listen to someone because he turns them on emotionally. There are still others today who follow after some school of thought. It is the popular thing today to cry, "Back to the Reformation!" If someone comes along preaching the doctrines emphasized during the Reformation he will get a great following among the people who think that the Reformation was the whole sum and substance of all great Christian truth.

Some people will pick other matters of doctrine to affirm. There are the Calvinists and the Arminians and the Dispensationalists—these represent some of the things held up as the "summon bonum" (the highest good) in theology. If you survey the church scene all over America today you will find people dividing up this way. Some say, "I am of Gothard," and others say, "No, I am of Bright." Still others say, "We are of Schaeffer," and others, "We are of Graham," or, "We are of C. S. Lewis."

Clearly Paul is deeply troubled by this. It is a serious threat to the life of a church to find people choosing favorite preachers to the degree that they do not want to listen to anyone else. Now, we all have our favorite preacher, and up to a point that is not wrong. There are some people who minister to us better than others, and it is only natural that we should listen to them and follow them. But it is the exclusiveness that Paul is concerned about here—people who do not even want to come to a service if someone other than their favorite is preaching. That is what Paul speaks about.

Christ Parcelled Out

In verse 13 Paul gives us three clues as to what is wrong with this kind of thing. To all of this he asks of Corinth, as he would ask of us,

Is Christ divided? Was Paul crucified for you? Or were you baptized in the name of Paul?

Here are our first clues as to what is wrong with this kind of cliquishness in a church. The first thing, Paul says, is that it tends to chop up Christ and parcel him out as though his person and his work came in various packages; thus you lose a true perspective of the whole of Christian theology. When you follow one man you are getting a view of Christ, but there is no teacher in the church who has ever come along—including the apostle Paul himself—who has ever set forth a totally complete view of Christ. That is why we have four gospels, because not even one of the disciples who was with the Lord was capable of giving us a complete enough view of Christ. It took four viewpoints to report his earthly life and ministry accurately enough to us. God, therefore, has designed that there be many teachers, many preachers, many viewpoints, in a church. In the Body of Christ at large there are many who can make a contribution to our understanding of Christ.

The second thing Paul says is, "Was Paul crucified for you?" There he indicates that the problem with cliquishness is that it tends to overemphasize the significance of the human leader. It builds him up too much; it makes him a rival, to some degree, of the Lord himself. People begin to think things about their favorite that are not true, and expect things from him which he is unable to deliver. I have had to do some degree of battle with this myself. I have had people say to me, "Oh, Mr. Stedman, when you speak I see things so clearly! I hang on every word you say. Whatever you say, I believe." (I have been trying for a long time to get my wife to accept that!) That is a very dangerous attitude, and yet we tend to think of individuals as being the channel by which deliverance can come to our heart.

But it cannot come that way. Paul is putting his finger right on the problem when he asks, "Was Paul crucified for you?" Not a single Christian teacher ever lived who can help us be forgiven one single sin, not one. Not a single teacher ever lived who can heal the hurt of a broken heart, or supply energy and adequacy to someone who feels worthless and unable to function in society, not one. Not a teacher among us today or at any other time is able to open the mind and the eyes of the heart and reveal to us the glory and majesty of God, not one. That is not the work of men; that is the work of God himself. He chooses various channels through which to work. We must allow him the privilege of doing that. They will not all be the same flavor; they will not all have the same characteristics. We reveal our immaturity when we insist that only those with certain characteristics are the ones we will listen to, or we feel can bless or strengthen our lives. No man is the Savior; no man can deliver us except Jesus. All are mere teachers; there is only one Lord. He said so himself. "One is your master; all of you are brothers."

Distorted Symbols

The third danger of groups is given in the latter part of verse 13, and on through the next few verses:

> . . . Or were you baptized in the name of Paul? I am thankful that I baptized none of you except Crispus and Gaius; lest any one should say that you were baptized in my name. [Then he thinks of another group that he baptized.] (I did baptize also the household of Stephanas. Beyond that, I do not know whether I baptized any one else.)

Here the apostle makes clear that the tendency among groupies is to distort the meaning of symbols. They take an innocent teaching medium (in this case baptism), and make it into an identification badge. Many of us are familiar with this common phenomenon of human psychology; some symbolic thing of use to us is so important that we finally make it a badge of the group to which we belong.

As a young Christian during World War II, I was stationed in Hawaii, and I became acquainted with the work of the Navigators. At that time it was under the leadership of its founder, Dawson Trotman, and it was my privilege and delight to be a close friend of his, to have spent a good deal of time with him and to come under the influence of his teaching and his methods. The Navigators in those days did a great work in the navy throughout both the Pacific and Atlantic oceans, and hundreds of young men were led to Christ through their efforts during the war years. I used to attend a Navigator group which met in Honolulu on Sunday afternoons. Sometimes two or three hundred sailors, all of them Christians, would be there. We had some great meetings and great times together. It was a glorious work.

But you could always tell the Navigators because there were three things that marked them. First, each had a Scofield Reference Bible tucked under his arm; that was the only "Authorized Version." Then every Navigator who was anybody at all had to have an index drawn in on the pages of the Bible, a kind of a ladder that gave you a clue to where the books were so that with your thumb you could turn up any book in the Bible almost instantly.

The third thing every Navigator had was a little black notebook covered in rough-grained leather. On opening it you found a loose-leaf notebook with many of the small, half-page materials on which the Navigators printed their Bible helps. Now these things were good. There was nothing wrong with them; they were helpful, but it was not long before they became status symbols, and they were used, not always intentionally, to put down those who did not have them. They became symbols of prestige that resulted in divisions among the men. Almost every group does this. Something shows up sooner or later as an identifying badge that marks them as "special." That is what they were doing with baptism here in Corinth. Some were saying, "Well, Paul baptized me." Others were saying, "Apollos himself baptized me." And there were some who said, "When Peter came through, he baptized me. And, after all, Peter even walked on water!" That was a mark of status with them, and Paul says it is all wrong. It would destroy the unity of the congregation and provide an inaccurate testimony to the Person of Christ before the watching world. So he says, "I didn't baptize many of you. I thank God that only a few of you can say that about me."

Now, in one verse he introduces the cure for these divisions (v. 17):

> For Christ did not send me to baptize but to preach the gospel, and not with eloquent wisdom [i.e., literally, "wisdom of words"], lest the cross of Christ be emptied of its power.

This introduces one of the greatest passages in the Bible, setting forth the difference between the wisdom of man and the wisdom of God. He says, in effect, "You don't cure divisions in a church by identification badges. Christ did not send me to take scalps or to cut notches on my gun handle as to how many converts I've won." (Now, he is not saying that it is wrong to baptize; he himself did it and acknowledges that he did. He does not say we should stop baptizing because of this problem.

He simply says, that is not why he was sent.) "I was not sent to emphasize symbols, but, positively, I was sent to preach a whole gospel, not even one emphasizing style (not in wisdom of words), but that which emphasizes content." The facts in the gospel are what will set us free, and particularly, he says, the word of the cross.

The cross of Christ is what will heal the fragmentation of Christians wherever they are. When you call them back to an understanding of the meaning of the cross, you will find all the divisions disappearing; they fade away like the morning mist. When you get men's eyes off the status symbols and call them away from following men to the Person of Christ and his cross, all the divisions will disappear. There has been no other cure that I know of through the years. The cross of Christ cuts across all human value systems. It wipes out all the petty distinctions that people make among themselves. The cross strips away our illusions and brings our pride tumbling down from that high place where it exalts itself against the knowledge of God. Paul is going to go on to describe this radical force so different from anything else in the world. No man would ever have planned the cross. If it had been left up to us to plan the program by which God would change the world we would never have included a cross. This is a radical principle that we need to thoroughly understand, because when we understand the cross there will be no room left for divisions.

2
—
God's Nonsense

We usually think of the gospel as something that non-Christians need to hear, but the New Testament makes very clear that it is also Christians who need to understand the gospel. Believing the gospel is not only the means by which you become a Christian; it is also the means by which you are delivered in your Christian life from all the causes of disagreements, factions, dissensions, pressures of lust, and so forth. The heart of the gospel, Paul says, is the cross of Jesus Christ, and he brings us to that in verse 17 of chapter 1:

> For Christ did not send me to baptize but to preach the gospel, and not with eloquent wisdom lest the cross of Christ be emptied of its power.

The theme of this next section is the power of the cross, and Paul is going to show us clearly, in a very profound passage, what the cross does in human thinking and in human affairs. The cross, of course, has become the symbol of Christianity today. People wear it on chains around their necks; we use it as decorations in various places. We have become so familiar with the cross that we have forgotten much of the impact it had in the first century. For these early Christians, and for those among whom they lived, it was a horrible symbol. We would get much closer to its impact today if we substituted an electric chair for the cross. Wouldn't it seem strange, driving across this country, to see church steeples with electric chairs on top?

The cross is not the whole of the gospel. Some people have misunderstood that from this letter, because Paul said that when he came to Corinth he came determined not to preach anything among them "save Jesus Christ and him crucified." Before this letter is over, however, the apostle is going to write a great section on the resurrection of Christ. That is part of the gospel, too. But the cross was particularly needed in Corinth, as it is needed in our American churches, because the word of the cross is the cure for all human division.

The Fundamental Conflict

Paul now goes on to speak of this astonishing power of the cross (v. 18):

> For the word of the cross is folly to those who are perishing, but to us who are being saved it is the power of God. For it is written, "I will destroy the wisdom of the wise, and the cleverness of the clever I will thwart."

The cross is significant in Christianity because it exposes the fundamental conflict of life. That is what these verses declare to us. The cross gets down below all our surface attempts at compromise and cuts down the basic difference behind all human disagreement. Once you confront the cross and its judgment of life, you are either committed to error or committed to truth.

We must understand very clearly what Paul means by "the word of the cross." First of all, it means the basic announcement of the crucifixion of Jesus. The cross is a fact of history. If you have come into contact with some of today's modern cults you know that what they present, basically, is philosophy: various ideas about human behavior and how to control it. A whole spectrum of religious groups is based upon various philosophical concepts.

But when you come to Christianity you do not start with philosophy. You start with facts—inescapable facts of history that cannot be thrown out or avoided. One of them is the incarnation of Jesus, the fact that he was born as a man and came among us through strange and marvelous circumstances. Another of the great facts of our faith is the crucifixion. Jesus died. He was nailed to a tree. It was done at a certain point of time in history and cannot be evaded. This fact is an essential part of the word of the cross, part of the gospel that we declare to people everywhere. Something strange happened to Jesus of Nazareth. He died a strange death. He did not deserve it, but by the judgment of the Romans and Jews alike he was put to death for a crime he did not commit. That is part, but of course not all, of the word of the cross.

This phrase primarily refers to the judgment that the cross makes upon human life. Paul later calls it "the offense of the cross." When you say Jesus was crucified you are saying that when the man universally acknowledged to be the finest man who ever lived took the place of any one of us, or any person who has ever lived, he deserved nothing but the instant judgment of God: death at God's hand. That is therefore a judgment on all of us. That is what people do not like about the cross. It condemns our righteousness. It casts aspersions on all our good efforts, wipes them all out and says they are totally worthless before God. A single individual, yielding to the God who made him, and filled with the power of God designed for him, is worth far more than all the created universe. But a man *without* God is a totally worthless being whose only value lies in the possibility that that divine life can be reinstated in him. That is the word of the cross, and that is what Paul means when he speaks of the cross as the symbol of the Christian life.

He goes on in this verse to tell us that this word always produces two reactions. It did so in the first century and still does today— exactly the same two. First, the word of the cross is folly to those who are perishing. The word *folly* here literally means "silly." It is silliness, absurdity, nonsense, to those who are perishing. If you have ever tried to witness to somebody who feels that he is a self-made man and worships his creator, you will have discovered the folly of the cross. To tell such a man that all his impressive record of achievement is worth nothing in God's sight, that it does not make him one degree more acceptable, that it is nothing but wasted effort, is to immediately run into the offense of the cross. He will call that doctrine silly, absurd: "You mean to tell me that all this impressive array of human knowledge and wisdom that has been accumulated for centuries, with all the great achievements of mankind to relieve human misery through the technological advances of our day, that all that is absolutely worthless? Nonsense!" That is what they said in the first century and that is what they say today. You may even be thinking yourself, "If that's what the Bible teaches, then I think it's ridiculous." That is the foolishness of the cross.

The other reaction is that the cross is "the power of God to those of us who are being saved." (Note that the perishing have not perished yet; they are on the way to perishing. Nor have the saved been fully saved yet; we are on the way to that final salvation yet to be realized.) But to us who are being saved, the cross is the key to the release of all God's power in human life. It is the way to experience the healing of God in the heart, the deliverance from the reign of sin, and the entry into wholeness, peace and joy. The cross is an inescapable part of that process.

Those are the two reactions. To prove that this is not something merely for a moment in time but always God's way with man, Paul quotes the words of God from Isaiah 29:14:

"I will destory the wisdom of the wise, and the cleverness of the clever I will thwart."

If you look it up in the Book of Isaiah you will find that it was uttered at a time when Judah was being confronted with an invasion. The northern borders of the land were being attacked by the Assyrian army, and all the statesmen and politicians of the day, including King Hezekiah, were trying to find a way out of this dilemma. (It reads very much like the present-day crisis in the Middle East.) They were trying to find a way by human ingenuity and political scheming to either make a mutual defense treaty with Egypt, or somehow turn off the wrath of the Assyrian army and thus escape imminent invasion.

But God spoke through the prophet Isaiah and announced that he would deliver his people without any help from the politicians. The Book of Isaiah goes on to record how God did that very thing. The Assyrian army came right up to the gates of Jerusalem and surrounded the city. King Hezekiah could see the hordes of Assyrians, mocking and taunting the Israelites. Their leader, Sennacherib, sent a letter to the king ordering him to surrender, but the king spread it out before the Lord and prayed over it. And God answered. He sent an angel who in one night slew 185,000 of the Assyrian soldiers. (History says that a plague broke out in the Assyrian camp, and overnight 185,000 died. The Authorized Version puts it in a rather remarkable way: "When they woke up in the morning, behold, they were all dead men.") God did exactly what he said he would do. He did not ask for any human help. He did it alone, and the land was delivered. Now, Paul picks this up and says it is the way God works, and especially, he works that way in the matter of human redemption.

Where Is the Wise Man?

That brings us then to Paul's analysis and examination of the wisdom of the age versus the wisdom of God. Now we are about to look at a very profound passage. It is one of the most amazing examinations of a problem that every generation, without fail, has to face: How much should we trust our own wisdom? How much reliance should we put upon our ability to solve our own problems in whatever realm or dimension of life we care to investigate? (This is a particularly helpful passage to students at school.) Paul answers in verses 20 and 21:

> Where is the wise man? Where is the scribe? Where is the debater of this age? Has not God made foolish the wisdom of the world? For since, in the wisdom of God, the world did not know God through wisdom, it pleased God through the folly of what we preach to save those who believe.

He begins with three questions, but essentially he is asking this one question: "What true standing does human wisdom give to you?" Here we come up against the matter of how much value are academic degrees. I am not setting aside degrees; they do represent something of value, but how much of the true value of a life can be detected by the degrees that a person has? The implication of these questions is: none!

Paul is referring to the two universal approaches to gathering knowledge and wisdom. The first is the scribal, or Jewish approach—the study of the wisdom and writings of the past. The Jewish scribes gave their whole attention to reading the Scriptures and ancient writings of wise men, trying to gather it all and reduce it to practical applications for their day. But Paul asks, "Where does that get you?" The answer is: nowhere! Not with God, anyway!

Well, what about the debater of this age? That was the Greek approach. The Greeks loved to get together to debate the philosophies of their day. We would call it the dialectic approach. Paul is raising the question, "Where does that get you?" Again, the implied answer is clearly: nowhere! What is it worth? Nothing! That is a harsh judgment, isn't it?

At this point we must make an important distinction. There is a difference between human knowledge and human wisdom. Knowledge is the discovery of truth, and God always encourages it; he gave us minds to use. God has set man on a search to unravel and discover the millions of secrets he has hidden in the universe—many of the greatest, I am sure, yet undiscovered. Man is given the gift of reason to search these out. To give yourself to a discovery of the laws of physics and what is behind matter is perfectly proper. To give yourself to investigation of the wonders of the human body, of medicine and pathology, is perfectly right. To set yourself to discover the secrets of the stars, or the secrets of the workings of the human mind and the psyche in psychology—these are all perfectly correct. But that is knowledge, the discovery of truth. Wisdom is something else. Wisdom is the proper use of truth. This is where scripture always throws down the gauntlet.

The Bible says there is something faulty about human wisdom—it does not know how to use truth. All truth discovered through human knowledge is misused, abused, twisted, and distorted. This needs especially to be emphasized today because so many Christians worship human wisdom and feel that secular writers know more about the use of knowledge than Christians do. There is no question that many secular writers do know a great deal more about truth than do many Christians. But what we must clearly understand, and what this great passage will help us understand, is that when it comes to the right application of truth, secular minds are for the most part juvenile. They are inept, they do not know what to do with their knowledge. And so are a lot of Christians who follow along these same paths, who have not approached the use of truth from the revelation and the wisdom of the Word of God.

Amazingly, even thoughtful secular writers will distinguish these differences. Recently I was reading an excerpt from Vance Packard's book, *The People Shapers*, in which he explores the possibility of molding the minds of men and altering human behavior by scientific process. He concludes with these words:

A person can be high in learning ability and memory, and still remain a fool. The two do not add up to either brilliance or wisdom in thinking. Until someone comes along with a pill for wisdom, we might better aspire to become a more human society, rather than a more brainy one.

In verse 20 the apostle asks another question, "Has not God made foolish the wisdom of the world?" He is asking in essence, "What is the true nature of human wisdom?" And his answer is, "Foolishness!" It is ridiculous; it always sounds impressive, it radiates optimism, and it even seems to work for awhile in a limited area of application. This is what confuses us so. But when it is all over it has succeeded in changing nothing. That is what we need to face. That is the fact which history confirms. Every generation wrestles with the self-same problems, and that remains true as far back as you can go into the farthest reaches of human history. That is why one generation never seems to learn from another. The great German philosopher, Hegel, was quite right when he said, "History teaches us that history teaches us nothing." That is why old age always points to youth and says "Won't you listen? Won't you pay attention?" And youth invariably points back and says, "Look what your philosophy made us! Look

where you got us! We're not going to pay any attention to you."
That is the story of history.

Winston Churchill once said these remarkable words:

> Certain it is that while men are gathering knowledge and power with ever-
> increasing speed, their virtues and their wisdom have not shown any notable
> improvement as the centuries have rolled. Under sufficient stress, starvation,
> terror, warlike passion, or even cold, intellectual frenzy, the modern man
> we know so well will do the most terrible deeds, and his modern woman
> will back him up.

The Stupidity of Ignoring God

Why is this true? In verse 21 the apostle puts his finger right on
the problem:

> For since, in the wisdom of God, the world did not know God through
> wisdom, . . .

That is the problem. What is the major fault of the wisdom of man?
Well, despite his pretentious claims to have penetrated the secrets
of life, he has failed to discover or even to acknowledge the greatest
fact of all—God himself. The great Being behind all that exists is
God, and for man to ignore the most important fact of all is nothing
but sheer stupidity. That is why, in our public school systems, there
is a conspiracy of silence to keep God out. No one hardly dares to
mention his name. Teachers are careful not to allow the investigation
of natural phenomena to lead to the conclusion that behind these
phenomena is a being of great wisdom, power and might. They use
euphemisms instead: "Nature, karma, destiny, fate." Or, if they are
driven into a corner, "Providence"—but not God. Now, that is another
incredible fact. In all the reasoning of the mind of man he fails to
discover the great Force behind all psychology, the great Reality behind
all the appearances that Science investigates. With all our brilliance
we end up like little children who fail to see a great giant towering
in our midst because we are so happily engaged in swinging on his
shoestrings. No wonder T. S. Eliot says in *The Rock:*

> All our knowledge only brings us closer to our ignorance, and all our igno-
> rance closer to death, but closeness to death, no nearer to God. [Then
> he asks the question that hangs over this whole generation.] Where is the
> life we have lost in living?

A Simple Story

Now what is God's answer to this? Well, Paul gives it to us in verses 21 through 25:

> . . . it pleased God through the folly of what we preach to save those who believe. For Jews demand signs and Greeks seek wisdom, but we preach Christ crucified, a stumbling block to Jews and folly to Gentiles, but to those who are called, both Jews and Greeks, Christ the power of God and the wisdom of God. For the foolishness of God is wiser than men, and the weakness of God is stronger than men.

What a strange answer that is! God has chosen to set aside both the searchings and the demands of proud, stubborn people who demand miracles or else they will not believe, in order to confront them with what is basically a simple story of a crucified Messiah. We had a clear example of these demands in recent newspaper reports of the discovery of a shroud marked with the image of a man, supposedly the burial shroud of Jesus. It immediately evoked tremendous popular attention. Why? Because something about us wants God to perform a miracle or else we will not believe. We are right where the citizens of Nazareth were when Jesus came among them. They asked him to do a sign, but he would not do it "because of their unbelief."

To the proud skeptics who demand miracles and to the foolish intellectuals who insist on explanations or else they will not believe, God gives the same answer. The story of a crucified Messiah is held out to them as the only hope for deliverance. It is preached by simple men and women, not brilliant people, not great, trained minds, not deep-thinking philosophers, but common, ordinary citizens—housewives, slaves, artisans, craftsmen, whoever, for anybody can tell the story of a crucified Messiah. And yet that story, believed in, effectively accomplishes what the wisdom of man and the power of man cannot do— salvation! People are actually delivered from themselves, and from their sins.

We all remember the mess of Watergate and the sickening discovery of a basic illness so deeply involved in our whole national life that it touched the highest office in the land. Associated with it was an arrogant, ruthless young lawyer named Charles Colson. We have heard the story of how the word of the cross reached that "hatchet man" of the Nixon administration, and how he is now devoting his life to the rescue of men in prison. He has been changed by the power of God.

I love to dwell on this because I think Christians have forgotten what it is God has put in their hands in the gospel. What a marvelous gospel this is! Paul seems, in verse 25, to bow before the wonder and majesty of this astonishing God who can devise such a simple but effective gospel.

> For the foolishness of God is wiser than men, and the weakness of God [the nonsense of God] is stronger than men.

What man cannot do, God accomplishes by a simple word about the crucifixion of Jesus and its judgment on the wisdom of man.

Here is what C. S. Lewis says about the nonsense of God in *The Problem of Pain:**

> It is hardly complimentary to God that we should choose him as an alternative to hell. Yet even this he accepts. The creature's illusion of self-sufficiency must, for the creature's sake, be shattered. And by trouble, or fear of trouble on earth, by crude fear of the eternal flames, God shatters it, unmindful of his glory's diminution. I call this "divine humility," because it's a poor thing to strike our colors to God when the ship is going down under us, a poor thing to come to him as a last resort, to offer up our own when it is no longer worth keeping. If God were proud, he would hardly have us on such terms. But he is not proud. He stoops to conquer. He would have us even though we have shown that we prefer everything else to him, and come to him because there is nothing better now to be had.

Thus "the word of the cross" shatters the pride of man. When we learn in it the truth about human life we find we are dealing with a reality that strips off the illusions and delusions of a secular age and introduces us to bedrock reality—the true view of life as God sees it. That is the beginning of our deliverance from evil.

---

* Published by Macmillan (New York: 1943), p. 97.

3

—

God's Tools

———————

I have entitled this chapter "God's Tools" because it deals with those whom God uses to change the world. I could have entitled it "God's Fools," because the startling truth Paul declares here is that God often prefers fools to use as tools when he wants to do a really great work in the world. Here are Paul's words (Chap. 1, v. 26):

> For consider your call, brethren; not many of you were wise according to worldly standards, not many were powerful, not many were of noble birth; but God chose what is foolish in the world to shame the wise, God chose what is weak in the world to shame the strong, God chose what is low and despised in the world, even things that are not, to bring to nothing things that are. . . .

The apostle is dealing with the wisdom of the world versus the inscrutable, marvelous wisdom of God, which is often regarded by the world as foolishness or silliness. These Corinthians were exalting the wisdom of the world, and so dividing into various factions, following certain men, and glorying in men's ability, power, and wisdom. To answer this the apostle shows us how God works, using a simple contrast; these Corinthians themselves are his "Exhibit A." He says, "Look at yourselves, consider your own call, look what has happened in your own life." He then points out two rather obvious but important facts they were evidently overlooking in their thinking. First, he says, "There are not many mighty among you, are there?" Fortunately, Paul did not say "any" mighty. Lady Hamilton, an evangelical believer

33

among the English nobility in the early part of this century, used to say she was saved by an "m," because if it had said not "any" mighty or "any" noble, she would not have made it.

There in Corinth only a few had some standing in the community. Sosthenes (he is mentioned at the beginning of this letter) and Crispus, who both had once been the rulers of the synagogue, were there and they, perhaps, were men of repute. At the close of the letter to the Romans (which Paul wrote while he was in Corinth), he mentions a man named Erastus, who was the city treasurer. A man named Gaius, who was evidently a wealthy businessman in Corinth, is also mentioned there. But that is about all the Scripture records of men who were of repute or knowledge in the congregation. The rest were the common, ordinary people of the city, those whom the world regarded as foolish. Many of them were slaves, perhaps, unknown people, "plain vanilla" people, like you and me.

Some of them were weak, the apostle says. They had no political or military clout; they were not men of influence, and they had no "in" with city hall. They were without power, apparently, to affect life around them, yet God chose them. They made up what we would call the working classes—artisans, tradesmen, the little people of the world.

Undiscovered Secrets

Paul points out that God even chose things "that are not to set at nought the things that are," that is, future events which had not yet come to pass, upon which great issues would ultimately hang. Perhaps Paul is referring here to certain technological secrets that had yet to be discovered. In those days they knew nothing about radio, television, and communications such as we know today, but all that was known to God. Perhaps some of the predictions of scripture about the last days rest for their fulfillment upon some of the things that have not yet been found. These are what God works with, "things that are not, to bring to nought the things that are." So, if you are feeling that nobody recognizes you, you ought to rejoice that you are a Christian because power and influence with men are not necessary for you to be greatly used of God. He often delights in setting aside the impressive things of men.

This does not mean that God does not use people of status and stature as well. He does, but only, remarkably enough, when they have learned that their usefulness is not derived from their position or their abilities, but rather from his presence in their lives. Is it not strange that we think so highly of the wisdom of the world when God thinks so little of it? Jesus said once, "What is exalted among men is an abomination in the sight of God" (Luke 16:15), and what Paul is saying here seems to flow from that fact. What men put great store by is often set aside totally by God; it is abomination in the sight of God.

Dr. Martyn Lloyd-Jones, who was for many years an outstanding pastor in London, says this:

> We Christians often quote "not by might nor by power, but by my spirit saith the Lord," and yet in practice we seem to rely upon the mighty dollar and the power of the press and advertising. We seem to think that our influence will depend on our technique and the program we can put forward and that it would be the numbers, the largeness, the bigness that would prove effective. We seem to have forgotten that God has done most of his deeds in the church throughout its history through remnants. We seem to have forgotten the great story of Gideon, for instance, and how God insisted on reducing the 32,000 men down to 300 before he would make use of them. We have become fascinated by the idea of bigness, and we are quite convinced that if we can only stage, yes, that's the word, stage something really big before the world, we will shake it and produce a mighty religious awakening. That seems to be the modern conception of authority.

Unfortunately, that is too true today; it seems to be the basic philosophy of the church. It is, "Seek ye first the Lily Foundation and all these things will be added unto you." I find people everywhere who seem to think that it takes money to do God's work, that nothing can happen unless you get money first. It seems to me that this is a reversal of the whole position of Scripture, for in Scripture you do not begin with money, you begin with ministry. Anybody can be a minister of God. That is the glory of the Church, because God has put us all in the ministry. If you begin to do what God wants you to do, right where you are, and God begins to work through you, all the money ever necessary to cause that ministry to grow to perhaps worldwide dimensions is always available. Money follows ministry, not the other way around. How far we seem to have drifted from this. I think God delights in every generation to prove again, by some unusual demonstration, this great principle that Paul declares. God deliberately chooses the weak and the obscure and uses them in great power to remind us that it is not status, prestige, bigness or money that makes ministry for God effective.

Take a Peanut

In my early Christian life I remember reading of the life and ministry of Dr. George Washington Carver, the outstanding Negro scientist, who in the early part of this century was used of God in great ways among the black people of the South. Dr. Carver, a great believer and a choice servant of God, said that one day he prayed, "Lord, teach me the secrets of the universe." He said God said to him, "George, that is too big a subject for you. I want you to take a peanut, that is more your size, and work on that." So he began to explore what was in the peanut, and now it is a matter of record that he found over 325 different uses for it. He revolutionized the technology of the South. God used this simple, humble believer to open secrets of the universe that he hid from everyone else.

Remember how Jesus once put it, "I thank thee, Father . . . that thou has hidden these things from the wise and revealed them to babes" (Luke 10:21). I have always loved that phrase from the eighth Psalm where David is rejoicing in the beauty and the glory of the heavens above.

> When I look at thy heavens, the work of thy fingers,
> the moon and the stars which thou hast established;
> what is man that thou art mindful of him,
> and the son of man that thou dost care for him?

Verse 2 of that psalm always puzzles people,

> by the mouth of babes and infants,
> thou has founded a bulwark because of thy foes,
> to still the enemy and the avenger.

What this refers to is that God chooses to open the mouths of children and mere striplings and use them, oftentimes, to do what the wise and the important have been unable to accomplish.

One of the greatest awakenings of the nineteenth century began in Cambridge University in England when D. L. Moody and his singer, Ira B. Sankey, came to that center of learning. In 1950 when I was traveling with Dr. H. A. Ironside, I met an Episcopal rector in Virginia who had been a member of that class in Cambridge when D. L. Moody came. He told us the whole University was outraged that this backwoods American preacher would dare to appear and speak in the center of culture of the English world. They well knew that he "murdered" the King's English. (Somebody once said that D. L. Moody was the only man he ever heard who could pronounce Jerusalem in one syllable!) So this rector said that he and others of his classmates who were not Christians determined that when Moody spoke in the chapel at Cambridge they would hoot him off the platform.

Moody began by asking Sankey to sing. (Sankey must have had a wonderful voice, because whenever he sang audiences quieted and listened to him.) As soon as he finished, Moody stepped to the edge of the platform and, looking directly at the students who were gathered there, he said these remarkable words, "Young gentlemen, don't ever think God don't love you, for he do!" This young man said that he and his classmates were dumbfounded by that beginning. Moody went on and in a few minutes he again said, "Don't ever think God don't love you, for he do!" Something about the very ungrammatical structure of these words captured them. The intense earnestness of this man spoke right to their hearts, beyond all the superficial, external things. That man said he later sought out Moody for a private interview, and Moody led him to Christ. A great awakening came to Cambridge University at the hands of that humble servant of God.

Now, God does this again and again to remind us that though he made the human mind, and he encourages us to use it to search for wisdom and knowledge, there is only one place we can learn to use this knowledge rightly—in relationship to the Lord Jesus Christ out of the wisdom and understanding of the revelation of God in the Scriptures.

Why does God do this? Why does God seem to be so against all the "wisdom of the world," as Paul calls it here? Is he jealous of man? Is he the kind of God who loves to put people down? It sounds almost vindictive, does it not? The answer is given to us in verse 29, where Paul says God does this "so that no human being might boast in the presence of God."

But why is God against human boasting? We are all experts at it, but God does not like it. Why? Surely he is not jealous of us; no, the answer is that human boasting is always based on an illusion, but God is a realist. Those who boast in themselves or in their abilities think they have some power in themselves to succeed, and God knows that this is a lie. They are deceiving themselves; they are living in a fantasy world. Therefore, the kindest thing God can do is to find a way to puncture that sinful pride, collapse that platform of prestige, and shatter that illusion of self-sufficiency. This he does by using the obscure and the weak and the things that are oftentimes regarded as foolish.

Some years ago I read an article by a businessman friend of mine who recounted his own experience in this regard. He learned this the painful way. He writes,

> It's my pride that makes me independent of God. It's appealing to feel I am the master of my fate; I run my own life, I call my own shots; I go it alone. But that feeling is my basic dishonesty. I can't go it alone. I have to get help from other people, and I can't ultimately rely on myself. I am dependent on God for my very next breath. It is dishonest of me to pretend that I am anything but a man, small, weak and limited. So, living independent of God is self-delusion. It's not just a matter of pride being an unfortunate little trait and humility being an attractive little virtue, it's my inner psychological integrity that's at stake. When I am conceited, I am lying to myself about what I am. I am pretending to be God, and not man. My pride is the idolatrous worship of myself, and that is the national religion of hell.*

That is right in line with what the apostle is telling us. God sets aside the wisdom, the pride, and the boasting of man because it is based upon an illusion, a fantasy, that men have in themselves power to act.

purpose of scripture

to teach us **To Walk in a Different Way**

Paul then sets forth for us in another beautiful passage the secret of true wisdom. What is it? It is the ability to recognize that though you may have little of what the world thinks it takes to succeed, if you have Jesus, and have learned to count on his power moment by moment, you have the secret of true success. Many Christians know that, but they do not act on it when the moment comes. The whole purpose of the Scriptures is to teach us to walk in a different way, to live by a different power and to do so with respect to everything we do. The simplest tasks are to be done in the power of Christ.

Look at what Paul says now, in verses 30 and 31:

> He [i.e., God] is the source of your life in Christ Jesus, whom God made our wisdom, our righteousness and sanctification and redemption; therefore as it is written, "Let him who boasts, boast of the Lord."

There is an interesting structure to the Greek sentence here. What Paul says is, "He is the source of your life in Christ Jesus, whom God made to be our wisdom, *even* our righteousness, our sanctification,

---

* Howard Butt, Jr., in an article in *CBMC Contact,* © 1954.

our redemption." In other words, righteousness, sanctification and redemption are the explanation of what wisdom involves.

Elements of Wisdom

You will remember that wisdom is the right use of truth, and it always takes three basic elements to be wise. First, there must be a true perception of what is, an understanding of the nature of reality. If you are going to be wise about any situation you may face, you have to understand what forces are at work, what is happening, what is involved and what is driving them. Therefore, one of the fundamentals of wisdom is the ability to distinguish the true from the false, to understand reality. ①

Second, there must also be a true evaluation of worth; you have to be able to distinguish between what is trivial and what is important. Have you ever had the experience of arguing with somebody, perhaps your wife, or your husband or your children, and it started out over some small matter but then you became very involved in it? You grew hotter and hotter, and they grew hotter and hotter, and soon you ended up nose to nose, shaking your fists at one another, with your voices raised. Suddenly it occurred to you, "What are we arguing about?" You began to see that you had built up a trivial matter into a mountain of meaning and it was foolish to do so. We are all guilty of that, but to act wisely you must be able to put things in perspective ② and keep them there so they do not get out of focus.

The third element of wisdom is the ability to blend the two essentials ③ of human life, truth and love, into that harmonious balance that keeps everything right on keel: to be honest yet patient, to be both frank and gracious. That is what we see so beautifully in Jesus. How honest he was, how frank he was, and yet he always had that gracious touch that was sensitive to the person to whom he spoke and the need of that person's life and heart. "Speaking the truth in love" is the sign of wisdom.

Christ has come to teach us how to live this way. The mark of somebody who is growing in Christ is that he or she is becoming able to exercise that kind of wisdom. And it begins, as the apostle tells us here, with the gift of righteousness. Christ is made unto us righteousness. Righteousness is really what we mean when we use the words "self worth," a full and loving acceptance in the eyes of God. It is a position to which we are able to return whenever we are threatened, or guilty or afraid, a position from which we can handle pressure.

If you feel worthless you cannot handle life, you lose the ability to function. You must have a sense of worth. The world says you have to earn that, but God says you can have it as a gift; it is yours already. Now, on that basis, start to handle life.

Then, wisdom moves into the process that Paul calls "sanctification." That is the daily manifestation of a Christlike character becoming more and more visible in our life—the outward product of the inward righteousness. We will find ourselves manifesting this character of Jesus more and more as we learn to handle life according to the way God teaches us. We will become more loving, more patient, more understanding, more insightful, more courageous. We are all in the process. No one has made it yet, but we are on the way.

And finally, it results in redemption. Redemption is the restoration to usefulness of something that has been rendered totally useless. Have you ever pawned anything? I have. Put something in hock and you get some money (never anywhere near what it is worth) from a pawnbroker. That object of value is useless while it is in pawn. It sits there, gathering dust on the shelf or in the shop window, until it is redeemed. But when you go back and pay the redemption price, you restore it to usefulness. That is what God is doing with us; he is restoring us to usefulness. We, who in the process of sin have been rendered useless, are gradually being restored. The day will come when restoration will be complete, body, soul and spirit, and God will open up to us an avenue of service such as we have never dreamed of, because at last we have been made useful once more.

That is the wisdom of God. The world cannot do that, can it? It uses people for a little while and then discards them as useless. But God's wisdom is such that through the processes of life he is gradually restoring us to usefulness (redeeming us), and he does it through this wonderful gift of righteousness and this process of sanctification. Thus, we ought to give thanks continually for what he is doing in our lives. How far superior is the wisdom of God to the wisdom of man! That is why Paul concludes this with these words, "Therefore, let him who boasts, boast of the Lord." It is the Lord who can change you, not you, yourself.

A Negative Note

Now, in chapter 2, the apostle is looking back to his first visit to Corinth:

When I came to you, brethren, I did not come proclaiming to you the testimony of God in lofty words or wisdom.

(Instead of "the testimony of God," some of the ancient manuscripts have the phrase, "the mystery of God," and I think, because of what follows, that is perhaps a better translation.)

For I decided to know nothing among you except Jesus Christ and him crucified.

That represents a deliberate decision the apostle made when he came to Corinth. He would not talk to them along the lines of the wisdom of men. He would not use flowery phrases and lofty, high-sounding words; he would not attempt to impress them with the beauty and the glory of Christian living, but he would start on the negative note of the cross of Christ.

To us, as to the Corinthians, the wisdom of the world always sounds impressive. We are exposed to it all the time through the media of newspapers, magazines, television, and even our conversations with one another. If you watch television you are encouraged to seek after "the good life," to become "beautiful people," to "live life with gusto," and to find the "real thing." We all know, of course, that using a different deodorant is not going to change life that drastically, or that changing your brand of perfume is not really going to introduce you into a world of romance and exotic excitement. However, we are continually exposed to this idea: if you only develop all your hidden powers you will find life the way you want to find it—there are things in you, in your personality, that need to be brought out.

There is a germ of truth there that the Scriptures recognize also. God made man a potentially wonderful creature, and it is not wrong to say there are hidden possibilities in every human being that need to be developed. Where the wisdom of the world goes astray, however, is in how to do it. The world promotes the idea that if we just know the right things, take the right course, get involved in the right program, use meditative processes and various other methods, we will achieve what we are after. It always sounds so beautiful. It is usually couched in colorful phrases and supported by clever arguments. It is confirmed on television and in color advertisements in the magazines by very impressive people and facts, so that it all seems right.

Things were no different in Corinth. When Paul arrived, the whole city was given over to exploring methods of fulfilling life by various philosophical schools, by giving themselves to fleshly indulgences in the worship of sex, and in various commercial and business enterprises by seeking after beauty, art, music, and the aesthetic things of life. That is why Paul made a definite decision not to speak in lofty, flowing phrases, or to tell people that all they needed was a little knowledge in special subjects. "But," he said, "I decided to know nothing among you except Jesus Christ and him crucified."

They Are Afraid He Is Right

As we have seen, the cross of Christ is a judgment on the wisdom of man. What do the smart, powerful people of the world do with Jesus of Nazareth? They crucify him! They reject him; they deny him; they put him to death if they possibly can. That is what they did in the first century and they still do today. Why? Because they think he is crazy? No, even today, nobody thinks Jesus was crazy. They resist him because they are afraid he is right. He threatens people. As we have already seen, the cross is the result of confronting the world with the ways of God.

I want to share with you a quotation from Dorothy Sayers, a very insightful writer and popular theologian who has done a fine job of defending Christian faith:

> The people who hanged Christ never, to do them justice, accused Him of being a bore—on the contrary: they thought Him too dynamic to be safe. It has been left for later generations to muffle up that shattering personality and surround Him with an atmosphere of tedium. We have very efficiently pared the claws of the Lion of Judah, certified Him "meek and mild," and recommended Him as a fitting household pet for pale curates and pious old ladies.

> To those who knew Him, however, He in no way suggested a milk-and-water person; they objected to Him as a dangerous firebrand. True, He was tender to the unfortunate, patient with honest inquirers, and humble before Heaven; but He insulted respectable clergymen by calling them hypocrites; He referred to King Herod as "that fox"; He went to parties in disreputable company and was looked upon as a "gluttonous man and a winebibber, a friend of publicans and sinners"; He assaulted indignant tradesmen and threw them and their belongings out of the Temple; He drove a coach-and-horses through a number of sacrosanct and hoary regulations. He cured diseases by any means that came handy, with a shocking casualness in the matter of other people's pigs and property; He showed no proper deference for wealth or social position; when confronted with neat dialectical traps, He displayed a paradoxical humour that affronted

serious-minded people, and He retorted by asking disagreeably searching questions that could not be answered by rule of thumb.

He was emphatically not a dull man in his human lifetime, and if He was God, there can be nothing dull about God either. But He had "a daily beauty in His life that made us ugly," and officialdom felt that the established order of things would be more secure without Him. So they did away with God in the name of peace and quietness.*

So when Paul came to Corinth he did not start with the "power of positive thinking," or even "possibility thinking." There is only one answer to what is wrong with us, and that is to lay hold, by faith, of what God has done on our behalf, and that is where Paul started.

What are the results of that decision? First, he says (verses 3–5),

> And I was with you in weakness and in much fear and trembling; and my speech and my message were not in plausible words of wisdom, but in demonstration of the Spirit and power, that your faith might not rest in the wisdom of men but in the power of God.

I think that ought to be one of the most encouraging passages to any of us who have tried to be a witness as a Christian. Speaking of the things of Christ and of God is easy in a church where you are gathered with Christian friends, brothers and sisters in the Lord. However, when you try to talk about these things with worldlings, people who have come from entirely different backgrounds, people who are committed to the philosophy of taking care of number one first, you find it difficult. You feel much personal weakness and fear and trembling. That is the way Paul felt, and that ought to be an encouragement to us.

Culture Shock

The reason he felt like this is that what he was saying to them was not in line with what they wanted to hear about themselves. It did not massage the ego of man. Paul deliberately rejected that approach (which is wrong because it does not help man), and began to talk about the judgment of God upon the thinking, the attitudes, and the wisdom of man. It left him feeling rejected, or more accurately, suffering from "culture shock."

---

* *Affirmation of God and Man* (New York: Association Press) p. 36.

When missionaries or business people go out into a different culture where the language and the whole system of purchasing things is different, where the way people relate to one another is different, it is common to experience what is referred to as "culture shock." (You can even suffer from this when you move from one part of this country to another where customs are different.) Now imagine what it is like if even the language is different. You have been used to communicating your value to people by the clever things you say, by the way you think, by showing compassion and friendliness and so on, and all of a sudden you cannot even conduct a conversation except on the simplest level of, "How much is this?" and, "I'd like so many of that," in the marketplace. All of the normally expected approval signs are missing. You begin to feel you are out of step; you feel rejected.

That is what Paul was suffering in Corinth. When he came, there was no great ego-pleasing reception for him, there were no dinners, there was no Academy Award, no sense of power or impact on this city. In Acts we are told that he came to Corinth from Athens. He had come alone to Athens after being driven out of Thessalonica and Philippi and Berea, and he tried to witness there in the Areopagus, the city council; and his witness, though it was true and based upon the cross of Christ, was not received. So he came away to Corinth, all alone, and moved into this great, bustling, beautiful, corrupt, powerful, commercial city, and tried to preach Christ.

He tells us that he felt fearful, weak, and ineffective. He felt his words were not outstanding; he felt he did not impress anybody. Have you ever felt that way? I have, many times. I have stood up to bear a public witness and I felt as if I had two tongues and they were stumbling over one another. I did not seem to have the right answers to things. I could only talk about how the gospel affected me; I felt as though I was doing nothing effective. Yet Paul was not discouraged, except at first. In the Book of Acts we are told that after he had been in Corinth for a few months the Lord Jesus appeared to him in a vision and strengthened him and said to him, "Do not be afraid, but speak and do not be silent . . . and no man shall attack you to harm you. . . ." That is a revelation of the basis of Paul's fears. He was afraid he was going to be beaten up as he had been in other cities. He was also afraid because of personal pride. He was afraid of being branded as a religious fanatic. He did not like those feelings; nevertheless, he faithfully began to talk about what God had said in Jesus Christ.

Soon there was a second visible result. Paul calls it the "demonstration of the Spirit and (of) power." As Paul told the facts and the story out of the simple earnestness of his heart, God's Spirit began to work and people started coming to Christ. You can read the account in Acts 18. First, the rulers of the synagogue turned to Christ, and then hundreds of the common, ordinary people of Corinth began to become Christians. Soon there was a great spiritual awakening, and before the city of Corinth knew what had happened, a church had been planted in its midst and a ferment was running throughout the city.

Real Evangelism

I believe this is God's continuous and perennial way of evangelism. Frankly, though I support fully the ministry of evangelists like Billy Graham, Luis Palau and others in their mass rallies, I recognize that this is not the primary means of evangelism intended in the New Testament. It is only possible when there has been a foundation laid by the individual approach that Paul is speaking of here. The real evangelism occurs by simple people like you and me sharing what has happened in our lives.

I remember when we first started Peninsula Bible Church in Palo Alto. In those early days of the '50s we used to have Bible Classes where people would gather in homes in a relaxed setting to reach their non-Christian neighbors and friends. God greatly blessed that witness. We had meetings and classes that sometimes grew to tremendous sizes. Because it was so open and so free, these people would get into discussions about the principles of life and Scripture that were so interesting and intense they would go on until 12:30 or 1:00 in the morning. And do you know what the greatest problem was? Christians! Christians who were uneasy about talking to non-Christians, who loved the comfort of being with people who thought alike, and who felt uneasy when anybody proposed an idea that was not in line with Scripture. We had a terrible time trying to educate Christians to be gentle and gracious with people who had a different viewpoint, not to strike them down or brand them as heretic or send them out angry or upset because of something that was said. But as they began to bear witness in a gracious way and talk about their personal experience of life in Christ, hundreds began to come to Christ.

Never in all our history as a church have we had an evangelistic meeting in the church building at PBC. Many are absolutely appalled at the idea that there is any way to reach people without an evangelistic service in the church. When I say to them that every year there are hundreds coming to Christ all throughout the whole Peninsula area at all levels and stages of life, and yet we never have had an evangelistic service, they shake their heads. Some have even walked away saying, "It won't work." But it has been working for many, many years.

That is the way Paul approached Corinth. There was nothing dramatic, there was no great awakening, but there was a quiet, resistless, surging movement of the Spirit of God touching and changing lives everywhere—a "demonstration of the Spirit and power." Paul was not holding great healing meetings or anything of that sort, but, as he tells us in the sixth chapter, some wonderful things were happening. He says, "Some of you were idolaters, some of you were adulterers, and some of you were homosexuals; some of you were drunkards; you were swindlers, thieves and robbers, and it has all changed. Such were some of you," he says, "but you were washed, you were sanctified, you were justified, in the name of the Lord Jesus." Dramatic things had been happening in their lives by this simple witness of the Spirit by the apostle in the midst of his own personal sense of weakness, fear and trembling.

I want to quickly state here that although Paul was preaching the cross of Christ, I am sure that he was not coming on with heavy-handed, threatening, condemning language. He was not preaching what we would call "hell-fire and damnation." He did not have to. Later on in 2 Corinthians he says his approach was "by the open statement of the truth, commending ourselves to every man's conscience in the sight of God." If you say to somebody, "You're a sinner. You're going to hell," you cannot expect them to say, "Oh! Am I? Help me! Save me!" They will get angry and turn their backs on you and walk off and say, "Forget it, fella." Paul was not doing that. Rather, he was saying, "Look, you folks, you only have to examine your own lives. How do you feel about what is happening to you? Are you happy?" They were not. They were empty, lonely, miserable, afflicted, falling apart and feeling it, and he just said, "This is why you are that way, and do you know that in the death of Jesus, God has wiped out all other approaches except through him, but in him you can have everything you want from God? Life can be filled with joy, peace, forgiveness, healing and wholesomeness." As Paul declared those words, a great desire was awakened in people's lives and they were coming to Christ by the hundreds. That is what happens every time people approach life with simple truth.

Some years ago I clipped these words from an article in *Eternity* magazine based upon the idea that truth is the best approach. The article was called "The Slickest Gimmick of All," and this is what it said:

> There is potency and wholesomeness in living life transparently—rather than endlessly erecting poses and postures and fraudulent pieties. This modern world of ours is generously supplied with pitchmen, con artists and those who have axes to grind. These are enthusiastically and persistently using the big lie on us. Hence, it is an arresting and refreshing experience to meet a person or a group that is authentic and transparently open.

That is how Paul came to Corinth. He knew no church could flourish in Corinth that did not recognize the weakness of the wisdom of men and rest instead on the power of God.

The Missing Links

By contrast, he now describes the content of that wisdom and power of God. Verses 6–10:

> Yet among the mature we do impart wisdom, although it is not a wisdom of this age or of the rulers of this age, who are doomed to pass away. But we impart a secret and hidden wisdom of God, which God decreed before the ages for our glorification. None of the rulers of this age understood this; for if they had, they would not have crucified the Lord of glory. But, as it is written,
> "What no eye has seen, nor ear heard,
> nor the heart of man conceived,
> what God has prepared for those who love him,"
> God has revealed to us through the Spirit. For the Spirit searches everything, even the depths of God.

Paul says he did not come with lofty words of wisdom, but that does not mean there is not a wisdom in Christianity. In fact, he says, the greatest wisdom of all, the wisdom of God, is there. He refers now to a body of truth which ought to be the standard curriculum for Christian education in any church. But there are thousands of churches today where you would hardly ever hear anything about this being taught. Yet look how Paul describes it. He says it is the "mystery of God," in verse 1; he calls it the "secret and hidden wisdom of God," in verse 7; the "deep things of God," in verse 10; the "thoughts of God," in verse 11; the "gifts bestowed on us by God," in verse 12; and "spiritual truths" in verse 13. Finally, at the end of the chapter, he says it is "the mind of Christ."

Now what is this that Paul is talking about? A lot of people think this is some kind of religious truth that only churchgoers would be interested in, but it is not. What he is talking about is basically the missing links of human understanding without which we are unable to function as God intended us. These are truths that people all over the world are searching for. If you come to people with a simple declaration of these truths, you will find they are always eager to hear. This is why churches that really expound the Scriptures never have any trouble filling their pews. This is the most attractive truth the world knows anything about. There is no need for a lot of showmanship and hoopla to get people to come out. Once they understand that you are talking about the secrets of how to be a person, how to live, how to get rid of guilt and fear and hurt, how to interact with individuals, how to love God and be filled with the love and power of God, they will be there; they will be breaking down the doors to get in. These are not "religious" truths. They are vital and essential truths about man and God and the universe. They are what I would call "the lost secrets of our humanity."

Notice some of these statements that Paul makes. First, these are permanent truths; they are not passing (v. 6),

> . . . it is not a wisdom of this age or of the rulers of this age, who are doomed to pass away.

In 1 John 2:17 we read,

> The world passes away, and the lust of it; but he who does the will of God abides for ever.

This is not a passing fad that will change in the next decade: this is truth that remains eternal and unchangeable forever.

Second, it is intended, Paul says in verse 7, "for our glorification." Now glorification means the fulfillment of all the possibilities that are in you, discovering the "real you," to put it in modern terms. These truths will bring this about when you learn them.

Third, this truth is not discoverable by natural processes. The rulers of this age know nothing about it. When Paul speaks of "the rulers of this age," he means more than merely the officials of the day. He is talking about the leaders of thought, the mind benders, the shapers of public opinion, the philosophers, the sociologists, the politicians. They do not know these secrets. They do not understand this body of truth, and that is why nothing they propose ever works in the long run. You cannot find them out by listening to the speakers around today, Paul says. Neither are they observed, he says, by the eye, or the ear, or by the reason. You will not get them in school or in any secular training. You will not learn them by observation of life. You will not learn them by studying the history of the past, or by hearsay. You will not get them by deep and profound thinking on your own level about the mysteries of life. Paul says that God has revealed them to us by his Spirit. He then introduces the great section on how the Spirit of God takes the Word of God and teaches the people of God, which we will come to in the next chapter.

This is what I consider the greatest truth ever set before men, this body of knowledge that Paul is talking about here. This is the value of coming to church and of Bible study, both personal and in groups. If you are involved in profound Bible study you are beginning to probe the greatest body of knowledge available to men anywhere; hidden secrets about life that will never be found out in the secular world around us, and yet, when understood, will lead you to fulfillment of joy and beauty, love and grace such as you never dreamed of.

4

God's Teacher

Everyone who heard Jesus teach must have been deeply impressed by the fact that he spoke with authority about things that other people knew nothing about. Remember that in the gospels he answers questions before they are even asked and accurately identifies people's motives. Even more than this, he speaks of unseen things with familiarity. He describes what God is like, and the nature of angels. He describes what happens after death. He predicts future events with pinpoint accuracy. At the close of his ministry, as he was about to leave his disciples, they were filled with foreboding and despair not only because of the loss of his presence but because of the loss of his wisdom and power. In the Upper Room discourse he said to them, "I will not leave you orphans: (I will not leave you alone). If I go away I will send another Comforter to you and he will guide you into all the truth. He will take of the things of mine and show them to you, and he will say to you the things that I have not been able to say." Remember that he said, "I have many things to say to you but you are not able to bear them yet. When the Spirit of truth comes, he will guide you into all truth."

In this section of 1 Corinthians 2, the apostle Paul is clearly referring to that promise of our Lord about the coming of the Spirit and what the Spirit would teach us. Verse 10,

God has revealed to us (these things) through the Spirit; for the Spirit searches everything, even the depths of God. For what person knows a man's thoughts except the spirit of the man which is in him? So also no one comprehends the thoughts of God except the Spirit of God.

This passage introduces us to our mighty teacher come from God, the Holy Spirit himself, who is to instruct us by the Word of God. He will lead us into the truth of God that will change our lives and expose us to this "secret and hidden wisdom of God." When you discover that, I want to tell you something: life is going to be exciting and adventurous, for this line of truth is designed to set us free, to let us be the men and women God designed us to be.

Notice how the apostle underscores here the Spirit's knowledge first, using an analogy: "No one understands the things of man except the spirit of the man which is in him." Have you ever tried to talk to your plants? Many people do these days. We are told that plants can respond to our moods and reflect our attitudes. I know a woman who even prays over each plant. I don't know what it does for the plant, but it probably helps her a great deal! But it is clearly evident that plants do not talk back. (If they do, give me a call right away! I'll see if I can help you.) Life is constructed at various levels; the higher can take hold of the lower, but the lower cannot reach up to the higher. We have plant and animal life, then human life, then angelic life, and finally, divine life. The higher can reach down to encompass the lower, but the lower cannot reach up to the higher. That is Paul's argument here. Though no animal can reach into the realm of human relationship and converse with us, other human beings like ourselves can.

Do you ever try to tell your troubles to your dog? I know people who do. I've done it myself. A dog is man's best friend; he seems so sympathetic. If you talk to your dog, he'll whine, wag his tail, and lick you on the face. He knows you're trying to get something across; he is trying so hard to understand, but he cannot comprehend the things of a man. If you sit down and tell your troubles to your wife, however, she will understand. Or if you tell your troubles to your husband, or your friend, they will understand. Fortunate is the man whose wife is his friend, or the woman whose husband is her friend. They can understand because the spirit which is in man shares a common basis of knowledge.

God Must Disclose Himself

But here is this great Being in our universe, this fantastic Being of infinite wisdom and mighty power who is God. How can we know anything about him? Paul's answer is that we cannot unless he discloses himself to us. You cannot find out God by searching. Man by wisdom does not know God. Man by investigation of all the natural forces of life will never find his way to the heart of God. God must disclose himself, must open himself to us. That he has done by means of the Spirit of God—the Spirit has come to teach us about God. The Lord Jesus appeared as a man in order that we might have a visible demonstration of what God is like. The simplest answer to the question, "What is God like?" is to say he is like Jesus, under all circumstances. But it is the work of the Spirit to show us what Jesus is like. Jesus said, "He will take the things of mine and show them unto you." You can read the historical record of Jesus, but the living Lord does not stand out from the pages merely by reading them. It is as the Spirit illuminates those pages that you find yourself confronted with the living, breathing Christ. That is the work of the Holy Spirit.

Paul describes the method that the Spirit has taken to do this fantastic thing. Verse 12,

> Now we have received not the spirit of the world, but the Spirit which is from God, that we might understand the gifts bestowed on us by God. And we impart this in words not taught by human wisdom but taught by the Spirit, interpreting spiritual truths to those who possess the Spirit.

Paul points out five steps here that the Spirit of God has followed to teach us this secret and hidden wisdom of God. The first step is that the Spirit begins with the apostles.

> Now we (apostles) have received not the spirit of the world, but the Spirit which is from God . . .

The "spirit of the world" is that intelligent, strange, but sinister being behind the whole thinking of the world. He is described to us clearly and vividly in Ephesians 2, where Paul says, "You (believers) he made alive, when you were dead through the trespasses and sins in which you once walked, following the course of this world, *following the prince of the power of the air, the spirit that is now at work* in the sons of disobedience" (Eph. 2:1, 2, italics mine). From this we learn that behind the strange, confused knowledge and wisdom of the world is a spiritual being the Bible calls the Devil. The world does not know that; worldlings are like so many dumb animals being led to slaughter without realizing where they are going. But Paul says that is not the spirit we have received. Remember how he put this to Timothy: "God did not give us a spirit of timidity but a spirit of power and love and self-control (or, a sane mind)" (2 Tim. 1:7). Jesus had told the disciples, "The Spirit is now with you; he shall be *in* you." And on the day of Pentecost the Spirit of God came in a new and fresh way. He had been present before in the world, but he entered into the disciples and from then on these apostles who were to give us the Scriptures were men and women filled with the Spirit.

A Totally Different Light

Then Paul tells us the second step—the Spirit of God taught them and illuminated their minds.

(We have received . . . the Spirit) which is from God, that we might understand the gifts bestowed on us by God.

He is not talking about spiritual gifts here; the context indicates that he is talking about the whole realm of knowledge and truth that God has given us, which these apostles had begun to understand.

Have you ever noticed in reading the gospels that the apostles did not understand Jesus when he taught? He baffled them; he puzzled them; he said things that left them scratching their heads. He angered them at times, upset them, and said things to people that sometimes embarrassed the apostles. On one occasion they turned to him and asked, "Lord, don't you realize you offended those Pharisees?" As if he did not realize that! But when the Spirit came on the day of Pentecost, suddenly all that Jesus had said began to make wonderful sense; thinking back over all they had heard from his lips, they began to see it in a totally different light.

That is the reason why, when non-Christians read their Bibles it seems to be a totally different book to them than it is to a Christian. Perhaps you have had that experience. Before you became a Christian you read the Bible and it was such a dull book; there was nothing exciting in it. Then you became a Christian; you received the Spirit, and the result was that the book came alive. Things that you once had puzzled over became clear, and you found yourself fascinated. A man said to me recently that he had just become a Christian and for four and a half hours straight he could not lay the Bible down because the Spirit was teaching him from its pages. This is what Paul is talking about here. The Spirit began with the apostles and they were illuminated by him.

Words That God Approved

The third step is the phenomenon mentioned in verse 13,

> And we impart this in words not taught by human wisdom, but words (implied here) taught by the Spirit.

One of the major arguments of our day is over the question of the inerrancy of Scripture. People are asking afresh today, "Is everything in the Bible true? Does the Bible speak with authority in every realm of life? Is it true in what it says about scientific, geographic, and astronomic matters, and the like? Or is it true only when it tells you how to get to heaven?" That question is answered by Paul's statement here. He says that when the apostles began to speak and to write the Scriptures, they did so by words "taught by the Holy Spirit."

I do not think he meant that the Spirit of God dictated the Bible to them. What he is really talking about is a process by which the Spirit of God awakened the minds of the apostles to understand truth, and they chose their own words to express it so that every apostle's personality comes through in the words he uses. And yet, in a strange and wonderful way, those words which the apostles chose are words that God himself approved. Therefore, they come from him not directly, but indirectly. Paul says to Timothy, "All Scripture is breathed out from God" (2 Tim. 3:16). If that is true, then it comes from a God who cannot lie, a God who makes no mistakes, a God who sees the end from the beginning, so every word in Scripture is true. As the apostles wrote these things down, therefore, we can trust what they had to say.

A young man was telling me how he has discovered that he does not always have to understand the Bible to benefit from its wisdom. He said, "I've learned that I don't always understand everything it tells me. But I know this: if I obey it, I will benefit from what it says." That is the truth, because it is the Word of God, the living Word, the Word of truth from the Spirit of truth.

Then there is a fourth step; Paul says,

> And we impart this in words not taught by human wisdom, but taught by the Spirit, interpreting spiritual truths to those who possess the Spirit.

The whole last phrase, "interpreting spiritual truths to those who possess the Spirit," is a translation of three words in Greek, and it is a difficult phrase to translate. If you have a Revised Standard Version, there are two other possible translations given in the margin. One is "interpreting spiritual truths in spiritual language," and the other is, "comparing spiritual things with spiritual." The verb that is translated "interpreting" here is really a word that means, "to fit things together." What I think Paul is describing here is the process of taking the wisdom of God—these great facts about our personalities, our makeup, and about God himself revealed in this secret and hidden wisdom of God—and fitting them to the circumstances and the personalities of each individual. In other words, making the Word living to us. That is the work of the Spirit of God. We have all had that experience, if we are believers.

Now, finally, (step 5) to do this, we must be indwelt by the Spirit as well. Paul uses a word here that indicates that. He calls us "spiritual people"; *pneumatikoi* is the word. It comes from the Greek word for spirit, which is *pneuma*. Who are the *pneumatikoi*, the spiritual people? Well, they are those who have received the Spirit.

One of the arguments of today is over the matter of how we receive the Spirit. Some tell us it must be a dramatic demonstration that results in speaking in tongues. I was talking with a girl not long ago who said, "You know, the evidence of receiving the Spirit is speaking in tongues." I said, "Do you mean that everybody who has not spoken in tongues does not have the Spirit?" "Well, no," she said, "I didn't mean that." "But you said that the evidence for receiving the Spirit is speaking in tongues," I replied. "Well," she said, "maybe there's something else there that I don't understand." I assured her that there was!

According to the Scriptures you receive the Spirit when you believe in Jesus. That is what he himself said. On the great day of the feast of the Tabernacles recorded in John 7, he said, "If anyone thirst, let him come to me and drink. He who believes in me, as the Scripture has said, 'Out of his heart shall flow rivers of living water.'" John adds, "Now this he said about the Spirit, which those who believed in him were to receive . . ." (John 7:37–39). And in the first chapter of his Gospel John says, "To all who received him (Jesus), who believed in his name, he gave power (power is the work of the Spirit) to become children of God" (John 1:12). Everywhere in the Scripture you find that the moment you believe the word about Jesus—who he is, what he did, and what he can do for you as Lord of your life—in that moment you receive the Spirit.

Scripture draws a beautiful analogy for us, comparing the new birth in Christ to a physical human birth. If you are a mother, you know that though the moment of birth was an unforgettable time, the moment of conception occurred without your even realizing it. In an experience of love, two tiny seeds joined together and a new life began by that union. It began to develop and grow, and soon it became evident to you and to everyone else that a new life was there. This is the way the Holy Spirit is born into our hearts. Nobody knows when it happens, but when the ovum of faith meets the sperm of the truth of God about Jesus, a new birth occurs; the Holy Spirit enters a life. Those who receive the Spirit then, are born again into a new creation, as Paul terms it; they are then "spiritual" people.

The apostle goes on in the next passage to contrast this with carnal Christians. Carnality is a state of temporarily not relating to the Spirit. But spiritual-minded Christians are those who not only have received the Spirit but, as Paul describes in Romans 8, "they have set their minds on the things of the Spirit." They listen to the Spirit; they hear the word of the Spirit; they believe the word; and they act upon the word of the Spirit. This whole body of truth then becomes active in their lives and they are changed.

There is the process. It begins for the apostles with the Spirit's indwelling and illuminating of their minds, so as to preach in words chosen by the Spirit, followed by the indwelling of every believer by belief in the word that the apostles preached, and the illuminating of the mind of each believer to understand truth as it fits his or her life directly. That is the process by which this great body of fascinating truth, the secret and hidden wisdom of God which is intended for our glorification, will begin to change our lives, our homes, our families, our community, our nation, and ultimately, the whole of the world.

The Natural Man

Now, in verses 14–16, we will learn why the world can never solve its problems, why it is locked into the same pattern of failure, generation after generation. The only breakthrough that can ever occur is to someone who opens his mind and heart to the word of the Spirit.

The unspiritual man does not receive the gifts of the Spirit of God, for they are folly to him, and he is not able to understand them because they are spiritually discerned. The spiritual man judges all things, but is himself to be judged by no one. "For who has known the mind of the Lord so as to instruct him?" But we have the mind of Christ.

In verse 14 the translation, "the unspiritual man," is not a very accurate rendering. The margin says "the natural man." That is a much better translation because what Paul is talking about here is man as he is born, as he is by nature. We were all of us, without exception, born natural men and women. Paul uses a descriptive and helpful word to understand what that is. The word translated "unspiritual" here is really the word *psychikos*, which derives from the root *psyche*, which means, of course, the soul. What Paul means is that the one who enters this world according to nature is operating from the basis of his soul and not his spirit. As God made man in the beginning, he was intended to be a threefold being—body, soul, and spirit—with the spirit as the highest center of the operations of his life, directly open to the revelation of God himself. In the Garden of Eden, Adam and Eve were both spiritual men and women, operating by the human spirit's contact with the living God who walked with them and talked with them. As someone has described it, when the Fall came, that spirit, that upper room, fell down into the basement, and man has been operating at the level of the second floor ever since. He is a second-story man, in every sense of the word, and that is the highest center of human functioning today.

The soul has three primary functions. The first and most notable quality about it is that it has the power to choose. It has a will, and we all recognize that. Even babies have their own will, which they exercise sometimes at the most inopportune moments. They will already do things that their parents do not want them to do, simply because they have the power of choice—one of the highest dignities accorded to mankind.

But that choice, that exercise of will, is made on the basis of two other functions of the soul. One is the ability to feel, the emotional capacity to have moods, urges, and desires, and this governs many of the choices of the natural man. We have all seen the bumper sticker that says, "If it feels good, do it!" That is a reflection of this natural philosophy which urges you to make your choice on the basis of your mood, your desire, your feeling of how you are at the moment.

There is another capacity of the soul, however, and that is the *reason*. Some people pride themselves on not making decisions on the basis of feelings. They think of themselves as logical, coldly reasonable people who decide on the basis of the facts. They sometimes feel very superior to all those poor people who simply "emote" as they go through life, making decisions on that basis. But again, the Word of God tells us that they need not feel so proud of themselves, because their reasoning power is limited. It functions only between two clearly marked dividers, birth and death—only in the realm that exists between those two poles. Therefore, everything the reasoning man sees is related to this life. His logical choices are made on the basis of goals centering around this life, goals such as personal success, fame, wealth, power, personal pleasure, and so forth. People who live like this are what we call men and women of the world. Their viewpoint is natural; it is instinctive with them; it is from birth. As someone has well put it:

> Into this world to eat and to sleep
> And to know no reason why he was born,
> Save to consume the corn,
>   devour the cattle, flock and fish,
> And leave behind an empty dish.

Shut Away from the Things of God

But according to this passage, the natural man has some severe limitations. Verse 14:

> The natural man does not receive the gifts of the Spirit of God, for they are folly to him, and he is not able to understand them because they are spiritually discerned.

Three things limit the natural mind: first, it is shut away from all the things of God, the whole realm of the secret and hidden wisdom of God that Paul has been describing. The natural man does not even know this realm exists. He thinks that all the bases on which he must make his choices are present before him now, such as his reasoning power, his emotions, and his ability to assess and evaluate life as he sees it. He is ignorant of a vast realm of information about us, about God, about the world and the way it functions, about the purpose of life, and about the end toward which all things are heading. For this reason, as we have already seen, he misunderstands much about life.

It is evident that he misunderstands marriage. He does not see it as a union designed to take two very different types of people and blend them together through a long process, sometimes involving much struggle and heartache, until a whole new being is formed to the glory and honor of God. To the worldly man, the natural view of marriage is that it is for his personal pleasure, so that another person might satisfy his needs. When that no longer happens, there is no reason to maintain the marriage. Many Christians are falling heir to this kind of thinking and even breaking up their marriages because they have allowed themselves to be seduced by the natural view of marriage.

The natural man misunderstands the power and purpose of sex. These days, many churches are debating whether they should ordain a man or a woman who has been and is an avowed, practicing homosexual. The only reason they are debating this thing is that they have forsaken to some considerable degree the revelation of the secret and hidden wisdom of God. Otherwise, it would not even be subject to debate, for the wisdom of God makes very clear that homosexuality is a violation of God's intent for mankind and a destructive force let loose in our society that tears down the very fabric of society by which we exist.

I read an article in the paper recently by a prominent woman pediatrician advocating openly and without shame that children ought to indulge in sex at an age as early as four or five years. And further, that incest between a father and a daughter is a good thing. Now where do those kinds of abominable ideas come from? Well, they arise from a failure to understand the secret and hidden wisdom of God, and a failure on the part of the church to adequately teach this so that it infiltrates society and affects the secular world around. Such abominations take root in our culture only when the people of God begin to drift away from their moorings in the Scriptures.

This is why the world misunderstands adversity. It does not see it as God's training ground. Trouble is regarded as an invasion of rights, as an alien invader that has no right to be there. The natural man's attitude toward God when trouble strikes is that of anger, hostility and resentment. Too often, it is also part of the Christian's attitude, because we have failed to hang on to those wonderful revelations of God by the Spirit in his Word.

Furthermore, not only is the natural man shut away from this, but going a step further, Paul says the natural man is *unable* to understand these things—they do not make sense to him. It is only as these principles permeate society as Christians live on this basis that he is able to see or accept them at all. Otherwise, he sees no reason whatsoever for these things. He cannot understand the things of God.

To the natural mind, such a thing as euthanasia—putting older people to death when they are no longer able to function quite as well as they once did—is regarded as the logical thing, the sensible thing to do. "Get them out of the way, they only clutter up the landscape." This is why abortion is so widely practiced and accepted in our day, because it is no longer seen to be what the Word of God clearly declares it to be—a taking of human life, a form of murder. But the natural mind does not see that. To the natural mind it seems to be logical and reasonable. This is ultimately what produces the macabre activity of Nazism in which a whole race of people is committed to the gas chambers. That kind of thinking arises because the natural mind does not understand the things of God.

The reason, Paul says, is very clear. These things are spiritually discerned; it is necessary to have the Spirit of God indwelling you in order to see and understand fully that these things are true. The natural man does not yet have the Spirit, so the only point of release for the natural mind at this point is to confront it with the person of Jesus. "What we preach is not ourselves," Paul says, "but Jesus Christ as Lord, with ourselves as your servants for Jesus' sake" (2 Cor. 4:5). That is where the world can be helped, for it is only by faith in Jesus that the Spirit of God enters the human heart. If there is no faith in Jesus, if there is no acceptance of him as Lord, the mind remains darkened. Although it may accept, because of popular pressure, the standards of Christian life, it is never fully convinced that they are right until the heart is open to the Spirit of God by faith in Jesus. Without this equipment of the Spirit the mind is unable to grasp what God wants to say to us.

If we stopped to think about it, we would realize that though we may be sitting quietly in our room, the air around us is charged with pictures and music and people's voices. The reason we do not see or hear them is that we lack for the moment the necessary equipment, but if we had a radio or a television set we could immediately pick up these sound and picture waves right out of the air as they pass through the room. So it is with the men and women of the world. Without the presence of the Spirit they lack the equipment to understand many of the things that Christianity says.

Open to the Spirit

Now in contrast, Paul returns to the spiritual man. Verse 15:

"The spiritual man judges all things, but is himself to be judged by no one. For who has known the mind of the Lord so as to instruct him?" But we have the mind of Christ.

Here the apostle uses still another word, not *psychikos*, "soulish," but *pneumatikos*, "spiritual." In the widest sense, Paul is talking about all Christians—anyone who possesses the Spirit of God. In the Book of Romans the apostle says that if anyone does not have the Spirit of Christ he is none of his—he is not a Christian, and yet, if we are led by the Spirit of God, we are the sons of God. Therefore, the presence of the Spirit of God in the individual life is what marks the difference between a true Christian and one who is not; and those who have the Spirit are spiritual men and women in the widest sense.

However, as Paul will go on to show in chapter 3, it is possible to have the Spirit of God but not always to obey him. Such a person is called a "carnal Christian," one who has the Spirit but does not walk by the Spirit. In a narrower sense, this is what Paul is speaking of here. To all who are open to the Spirit, who obey the Spirit, who are led by the Spirit, these three great possibilities are true.

First, they are able to judge all things on a moral basis. That is a remarkable statement, because when Paul says all things, he means *all* things. Christians who thoroughly understand the revelation of God in the Scriptures by the Spirit are rendered able to pronounce a moral or ethical judgment in any area of life. That does not mean at all that a Christian knows everything. Christians do not automatically understand all scientific knowledge, all physical or musical knowledge. If you think that by being a Christian you are able to know everything, someone will quickly disabuse you of that. What it means is that since everything has an ethical or moral dimension, it is the task of the Christian, indeed the privilege of the Christian, to point out to himself and to the world around what is the right and the wrong way to use things. Thus, he is the judge of all things in that realm. He must, therefore, pronounce the final ethical judgment in these areas.

Now, this is not something automatically yours because you are a Christian. There are probably millions of Christians who are not fit to judge ethics or morals because they do not obey the Spirit, or even know all that the Spirit has said. They do not study nor understand their Bibles. Therefore, they are not able to judge in this area. Nor does it mean that you need to quote only one or two verses of Scripture to prove that something is right or wrong. That is called "proof-texting," and it is one of the most abominable practices in the world today. If you merely take a verse here or there to support some particular cause, you can prove almost anything by the Bible. But that is a terrible abuse of Scripture.

The spiritual man is the man who has thoroughly studied the mind of the Spirit as he has spoken in the Old and the New Testaments. He is, furthermore, willing to be taught by the Spirit. He prays, he searches diligently and waits before God for an understanding, an illumination of his mind; he tries to understand the problem before him, and only then makes a pronouncement that could be called the judgment of the Lord.

It is this ability to judge all things in an ethical dimension that makes it possible for Christians, when the whole world is saying abortion is right, to stand up and say it is wrong. It is this ability that makes a Christian able to declare that homosexuality is wrong, no matter how many laws are passed favoring it. You can pass laws that make it legal, but you will never pass any that will make it moral. It is this ability to judge all things in an ethical dimension also that makes it possible, in fact, necessary for a Christian to say that heavy-handed materialistic greed is *wrong*, that conniving and wheeling and dealing in business to manipulate people to do what you want is *wrong*, and that social oppression is *wrong*, and that bigotry of every type is *wrong*. It is the Christian who is to say that, based not upon the wisdom and thinking of the world, but on the secret and hidden wisdom of God.

The second thing Paul says about the spiritual man is that he is not subject to judgment himself. This means, of course, that there are times and occasions when he will be beyond and above the law. Now if you think that means all law, and you go out and try to live on that basis, you soon will have plenty of time to think it over and no one will bother you during the process! But there will come times when even the Christian must act against the law. This raises the whole civil disobedience question, and that is discussed in the Scriptures in various places. There are times when the laws of the land become oppressive, anti-Christian. Then there is a Christian way of response. It is not demonstration, it is not violent protest of any sort, but it is quiet insistence that says his conscience must be taught and instructed by the Word of God or nothing will move it. You see it in Martin Luther as he stood before the Diet of Worms at the great cathedral on the Rhine with the authorities of Europe assembled there, including the Emperor of the Holy Roman Empire. Luther declared, "Unless my conscience be taught and corrected by the Word of God, I will not change or recant anything that I have written. Here I stand: I can do no other, God help me." Now that is the Christian who is no longer subject to the judgment of the world, for he acts on the basis of the wisdom and knowledge of God. And Paul supports this; he says, "For who has known the mind of the Lord so as to instruct him?" Wisdom from this source is beyond challenge, for it comes from God himself who is the ultimate realist, who sees life exactly as it really is.

The Mind of Christ

Then the apostle concludes by saying probably the most daring thing that has been said in the Bible: "But we have the mind of Christ." We have the very way of thinking about life that Jesus himself had, with that keen ability to observe what was going on around him, that ability to evaluate the changing standards of men and to come right through to the very heart of the thing. That is the mind of Christ, the ability to know what was in man. He needed no one to tell him because he understood men. That is the mind of Christ.

The mark of it, of course, is that we will behave as Jesus did. In the midst of this present world we will be compassionate when others are severe; we will be severe when others are tolerant; we will be kind to the ugly, the poor, the obscure, the people of no ability or power, but we will be frank with the rich and the powerful and the mighty. That is the mind of Christ. I submit to you there never was a more radical proposal to change the world than that brief statement—to act according to the mind of Christ. Here is the true way to radically affect the world of our day. That is what God sends us out to do.

I freely admit to you that there are few of us who in any degree manifest this consistently. We are all in the process of learning, and nobody can hold himself up and say that he always operates this way. But to the degree that we are learning to fashion our lives according to the revelation of the secret and hidden wisdom of God, we are letting loose in this world the mind of Christ. What a powerful effect it will have upon society! This is the privilege of the spiritual man, who is able to operate in the midst of the confusion of life today in such a way as to call men back to reality, away from the confusion and the illusion and the delusions by which the world lives, to the realities of life as it is in Christ. What a privilege!

5

Carnal and Spiritual Christians

What is the trouble with the church at Corinth? Well, as the apostle has told us, by now they should have been governed by spiritual thinking; they should have understood what God had revealed to them in the Scriptures in such a profound way that their outlook would be controlled by this kind of thinking in everything they did. But instead, they are still operating on the natural philosophy of the world around, and they have brought that thinking into the church.

Of the Flesh

Paul says in plain language in chapter 3 that this is all wrong:

> But I, brethren, could not address you as spiritual men, but as men of the flesh, as babes in Christ. I fed you with milk, not solid food; for you were not ready for it; and even yet you are not ready, for you are still of the flesh. For while there is jealousy and strife among you, are you not of the flesh, and behaving like ordinary men? For when one says, "I belong to Paul," and another, "I belong to Apollos," are you not merely men? (vv. 1–4)

Notice that Paul uses the phrase "of the flesh" three times. That phrase represents the problem here at Corinth. The apostle actually uses two different Greek words translated "flesh" here, and though they are closely related, there is a difference between them. The first one is the word *sarkinos*, which comes from the Greek word for flesh, *sarks.* We could translate *sarkinos* into English by the word *fleshy.* Paul is not putting them down when he uses this word, he is merely recognizing their nature—they are fleshy people; they are of the flesh. All Paul says is, "I could not speak to you as spiritual men because you are fleshy men." In other words, he began where they were, and he preached Christ to them. Even after they came to Christ, he recognizes they still had not advanced very far beyond the normal, natural outlook of flesh and blood.

He is careful, however, to indicate they were not unregenerate after he had brought them to Christ. He calls them "brethren," and he says they are "babes in Christ." They are in Christ, but they are babies. That is the problem. Paul was preaching and teaching in Corinth for a year and a half, but in all that time they never advanced far beyond babyhood. They were still governed by the thinking of the flesh. So in the second part of this section where he refers to the flesh again twice, he uses a slightly different word. It is not *sarkinos* here, but *sarkikos,* which comes from the same root but means "dominated by the flesh." The Latin word for flesh is *carne* and that is why in some versions this is called "carnal." It should be translated "fleshly,"

. . . for you are still fleshly. While there is jealousy and strife among you, are you not fleshly, and behaving like ordinary men?

Someone who is still fleshly or carnal after he has become possessed by the Spirit is one who is still thinking like a natural man. We see the same divisions in Romans 8 where Paul speaks of those who are no longer of the flesh, i.e., they are regenerate but they walk "according to the flesh" instead of "according to the Spirit." Paul is using the same terminology in each case.

What is this like, this condition of carnality or fleshliness? Well, Paul describes it first as "spiritual babyhood." Now there is nothing wrong with babies; everyone starts out that way. Babies are delightful little creatures, up to a point, but they require a lot of care. They are messy; they burp, and they spill over in various ways. Someone has described a baby as a digestive apparatus with a loud noise at one end and no responsibility at the other! No one minds that when babies are little; we all must have that kind of care, and even a young father will learn to change diapers. But when that condition goes on and on and on and the baby becomes 5, 10, 15, 20 years of age and it still requires the same amount of care (you are still changing diapers!) it is a different situation altogether. That is what Paul is talking about here—spiritual babyhood that continues too long and that requires milk instead of meat. That is a very important distinction.

The Elementary Doctrines

In chapters 5 and 6 of the letter to the Hebrews, you also have a helpful explanation of what these terms mean. This was the problem with the Hebrews, too. They were spiritual babies; they had a case of arrested development. That passage also says, "You need milk." Well, what is milk? Hebrews 6 tells us that it is "the elementary doctrines of Christ," and it goes on to list them for us. The first one consists of evangelistic preaching, i.e., telling people how to become Christians.

One of the most dangerous and, I think, deadly things in the Church is the habit that thousands of churches have of preaching the gospel over and over every Sunday morning. For this reason Christians never grow up; they never get out of spiritual babyhood because all they hear is how to become a Christian. Now that is all right for babies; that is what leads them to Christ and establishes them, but evangelistic preaching is only milk. Hebrews goes on to say that teaching concerning rituals like baptism and laying on of hands (probably for healing), and all such emphasis on rituals and ceremonies are part of the milk that babies need. It is not yet meat, the strong food that is required for maturity. Hebrews 6 tells us also that truth about the resurrection and the last judgments (about prophecy and eschatology), is all milk. It is designed to get believers started in the Christian life, but it is no way to build maturity as a Christian. Yet, across America there are thousands and thousands of churches that spend their whole teaching period, year after year, in investigating more about rituals, ceremonies, baptisms, prophecy and prophetic matters, and evangelizing. That is milk.

What is meat? Meat is preaching that unfolds the full riches and magnificence of the gospel so that people grow up. They stop being children, as Paul says in Ephesians 4, ". . . no longer (to be) children, tossed to and fro and carried about with every wind of doctrine" (Eph. 4:14). That requires the meat of the Word.

Christ died for my sins; that is milk. We died with Christ to sin; that is meat. That is what will free me from habits and attitudes that are irritating to others and that make me difficult to live with. The knowledge of the gifts of the Spirit—that is milk. These Corinthians had that knowledge. Paul says right at the very beginning that they had all the gifts present among them so that "you are not lacking in any spiritual gift." What they did not understand was how to produce the fruit of the Spirit, which is love. That is meat. Later on Paul will discuss the gifts of the Spirit, and then he will say, "And I will show you a still more excellent way." That way is love. When you rejoice in hope of sharing the glory of God, that is milk, that is looking forward to the glory coming at the end of life. But when you learn to rejoice in your sufferings because you know God is working out something in your life which nothing else could do, that is meat. That is growing up as a Christian.

Now the mark of spiritual babyhood, Paul says, is jealousy and strife. Where you have baby Christians who are all too long in that condition, you will always have divisions, factions, strife, and breaking into little cliques and groups in the church. This arises out of a sense of competition. That is what Paul says here.

> For while there is jealousy and strife among you, are you not of the flesh, and behaving like ordinary men (still unchanged in your thinking)? For when one says, "I belong to Paul," and another "I belong to Apollos" (there you get the competitive spirit), are you not merely men?

The whole world functions on the basis of competition. Out there in your job you are up against the sharp, "dog-eat-dog" type of aggression, competition that exists for jobs and the in-fighting that goes on in the office to see who is going to get the next promotion and how to cut one another out (we have all become skilled at that)—but that is not to be carried over into the church. Nor is it, by Christians, to be indulged in even in the world. The whole purpose of the Spirit of God is to change our way of thinking so that we are no longer operating out of competition, but of cooperation.

In this next passage Paul brings out beautifully the spiritual view of relationships. I know pastors who live in fear some layman will have a ministry that will outshine theirs so they are afraid to let people meet in homes or discover their spiritual gifts and go to work for the Lord. There is a sense of rivalry and competition in the church. I know of Christians who are unwilling to use their spiritual gifts unless they can do so in large meetings or somehow be the center of attention. They are not interested in small, obscure places.

Some time ago I ran across this little poem. I thought it expressed this very well:

> Father, Where shall I work today? And my love flowed
> warm and free.
> Then He pointed me out a tiny spot and said, "Tend
> that for me."

I answered quickly, "Oh, no, not that. Why, no one
> would ever see,
No matter how well my work was done. Not that little
> place for me."
And the word He spoke, it was not stern. He answered
> me tenderly,
"Ah, little one, search that heart of thine. Are thou
> working for them or me?
Nazareth was a little place, and so was Galilee!"

Author Unknown

The spirit of carnality has invaded the church and made us rivals one of another, but how truly the spiritual-minded person lays that all aside and begins to operate, no longer in competition with anybody, knowing he or she is unique, with uniquely chosen gifts that no one else has exactly in the same combination. We do not need to be in competition with anybody at all. Each has something unique to do that only he can do.

That is what Paul goes on to describe,

> What then is Apollos? What is Paul? Servants through whom you believed, as the Lord assigned to each. I planted, Apollos watered, but God gave the growth. So neither he who plants nor he who waters is anything, but only God who gives the growth. He who plants and he who waters are equal, and each shall receive his wages according to his labor. For we are fellow workers for God; you are God's field, God's building (vv. 5–9).

Paul is looking now on the true view of ministry and ministers. He does not mean by ministers only the apostles or only a select group called the clergy, the pastors. This devilish idea that has possessed the church sees the clergy as people with a special pipeline to God. That idea is never found in Scripture. No, in Scripture all Christians are in the ministry, everyone without exception. All are given gifts by the Spirit. All are expected to have a function, a service that God uses. It does not have to be in the meeting of the church. It is out in the world, anywhere you are.

The Highest Rank

So how are we to view one another? As big shots striving to see who can get the most recognition; as dignitaries with special dress to indicate our rank and style of life? Are we to be the "heavies," the bosses, the brass? No. Paul says we are servants. That is all. Everyone, servants of Christ. That is the highest rank possible in the church, and everybody has it to start with. Therefore, there is no need for competition or rivalry. We are all servants of Christ. Jesus himself told us what our attitude is to be: "The Son of Man," he said, "came not to be ministered unto but to minister, and give himself a ransom for many." And again, "One is your Master, and all of you are brethren."

What is your reason for going to church? Is it that you might have a blessing, or is it that you might be a blessing? The attitude of a servant is always, "What can I do for another?" In the process you find yourself abundantly ministered unto. We hear so much today of this attitude that insists that "everything has to meet my needs." But the apostle is telling us that this will bring nothing but trouble in the church; it creates divisions and factions. We must come to see each other as servants of Christ, mutually living and ministering to one another as God gives us opportunity. This is what the Lord himself demonstrated for us. Are we in competition? "No," says Paul, "we're in cooperation. I planted; Apollos watered; but God gave the growth. We are doing different things, but we need each of them."

It is one of the glories of the church that nobody does the exact same thing. Churches that try to turn out people who all look alike, dress alike, carry the same kind of notebook, speak the same kind of language, use the same version of the Bible, are missing what God has in mind because we are all to be different, yet working together and needing one another. Paul will develop this much further in chapter 12.

The evangelist plants, the Bible teacher waters. Well, which is more important, Bible teaching or evangelizing? Paul's answer is, neither. God can do away with both of those. The important thing is not what either can do, but what God alone can do, which is to take truth and change lives with it. Evangelists cannot do that; Bible teachers cannot do that; only God gives increase, opens the mind, changes the heart and makes people different.

It is evident that God can dispense with both the planter and the waterer in nature. Out in the wilderness, *he* plants, *he* waters, and *he* gives the increase. God can do it all. So Paul is putting us in our proper place as regards people. When we ask who is more important, Paul or Apollos, Bill Gothard or Billy Graham, it is like asking which blade of a pair of scissors is more important, or which of my pant legs is more important? I need both. So it is not the people who are important, it is God who works through the people. Therefore, to give glory to men as though they were all-in-all (honor is right to give to those to whom honor is due), to exalt one as more important than another, is wrong. Paul says we are equal. "He who plants and he who waters are equal, and each shall receive his wages according to his labor," i.e., they are equally in need of the grace and the power of God, and shall receive the same according to their need.

Finally, his view is that all of us share the same high privilege. "We are God's fellow workers." Isn't that amazing? Nothing is more important in all of life than that. Think of the privilege of being a fellow-worker with God in this day and age! When at last it is all over and we stand before the King, the greatest honor ever accorded us will have been the honor that we have had of bearing his name and being an instrument of his grace here on earth, where we live, where we work, in our family.

Two Views of the Church

"You are God's field," Paul says. "You are God's building." Here are two equally valid views of the church. In the field, Paul is thinking of evangelism, of the increase. As a farmer plants his crop year after year it increases as he plants, so each year he is able to plant more because of the increased seed he gets. So the church spreads and increases numerically as we work within it, building one another up and teaching the truth of God. That, in turn, is imparted to others who are reached by neighbors and friends and thus the church increases. You are God's field. But you are also God's building, which, Paul says in Ephesians, ". . . grows into a holy temple in the Lord; in whom you also are built into it for a dwelling place of God in the Spirit" (Eph. 2:21, 22).

As we minister according to our gifts, where we are, we are learning something. We are being changed. We are being shaped and fashioned and chiseled off a little here and put in the right spot there, until the whole temple grows to be a manifestation of the wholeness of God. That is why, as the church functions in the way the Bible outlines, we become more and more like Christ. We manifest his qualities; we become a wholesome, healed people, a community that has learned to live together in forgiveness, friendship, compassion, love and mercy toward one another. As that becomes visibly manifest, the whole world begins to prick up its ears and watch and listen, for it discovers that is where God is. God is dwelling among his people and we are built up into God's building.

When our Lord said, "I will build my church and the gates of hell shall not prevail against it," he meant the church is people. The remarkable thing about the church is that it is a growing building, growing through the centuries, made up of people whom Peter calls "living stones" who are built into this mighty temple of God. Our Lord is still building his church, which he started back in the first century when the foundations were laid. That building has been going on, stretching through the centuries ever since, and now, perhaps, we are finishing off the roof. The building is almost complete it seems to me, but it is *one* building, *one* church.

An Invisible Union

Paul describes this now, in verses 10 and 11:

> According to the commission of God given to me, like a skilled master builder I laid a foundation, and another man is building upon it. Let each man take care how he builds upon it. For no other foundation can any one lay than that which is laid, which is Jesus Christ.

What a strange building the church is! It is not made of wood, or of stone, least of all of glass. It is made of people, and it consists of an invisible union among visible people, so in some sense the church is both visible and invisible. You can see the church because the people of God gather in one place, and yet you cannot see the church because it is made up of only that spiritually wrought tie that binds us together in sharing the life of Christ. That truly constitutes the church.

That union is manifested in three distinctive ways. First, we can refer to the church as the total union of all believers of all time, both on earth and in heaven. Paul speaks of the church in that regard in Ephesians where we have a picture of the whole temple of God in which God dwells.

Then, of course, there is the manifestation of that church as an individual congregation. In this sense the church consists of any two or three Christians gathered in the name of the Lord. Jesus said, "Where two or three are gathered in my name, there am I in the midst of them." Christians meeting in a home deserve the name of a church because they are a manifestation of this strange living union that our Lord is talking about. Every congregation is that kind of a church.

Still further, as this letter makes clear, every individual believer among us is a picture of that church. Paul will say in the sixth chapter of this letter, "Do you not know that your body is a temple of the Holy Spirit . . . ? You are not your own; you were bought with a price."

In that sense every one of us is a church, a dwelling place of God by the Spirit, and when Scripture speaks of the church it has all three of these in mind.

Now in all or any of these manifestations the matter of first importance is the foundation. The apostle clearly emphasizes what that foundation is. He does not leave it to debate; it is stated as plainly as it can be (v. 11):

> For no other foundation can any one lay than that which is laid, which is Jesus Christ.

His person, his life, his doctrines, his teachings, his resurrection, his ascension, his return by means of the Holy Spirit to make himself universally available among us, his coming return in person from heaven—all that is included as part of the foundation. The teachings concerning Jesus were given to us by the apostles, but they focus on the person of the Lord. Every church that departs from teaching about Christ and his work, his person and his resurrection, begins to slide away from the foundation and soon becomes tottery and wobbly, and finally collapses and crumbles into nothing. Every individual who is not built upon that foundation will find his life crumbling and failing ultimately. So our Lord is to remain always present as the foundation of the church, the God and Lord of the universal church, the head of the local body, manifesting his presence, his power, and his guidance throughout that body, and the Master and Savior of every individual heart which has come to know him. That is the foundation.

That foundation, of course, basically consists of Jesus as revealed in the Scriptures. They are the only witness to the true foundation of the church. They were given to us by the apostles and as such they constitute an unshakeable foundation. That is why every church, either local or universal, or any individual who does not base his life upon the Jesus of the Scriptures, soon begins to waver. Today we hear the words "Jesus" and "Christ" used in many ways not reflected in the Scriptures, but the only foundation God ever recognizes is the apostolic Christ. "No other foundation can any one lay," Paul says. That is the foundation, and this is why we must keep Jesus central in all things.

Master Contractor

Paul calls himself here "the wise master builder," and the word for master builder, *architectron* is the word from which we get our word *architect*. But he really uses this word in a different sense than we use the word *architect* today. To us an architect is the man who thinks up the building. He conceptualizes it; he plans it and draws the designs for it. In that sense, of course, God is the true architect of the church. The Lord Jesus said, "I will build *my* church." He has conceived it; he has designed it, has planned its structure, programmed its activities, and he continues to do so, thus he is really the architect.

The term I think we would use here for Paul is "contractor." Paul is a master contractor. He is skilled; he knows his business; he is filled with grace; he is helped by the power and the Spirit of God. He comes equipped to go to work and lay the foundation as he did in Corinth and everywhere else he went, preaching and teaching the doctrines of Christ. Many people think of a preacher as an individual with a dark suit on, who has an unclear mind, and always speaks with a holy groan. But we ought to think of a preacher as a man who wears a hard hat and a carpenter's apron and carries a saw and a hammer. He is building something. That was what Paul was doing. By preaching and teaching the doctrines of Christ and enabling people to practice these, he, together with the other apostles, laid the foundation of the church.

Now the purpose of a foundation, as Paul makes clear, is to build something on. You do not lay foundations and then walk off and leave them. If you do, it is a sign you have run out of money; you are not able to finish what you have started, and God does not do that. The apostles laid the foundations in giving us the Scriptures during the first century in order that they might be built upon, and the church rises upon that foundation. As believers are added to it, and as they become mature and strong in Christ, love and compassion, mercy, truth and grace begin to flow out of their lives instead of confusion, weakness, hostility and anger and all the things that were once there. So the church rises and takes shape as the building of God.

But who builds upon the foundation? Paul says, "I laid the foundation, and another man is building upon it. Let each man take care how he builds upon it." Obviously he has in mind Apollos and Cephas and some of the other teachers in the church at Corinth. There probably were many in Corinth who were teaching and preaching the doctrines of Christ and thus building on the foundation of personal faith in Jesus Christ which the apostle had laid. But this would also apply to almost any Christian, because we are all working with each other. There is a sense in which we disciple one another. Nobody is solely the "discipler" and somebody else the "disciplee." I have learned when I take on a young man to train or disciple that it is not very long before he will start discipling me as well. He will have insights and understanding of the Scripture that I need, and so we begin to build into one another's life. The great question that Paul raises here is, "What are you doing to one another as you build into one another's lives? They have an effect on you; you have an impact upon them." Everyone is faced with this great question here, "What is my impact? What am I building with? What kind of material am I putting into another person's life?"

Building for Eternity

Paul gives us the choices, in verses 12 and 13:

> Now if any one builds on the foundation with gold, silver, precious stones, wood, hay, stubble—each man's work will become manifest; for the Day will disclose it, because it will be revealed with fire, and the fire will test what sort of work each one has done.

Each one of us has an influence on someone else in the body of Christ. It may be on our children, parents, friends, companions, wives, or husbands. We are building upon the foundation which has been laid in their lives. "What are you building with?" That is the great question. There are two types of material. One is permanent—gold, silver, precious stones. By "precious stones," I do not think Paul means jewels, like rubies, diamonds, and emeralds. The word really refers to those large building stones carved out of granite or marble that are put upon a foundation to raise the walls and complete the edifice. They were costly stones because they required a great deal of work in quarrying and shaping and fitting them into the place where they ought to be. That is what Paul has in mind. The thing characteristic about gold, silver, and costly stones is that they withstand the fire. Such materials are permanent; they never fail or slip off the foundation; they are in line with the nature of the foundation.

The other three, of course, are exactly the opposite. They are highly combustible material—wood and hay and straw ("stubble," the King James Version calls it)—all very temporary.

These are symbols of course, but what do they refer to? What is the permanent material with which we can build into each other's lives, as opposed to the perishable? I do not think we have to debate that. It is what Paul has been talking about all through this whole section. The permanent is that secret and hidden wisdom of God which he said was, ". . . decreed before the ages for our glorification" and is revealed only by the Spirit through the Scriptures. If we build into each other's lives on the basis of that philosophy, what we build will endure the test of the fire.

On the other hand, the perishable is the "wisdom of the world," as Paul calls it, the wisdom of speculations and traditions, the changing philosophies of men. Every person sooner or later comes up with the same question, "Who am I? Why am I made this way, with this name and this color skin and why have I appeared in history at this point?" As people ask these questions, they begin to come up with answers, all of which conflict with one another. These reflect the shifting, impermanent philosophies of men. If you try to build your life on them, they will all disappear in the fire of testing.

But on the other hand, listen to the wisdom of God, Paul says. God is saying in effect, "Look, if you will just shut up for a minute I'll tell you who you are. I made you. I know what you're for. I know what you can do and how you fit and if you'll listen I'll tell you. You'll not only find out who you are, you'll find out who I am, and you'll discover that you can't find out who you are until you know who I am. I'm behind all things. I've brought all things into being and all things function within my will and purpose. All things will end in the objectives that I have set up. You can find yourself when you find me." That is what Paul is talking about.

One of the most devastating problems in our world today is the number of marriages which are threatened. Why are they threatened? Well, because they have all partaken to one degree or another of the current changing ideas reflecting the spirit of the age, which say that marriage is a way of enjoying yourself with another person. It is designed for sexual satisfaction. It is having somebody to meet *your* needs. Marriage is being in love and being happy together and if you are not happy or you are not in love any more, then forget it and marry someone else. That is why marriages are crumbling. They reveal what this very passage is telling us—that such ideas are impermanent, they do not last, they crumble and fall. It is improper material with which to build upon the foundation.

What lasts? God's insights into marriage, God's understanding of what is required for two people to become one flesh! God alone can show you how to lay hold of power and resources that make you able to do even things you do not want to do. That is "the secret and hidden wisdom of God." Without it marriages break up and churches fall apart, split and divide. Individual lives grow cold, lonely, despairing, unhappy and miserable. How appropriate is Paul's description of God's wisdom as "gold, silver and precious stones." These remain permanent, solid and sure!

Reflecting the Secrets of God

What Paul is asking us is, "You who preach and teach in the church (including me), what is the source of your teaching? Are you understanding these great secrets of God revealed through the Spirit, and do you reflect them in your teaching of the doctrines of Christ? Are you understanding that man is not to be exalted and/or to concern himself about status and titles, degrees and traditions? Has the word of the cross come to you, the word that cuts beneath all human attainment and sets it totally aside?" That word causes us, in fear and trembling, to declare what God is ready to do in our midst, not how much we can impress others by what we are going to do for God. That is the "word of wisdom," the "gold, silver and precious stones." This is what will endure and build up the church to last from age to age.

But do you know what we often want? What I frequently want is to find a way to indulge in all the love and pleasure of the flesh, to give way to my temper and to my desires to acquire comfortable things, to enjoy life with all its pleasures and at the same time, have a compassionate heart and the loving, joyful, peaceful, serene spirit of a Christian who is walking in the power of God. Isn't that what you want? Sure you do. But do you see what the apostle is saying? It is one or the other. If you are not building with gold, silver and precious stones into your own or another person's life, you are building with wood, hay and stubble. There are no other choices. That is why Paul says you must "take care" how you build the church.

Exam Time Is Coming

Now, why? Well, Paul says our motivation for true work is that examination day is coming.

> If the work which any man has built on the foundation survives, he will receive a reward. If any man's work is burned up, he will suffer loss, though he himself will be saved, but only as through fire (vv. 14, 15)

What do these words mean? Remember that Paul says in 2 Corinthians, "We must all appear before the judgment seat of Christ" (5:10). In John's Book of Revelation he describes the Lord before whom we appear: "His eyes are like a flame of fire" (1:14). Those flaming, searching eyes are going to examine all our Christian lives, what they have been made of, what we have been building with. Paul says in 2 Corinthians, "Then we shall receive the things done in the body whether they be good or bad"—the same two categories—whether they be built on the basis of the revelation of the mind and Spirit of God (gold, silver and precious stones), or whether they reflect the current philosophies of the spirit of the age around us. If it is good it will endure; it will stand the test, and we will be given a reward.

What is the reward? Do you know what I think it is? The Scriptures do not tell us flat out, but I think there are hints that indicate what it is. When Paul wrote to the Thessalonians he said, "Are you not our crown of rejoicing?" I think the reward is simply joy, joy over having spent your life in a way that counts. Did you ever watch a winning team at the end of a game? Do you notice what they do? They go crazy. Grown men jump on each other's backs; they pound one another and hug one another and even kiss one another. They jump up and down like little kids in a candy store. Why? They are filled with joy because the efforts they put forth produced results: it was satisfying to them. That was their reward.

Did you ever watch the losing team? They slink off; there is no jumping around and slapping one another on the back. No. Sadness and gloom prevail; they are ashamed because all their efforts were to no avail. It was all wasted effort. Now each of us will have some of both in our lives. There is no Christian who will not have some degree of gold, silver and precious stones because God guarantees it by having come into our lives. But there can also be a lot of wood, hay and stubble, too, built upon the philosophy of the flesh instead of the Spirit. John says, "Let us so live that we shall not be ashamed before him at his coming."

What is your life going to count for? That is the question. Every one of us is investing his life in something. You cannot live without making an investment. Will it be permanent? Will it abide? Will it stand the test? In the great day when all the universe sees things the way they are, will you be filled with joy that your life was invested in what stood the test and contributed to the glory of the Lord himself? Or will you be ashamed that you wasted much of those years making an impression on men and teaching and influencing others to do so,

and it was all burned up in the fire? You are saved, but as though
you had to run through the flames and lost everything besides?
Martha Snell Nicholson has put it this way:

made a
commitment,
but not
grown —

When I stand at the judgment seat of Christ
And He shows me His plan for me,
The plan of my life as it might have been
Had He had His way, and I see

How I blocked Him here, and I checked Him there,
And I would not yield my will—
Will there be grief in my Saviour's eyes,
Grief, though He loves me still?

He would have me rich, and I stand there poor,
Stripped of all but His grace,
While memory runs like a hunted thing
Down the paths I cannot retrace.

Then my desolate heart will well-nigh break
With the tears that I cannot shed;
I shall cover my face with my empty hands,
I shall bow my uncrowned head . . .

Lord of the years that are left to me,
I give them to Thy hand;
Take me and break me, mould me to
The pattern Thou has planned!

6
–
How to Destroy a Church

Through the centuries many have been building on the foundation that Paul and the other apostles laid. The great leaders, teachers and theologians, some of the great churchmen of the past—Martin Luther, John Calvin, John Wesley, George Whitfield—a great host have built upon it so the church has risen through the centuries. But always, as the apostle now tells us, there is a danger involved to anyone who would come against the church that God is building.

> Do you not know that you are God's temple and that God's Spirit dwells in you? If any one destroys God's temple, God will destroy him. For God's temple is holy, and that temple you are (vv. 16, 17).

There is no doubt that Paul has the congregation at Corinth in mind when he says this. "You as a people," he says, "functioning out in the world, at your work, wherever you are—you are the temple of God." In a sense this also applies to every individual, as Paul says plainly in chapter 6, "Do you not know that your body is a temple of the Holy Spirit within you, which you have from God?" (v. 19).

Some time ago I attended a conference of the Fellowship of Christian Airline Personnel and a number of the pilots and flight attendants were sharing some of their experiences as Christians in the airlines. One beautiful stewardess told us that one day she was serving coffee and as she came down the aisle a man looked up at her and got her attention. He then opened his hand and showed her an explicitly sexual object and she immediately got the implication. It shook her, and she did not know what to do for a moment.

She turned and went to the back of the plane to recover herself and she prayed and asked God to show her what to do, because she had to go up to that man again. She went back and knelt beside his seat and looked him right in the eye and said, "Sir, I saw what you showed me and I understand what you mean, but there is something you need to know. I am a Christian and my body is the temple of the Holy Spirit and God says he is going to destroy anyone who damages his temple." The man began to stammer out an apology, and she said, "I understand. Don't say any more. I just want you to know that." Later she gave grateful thanks that the Lord had laid that verse on her heart because it served to deliver her from both the embarrassment and the threat of that situation.

That great truth lies at the base of all that Christians do. Their bodies are temples of the Holy Spirit, and when Christians, with the Spirit indwelling them, gather, the whole congregation becomes a great temple of the Holy Spirit, the center of the presence of God. "Where two or three are gathered together, there am I in the midst of them," Jesus said.

But according to this verse it is possible to "destroy" the temple of God. (The word is not really "destroy," meaning "to eliminate or break apart." The word is everywhere else in the Scriptures translated "corrupt." It means to damage, to injure, to harm the temple of God.) Nothing can actually destroy that temple. Jesus said, "On this rock I will build my church and the gates of hell shall not prevail against it." No matter what force is brought against the church, nor how powerful may be its adversaries, nothing can destroy the temple of God. But it can be damaged, it can be injured, and that is what Paul is talking about here. He says it is a dangerous thing to destroy or corrupt the temple (the church of God). God takes a dim view of anyone who does so and he will do something about it.

We have a dramatic example of that in the fifth chapter of Acts where Ananias and Sapphira indulged in a little hypocrisy. They pretended to a level of dedication and commitment which they really did not fulfill, and Peter, by the insight of the Holy Spirit, pronounced them guilty. Instantly, they both fell dead at Peter's feet. That was not intended to be the model of what the Spirit is going to do every time there is hypocrisy in the church, because he has never done it since. But it is intended to be a message from God as to what happens spiritually in a church when hypocrisy is allowed to pervade the thinking of the congregation. Something dies; something is damaged; some injury occurs, and God takes it very seriously.

Living by the World's Wisdom

How do you damage the church? How do you corrupt the congregation? I think the answer is clear from the context; corruption takes place when someone introduces the wisdom of the world into the life style and the practice of a congregation. If someone individually chooses to live according to the wisdom and the practice of the world, he begins to corrupt and damage the church. He is building with shoddy material, with wood, hay and stubble which will not stand the test of the fire and therefore he is marring the building of the church. When someone seeks to make the church impressive and powerful by the methods and the standards of the world, compromising with the spirit of the age, he is corrupting and damaging the church.

Let me give you some practical examples of this. What is happening in our own day is what was happening in that first-century world as well. For one thing the church is damaged when within the congregation people begin to treat each other in the same way that they treat one another out in the world—by recognizing distinctions between colors and classes and carrying these over into the life of the church.

Here in this country it has become evident that the churches, not only of the south but in many other parts of the country as well, do not believe the Word of God about those brothers and sisters in Christ who have a different color of skin. They have treated them in the same way the world around was treating them—making distinctions and putting them down at a lower level of life. This has damaged and injured the whole world because the church is at the very center of life and the world around reflects, to a great degree, the condition of the church. It produced an explosive situation in which our nation was torn apart because the church allowed a worldly philosophy to come in and govern the conduct and behavior of Christians.

This also happens when a church insists on having a hierarchy in the government of a congregation—someone at the top, someone in authority over everyone else. This is wrong, as our Lord said: "The kings of the Gentiles exercise lordship over them, and those in authority over them are called benefactors. *But not so with you;* rather let the greatest among you become as the youngest, and the leader as one who serves" (Luke 22:25, 26). Yet how widely that has been ignored and how many churches still today have brought the hierarchical structure of the world's government into the church. As a result the church is severely damaged.

This happens too when a church permits the lax moral standards of the world to go unjudged within the congregation. (Paul is going to deal more extensively with this as he comes into the next chapters.) It is happening all around us today. Sexual practices widely tolerated in the world are admitted into the church and Christians allow themselves to practice these kinds of things. This damages the church and tears it apart; it destroys and mars what God is doing.

Corruption happens when you substitute secular insights and secular authority for guidance in the matter of counseling and discipline problems in a church. This is happening widely in our day. Much of secular counseling is designed to build up the flesh, to make people self-confident. The church forgets that the secular viewpoint is narrow and limited. It does not take into consideration all the factors of human life and make-up as God has designed it. Apart from that understanding, operating only on that very narrow, limited viewpoint, severe damage is done to people in counseling. Although there may be momentary or temporary help, they are trapped on a plateau from which they cannot escape and this has the effect of damaging the church.

Another common way of damaging the church today is to allow a congregation to drift into a "mechanical" worship. Perhaps nothing is more deadly than to permit people a kind of outward compliance with the matters of worship and service without any inward, heartfelt commitment to it. That will destroy a church.

Threatened in Their Worship

When Paul wrote to the church at Colossae he saw them severely threatened by three things in their worship together. One threat was formalism. They were going through ceremonies and rituals in a set way as though that was what God was after, and they were not manifesting the change of heart that these things represented. That formalistic pattern of worship is a destructive thing to the life of the church which God is seeking to build.

The second threat was emotionalism. Many of the Colossians were caught up in a kind of mystical experience and had forsaken a proper clinging to the Head of the body, who is Jesus himself. That was destroying the church, as it does in many places today. And the third threat was asceticism, a legalistic spirit that was taking pride in its dedication and its willingness to give up many things; to go in for fasting and beating the body, and not touching certain things. They were glorying in their self-denial. The apostle saw the church being choked and sabotaged by these kinds of practices.

Now according to Paul, God takes this seriously, and he does something about it. Paul says, "If any one destroys, or corrupts, God's temple, God will corrupt him." What does he mean? I think it is set forth back in verse 15: "If any man's work is burned up, he will suffer loss . . . ."

A couple of years ago I was in Australia preaching in a downtown Melbourne church—a building that was rightly known all through the city for its beauty. I was staying in the home of one of the lay leaders of the congregation, a man who was known all through Australia as a leading churchman. He had given himself to many of the programs that the denomination had sponsored and he was leaned upon heavily as a leader in this field. He was also a very intelligent man, and, I think, a deeply devoted man.

That night I preached on Paul's experience of discovering how all his zealous effort on behalf of God was set aside in the early part of his ministry. How painfully he had to learn that all these things he counted upon from his past—his dedication, his ancestry, his morality, his background as a Hebrew of the Hebrews, etc.—all were set aside. He had to come at last to learn that the only thing which counts is what Christ was ready to do through him, as he puts it in 2 Corinthians, "Nothing coming from me, everything coming from God."

As he was driving me home afterward this man turned to me and said, "You know, if what you said tonight is true, and I think it is, I have wasted my whole life." I do not think that was true because I knew his heart already, and I knew God had used him greatly in certain endeavors. But he caught, perhaps for the first time, a glimpse of the fact that effort put out to impress people as to what the church is like is wasted effort—it is wood, hay and stubble that comes to nothing in the measurements of God.

Paul now moves on to the logical answer to this in verse 18. What are you going to do? What is God's demand upon you if this is the danger under which we live? Paul says in verses 18–21:

> Let no one deceive himself. If any one among you thinks that he is wise in this age, let him become a fool that he may become wise. For the wisdom of this world is folly (foolishness) with God. For it is written, "He catches the wise in their craftiness," and again, "The Lord knows that the thoughts of the wise are futile." So let no one boast of men.

There are two things Paul says to do if you catch yourself in this sort of thing—and we all do from time to time. We all think we are making an impression for God, doing great things for God. Yet, down in the heart, hidden from others around us, is an ambition, a desire for prominence. Paul says, "Stop kidding yourself. Don't let anyone deceive himself in this. You may be greatly impressing men, but God is totally unimpressed. You may think you are a great success but God is sadly shaking his head over what he sees. God cannot be fooled. He knows the heart. Others may give you tremendous applause and recognition, but if it is not coming from the sense of dependence on the wisdom and the power and the working of the Spirit of God; it is all wasted effort, coming to nothing."

[margin note: God knows the heart—]

Choose Foolishness

Secondly, Paul says, "Deliberately choose what the world says is foolish. If any one among you thinks that he is wise in this age, thinks he's got it made, thinks he understands the methods to move people and motivate them, let him become a fool that he may become wise, for the wisdom of this world is foolishness with God."

I was in the state of Washington a while back and a pastor I met there told me that another pastor in town asked him once, "What are you doing over there in the church?" So he told him, "We're trying to share one another's problems. We pray for one another and we're trying to meet each other's needs. We have a service where we try to talk openly and honestly about where we're struggling and where we're really messing up in our homes and our marriages." The other pastor said, "There's no other church in town that will act like that. Why do you do that?" And the first pastor said, "Because the New Testament tells us to." This other man said, "You won't get anywhere with that approach." But the first pastor said, "I determined that I was going to keep right on whether I got anywhere or not, because that is what God said to do."

Now that is "becoming a fool in order that you might become wise." That is choosing what the world and the worldly church says is foolish. Because the Lord says it is right, be willing to act upon it.

I think of that word in Hebrews about Moses growing up in Pharaoh's court. There came a day when, it says, "He counted the reproach of Christ greater riches than all the treasures of Egypt" (Heb. 11:26). There was a moment when he renounced the allure of the world that he might suffer loss with the people of God for a season. How richly he won because of that.

I will never forget in my own life as a young Christian many years ago hearing George Beverly Shea sing the words for which he became famous. They spoke volumes to my own heart along this line.

> I'd rather have Jesus than silver or gold.
> I'd rather have him than have riches untold.
> I'd rather have Jesus than houses or lands.
> I'd rather be led by his nail pierced hands
> Than to be a king of a vast domain
> And be held in sin's dread sway.
> I'd rather have Jesus than anything this world affords today.

That is what Paul is talking about. Never mind what the world thinks, never mind what the world says, for the wisdom of the world will prove to be foolish in the end.

Are they not remarkable, the foolish things worldly people and worldly Christians will do to keep up with the styles? Do you know what they have now to keep up with the fashion? Chest wigs! If you do not have hair on your chest you can buy a wig for it. The style today is open shirts with the hair visible and some men will not open their shirts because they do not have hair on their chests. Well, you can remedy that. You can buy a chest wig and nobody will know the difference. It will stay on even when you are swimming, they advertise. Nobody will laugh at you again. Isn't that wonderful?

How ridiculous, how foolish are the ways of the world. That is what Paul is saying. "The wisdom of this world is folly with God." Quoting from Job he says, "God catches the wise in their craftiness," and then from Psalm 94, "The Lord knows that the thoughts of the wise are futile." The word *futile* is really, a breath, a puff of air. The words of the wise in the world are like a breath of air, a puff—it is gone, instantly; it changes to something else. Those who give way to that not only damage the church but they give way to that which in the end proves to be a wasted life.

Gain the Whole World

Now, in contrast, Paul moves on to show you what happens when you choose the wisdom of God and the ways of God.

> For all things are yours, whether Paul or Apollos or Cephas or the world or life or death or the present or the future, all are yours; and you are Christ's; and Christ is God's (vv. 21–23).

You end up gaining the whole world. That is what Jesus said—"The meek shall inherit the earth." What a broad vista opens up to us in these words! All the world or the worldly church can offer you is fame, pleasure, honor, or wealth. If you want it badly enough, you will probably get it. But that is all you will get.

Jesus said that if you do your giving to be seen by men you have your reward. That is it. You will never get another one; nothing waiting for you beyond, no treasure laid up in heaven. If you do your praying to be heard by men so that you get a reputation for piety and godliness, well, you will get the reputation but that is all you get. It is the world that is narrow; it is the world that is crabbed and withered and limited in its whole approach, but, as Paul reveals here, those who choose God never lose.

This is right in line with Jesus' great principle, "If you save your life you will lose it, but if you give up your life for my sake you will save it." Paul looks all around and says, "He who lets God choose ends up with everything. Why do you divide between Paul and Apollos and Cephas and choose one among them? You can have them all," he says. "They are all yours. Paul, who planted, his whole ministry is yours. Apollos, the waterer, his ministry is yours; you can get the benefit of it. Cephas, the rock, whatever there is of value in his ministry is yours. In fact the whole world is open to you. Led of the Spirit of God you can go anywhere you want and God will give you things that money cannot buy."

I have had the experience many times of enjoying things that millionaires own but I get to use—they do not. The world is yours. Life with all its possibilities is open before you. God can lead you into where the real living is. Even death with its threat is already mastered; it is already yours. When you come to it, it will minister to you, not take from you. It will bring you into glory. The present, the future, all things are yours because you are Christ's, and Christ is God's and therefore everything he owns is yours. All things belong to you because you belong to the One to whom all things belong.

That is an incredible vista, isn't it, and yet those words are true. That is what God has in mind for his people. As we choose our life style, do we have the faith and the courage to set aside the life style of the world around us, and walk with God? When we do, all that God possesses becomes ours. We become children of a heavenly King who makes it all available to us.

7

The True Minister

In the first seven verses of 1 Corinthians 4 we have a passage that gives us the true view of a minister of Christ. There are many stereotypes abroad today as to what a minister is. One stereotype is that he is a producer of hot air, a gas bag, saying things that have no real significance, "a holy groan in a black suit." I read another definition of a minister as "a mild-mannered man standing before mild-mannered people and exhorting them to be more mild-mannered." What an exciting concept of a Christian leader!

These Corinthians to whom the apostle Paul was writing thought of ministers of Christ as big shot traveling preachers who had their partisans in every church and who were known for their knowledge or their eloquence. At great length Paul has pointed out the danger, the weakness and the error of that position, and now in chapter 4 he corrects it by setting before them the true view:

> This is how one should regard us, as servants of Christ and stewards of the mysteries of God. Moreover it is required of stewards that they be found trustworthy [or faithful] (vv. 1, 2).

Here are the responsibilities of ministers. In verses 3 through 5 Paul gives us the proper evaluation of ministers, and in verses 6 and 7 the freedom which they will exercise when the congregation sees them in the proper light.

When I use the term "minister of Christ," I am not speaking of the traditional concept of a full-time employee of a church who is kept around to do the preaching, the teaching, the counseling and to run the mimeograph machine. Unfortunately that is a widespread concept of what the pastor ought to be and I run into it in many places.

This concept, of course, is totally unknown in the New Testament. The idea of having a single pastor, *the* pastor, is an unbiblical imposition that has come into the church only within the past 400 years. A minister of Christ in the New Testament churches was anyone, *anyone*, who by virtue of a gift of the Spirit was a preacher or a teacher of the Word of God. That is what Paul is talking about here.

In this sense we are all ministers of Christ. Every Christian is in the ministry—I have said that many times. But there is a special sense—Paul is dealing with it here—wherein those who have the gift of teaching or preaching ("prophesying" as it is called in Scripture), have a special function within the body of Christ. There are dozens of ministers like that in every church.

How are we to look at such people and what are we to think about them? Paul deals with this first. Who are these people? Should we call them bishops? Are they wardens, as the Episcopalians might call them? Are they doctors, rabbis, popes or even senior pastors? You do not find those titles in the Scriptures. (Bishops are referred to, but not in the usual sense that we think of them today. Bishops were not in oversight over more than one church. They were the equivalent of elders and overseers.)

Under-rowers of Christ

The word the apostle uses here is a remarkable one. He says, "We want you to look at us as servants of Christ." The word for servant is the Greek word *huperetes,* which literally means "an under-rower." Now everyone in Corinth understood what the word meant. Corinth was where the war galleys of the Roman Empire crossed the isthmus that separated the Ionian Sea from the Aegean Sea, and the Corinthians knew that the lowest deck of a war galley was made of single rows of benches on both sides of the ship where the rowers sat. Then on a little deck raised up above them all so that each rower could see him was the captain of the ship. It was the rowers' task to row according to what he said. If he wanted the ship to move then they were to row; if he wanted them to stop they had to stop instantly. Their whole business was to obey his orders. Now that is the word that Paul chooses to describe those who are teachers, preachers and ministers of the

Word of God within the congregation of the church. They are "under-rowers" of Christ.

This word is used in other places in Scripture also. When our Lord stood before Pontius Pilate and Pilate asked him if he were a king, Jesus said, "My kingship is not of this world; if my kingship were of this world, my servants *(huperetes)* would fight," i.e., "If my kingdom were an earthly kingdom and I told my servants to fight that is what they would do. They would obey what I said."

This word is used again in the account of Paul and Barnabas as they go out on the first missionary journey. Luke tells us that they took with them a young man named John Mark to be their "minister" *(huperetes)*. Did that mean that he was to be in charge of the devotions every morning? No, it meant that he was the one who got the airline tickets, checked their baggage, and made hotel reservations, ran the errands and did what they told him. Paul says, "That is what we want you to think about us. We are not big shots, we are not among you as domineering leaders. We are servants of Christ, under-rowers with our eyes fixed on him. What he tells us to say, that is what we are to say, and what he tells us not to do, that is where our limits are. That is what we want you to think about us as you see us ministering among you."

From this flows what I think is the biblical independence which ministers of Christ have, using that term in its widest sense. They are not to be servants of the Board, for the members of the Board themselves, the elders, are joint ministers of Christ with them. Ministers are not to be servants of the congregation, and least of all the denomination. They are servants of Christ. In Galatians Paul says, "If I were still pleasing men, I should not be a servant of Christ." There he draws a sharp contrast. They are not to be paying heed to what the congregation or any one group within the congregation wants to hear, but they are to say what the Lord tells them to say. That is what the servant of Christ, the under-rower of Christ, must do. I have never valued anything more in my whole life than the fact that I belong with that crowd. I see myself as an *huperetes,* an under-rower of Christ, and it is my responsibility to say and do what he tells me to do.

A young pastor at a pastors' conference once said to me, "What would you do if you were in my shoes? My Board called me in and said to me, 'Look, there are some things we want you to understand. One is that this is our church; it is not your church. We were here before you came and we are going to be here when you leave; therefore, we expect you to do what we want you to do and not what you think you ought to do.' What would you say to a church like that?" I told him that I would call together the elders of the church and I would say to them, "Brothers, I think you are suffering from two very serious theological errors. One, you think this is your church, but it is the Lord's church. All churches belong only to him; they do not belong to the people; they are not a democracy owned by the congregation. Jesus said, 'On this rock I will build *my church* and the gates of hell shall not prevail against it.' So all of us are under the authority of the Lord of this church and it is his work to tell us what he wants the church to be and not our job to tell him what we think it ought to be.

"The second error is that you think you hired me to work in this church, but you have not. I did not come on that basis. I have joined you to share the ministry with you. I appreciate the fact that you have set me aside and given me support from the congregation so that I do not have to spend time earning a living but can devote my full time to the ministry of teaching and preaching. If you will not accept those terms then I will have to look elsewhere. I cannot work on any other terms because that is what the New Testament says."

He went back to his church and they fired him, but now he has another church and he made his stand clear from the beginning and things are working out very well with him.

So much for the status of the under-rowers. They are not unusual; they are not above anybody; they are not authorities within the church. They are under-rowers of Christ. Their accountability is to him.

Now what is the responsibility of a minister of Christ? Here Paul uses another term. He calls them "stewards of the mysteries of God." Isn't that an enchanting term? The word for steward is *oikonomos*, meaning "housekeeper." Today I think the nearest equivalent would be "administrator," but perhaps we get at the heart of this when we come right back to the old biblical word "steward" or "stewardess." We know what they are. When you are on an airplane you find a stewardess or a steward who serves coffee, tea, milk (and other beverages) and a tray of food at the proper time. They have been entrusted with certain valuable commodities which they are responsible to dispense. That is what a steward is and that is exactly in line with this New Testament picture.

A minister of Christ, whoever he or she may be within a congregation—and it does include women—is to be a steward entrusted with what Paul calls "the mysteries of God," that secret and hidden wisdom of God, these valuable truths which are only found in the revelation of the Word of God and nowhere else. They are responsible to dispense them continually to the congregation so that lives are changed and lived on the basis of these remarkable truths.

The Mysteries in Our Care

We have already seen what they are—truth about life, about our families, about God and ourselves. Let me remind you of some of them. There is the "mystery of the kingdom of God." How often that is mentioned in Scripture. What does it mean? Well, it means God at work in history, how he is working through the events of our day to carry out his purposes. It is the business of a minister of Christ to unfold that mystery to people and to help them to understand these events. The world interprets them on other grounds but God is intending to use them in a quite different way. That is the business of a minister of Christ, an under-rower of Christ, a steward of the mysteries of God.

There is the "mystery of iniquity," of lawlessness. This is the explanation we desperately need of the nature of evil. Why are we never able to make any progress when it comes to solving human dilemmas; why does every generation without exception repeat the struggle, problems and difficulties of the previous generation? We do not have instinct to guide us as the animals do, and we never seem to learn from the past. As the philosopher Hegel put it, "History teaches us that history teaches us nothing." We wrestle endlessly, over and over again, with the same basic struggles and problems. There is no advance. Why? Because of the mystery of lawlessness, that evil, invisible panoply of remarkable beings who are constantly twisting and distorting the thinking of men. They lead us down garden paths into error and illusion and cause us to see things out of proportion and out of relationship with reality. We assume that something is true when it is not and act on that basis. That is why we get mixed up all the time. You will never understand why if you do not understand the mystery of lawlessness.

Then there is the opposite of that—the "mystery of godliness." This is the remarkable secret that God has provided by which a Christian is enabled to live right in the midst of the pressures of the world (with all its illusion and danger), and yet not run away from it but refuse to conform to it and do so in a loving, gracious way. What is the secret? It is the secret of an imparted life—"Christ in you, the hope of glory." Christ in you, available to you—his life, his wisdom, his strength, his power to act available to you to enable you to do what you do not think you can do at the moment, but when you choose to do it you find you have the strength to perform. That is the mystery of godliness, the most life-transforming doctrine that has ever been set before man, radical in its effect.

Then there is the "mystery of the church," that strange new society that God is building which is to be a demonstration of a totally different life style before a watching world and which is to resist the impact of the world and instead be an impact upon the world around to change it. That is a great mystery. Those who are called to teach this and preach this in a church congregation are stewards of that mystery. They are entrusted to set it out and to help people to face the facts of life without fear so that all can experience both the ecstasy and the agony of Christian experience.

That brings us to the third part of the responsibility which is, "Moreover, it is required of stewards that they be found faithful." Faithful at what? Faithful at dispensing the mysteries so people understand them. You may fail at many things as a teacher, a preacher, a leader of a class. You may not make it in many areas but do not miss it in this one. Be sure that you are setting forth the mysteries of God. That is what you will be judged on. You are being "a good steward of the mysteries of God" if you set forth these truths.

Subtle Pressure

Paul now turns to a common problem, and that is the evaluation of the minister. Who is to do this? The remarkable thing is that we have hundreds of volunteers—everybody wants to get in on the act of how to judge the minister as to his or her faithfulness. The result is a kind of subtle but constant pressure upon everyone who is called to this kind of ministry.

> But with me it is a very small thing that I should be judged by you (Can you imagine how popular that verse was in Corinth? Can't you see them memorizing it and carrying it around with them on little cards?) or by any human court. I do not even judge myself. I am not aware of anything against myself, but I am not thereby acquitted. It is the Lord who judges me. Therefore, do not pronounce judgment before the time, before the Lord comes, who will bring to light the things now hidden in darkness and will disclose the purposes of the heart. Then every man will receive his commendation from God (vv. 3–5).

The first pressure Paul mentions is congregational evaluation, and he puts it at the very bottom of the list. "It is a very small thing," he says, "what you think about me. I know you are thinking about me and I know what you think, but I want you to know I do not think it is very significant."

Stuart Briscoe says there are three kinds of congregational pressure—there is adulation, which swells the head; there is manipulation, which ties the hands; and there is antagonism, which breaks the heart. I have experienced all three of those, as everyone has who seeks to teach and preach the Word of God.

There is adulation. There are always those people—they mean to be encouraging and within certain limits they are encouraging—but they will say nice things all the time, sometimes heaping it on until it begins to swell the head. Many a young pastor and many a teacher within the church has been ruined by too much adulation. It is so easy to start preaching to it, wanting to hear words of praise, and passing over truth that would be unpleasant. Evaluation by the congregation is a subtle pressure.

Then there is manipulation. Every congregation has its "power structure," people who seek to manipulate and to influence the teaching and the preaching. Sometimes they do it by personality, sometimes by a display of wealth, sometimes by perseverance, hounding you until you begin to give heed to what they say. There are many ways of putting pressure on a preacher or a teacher to stop being an *huperetes* of Christ. You begin to preach to accommodate; you pass over unpleasant doctrines, passages that deal with issues that would create controversy within the congregation, and this is deadly. It destroys the congregation and the life of a church.

Manipulation ties the hands. I have met young pastors across the continent who are ready to quit the ministry because they have run up against the power structure in their church. It has tied their hands and they are ready to quit. They have forgotten they are *huperetes* of Christ, and that he will see them through. But they give up and quit the ministry instead.

And then there is antagonism—outright, sharp, open-faced opposition. A young man once told me about his experience when he was on the staff of a church. He said one of the elders stopped him one day and said, "Where are you getting all these ideas? Have you been down to Stedman's church?" The young man answered truthfully, "No, I haven't." The elder grabbed him by the shirt front and said, "I want to tell you something: if I ever hear that you are going down to Stedman's church and coming back with some of those radical ideas, you're out!" Now that is antagonism; that is pressure upon the minister. This is what Paul is speaking of. It breaks the heart of a young pastor or teacher.

Next, Paul speaks of societal evaluation. "But with me it is a very small thing that I should be judged by you *or by any human court.*" Literally, it is "by man's day," the view that mankind in general has of a minister. Have you ever noticed the attitude displayed toward ministers in the movies or on television? Usually it is a kind of contemptuous, disdainful putdown. On the other hand, sometimes a church begins to make an impact upon its community and everybody in the world outside begins to patronize it, praise it, talk about it and flatter it. Again, you are tempted to speak so as to get these encouraging, helpful things said about you. Maybe you will get your name in the paper and perhaps some recognition by a denomination or by some other group across the country; you will build a reputation. This is a deadly, dangerous thing in a church. Paul says, "Don't pay any attention to it. I don't allow myself to. I'm not affected by any human court. It doesn't make any difference to me."

The Paul says, "I do not even judge myself." Now he does not mean he does not look at himself and evaluate what he is doing because he tells us that he does so in other places in Scripture. He also tells *us* to do it. He says, "Examine yourselves whether you be in the faith or not." What he means is that he does not take any final notice of this kind of judgment. He realizes it is incomplete. There is often a blindness about ourselves; we are blind to our faults and failures, and he knows it.

We are also sometimes unaware of our successes. There have been times when I thought I had totally failed in the preaching of a message, and yet I have seen many instances when that very occasion was the means of reaching people in a remarkable way. I have discovered, as Paul must have discovered, that you cannot accept your own judgment of yourself

Paul says he is "not aware of anything against himself" at this moment. He has dealt with all the Lord has ever shown him about himself. He is not aware of anything, but he knows that he is not acquitted by that. He is not home free because he does not know there is anything wrong at the moment. He says the only evaluation that really counts is the Lord's—"The Lord is judging me." This is present tense; it is something that is going on all the time. In the privacy of his own heart and conscience he says that as he exposes himself to the Word

of God and the Spirit of God speaks in his heart, he becomes aware
of the Lord's evaluation.

The Motive That No One Knows

Then Paul extends that on to the great day coming when all will
be made public. His advice to the congregation is, "Wait until then
before you pronounce judgment on the ministers of Christ. Do not
pronounce judgment before the Lord comes, who will bring to light
the things now hidden in darkness." That does not mean evil, necessarily. It means the motives that no one knows; even the man himself
does not really know what is going on, or why he does things—"(The
Lord) will disclose the purposes of the heart. Then every man will
receive his commendation from God."

I often try to think of this. I live continually in the awareness that
one of these days my whole life is going to be examined by my Lord.
He is going to walk with me back through all the record of the years.
There are some things that I would not want him to see, but I have
already faced them so I am not afraid; he has already seen them.
There are other things that I am anxious for him to see. I think he
is going to praise me for them, but I may be wrong. He may come
to them and instead of saying anything he may silently look at them.
He does not condemn me, but he goes on, and I am disappointed. I
think, "Oh! Lord, I thought I had it that time." Then he will come
to some area that I think is unimportant and he will say, "Ah, that
was the moment. You pleased me then. You were not looking for
self-glory; you were not looking for a pat on the back; you did not
want anything out of it for yourself. You did it for me and you did
not feel very good about it afterward, but I did." "Then every man
will receive his commendation from God." He does not condemn us;
he commends us. His condemnation comes only in his silence about
the wasted areas of our lives.

Now let us clear one thing up very plainly here. Paul is not saying
that we are not to judge the actions of men when they do wrong. In
the next chapter he scolds this church because they do not judge
the actions of a man who has done something wrong in the church.
So he is not saying that we are not to judge actions. What he says
is, do not judge motives, do not assume that you know what has made
somebody act the way they have. I find this is a common, constant
temptation among us.

That brings us to verses 6 and 7 where the apostle sets forth the freedom that will be enjoyed by a minister when the congregation begins to think rightly about him as Paul has described:

> I have applied all this to myself and Apollos for your benefit, brethren, that you may learn by us to live according to Scripture, that none of you may be puffed up in favor of one against another. For who sees anything different in you? What have you that you did not receive? If then you received it, why do you boast as if it were not a gift? (vv. 6, 7)

A right attitude makes a difference as to what the congregation thinks and the way they treat the ministers in their midst. The first thing it will do is to eliminate rivalry among them. How many churches have been split right down the center by a rivalry developing between teachers and pastors? That is eliminated when the congregation refuses to be "puffed up in favor of one another," when they are bound by the word of Scripture how to think of men and they refuse to take sides and to choose favorites. If the congregation watches itself it can free the ministers in their midst so that there is no sense of competition and rivalry between them.

And then, second, it will have an effect upon the minister himself. It will destroy his tendency to personal conceit if he begins to think rightly about himself. Paul asks some searching questions here: "What have you that you did not receive, you people with gifts of teaching and preaching and prophesying? Where did you get those? You were not born with them. These are spiritual gifts imparted by the Holy Spirit. He could have given them to somebody else. He still could, perhaps; therefore, how foolish to boast because God has used you in a ministry of some sort. It is only the Lord himself who has done it. How foolish it is to make anything of that, to be proud over what God has given!"

I heard of a young preacher who preached a message to a congregation on a special occasion. God richly blessed the message and it hit with great impact. The young man enjoyed the obvious appearances of success, and afterward, going home with his wife, and evidently thinking over and enjoying the results of that powerful ministry in his own heart, he said to her, "I wonder how many great preachers there are in the world?" His wife replied, "One less than you think!"

What a foolish thing it is to view our gifts as though we were responsible for them. What a freedom can be found in a congregation concerning those who teach and preach among them if we will see them as people to whom God has given his gifts. If we take this view, the men and women themselves will refuse to take any credit for the ministry and for the gift that God has given them.

8

A Father in Action

In this section of 1 Corinthians the apostle is dealing with the problem of a complacent church, that is, a church filled with complacent Christians. This was also the problem of the church of Laodicea (Rev. 3), a church that was saying, "We are rich; we are filled; we have everything." But the Lord says, "You do not know what you are like. You are deceiving yourselves."

This is the ancient problem of spiritual lukewarmness, of being neither cold nor hot, but something in between, which is nauseating. I think the problem that most discourages people from turning to the gospel of Christ today is this very problem of half-warm Christians. They are not alive, alert, on fire for God, or ready to serve him, but they are not turned off either. They are in between, a kind of nauseating experience of spiritual life.

Paul now describes that condition and its cause in chapter 4:

> Already you are filled! Already you have become rich! Without us you have become kings! And would that you did reign, so that we might share the rule with you! (v. 8).

There are two marks of complacent Christians in this verse. The first one is that they have a sense of having arrived. You meet such people today, people who seem to feel they have it made; they have learned the whole truth; there is nothing you can tell them that they have not already learned; they think of themselves as rich.

Many things can give a Christian a sense of being rich. Sometimes it is pride in numbers or size. At Laodicea it was material possessions.

97

"We are increased with goods," they said. "We have a tremendous budget; we can do what we want; we do not need God anymore." Their pride in affluence gave them a sense of complacency so that the Lord had to say to them, "You have no idea what you are really like—you are poor and blind, pitiable and naked, and spiritually poverty-stricken." Affluence can do that to a church. It is always a problem.

Sometimes it is prominence that gives this sense of complacency. Peninsula Bible Church, where I have been a minister for many years, is known all over the world. We have a great reputation as an active church, a Bible-teaching church, and people in the congregation soon begin to think, "We have arrived; we have no further to go," and pride of complacency begins to appear.

At Corinth, however, the problem was none of these: at Corinth they were complacent over possessing all the gifts of the Spirit—they had them all. Can you imagine their advertisements in the "Corinthian Bugle"? "Come and Visit the Total Church—The Church That Has It All!"

We hear a great deal today about the gift of tongues. Corinth had tongues, and with it they had miracles and healings and prophesying plus many of what they regarded as lesser gifts—the gifts of helps and administrations, wisdom and knowledge, teaching, service, and giving. All the gifts were present, as the apostle Paul says in the very first chapter of this letter: "You are not lacking in any spiritual gift" (v. 7). I am sure their meetings were interesting, even exciting, but they were forgetting and already losing a sense of evangelism and of service. The church was in danger and Paul wrote to them to point this out. The first mark, then, of a complacent Christian is that he feels he has arrived.

The second mark, Paul says, is an "exclusive advance." "Without us," he says, "you have become kings!" They no longer needed Paul or any of the apostles, and there was no need for other Christians or any communication with the body of Christ around them because they were too far ahead of everybody else.

I think you will recognize this as a prominent tendency among many today. Christians who start out as alive and vital can become so in love with their own teaching that they begin to develop exclusive attitudes. They tell people they are the only "true" church. They have the only "apostolic" ministry, and there is no need of anyone else anymore. That is the danger of complacency, and as the apostle shows us here, it is always a sign of sinful human pride and a complacent spirit—and it is an offense to the Spirit of God.

As victims of the world's illusions, these Corinthians loved to dream of getting some special ability that marked them out as different from others. They had developed a smugness and a sense of satisfaction. They were living in a dream world and acting as though the millennium had already arrived.

Paul brings them (and us) back to reality with a jolt, in verse 8 and following: "And would that you did reign, so that we might share the rule with you!"

"I wish the millennium were here," he says. "We would love to enter into it with you, but it is clear it is not here yet. Would that it were." He continues in verses 9 through 13:

> For I think that God has exhibited us apostles as last of all, like men sentenced to death; because we have become a spectacle to the world, to angels and to men. We are fools for Christ's sake, but you are wise in Christ. We are weak, but you are strong. You are held in honor, but we in disrepute. To the present hour we hunger and thirst, we are ill-clad and buffeted and homeless, and we labor, working with our own hands. When reviled, we bless; when persecuted, we endure; when slandered, we try to conciliate; we have become, and are now, as the refuse of the world, the offscouring of all things.

What a stark contrast! "There is the real world," Paul says. "It is tough and ruthless. On the surface it can appear to be kind and responsive, but underneath the velvet glove is an iron fist that can smash and crush without compunction. You in your dream world are just kidding yourselves. Earth is a battleground and we apostles are fighting the battle. We are living in the real world, and it is not like yours at all." So Paul brings them back to reality.

Christians on Exhibit

Notice three things here that he teaches us about the apostles. First, "We apostles," he says, "are pattern Christians; in effect, God has put us on exhibit in order that we might demonstrate certain things. He has exhibited us last of all, like men sentenced to death . . . we have become a spectacle. . . ." The word *spectacle* is the word from which we get our word *theater*. He is saying, "We have become the theater of the world, and when you look at us you will see what life is really like."

That is why the apostles are so important in the new Testament and to all the church ever since. They are "pattern" Christians. They are not, as we often imagine, super saints who live at a level that no one else can hope to attain. They were sent out to live, like our Lord, in the very teeth of the reality of life to show us how to handle it.

Notice that Paul calls the apostles, "men sentenced to death." Now men sentenced to death never deal with trivialities; they use their time to proper purpose. If you were sentenced to death you would not concern yourself with where your next ice cream cone was coming from. You would want to see that your relationships with others were right, and that your property was properly disposed of. You would be concerned with what was coming and what you could do about it, and what would happen after you were gone. Paul says that was the way the apostles lived—in the reality of life, not dealing with trivial things but using their time on the things that count.

I am sure he is thinking of the gladiatorial combats that were held in the great Coliseum when, as a final act, two gladiators, both of them condemned to death, would engage in mortal combat. They would stand before the great assemblage and salute the Emperor, crying, *"Morituri te salutamus."* ("We who are about to die salute you.") Paul is thinking of that as he writes about himself, "We are set forth as men who have already died, in a sense, so we are not wasting our time; we are dealing with reality. We love not our life unto death; we want to make every moment count."

Notice that apostles, he says, are persecuted Christians (v. 10):

> We are fools for Christ's sake, but you are wise in Christ. We are weak, but you are strong. You are held in honor, but we in disrepute.

By this he indicates that there is something about the gospel that will always make us unpopular. This is the problem, isn't it? Nobody likes to be unpopular. We all want to be accepted, but sooner or later we are going to be put in a spot where, if we are going to be true to what our faith says, to our Lord, to what we have learned in the Word of God, we are going to find people ridiculing us.

Sold Out to the World

Now nobody likes that, but it constitutes *the* great test of life: whether we are willing to bear reproach for Christ's sake. These Corinthians had sold out. They had so compromised with the world around that the world was not persecuting them anymore. The world did not laugh at them. They had adjusted their teaching so that worldly wisdom penetrated everything they said and did, and the world thought it was great. They had adjusted their actions so that nobody was offended by them, and they never had to tell anybody that something was wrong. As we will see in the succeeding passages, the Corinthians put up with anything in the church; they never told anybody they were doing wrong. So, Paul says, "The world calls us fools and treats us with dishonor, but you, you are treated as wise and as understanding; as strong, and we are weak."

A Christian lawyer friend who lives and works right in the midst of the world and who yet has a very deep commitment to the things of God and of Christ was discussing with me some of the ways that people—especially Christians who long for the favor of the world— look at other Christians. He said to me, "I get so tired of being treated like the village idiot every time I try to take the Bible seriously." Now that is the treatment you will get, but you have to be ready to be the village idiot and not mind it at all, because it is the other group that is wrong.

This is what lies behind many of the issues being debated in the church in our day, this unwillingness to be laughed at by the world. Behind the inerrancy issue that is raking the Church, behind the evangelical feminist issue, behind the homosexual issue and the issue of women elders, is this love of the world's approval, this desire to be like others, this unwillingness to bear reproach for the name of Christ. But Jesus himself told us that it would be there: "in the world you shall have tribulation, but be of good cheer, I have overcome the world" (John 16:33).

The third thing the apostle points out is that apostles are "peculiar" Christians—they do not act normally. Read this again:

> To the present hour we hunger and thirst, we are ill-clad and buffeted and homeless, and we labor, working with our own hands. When reviled, we bless; when persecuted, we endure; when slandered, we try to conciliate; we have become, and are now, as the refuse of the world (trash, rubbish) the offscouring (the scrapings of the plates after a meal, the garbage) of all things.

That does not sound like us, does it? I was thinking of this verse the other day while lying in my new hot tub. The temperature of the water was 103 degrees and the jet was massaging my body and I was thinking of Paul who was hungry, thirsty, ill-clad, buffeted, and homeless. Now my hot tub was a gift from some very loving and generous friends and I am enjoying it, but lying in it I was thinking, "Is the 'hot tub' life style wrong?"

That is a question we are all going to have to face one of these days, is it not? We have so much: is it wrong to have so much when the rest of the world has so little? Some Christian periodicals today are telling us, "Yes, it is wrong. We have no right to this kind of affluence." They tell us that Christians ought to take a vow of poverty, in effect, and give away their riches and live at the lowest possible level of existence. And I must confess there are times when I wonder if they are right.

I agree that we need to rethink this issue and I think it will be consistently faced by the church in the days to come; it has to be faced. And yet I am not at all sure they are right. C. S. Lewis said that the devil always sends error into the world in pairs which are opposites. His strategy is that you will get all concerned about one and back right off into the other. That is the danger: that we will get so guilty over our affluence that we will back off into a kind of enforced poverty which is just as extreme and just as dangerous. But having said that, it still is true that we have to be very careful in this, as the Scripture warns us.

Despite this passage there are places where Paul says that at times he abounded. He had to learn how to handle it. He writes to Timothy and says, "God gives us richly all things to enjoy," and therefore to enjoy them is not wrong. So we must preserve a careful balance. I know that I must hold things loosely; I must not covet them or crave them if I do not have them. I must be willing to lose them without any complaint or sense of deep loss. They are just things; that is all.

But notice, the important thing here is not how we react to affluence: the important thing the apostle is underlining in this passage is how we respond to mistreatment. That is the indication of a true Christian life style. "When we are reviled, we bless," he says. "When we are persecuted, we endure. When we are slandered (lied about), we try to conciliate." That is the key; that is the heart of the issue. When you are treated like rubbish and garbage, do you try to get even? Do you try to reply in kind: "I'll give as good as I get; I'll let him know how it feels"? Or do you, as the apostle learned to do, try to work it out and try to heal the hurt? That is authentic Christianity; that is a true Christian life style.

Admonished As Children

So Paul has examined this complacent spirit here and shown us the cause. Now, as he calls us back to the real world, he shows us the cure.

I do not write this to make you ashamed, but to admonish you as my beloved children. For though you have countless guides in Christ, you do not have many fathers. For I became your father in Christ Jesus through the gospel. I urge you, then, be imitators of me. Therefore I sent to you Timothy, my beloved and faithful child in the Lord, to remind you of my ways in Christ, as I teach them everywhere in every church. ("You are getting no special treatment here. I am not just zeroing in on you— this is the way I talk to all the churches.") Some are arrogant, as though I were not coming to you. But I will come to you soon, if the Lord wills, and I will find out not the talk of these arrogant people but their power. For the kingdom of God does not consist in talk but in power. What do you wish? Shall I come to you with a rod, or with love in a spirit of gentleness? (vv. 14–21)

At a Pastors' Conference some time ago we were examining the principles by which you work out problems of personal relationships—how to handle people who are near you, especially within a family circle. Four principles emerged from various Scriptures. They are to be in evidence if you are approaching these sticky, difficult personal relationship problems as a Christian.

Now when I was looking through this passage in 1 Corinthians, I was struck by the fact that all four of those principles are present here. The key is in these words in verse 14, "I admonish you as my beloved children." He says, "I am your father and you do not have many fathers. I led you to Christ; you came to new life with me as your teacher. I did not give you the life (it came from God), but I led you to it." (Neither do a mother and father give life to their children; they are merely the channel through which it comes.) "But I am your father," he said. "You may have ten thousand instructors and teachers, but you will never have another father in Christ. That is my relationship to you, and that is why I talk to you the way I do. I am not trying to shame you; I am not trying to make you cringe and feel awful and crawl away; I am simply trying to bring you to reality, and as a father to heal the thing that is destroying and damaging you and your life."

The first principle to come out at the conference mentioned above was that in dealing with another person you should try to convey some sense of confidence and love first. Never wipe somebody out: "If you are going to act this way I don't want anything to do with you again. Get out of my sight." Paul never does that. Rather, he says, "You are my beloved children." At the point of sharpest censure you find this term of deepest endearment. Isn't that amazing?

The second principle was: present a model. Notice how Paul does that here: "Be imitators of me. I sent Timothy to you to remind you of my ways in Christ. I do not want you to follow what I say; I want you to follow what I do."

Now that statement troubles some of us. Many people think Paul is conceited when he says that. But he is not. He is recognizing the universal psychological principle that people will always follow what you do, not what you say. You can talk your head off to people but if your life does not reflect what you say, they will not follow you; they will pay no attention to it, because coming through all the time is that nonverbal communication that is saying, "Yes, I am saying all this to you, but it is not really very important because I do not bother to do it myself." You have no right to talk if you do not do what you say. Many parents have kidded themselves into thinking they were teaching their children what was right when they told them what to do, but never did it themselves. The child picked up all the vibes that were coming through and did just what the parents did. So the second principle is: present a model.

The third principle was to preserve liberty. That is, do not box someone in so they have no choice in the matter. Allow them to have a choice as to what they do or do not do. Notice how Paul does that here. "I admonish you," he says. "I do not command you. I admonish you; I urge you, but the choice is yours. What do you want? Shall I come to you with a rod or with love in a spirit of gentleness? You have the liberty to choose." What an important principle that is. Everybody resists being compelled to do things, but Paul does not threaten sanctions or punishment. He simply says, "You have the choice to make and it is up to you to choose."

And then the last principle was: confront realistically. That is, strip off all the illusions and bring things down to the way they are. That is what Paul says, "When I come I will find out not the talk of these arrogant people but their power. For the kingdom of God does not consist in talk but in power." What is the fruit of your life? Jesus said, "By their fruits you will know them." Do not listen to their words. Many a person has been deceived by the smooth talk of someone who leads him along with deceptive words that sound wonderful. But the thing to do is to ask, "What has happened as a result of all these good words?" Talk is cheap, but change requires power.

If we are unwilling to confront another with the reality of a situation we simply perpetuate his own self-illusions; he goes on thinking everything is fine when it is not. Sooner or later when the collapse comes he is shocked, startled, and shattered by the revelation of what has been going on all the time. This is why everywhere in the Word we are encouraged to admonish one another in love, to reprove and rebuke one another with all faithfulness in love. What a helpful ministry that is. Paul says, "When I come, that is what I am going to do with you."

This is the way he deals with the problem of complacency. The hunger of his heart is that these Christians will be really effective for Christ.

9
—

Scandal in the Church

Chapters 5 and 6 introduce a new section of the letter to us. Prior to this the apostle has been dealing with pride and its consequences in the Corinthian assembly. Now he turns to a related theme, but one that is somewhat different: lust and its problems.

One of the growing problems the church is facing today is what to do about the frightening increase in sexual immorality among Christians. We hear of Christian leaders who have forsaken their wives, run off with a secretary, fallen into homosexuality, or are facing some kind of a moral crisis in their churches. Many are properly concerned about this and wondering why it should be.

In 1 Corinthians 5, we find the apostle Paul dealing with that very problem. These great Greek cities such as Corinth and others were given over to the casual acceptance of sex outside of the marriage relationship. As you know, there was in Corinth a temple devoted to the worship of sex, the temple of Aphrodite; therefore, it was a common thing for Christians to be tempted in this area. Many of them had indulged themselves in constant sexual liaisons before they became Christians and it was difficult for them to break these habits. If we think we have difficulty in these areas today, we are no different at all than these Corinthians.

The Christians in Corinth also were expected to meet the same demands for chastity and purity that we are called upon in the Scriptures to meet today. It was more difficult for them in some ways than it is for us, and yet the damands were the same. God has not changed;

the world has not changed; and as we read this passage we can see that we are dealing with a very present and current problem.

In the opening words of chapter 5 the apostle describes the specific nature of this problem in Corinth:

> It is actually reported that there is immorality among you, and of a kind that is not found even among pagans, for a man is living with his father's wife (v. 1).

This is what we would call "incest" today, and incest is increasing in frequency in our country to a frightening degree.

Beyond Shock

The woman mentioned in this letter, of course, was not the man's mother but his stepmother, his father's wife, and this was, therefore, a clear-cut case of adultery. But the additional element of the marriage relationship turned it into something even worse, incest. Paul is disturbed by this—I would not say he was shocked because I think at this stage of his career he was probably beyond shock. He had run into everything. When he says, "It is actually reported," he is not reflecting shock. It should more accurately be translated, "it is commonly reported among you"; this matter was notorious in Corinth.

As he points out, this was something that even that pagan environment would not look upon lightly. It is rather interesting that even in our own day the most degrading epithet anyone can apply to another is to suggest that he is sleeping with his own mother.

But the only ones in Corinth who were not shocked by this were the Christians in the church, and this is what bothers Paul the most. They were taking it lightly; they were even boasting in their attitude toward this and how they were handling this problem.

In verses 2 through 5 Paul describes what they were doing and what they should have been doing about this matter:

> And you are arrogant! Ought you not rather to mourn? Let him who has done this be removed from among you. For though absent in body I am present in spirit, and as if present, I have already pronounced judgment in the name of the Lord Jesus on the man who has done such a thing. When you are assembled, and my spirit is present, with the power of our Lord Jesus, you are to deliver this man to Satan for the destruction of the flesh, that his spirit may be saved in the day of the Lord Jesus.

They were boasting in their tolerance of this condition, as many people do today. Many have a mistaken notion that rather than condemning such immorality, the church ought to express understanding of the pressures and the difficulties of living in our world. They feel we ought to say nothing about this; let the individual work it out on his own. This is what was happening in Corinth. They thought they were showing love and understanding by their casual attitude toward this sin.

I have met church boards like this. In one church where I was involved briefly, the young pastor had been caught up in immorality. The board of the church was very casual about it. I reminded them of this very passage, and the chairman of the board said to me, "Well, he's a young man and, after all, boys will be boys." That reflected something of the attitude here at Corinth.

Now I know that this attitude of tolerant acceptance is often a reaction to another wrong approach, which is self-righteous condemnation. Such a censorious reaction of horror, usually because of offended pride, cuts the individual off and has nothing to do with him anymore. That is wrong, too, and there is nothing of that in what Paul expects of this church in Corinth. I have met people who have been deeply hurt and terribly injured by the harsh, critical judgment of boards and leaders who have thrown them out without trying to understand the pressures they were facing. One is the antithesis of the other.

Paul now shows us what the true attitude of a church ought to be when immorality rears its head: it ought to be grief. "Ought you not rather to mourn?" he asks. There ought to be shock and hurt not only for the persons involved in this but also for the church and for the Lord himself that the cause of Christ is damaged in the eyes of the community by these deeds.

The reason this was so hurtful in Corinth was that the church was permitting it to happen. They were, therefore, participators in this evil thing. The church ought to mourn that such a thing can happen in its midst and that there is not more help and protection afforded for it. So Paul says there ought to have been sorrowful prayer about this.

This is surely what he means when he writes to the Galatians, referring to an individual involved in a case like this: "If a man is overtaken in any trespass, you who are spiritual should restore him in a spirit of gentleness. Look to yourself, lest you too be tempted" (Gal. 6:1). That is facing the fact that you could be involved in something like this too. So the proper attitude in handling a situation like this is never one of, "Well, we would never do a thing like that," but rather one of, "Yes, we understand the pressures; we know what you have been up against. We are tempted ourselves; we could fall under the right circumstances. We do not trust ourselves any more than we trust the flesh in you, but nevertheless we cannot permit this to go on this way." There must be a right attitude.

A Right Basis for Discipline

There are four clear, practical steps to be taken when immorality is present. The first one is that there must be a right attitude. We must mourn and feel grief, instead of harsh, critical judgment or toler- ant, casual love. Second, there must be a right basis for discipline. Notice what the apostle does not say. He does not say to these elders, "Now you elders get together and decide among yourselves what you ought to do about this. Whatever you feel is right, you carry it out. If you decide that he ought to be excommunicated, if you decide he ought to be fined a certain amount, well, that's fine. Whatever you decide to do is all right." No, it is never left up to individual judgment as to what to do. What Paul clearly indicates is that they have already been told what to do; they should just do it. He speaks "in the name of the Lord Jesus . . . by the power of our Lord Jesus . . . by my spirit present with you." In other words, apostolic and divine authority has already spoken in these areas; therefore, follow it through.

In Matthew 18 the Lord Jesus tells us what to do in cases like this. "If your brother sins against you," he says, "go and tell him his fault, between you and him alone." Do not spread it around; do not ask for prayer about it; do not talk about it; go to the one who is doing the wrong.

This wrong, by the way, is not a matter of personal injury, something that has offended you, or some way the person has acted that you think is inappropriate. Here Jesus is talking about things that the Word of God has already judged. You are to "go and tell him his fault, between you and him alone." If he hears you, "you have gained your brother." That is enough; it does not need to go any further; no one else needs to know about it. But if he does not hear you, Jesus says, take one or two others and go and tell him his fault again and discuss it among yourselves. (You need two or three to avoid what often develops when two people argue. One says, "I already said to you this and this." The other fellow says, "No, you did not say that at all, you said this and this.") But two or three are there as witnesses that what was said was exactly what was really said. This is an attempt to help a person see what he is doing and if he listens, that is the end of it.

Hundreds of cases of incipient immorality have been nipped in the bud, as it were, by Christians who faithfully go to somebody and tell him that what he is doing is wrong. That is the healthiest thing a church can do and Christians can do with one another. It saves scores of cases like this that would come to ultimate heartbreak if they were allowed to proceed.

But the Lord goes on. "If he refuses to listen to them (the small group that has come to him), then tell it to the church." Then it must become public; the individuals involved must sense the censure of the church, the feeling that this is not acceptable behavior to other Christians.

Now again, this is not to be done in a spirit of self-righteous complacency or critical judgment. It is to be done by lovingly stating that this is wrong; it is unacceptable behavior. It cannot be allowed to continue even though you understand the pressures and the problems involved in it. Therefore, it is to be told to the whole church. Everyone in the church, then, becomes responsible to try to help that individual to recover from this terrible situation.

Jesus then gives the final step: if he will not hear the church then "Change your attitude toward him" the Lord is saying, "let him be to you as a Gentile and a tax collector, as a sinner." In other words, let him be unto you as though he is not a Christian at all. He has declared himself not to be a Christian by his actions, even though he claims yet to be a Christian by his words. You are to treat him as one who is not yet a Christian, but that does not mean with scorn, or with judgment, or with any kind of retribution. Recognize that he has deceived himself, and he is not really born again. Understand that he does not yet know the basis for purity and needs to be born again.

This is what Matthew 18 is saying, and clearly it is a parallel passage to what we have here. Paul knows by now that this is a well-known matter. It has come now to the place where it ought to be dealt with by the church. Since the church has been involved in this whole process of accepting and tolerating this situation, it has now come to the final step Jesus has set forth. That is what Paul means when he says there is to be a proper basis for action. It is on the basis of what the Lord has said and not what the individuals themselves may feel.

I know many people have tried to apply Jesus' words, "Judge not that you be not judged" (Matt. 7:1) to a situation like this. But our Lord is clearly talking there about individual judgment of another on the basis of what offends you, whereas here he is talking about something he has already judged. The church is responsible to carry out that judgment, as Paul will make crystal clear throughout this passage.

Out into Satan's Dominion

So step number three in this passage is: there must be a right action. ③ There must be a right attitude; there must be a basis for discipline; and there must be a right action taken. Here it is:

> When you are assembled, and my spirit is present, with the power of our Lord Jesus, you are to deliver this man to Satan for the destruction of the flesh, that his spirit may be saved in the day of the Lord Jesus (vv. 4, 5).

Three times in this passage the apostle says very clearly what action is to be taken. You have in verse 2, "Let him who has done this be removed from among you"; you have in verse 13 (the last verse of the chapter), "Drive out the wicked person from among you." Those two commands, which sound rather harsh and almost seem to describe a kind of physical exclusion, are softened and corrected and amplified by this central statement here in verse 5, "deliver this man to Satan for the destruction of the flesh." Now that helps us to understand what this action is to be, because, as we read in Matthew 18 and also here, the Scripture always regards the world as Satan's dominion.

There are two kingdoms at work in life: the kingdom of Satan and kingdom of God. They intermingle; they are working all the time, everywhere, and though you cannot separate them by sharp lines of demarcation from the standpoint of geography or personality, nevertheless they are sharply separated in their philosophy. What Paul is saying here is that the church is to put the man back, in its thinking, into the realm of Satan's control. He has never really left it; his persistence in evil has demonstrated that he has never really left Satan's world. Therefore, the church is to regard him as back under that control, and publicly the church is to recognize that he is not a Christian. He is, as Jesus says, like a Gentile, a tax collector, a sinner, unregenerate, and therefore he is not to be treated any longer as though he were a Christian.

Now I realize that there is always great pressure not to take a public action like this. People are offended by being made a public example. When our church has had to do this on several occasions we have been actually threatened with lawsuits if we took a public stand in this direction. This is why the apostle adds the words, "(take this action) with the power of our Lord Jesus!" You are not taking it as a group of people, an organization voting on one of its disobedient members. You are taking it as the church of the living God, among whom the Lord Jesus is present as he said he would be, with power to control the results and to guard and protect if you will be obedient to him. Therefore, the church is to act, regardless of what the threat may be, because the church acts by the power of the Lord Jesus.

This action does not mean physical ejection. The individual may continue to attend but he is to be treated and regarded in a different light. Usually, however, this almost invariably means that the individual, feeling the censure of the church, withdraws himself. If so, then he is allowed to go. There is no punishment ever assessed; there is no ceremony of excommunication to be carried out. That kind of a thing represents a misunderstanding of this passage.

Thus we have three of the steps: a right attitude; a right basis for action; and a right action to be taken. There is one more, and Paul indicates it in verse 5: it should be for a right purpose, ". . . that his spirit may be saved in the day of the Lord Jesus."

Why does the church take this action? Well, not just to get rid of a troublemaker or merely to show itself clean in this regard, but rather to reach the individuals involved and so deal with them that eventually they will see their wrongdoing and repent. All judgment ends at repentance; all discipline ceases when repentance occurs. The hope here is that when you put someone back into the world, as it were, under Satan's control, that he will learn what worldlings will learn if they live long enough: the philosophies they are following are delusive, empty, and vain, and when they find themselves drained, jaded, and empty of heart, they will turn back to the living Lord and their spirits will be saved in the day of the Lord Jesus. When he comes or when they meet him in death, their spirits will be saved even though their lives have been wasted. This is the hope and that is the purpose for church discipline.

Reasons for Action

Now the apostle follows with an explanation for the severity of this kind of action. When a church is involved in this sort of thing many people raise the question of why the church should act so severely. Here Paul gives three excellent reasons why the church must take action:

> Your boasting is not good. Do you not know that a little leaven ferments the whole lump of dough? Cleanse out the old leaven that you may be fresh dough, as you really are unleavened. For Christ, our paschal lamb, has been sacrificed. Let us, therefore, celebrate the festival, not with the old leaven, the leaven of malice and evil, but with the unleavened bread of sincerity and truth (vv. 6–8).

The imagery is clearly borrowed from the Feast of the Passover when the Jews, remembering their deliverance from Egypt, would take the blood of a lamb and sprinkle it over their doorposts so the angel of death would "pass over." Then they would gather and eat the meat of the lamb that had been roasted. Before this they would go through the house with a candle and search out all the leaven that was in the house, for the Lord had said they must never eat the feast with leaven.

Leaven is yeast, and even today Jews will go through their houses and look for any form of leavened bread that may be present before they celebrate the Passover. Leaven is consistently used throughout the Scriptures as a symbol of evil. Paul says the problem is that "a little leaven leavens the whole lump." Therefore, the first reason action must be taken is to arrest the tendency to spread the infection throughout a whole congregation.

I have mentioned that we have had to take action like this on two or three occasions. Though it was painful and hurtful and there was great grief involved in it, the effect was an almost instantaneous cessation of the spread of evil throughout the congregation. People think twice before they begin to get involved in extramarital affairs or consider divorce or fall into homosexuality or other sexual sins. Sexual sins, of course, are not the only ones that call for judgment though they are probably the most common form today. This is the first reason the church must act, lest the infection begin to spread and "the little leaven leavens the whole lump."

The second reason is that judgment makes possible the demonstration of reality. As Paul says here, "Cleanse out the old leaven that you may be a new lump, *as you really are.*" The community was getting a wrong idea of the church. It did not see them as having solved the problem of how to handle sexual drives. It saw them as being as much a part of the problem as they themselves were and yet, as Paul will say in the next chapter, Christ had cleansed them, he had changed them: "And such were some of you. But you were washed, you were sanctified, you were justified in the name of the Lord Jesus Christ." But that is not evident while this tolerance of evil is going on. The world has no idea that there is any way to escape the power of sexual lust. "Therefore," he says, "the church must judge this kind of thing that it might be evident what you really are—that you have been given power to handle these drives and to be pure and chaste in the midst of immorality. For that is what you really are."

The third reason is that judgment permits the celebration of Christian deliverance and liberty. "Let us, therefore, celebrate the festival, not with the old leaven, but with the unleavened bread of sincerity and truth." "Celebrate!" he says. That is possible in a church when it begins to live on this basis in the eyes of the community and before the Lord. An element of joy comes into their midst, and they begin to celebrate that freedom.

I have noticed that congregations that refuse to act along these lines are usually grim. Their worship is dull and there is little joy. What brings joy into a congregation is not the sense of having achieved some degree of morality on its own, but of having been washed, cleansed, freed by the grace of God. All the ugliness of the past is washed away; it disappears from among you and that allows for a free spirit of celebration and of joy.

Now the concluding section of chapter 5 describes the limits of church discipline:

> I wrote to you in my letter not to associate with immoral men; not at all meaning the immoral of this world, or the greedy and robbers, or idolaters, since then you would need to go out of the world. But rather I wrote to you not to associate with any one who bears the name of brother if he is guilty of immorality or greed, or is an idolater, reviler, drunkard, or robber— not even to eat with such a one. For what have I to do with judging outsiders? Is it not those inside the church whom you are to judge? God judges those outside. Drive out the wicked person from among you (vv. 9–13).

In verse 9 Paul refers to a previous letter of his that is lost to us. No one knows what it said other than this reference to it. Yet in it Paul had evidently said something about not associating with immoral people and the Corinthians had taken it to mean (as many Christians seem to feel today) that they were not to have anything to do with worldlings who lived on a lower level of morality.

I am amazed at how the very attitude which Paul was attempting to correct here in this letter has pervaded the evangelical world. I meet people who refuse to have anyone come into their homes who is not a Christian. They want nothing to do with anyone who lives in a way offensive to the Lord. In my early pastorate I remember going to a couple and asking them to open their home for a Bible class. The lady looked horrified and said, "Oh! I could never do that." I asked, "Why not?" "Why," she said, "people who smoke would come in. My home is dedicated to God and I am not going to have any smoking going on there."

Well, that is a misunderstanding of the very thing Paul is talking about. We must not avoid the world—we were sent into it. The Lord Jesus said to his disciples, "Behold, I send you forth as sheep in the midst of wolves." That is where we belong. Their habits may be offensive to us, but that is understandable. We do not have to pronounce judgment on them; God will do that, Paul says here. We are to love them and understand that they do not have any basis of knowledge so as to change. We are not to demand it of them before we begin to show friendship and love and reach out to them to help them to see their need, to see the One who can answer the hunger of their hearts. No, we are not to judge the world, but we are to judge the church. Paul says, and we are to do it on a clear-cut basis.

By the way, in referring to the world here, Paul mentions three characteristic sins that are very revealing:

> . . . not at all meaning the immoral of this world, or the greedy and robbers (that is really one phrase taken together, the greedy and grasping), or idolaters.

There you have the world characterized for you: the sins of the body (immorality), the sins of the mind or heart (greedy and grasping attitudes), and the sins of the spirit (idolatry, another god). The offense against yourself, the offense against your neighbor, and the offense against God himself—those are the characteristics of the world.

What we will offer them is the gospel, not condemnation but the good news. But we are to judge the church for specific wrongdoings. Notice how Paul lists them. It is not because they are hard to live with or they are impatient people or they are obnoxious Christians— you are not to judge them on that basis. But if they are immoral, or greedy, or idolaters, or revilers (constant critics, running everybody down), or drunkards, or robbers, then they are to be judged by the action of the church in the way he has indicated, even to the point of social pressures. "Do not even eat with them," he says. If they will not listen, then withdraw from them. It comes at last to ultimate exclusion, as he has indicated in this passage.

What health would return to the world and to the church if the church would behave this way! The reason the world is going downhill rapidly is because the church does not maintain the standards God has given us here. The purpose of a passage like this is to call us back in all honesty to what God has given us, so that we recognize the unique position the church holds in the world today when it begins to walk in the beauty of holiness and enjoy the privileges God has given to us. When we live in victory over the forces that destroy others, then people see that there is meaning and purpose and reason for the salvation we profess to have.

10

Two Kinds of Lust

The apostle Paul deals with the problem of lawsuits among brethren in the passage we come to now. Recently two Christian organizations involved in smuggling Bibles behind the Iron Curtain were suing each other before the courts in libel actions for damages. I wondered if they had spent any time reading the Bibles they smuggle, for in this passage Paul clearly says that lawsuits between believers are definitely wrong.

The apostle seems to change his subject in this section. In chapter 5, he was talking about lust among Christians at Corinth. In the closing part of chapter 6 he returns to that subject and deals with prostitution in Corinth. But in between, the first eleven verses of chapter 6 are dealing with lawsuits among brethren.

We might well ask, "What has that got to do with lust?" The answer is that the greed which prompts lawsuits is a form of lust. Lawsuits usually arise out of greed, or covetousness. A lawsuit is an attempt to force another person to yield to you what you regard as your right. The dictionary defines lust as "obsessive craving or desire," so it is apparent that someone who is greedy, especially regarding material matters, is guilty of a form of lust, of making things more important than people.

These first eleven verses divide naturally into three subdivisions. The first thing the apostle says is that lawsuits among brethren are stupid, foolish. Second, he says, lawsuits are shameful. Finally, Paul

117

says, they even raise suspicions as to the spiritual state of the ones involved.

Notice how he brings in this subject:

> When one of you has a grievance against a brother, does he dare go to law before the unrighteous instead of the saints? Do you not know that the saints will judge the world? And if the world is to be judged by you, are you incompetent to try trivial cases? Do you not know that we are to judge angels? How much more, matters pertaining to this life! (vv. 1-3)

The apostle does not use the word *stupid* here, but his implication is that these people are very foolish. They were obviously engaging in lawsuits, dragging each other before the Roman courts, washing all their dirty linen in public by going to secular courts to settle their problems. This, the apostle implies, is foolish, for two reasons.

First, it is an audacious act of boldness. "Dare any one of you, having a grievance against his brother, take it to a law court to settle?" This is an outrageous act, a bold, daring thing to do. Paul implies that one who does such a thing has reached the point of not caring what anyone thinks or feels; he is acting regardless of the injuries that may be done to others.

Paul then suggests in the two questions he asks that anybody who does such a thing is really an ignorant person: "Do you not know that the church is going to judge the world, and do not you know that the church is going to judge angels?"

In this chapter there are six occasions where the apostle asks the question, "Do you not know?" These questions imply a certain degree of knowledge that the Corinthians ought to have had. "Do you not know," he says, "that the saints will judge the world?" Surely he is referring to those passages, both in the gospels and in the epistles, where we are clearly told that when the Lord returns the saints are going to share the throne of judgment with him. We are to rule with Christ; we will, therefore, enter into judgment with him.

Learning How to Judge

Exactly how we will do this we are never told. Whether we are to be assigned a literal throne to sit on or whether the throne is only a symbol is not made clear. What is clear is that we will enter into the mind and heart of God as he examines the thoughts and innermost desires of men. In chapter 4 Paul said that we are not to judge before the Lord comes who will examine the motives, the hidden things of the heart. But now we are learning how to do that, and that is the point Paul is raising here.

He does not mean to put down the systems of justice that were practiced in that day or any day. Paul admired and honored Roman law—he himself called upon it for defense on occasion—but he is saying that human law by its very nature has to deal with relatively trivial and superficial things. It deals with actions, not with urges and deep, hidden desires and motives. The law specifically prohibits the jury or the judges or the defense attorneys or anyone from probing too deeply into motives. Intent has to be established, but they cannot presume to judge why people act the way they do. The law is restricted to judging actions as to whether they are injurious to others or not. Therefore, human law operates at a rather shallow level of judgment.

Paul is saying, "If you are learning during the course of your life how to go deeper than actions, how to understand why individuals act the way they do, and what is wrong and right about feelings and desires, then surely you ought to be competent to judge these simple cases among yourselves that deal with actions."

Then the apostle goes even further and asks, "Do you not know that we are to judge angels?" Think of that! We do not know much about angels. They are beings of a higher order than we are. They are not only different from us in culture, they are different in their very nature, and yet the amazing statement of Scripture is that God is preparing a people who will be so capable of delving into the motives of all beings that some day they will participate with him in judging the angels that have fallen.

There are two references in the New Testament to the judgment of angels. We are reminded in 2 Peter that, "God did not spare the angels when they sinned, but cast them into hell and committed them to pits of nether gloom to be kept until the judgment" (2:4). And in the little book of Jude we are also told of ". . . the angels that did not keep their own position . . . have been kept by him in eternal chains . . . until the judgment of the great day" (Jude 6). Therefore it is the duty of all believers to learn how to judge—that is one of the major reasons we are here on earth.

You can see Paul's argument then: "Is it not rather ridiculous that you people who are going to have to deal in such difficult matters as the judgment of the world and of angels cannot even settle these little squabbles among yourselves?" It is almost as if a mathematician who works with great computers were to call in a ninth-grader and ask him for help to balance his checkbook. Paul's argument is that it is stupid to have the world judge between brothers.

I do not think he means that Christians are never to go to law; sometimes that is impossible to avoid. Paul is not saying that it is wrong for Christians to settle claims with non-Christians before courts of law. It is between believers that it is wrong to go to law. Paul himself on one occasion stood on his rights as a Roman citizen and appealed to the court of Caesar for a final judgment.

Now Paul goes on to say further that lawsuits between brothers are shameful:

> If then you have such cases, why do you lay them before those who are least esteemed by the church? I say this to your shame. Can it be that there is no man among you wise enough to decide between members of the brotherhood, but brother goes to law against brother, and that before unbelievers? To have lawsuits at all with one another is defeat for you. Why not rather suffer wrong? Why not rather be defrauded? But you yourselves wrong and defraud, and that even your own brethren (vv. 4–8).

You can almost hear Paul's shocked tone of voice; he cannot believe that these Corinthians will actually forsake the cause of Christ to this degree.

Paul points out four things here. The first is that lawsuits are shameful because they stoop to a lower level of judgment. What Paul means by "those who are least esteemed by the church" is the secular judges who are presiding over the courts of law in the world. He does not mean to dishonor them, as I have already said. He recognizes the limits of human law, but he is saying that a secular judge who does not understand the relationship of one Christian to another, who has no concept of the fatherhood of God and the family life of believers, who does not understand that we are members one of another, and who does not understand our relationship to Christ, is, therefore, not to be highly esteemed as a judge of matters concerning believers.

An Ignored Alternative

Second, he says these judgments and lawsuits between believers ignore a possible alternative that could be adopted. Suppose you have an agreement with a brother in Christ and he ends up owing you money. He has the money but he chooses to use it for other reasons. The world would say, "Take him to court; that is what the courts are for; you can get your rights that way."

But that is the very thing the apostle says is not right for Christians. In fact, he says, when you do this you are passing by an alternative, and he suggests it here: "Can it be there is no man among you wise enough to decide between members of the brotherhood? Why do you not select somebody in the congregation who understands the whole matter of relationships among Christians and ask him, or perhaps a group of people, to decide for you?"

I am amazed at how little this is practiced today. I have been asked to serve in this capacity a couple of times, but it is very rare. Yet I think it ought to be more common; elders ought to expect to be asked to serve in this capacity. Disagreements among Christians will come, and they do need to be adjudicated. The apostle's point is that you have people available far more competent to settle these than any secular law or court. Therefore, he suggests, why not do that?

The third thing Paul has to say about this (v. 7) is "To have lawsuits at all with one another is defeat for you." No matter who wins the lawsuit the gospel is still going to suffer. In the case of these two Christian organizations I mentioned, it really does not make any difference which one wins. The cause of Christ has already been degraded in the eyes of the watching world; no matter who wins the case there are people who have been turned off already by the fact that believers are fighting each other in this open, aggressive way.

What a lawsuit says to the watching world is, "Christians are no better than you are; they, too, have to have a judge settle matters between them. What have they to offer us?"

Consider the Damage

Finally, Paul says, there is still another alternative: "Why not rather suffer wrong? Why not rather be defrauded? But you yourselves wrong and defraud, and that even your own brethren." What he is suggesting here is that to accept personal loss is preferable to going to law when you consider the damage that would be done to the Christian cause by bringing them to secular courts to settle. After all, what is the loss of a few hundred dollars or a thousand dollars, or a hundred thousand dollars, if the whole cause of Christ and the gospel is going to be degraded in the eyes of those who need it in the world around?

Dr. H. A. Ironside, with whom I traveled once, told me of an incident in his own life. When he was only eight years old or so his mother took him to a meeting of the brethren, who were discussing some kind of difficulty among themselves. Young Harry Ironside did not know what the trouble was but it was clear they were deeply disturbed. He said that one man stood up and shook his fist and said, "I don't care what the rest of you do. I want my rights! That's all! I just want my rights!"

There was an old half-deaf Scottish brother sitting in the front row, and he cupped his hand behind his ear and asked, "Aye, brother, what's that ye say?" And the fellow said, "Well, all I said was that I want my rights. That's all." The old man said, "Your rights, brother, is that what you want, your rights? Why the Lord Jesus didn't come to get his rights. He came to get his wrongs, and he got them." Harry Ironside said, "I'll always remember how that fellow stood transfixed for a little while. Then he dropped his head and said, 'You're right, brother, you're right. Settle it any way you like.' " And in a few moments the whole thing was settled.

What we should never forget is that as believers we are called to demonstrate a different life style before the world, one in which we are ready to surrender personal rights for the cause that we serve. Paul is going to develop this more and more later in his letter. There is nothing more characteristic of a believer than his willingness to surrender some personal right, even to his own hurt, so that the cause of the gospel may prevail.

A Christian businessman told me that whenever people accuse him of overcharging or of taking advantage of others in business, he says to them, "Well, how much is involved?" When he learns the amount he says, "Let's forget it. I don't want that money. I don't agree with you, but if you feel it is yours I would rather you had the money than fight with you." Often it shocks the individual involved and opens a door for a witness that had never opened up before. This is what Paul says is more important.

But he is still not through. He has a third area to discuss:

> Do you not know that the unrighteous will not inherit the kingdom of God? Do not be deceived; neither the immoral, nor idolaters, nor adulterers, nor homosexuals, nor thieves, nor the greedy, nor drunkards, nor revilers, nor robbers will inherit the kingdom of God. And such were some of you. But you were washed, you were sanctified, you were justified in the name of the Lord Jesus Christ and in the Spirit of our God (vv. 9–11).

What ties this section with that which has gone before is found in verse 8, "But you yourselves *wrong*," and the word in verse 9, "Do you not know that the *unrighteous* will not inherit the kingdom of

God?" Those are the same basic words. What Paul is really saying is, "Look, when you are so aggressive in defense of your own rights that you take another brother to law before a secular court, you are wronging that brother. Even though you may be right in your cause, you are wronging your brother. That unjust action gives rise to the question, 'Have you yourself ever been justified before God?'" To treat another unjustly makes one ask if you have ever been justified, and he says the *un*justified, the *un*righteous, the *un*regenerate cannot inherit the kingdom of God if they are committed, as a life style, to these things that he lists.

Discontinued Life Style

Now he surely does not mean that those who have been involved in these things cannot be saved, for he goes on to say, "such were some of you"; they have come out of it. But what he is saying very clearly is that these things cannot be continued as a life style for Christians. Conversion makes a visible difference, and if it does not, there is room to question whether there has ever been a conversion.

You recall the incident in Luke 19 when Jesus came into Jericho and he saw Zacchaeus, the tax collector, up in a tree. Jesus called him down and went to his home for lunch. Afterwards Zacchaeus came out and began to give away his money. He began to repay those from whom he had stolen, not only the amount he had stolen, but four times as much. No one has ever doubted that Zacchaeus was converted from that day on—it changed his whole life. His attitude changed so completely that his behavior began to alter almost immediately.

In 2 Timothy 2 Paul writes, "God's firm foundation stands, bearing this seal: 'The Lord knows those who are his.'" (That is God's side of it. He reads the heart, but you and I cannot see that. But, Paul continues), "Let every one who names the name of the Lord depart from iniquity." That is the way to tell if somebody is a believer in Christ. To go on living in a life style involving fornication, idolatry, adultery, homosexuality, thieving, greediness, alcoholism, reviling, stealing, robbing, is entirely incompatible and inconsistent with a Christian profession. It is to give testimony that the person has never become a Christian.

Paul closes this on a rather practical and positive note: "Such were some of you." He says, "Because you are carrying personal quarrels so far as to get involved in lawsuits you are really giving testimony that you never were changed. But that is not true of most of you; 'such were *some* of you'."

"Such ones," he says, "were washed, they were sanctified, they were justified in the name of the Lord Jesus. For this reason I can count on the fact that they will change their way of life."

He lists here the three things that produce the change, not in the order of their experience, but in reverse order. It all begins with justification, "You were justified," he says. "You came to the place where you quit trying to earn your salvation. You acknowledged the fact that Christ had paid your debt for you, and on the basis of your trust in what he had done for you, God made you righteous. God gave you the gift of full acceptance before him, and you were justified. Then that began the process of becoming sanctified. The Holy Spirit began to lead you to change your attitude and your behavior."

Finally, there is a washing. One actually changes his behavior; he starts acting differently. That was what was happening here in Corinth. These people were behaving quite differently. They had actually been cleansed by the change in their hearts made by the Lord Jesus Christ and the Spirit of our God. That is what conversion and Christianity are all about.

Now Paul returns to the subject of sexual immorality. As a consequence of his teaching in Corinth, the church there had begun to challenge the sexual looseness of the city. But there were some in the church there who said that Paul had laid a groundwork for viewing some of the sexual practices of Corinth as being right and proper for Christians. Some of the people were actually quoting him to support what they believed. Beginning with verse 12, Paul refers to those quotations they were attributing to him:

> "All things are lawful for me," but not all things are helpful. "All things are lawful for me," but I will not be enslaved by anything. "Food is meant for the stomach and the stomach for food"—and God will destroy both one and the other. The body is not meant for immorality, but for the Lord, and the Lord for the body. And God raised the Lord and will also raise us up by his power (vv. 12–14).

Notice the quotation marks around the words "all things are lawful for me." These reflect the editors' opinion that the Corinthians had heard these words from Paul, and were repeating them constantly within the church. It is very likely that they echoed something Paul had said because this was part of his teaching about the grace of God: "All things are lawful for us."

The difference between legalism and true Christianity is right at this point. The legalist looks at life and says, "Everything is wrong—unless you can prove from a verse of Scripture that it is right." It is a negative approach to life; it says everything that is fun is either illegal, immoral or fattening. But New Testament Christianity says, "Everything is right: God made the earth and everything in it and everything is right—except what the Word of God labels as wrong." That is an entirely different point of view, opening the whole world to exploration and discovery and enjoyment, except for a very limited part which Scripture clearly labels as wrong.

These people were saying, "Paul himself said 'All things are lawful for me.'" Their argument should sound very familiar to us today. They were saying that sexual freedom, i.e., sex outside of marriage, is theologically sound. Their argument probably went something like this: "The law of Moses tells us that it is wrong to commit adultery. (*Adultery* here is a broad word referring to any kind of sexual wrongness.) But Paul taught us that when Christ came into our life the law ended its reign. We are no longer under the law; we are no longer under this commandment not to commit adultery. Therefore, by Paul's own words, we are free to indulge in some of these sexual practices that are so widely accepted in Corinth."

In Paul's answer, notice first what he does not do. He does not say, "Now that you are a Christian we have a new rule for you. You must not do such and such." Paul never retreats into legalism. What he does say is, "Yes, you are right, but you need to understand that truth must always be balanced."

The Same Distance Down

When I was a boy I used to enjoy walking along the back fences in the city of Denver. I could go for blocks on the back alleys. I enjoyed doing it, but it was a very narrow path. Jesus said the Christian life would be like that. He called it "a straight and narrow way." The problem is to keep from falling off, and either is equally dangerous; it is the same distance down. Christians ought to remember that the pathway of liberty is always narrow. It is a freeing and exhilarating path to walk, but you can easily fall off into one error or the other.

Liberty is liberty only, the apostle insists, when it is balanced between two extremes. These people in Corinth were saying, "The law is an extreme; it makes a rigid demand on my life that I or nobody else can live up to." And that is true—the law is an extreme. When you understand the impact and import of the Law of Moses, the Ten Commandments, you find they are so easily and quickly broken that there is not an individual in the world who has ever lived up to them except the Lord Jesus himself. "You are right," Paul says, "the law is an extreme, but license is an extreme too." "All things are lawful," he quotes, "but they are not helpful." The moment your liberty begins to hurt you or someone else, you have fallen off into license, and you are in the same trouble you experienced under law.

"Further," Paul says, "the things that are not helpful are always enslaving. 'I will not be brought under the power of anything.' " Notice how beautifully he is balancing truth here. The things that hurt you have a tendency to be habit-forming. Have you noticed that? They hurt you, but they are fun. They give you a certain degree of pleasure, which is why you do not mind the hurt so much, but that degree of pleasure is habit-forming, either physically or emotionally. The apostle says, "But we are interested in true liberty. We must remember, therefore, that truth can be lost on either side of the fence."

There was another impressive-sounding argument there in Corinth about which they had written to Paul. "Food is meant for the stomach and the stomach for food." Notice the quotation marks around that; that is what they were quoting from Paul. It meant, the stomach was designed for food, and food is obviously designed for the stomach, so it is natural and right to satisfy your hunger need whenever it arises. We all run to the refrigerator when we get hungry. Nobody raises any objections or charges us with immorality when we do that. How many times have you heard the argument that sex is like that? Sex organs were made for sex; therefore, it is natural and right to satisfy them, and when you feel the urge it is okay to merge. That is what they say, isn't it?

A Permanent Plan for the Body

Now the apostle's answer to that is a profound revelation of the difference between our food appetites and our sexual appetites. Here we enter into an area of revelation where it is evident that the Word of God sees far more profoundly into the nature of our humanity than anything in the world around us. Here, by contrast, you can see the shallowness of the world's view of sex.

Paul's answer is very brief: "True," he says, "food is made for the stomach and the stomach is made for food, but God will destroy both one and the other." In other words, that is only a temporary arrangement. It is true that the stomach and food were made for one another—

and God obviously did that—but it is only true for this life. There is coming a day when God is going to destroy both the food and the stomach. God has no permanent plan for the belly, but he does have a permanent plan for the body. The body, quite apart from its digestive apparatus, has a reason and purpose in God's program.

But sexuality is much more profound and touches us at a much deeper level. Sexuality, according to the Scriptures, pervades our whole humanity. It touches us not only in terms of the body (physical), but also in terms of the soul (the *psyche*), i.e., our social relationships with one another. Even more profoundly, sex characterizes and touches us at the level of the spirit (the *pneuma*) as well.

Did you ever realize that the Bible teaches that worship is a form of sexual expression? The basic definition of sex could be stated as the urge to merge. You can see that going on in terms of friendship. If you sit down with friends you want to share; you want to hear what they have been doing and tell them what you have been doing. You want to hear their opinions about certain things, and you want them to listen to yours. Friendship consists of the interchange of one life with another at the level of the soul, expressing itself as mind, emotion and will. Now, what is worship? Worship is a hunger to be possessed by God and to possess all there is of God. The worshiping spirit cries out, "O Lord, come take me, use me, possess me." God, in turn, gives us the beautiful promise that he is available to us, to be experienced by us and to relate to us. Jesus put it in the most precise way when he said that the deepest relationship possible between a human being and his God is: "You in me and I in you."

We are taught by the world that sex is that which touches us only at the physical level. In the modern movements of today that call themselves "Sexual Freedom Movements," "Feminist Movements," "Woman's Rights," and other things, we are being told that sexual differences between the male and female are basically superficial. At heart, they say, we are all human beings. But the Word of God never tells us that. In the Scripture, from the very moment that man appears on the scene until we are carried into the reaches of eternity, man appears as two sexes: "Male and female created he them." That division is pervasive; it runs through our whole being. We are not only physically different, male and female in our physical bodies, but we are different in our attitudes, our emotions, our reactions. We are different in the way we worship God, and the way we enjoy him and respond in worship, as well. God likes it that way and God made it that way. Sex therefore represents a far deeper and more significant appetite than that for food and drink.

Made to be Possessed by God

Paul points out that God has a purpose for the body beyond this present life. He says, "The body is not meant for immorality, but for the Lord, and the Lord for the body." Notice the parallel there. They were saying, " 'Food is meant for the stomach and the stomach for food.' They are obviously designed to be together." Paul says, "All right, now carry it further: the purpose of the human body is not sex expression; it is to be the possession of the Lord himself—that is what your bodies were made for." There is a dignity about humanity that is far greater than any animal can claim. Humanity is made to be indwelt by God. That is the most exciting, the most remarkable, the most revolutionary teaching in the Word of God.

As Paul brings out, God has a purpose for the body; he is going to raise it up. He raised up the body of the Lord, and he will raise us up also. Sexuality, which penetrates our whole being, will not be expressed on the physical level in the resurrected body, but it will have its expression at the soulish and the spiritual levels. God has a purpose for it in the life to come. That is why we are given physical sex. It is designed to teach us what we are like, who we are, what our role is, in the life to come.

Male organs are external in order to emphasize, as one of the marvelous visual aids that God is always employing, that the male role is one of visible leadership. He is designed to take the initiative, and yet to do so with tenderness and gentleness. Any physical sex within marriage that is conducted without both firmness and tenderness becomes destructive and creates difficulties within the marriage.

Female organs are internal, hidden, to indicate the role of women as being inwardly sensitive, far deeper emotionally than men, more subjective, contributing deeper insights than man ever does, having a greater sense of compassion, and responding to that which leads. All this is designed to teach us truth about our relationships with one another and with God himself. That is why, throughout the Scriptures, God appears in relationship to the Christian as the lover, the aggressor, the male. We are the bride, the responders, the followers, and that role is consistent all through the Scriptures.

Paul is thus underscoring in these brief words the tremendous mystery of sex; that it is the very secret of life itself. To misuse it is to miss the beauty of it. Its beauty is destroyed and defiled when it is indulged for self-satisfaction only, or without the full commitment that marriage represents. (Paul is going to have a lot more to say about this when he gets into chapter 7. He will take up, in detail, the mutual sex roles of husband and wife, which we will look at with the same frankness as the Scripture does.)

But now, Paul moves on to attack the problem of prostitution that was present there in Corinth. The glory of the Scriptures is that they never present a principle without bringing it right down to where the rubber meets the road and applying it to life itself. That is what Paul does now with the widespread problem of temple prostitution:

> Do you not know that your bodies are members of Christ? Shall I therefore take the members of Christ and make them members of a prostitute? Never! Do you not know that he who joins himself to a prostitute becomes one body with her? For, as it is written, "The two shall become one (flesh)." But he who is united to the Lord becomes one spirit with him (vv. 15–17).

In this passage Paul describes fornication as a horrible sin which involves taking a body, which is the personal property of Jesus himself, and using it in a relationship with a godless woman. He suggests it is equivalent to involving the Lord of Glory in a dissolute and reprehensible act. That is what every act of prostitution and every act of fornication involving a believer is.

Dr. J. A. Schep, in the book *The Nature of the Resurrection Body* says,

> Sexual intercourse always effects a complete union of the two persons involved, and thus is quite different from eating or drinking something. Becoming one *flesh* with a harlot means becoming one body with her, i.e., being united with her in every respect, in her shameful sinning as well.

This is the thing that raises Paul's expression of horror: "Never! Who would want to do a thing like that?" Notice that Paul goes clear back to Genesis here. He takes that governing word spoken to Adam and Eve in the Garden of Eden, "The two shall become one flesh" (which describes marriage), and he applies it here to a passing liaison with a common street prostitute. Something goes on in the act of sex that creates a union far deeper than the merely passing pleasure of the moment. It is part of that whole mystery that God designed and set forth at the beginning in the Garden of Eden. Thus it has tremendous effect upon those who give themselves to such a practice.

This is a profound insight that we need to take very seriously these days. The apostle Paul is telling us that something happens when you indulge in sexual relationships that even callous worldlings can recognize. Men who live sexually promiscuous lives have told me that even the most casual sexual liaison results in a change that is evident when they meet the girl later. There is a deep sense of having shared a mystery together—an intimacy that can never be forgotten.

But the Christian's relationship with his Lord, in contrast with the sexual relationship, is one of spiritual identity. These are probably among the most revolutionary words ever written in the Word of God or anywhere in the whole world of books. Paul says,

> The body is not meant for immorality, but for the Lord, and the Lord for the body.

And also in verse 17,

> . . . he who is united to the Lord becomes one spirit with him.

The Lord is a Spirit, and we are human spirits. When regeneration occurs there is a fusing of identity. This is what Peter refers to in his letter as having "become partakers of the divine nature." Think about that for a minute. What a fantastic statement it is! We have an ability, a capacity within us, to fuse with the very nature of God so that there is no distinction left between us and him as to identity. We are one spirit and from there on that becomes our true "I," our true identity.

This is what forms the basis for the New Covenant in the Word of God—the availability of the life of God to the believer so that he faces every situation and every circumstance with a new power and a new ability to act; a new ability to understand and see things he never saw before.

A fantastic inward change takes place that means our spirits have fused with his Spirit and from then on one can hardly tell the two apart—we are one spirit with him!

That truth serves to highlight the terrible effects of fornication which, at Corinth, took the form of prostitution. "Shun immorality." ("Flee fornication" is the actual term.) That is Paul's apostolic advice as to how to handle sexual desire when it is not able to be expressed within marriage. "Get out of there," Paul says. "Don't fool around with it; don't play with it." If you are in a parked car and you are beginning to get aroused, start the engine and drive home. If you are reading a magazine and you run across something obscene, get rid of the magazine. If you are watching television and it presents erotic material so that you find yourself aroused by desires, change the channel, or go read a good book!

"Flee immorality"—that is the advice everywhere in the Bible. Do not try to fight with it; do not try to overcome it; do not try to suppress it. Get away! These are subtle, powerful forces, and the widespread destruction we see in lives around us is ample testimony to the subtlety with which they can conquer us.

Not Like Other Sins

Then Paul goes on to say something very interesting:

> Every other sin which a man commits is outside the body; but the immoral man sins against his own body (v. 18).

Many people have struggled with that verse because it seems to suggest that fornication (sexual promiscuity or sexual indulgence outside of marriage) is unique in its effect upon us. It is not like other sins, for it is against the body, and yet we know that other sins affect our bodies. Drunkenness, for instance, will destroy the human body. You only have to take a walk through skid row somewhere to see the awful effects of drunkenness upon the human body. And there are other sins that affect the body. Drug abuse can destroy the mind, twist the features and turn the individual into a twitching, nervous wreck. Why didn't Paul mention that? Drug abuse was known in his day. Even gluttony can destroy the body; even too much hard work will destroy the body. So what does Paul mean when he says other sins are "outside the body" but fornication is a sin against the body?

The answer is given in verse 19:

> Do you not know that your body is a temple of the Holy Spirit within you, which you have from God? You are not your own; you were bought with a price.

That is why fornication is different from other sins. Here again Paul is reflecting on the fact that human nature is different than animal nature. It is unique in its marvelous capacity to hold God, to be intimately related to the greatness of the majesty and glory of God. It becomes a temple, for God dwelling in something transforms it into a temple. But fornication defiles that temple. It involves the body of a person who is the temple of God in a wrong union. Therefore, fornication is basically the sin of idolatry. That is why in Colossians and other places the apostle refers to "covetousness, which is idolatry." He means sexual covetousness, the desire for another person's body, which is a form of idolatry.

It is idolatry, the worship of another god, the substitution of a rival god, which defiles the temple. That is why fornication has an immediate and profound (but subtle) effect upon the human psyche. It dehumanizes us. It animalizes us. It brutalizes us. Those who indulge in it grow continually more coarse, less sensitive, are more self-centered, more desirous of having only their own needs met.

A beautiful young couple came to me not long ago. Both of them were Christians; they had formed a close friendship, and they were enjoying one another greatly. They were growing in the Lord and heading for marriage. But then something happened. They began to fight, and I did not know what it was all about. Finally they brought one of their quarrels to me and in the process of working it out I asked them, "Are you having sex together?" They admitted they were. I said, "Well, this is the result of it. It is destroying your relationship." They did not believe me and went on. Sure enough, soon their relationship ended with great hurt on both sides, and the woman in particular was damaged by this. That is what fornication does. It defiles the temple and destroys the person.

Paul closes with a beautiful summary,

> You are not your own; you were bought with a price.

That is basic Christian truth. It is something every Christian ought to remember every day of his life. You have no final right to yourself. God has ordained that there are decisions that only we can make. He does not take away our right of choice. But, he says, we shall have to account for the decisions we make. Because he has bought us and we are his by right of creation and of purchase, God always reserves the right to send us where he wants us to go. He reserves the right to take away from our life whatever he sees is harmful or injurious to us, whether we like it or not, to give us both blessing and trouble alike as he sees what we need, and to guide us as a loving Father to the place where we recognize that he owns us, that we belong to him. God is glorified when any individual Christian lives on that basis: "Lord, you are the Lord of my life."

Therefore, in verse 20 Paul says:

> . . . glorify God in your body.

That is what will make the world see that there is something different about Christians—Christians have discovered the lost secret of their humanity. God has come to dwell in his temple again. That temple should be maintained without defilement, not offering it to another except as God himself has ordained in the beautiful sacrament of marriage.

11

Answers on Sex and Divorce

In the seventh chapter of 1 Corinthians we plunge into an explicit and forthright passage dealing with sex in marriage, followed by answers to the Corinthians' questions on divorce. Some Christians are squeamish about hearing the subject of sex taught and preached, but the very fact that the Word of God, in all its purity and wholesomeness, treats this subject ought to correct that attitude. Besides, it is a passage of crucial significance for our day.

You will remember from the first part of this letter that three young men—Stephanas, Fortunatus, and Achaicus—had brought a letter from the church at Corinth asking the apostle certain questions. Paul has not yet touched upon these questions; he wants to build up to the subject with some very necessary and honest dealing with the problems they had *not* asked about, and some revelations of truth that they needed to know.

But at this time he turns to the letter and begins to answer their questions:

> Now concerning the matters about which you wrote. It is well for a man not to touch a woman. But because of the temptation to immorality, each man should have his own wife and each woman her own husband (7:1,2).

Question number one on their list seems to be something like this: "In view of the sexual temptations we face in Corinth, is it perhaps better to take a vow of celibacy, renounce marriage for life, and withdraw from all contact with the opposite sex?"

That question probably arose from the difficulty that some were

133

having handling their sexual drives. They were facing temptation in these areas every time they turned around, just as we do today, so some of them were saying, "Rather than struggle all the time, why not just forget the whole thing; get away from the opposite sex, and live as a monk?"

This attitude is commonly held. It is what gave rise to monasticism in the Middle Ages and was a popular practice at that time. People withdrew from all contact in this area, viewing sex itself as defiling, dirty, and unworthy. They regarded the celibate state as a higher level of spirituality. They moved out of the world and built monasteries where men could live with men and women could live with women so as to remove them from all contact with the opposite sex and (they thought), all struggle in the area of sex. But it did not work, and it never will work. It is never God's intention for the sexes to live separately—he made them in the beginning to be together. Monasticism proved to be a disaster, for you cannot run away from drives that are within you, and Scripture clearly recognizes this.

Nothing Wrong with Celibacy

Paul's answer, given in the first verse, is that there is nothing wrong with celibacy. "It is well for a man not to touch a woman." He stresses that it is all right to be single. Nevertheless, he says, because of the temptations that abound, marriage is preferable in a place like Corinth. Some have taken that to mean that Paul had a very low view of marriage, that it was a kind of a second-best state of affairs, but they have missed the whole thrust of this passage; they have ignored the context.

It is true that the apostle, at least at this time, was unmarried himself. There is some evidence that he might have been married at one time in his life. It was a custom among the Jews for young men to marry. Furthermore, Paul had been a member of the Sanhedrin, because he tells us that he gave his vote against the Christians. To be a member of the Sanhedrin required marriage, so it is probable that he was married at one time. What happened to his wife is one of the great mysteries of all time. Tradition does not tell us. Scripture does not even mention it. Whether she died, or left him when he became a Christian, we have no way of knowing. (That is one of the first questions you can ask the apostle when you meet him in heaven.) But at this point, anyway, he was unmarried, and he glories in his singleness. Several times in this chapter he will tell us that he considered it an advantage to be single.

So he starts with this statement, "It is well for a man not to touch a woman." "Touch" is a euphemism for sexual intercourse. It does not mean that it is wrong for a male to lay his hand on a woman's shoulder or arm or whatever may be normal in friendship. Paul is saying here that to abstain from sex is not harmful and is not wrong, but if one abstains, a celibate life must be lived in chastity, as he has made clear in the previous section.

But, he says, marriage is proper too. Here in this passage he is not primarily talking about marriage; he is dealing with sex in marriage. The context makes it clear that sex is the subject he is discussing; therefore he takes up here the proper use of the body's sexual powers. He has covered sex outside of marriage in chapter 6, and now he discusses it within marriage. (If you want to know what Paul thought of marriage itself, read the fifth chapter of Ephesians. There is found an incomparable passage of tremendous beauty setting forth the glory of marriage as a picture of Christ's relationship with his church.)

The apostle now says three things about sex within marriage. The first one is suggested here in these opening two verses. Sex within marriage, the apostle implies, does permit relief from sexual pressures. Now he does not suggest that one should get married to be free from sex drives. That should never be the sole reason for marriage and no part of Scripture ever teaches such. What the apostle is saying is that being married does help one in this area. It helps to be married when you live in a sex-oriented society.

Several things are indicated by this. First, it answers the claims of some, notably the Roman Catholic church, that sex was given to us only for procreation purposes. Children do come from sex. Let us not hide it; the stork story has been blown! But that is not the only reason sex was given to us. It is clear from a passage like this in which married couples are urged, even commanded, to experience sex together and frequently—not just once in a great while when a child is desired—that sex is given to us for more than merely carrying on the race. It serves another function within marriage: to provide pleasure to one another.

When I was a young Christian in my early twenties I was given a book to teach me how to handle sex drives and what sex was for. It was called *The Way of a Man with a Maid.* It had some helpful things to say, showing that sex is a gift of God. But it also taught that the best marriages are based upon having sex only when you want to have children. I did not recognize how wrong this was at the time because it was a highly respected book and it seemed to be in line with biblical teaching. I have since come to see that it represented a terrible distortion of the biblical position on sexuality. There is a wealth of literature available today that much more accurately reflects biblical teaching on this subject.

One thing is clear from this passage: sex in marriage is given to us for the mutual pleasure of those involved. It is the highest form of physical ecstasy, without a doubt. It rates as the number one recreation of the world; it always has and it always will. God likes it that way; he designed it so. He gave us our erogenous zones and permitted them, yea, intended them, to be aroused and excited. He designed human beings to experience the exquisite ecstasy of orgasm, but he intended it to be protected, and experienced only within the walls of security which marriage provides.

Within marriage bonds sex is an exquisite pleasure which a married couple are to experience frequently, as frequently as they mutually desire. This is what is meant in Hebrews 13:4, which says, "Marriage is honorable in all, and the bed undefiled" (KJV). Those who twist certain passages of Scripture to indicate that sex should be kept secret and not openly discussed even in marriage are mistaking and missing the whole purpose of Scripture's teaching on the subject.

A Freely Offered Gift

Having said that marriage is a way of relieving sexual pressures, Paul now says something else very significant. He says sex in marriage is designed of God to teach us something about ourselves as well as to fulfill a need in our partners:

> The husband should give to his wife her conjugal rights and likewise the wife to her husband. For the wife does not rule over her own body, but the husband does; likewise the husband does not rule over his own body, but the wife does. Do not refuse one another *(or to put it more bluntly, as the Greek actually does and as we read in the King James Version, "Defraud ye not one the other")* except perhaps by agreement for a season, that you may devote yourselves to prayer; but then come together again, lest Satan tempt you through lack of self-control (vv. 3–5).

The major thrust of that paragraph is that sex in marriage is designed for the fulfillment of each partner. There are several important statements here. First, notice that Paul does not say to the husband or the wife, "Demand your sexual rights." As a marriage counselor I have been involved in scores of cases where one of the major problems of the marriage was that one partner, usually the man, demanded sexual rights from his wife. (Occasionally it has been the woman who was the agressor.) Nothing, perhaps, is more destructive to marital happiness than for the male to demand that his wife submit to him in this area whenever he feels like it. This is to mistake the use of this passage. In describing the wife as not ruling over her own body, Paul is not giving license to the husband to demand sex whenever he wants it. That is to destroy the whole beauty of sex in marriage.

What the apostle says is that each has the right to give to his or her mate as a gift, the fulfillment of sexual desires—and one's responsibility is not to the mate but to the Lord to do so. It is the Lord who asks us to give this gift to our mates in marriage, and thus to make sex an experience of mutual fulfillment and satisfaction. Thus sex in marriage is a gift that you are to freely offer to each other. It is not a selfish, self-centered satisfying of your own desire.

Understanding this will make a big difference in many marriages, and if you reflect on it a moment you will see why. Sex is given to us to teach us how to relate to one another psychologically, and also how to relate to God spiritually. We have no real ability to fulfill ourselves sexually. We need another to minister to us, and that is how God teaches us to fulfill the basic law of life. Jesus said, "If you save your life you will lose it." If you try to meet your own need, and put that first in your life, the result will be that you lose the joy of life and lose everything you are trying to gain. Instead of finding fulfillment you will find emptiness, and you will end your years looking back upon a wasted life. That is not merely good advice—that is a law of life, as inviolable as the law of gravity. The only way to find your needs met and yourself fulfilled is to fulfill another's needs. That is what is meant by verse 4,

> For the wife does not rule over her own body, but the husband does; likewise the husband does not rule over his own body, but the wife does.

This is not saying that you are slaves of one another. It is declaring that the power to give fulfillment to your mate lies with you. He or she cannot fulfill himself or herself in this area. It is impossible. That is why sex with yourself, solo sex, masturbation, is a drag. It does not go anywhere. It is a dead-end street. It is a momentary, mechanical fulfillment that leaves one psychologically unfulfilled.

God made us to need someone else to fulfill us sexually. This is why unresponsiveness on the part of a partner in sex always creates a problem in marriage. Frigidity, of whatever type it may be or for whatever cause, creates deep-seated psychological problems in a marriage and a rift occurs. God has given us the ability to give the gift of love to another person and the joy of doing so is what creates the ecstasy of sexual love in marriage.

So important is this to marriage that the apostle goes on to say that it takes precedence over everything else except an occasional spiritual retreat for prayer.

> Do not refuse one another except perhaps by agreement . . . .

If you are going to cease sex, it has to be mutual. You must not deny your partner the right to this kind of enjoyment. To unilaterally refuse to involve yourself in sexual union in marriage is to violate this command of God, and to hurt the marriage very severely. So Paul says, "Don't do that"—with one possible exception. If you both agree to it and if you do so only for a brief season and for a spiritual reason, such as to have more time for working out a special problem in prayer, then it is all right. But frigidity can be such a destructive thing in marriage that Paul says, "Be careful. Don't continue it very long, and by all means come together again lest Satan be given an advantage over you." Those are very wise words for Paul is underscoring here much that is causing problems in marriages today.

Illustrations of God

Now he says a third thing about sex in marriage which is very important:

> I say this by way of concession, not of command. I wish that all were as I myself am. But each has his own special gift from God, one of one kind and one of another (vv. 6, 7).

Paul is saying that sex in marriage manifests a special gift of God. Marriage itself is a gift from God, just as singleness is. Some have one gift and some another, but both express some unique quality about God himself that is intended to be manifested by that state. The word *this* in verse 6 looks not just to the immediate context but clear back to verse 2 where Paul talks about the gift of being married versus the gift of being single. What he is saying is, "Marriage is not for all." Paul himself glories in being single, but both states, singleness and marriage, are a gift from God, and sexuality in marriage reflects a special beauty of God; it illustrates something about God. I think it illustrates the unique relationship within the Trinity, and also, as we are told in Ephesians 5, between the Lord and his people. It illustrates a oneness of spirit and identity of person that can only be manifested when two human beings, weak and struggling and failing in many ways, nevertheless learn to live together and love one another despite the problems and the heartaches they experience.

On the other hand, singleness without sex reflects another beauty of God. It permits a quality of dedication to a single goal that is often highly admired by everyone around. We all know people like this who have never married, who have given themselves to achieve a certain goal in life. This too illustrates truth about God, his single-minded devotion to his determined ends. So both these states of life are gifts from God and we must view them as such.

This brings the apostle to a related matter which he takes up in verses 8 and 9. What about the sexual lives of people who once were married but now are no longer? (Later on in this chapter Paul is going to talk to the unmarried, those who have never married. He calls them "virgins." Here, obviously, he is talking about those who once were married, the divorced and widowed.)

> To the unmarried and the widows I say that it is well for them to remain single as I do. But if they cannot exercise self-control, they should marry. For it is better to marry than to be aflame with passion.

The King James Version puts it, "It is better to marry than to burn." I remember hearing a sermon years ago from a country preacher in Texas on the text, "It's better to be married than to be burned." All the young people in his church went out and got marriage licenses right away! Nobody wanted to be burned. But that, of course, is not what Paul is talking about.

He is talking about "burning" with passion. Paul is saying here that if you have been married and now are no longer, he understands that your sexual lives have been fully awakened by marriage. You are used to finding sex drives and pressures met, and now suddenly, deprived of your mate either by divorce or by widowhood, you no longer have a way of satisfying these desires. What about such persons?

This can create quite a problem. Years ago I read Catherine Marshall's book written shortly after the death of her famous husband, Dr. Peter Marshall, and with all frankness she said that her awakened desires for sexual love from her husband was a real problem in her life. Many a widow struggles with this; many a divorcee has agonized over it.

The apostle's word is, "If it is possible, remain single. Having learned many great lessons from life, you can now give yourself more fully to the work of the Lord than you ever were able to do before. This is your opportunity." I should state here, however, that in the letter to Titus Paul commands *young* widows to remarry. He says that would be much better for them. But if you are older and have lost your mate, then his advice is to remain single. That is best. But if the physical struggle is severe, then marry again. There is nothing wrong in it. Thus he graciously, and with the wisdom of God himself, encourages and gives advice to people who have once been married.

It is clear as you look back at this passage that the essence of marital happiness, sexually, is made up of three ingredients. First, love to God. The body is made for the Lord; therefore, what the Lord wants you to do with your body should be all-compelling. It should govern your decisions.

The second ingredient in sexual happiness is a discipline of self—a willingness to put your own needs second to those of your mate in this area, and to give yourself, to give the gift of beauty and love and fulfillment to your mate as he or she desires.

In a good marriage, of course, a husband and wife are always giving gifts to one another, buying little trinkets here, bringing home something from a trip, seeing something in a market or a bargain store that you think your mate will enjoy. That is a way of saying to your mate, "I'm thinking of you. You are important to me. I love you."

The greatest gift along that line is sex if it is given with that same spirit of willingness to give pleasure. Nothing is more important than that, but it calls for a refusal to indulge in mere self-satisfaction. The third ingredient, therefore, is mutual respect.

Love to God, discipline of self, and a mutual respect for one another—these help two lives to learn to unite in the Lord. That is the most beautiful thing God produces on this earth. If you have ever seen an old married couple who have been in love for years and have learned how to relate in happiness, peace and joy to one another, you know something of the quiet beauty of that relationship. It blesses everyone who sees it, and that is what God desires for marriage. Examine your own marriage in the light of this, or if you are not yet married and you feel God is heading you that way, think these things through.

Now Paul leads us into confrontation with one of the major social problems of our day, and that is the breakup of marriages. The divorce statistics today are frightening. I saw a cartoon in the newspaper that showed a father speaking to his daughter just before her wedding. He said, "Try to make it last, dear, at least until I can pay for the wedding!" I think that summarizes the attitude of many today toward marriage.

Yet with this widespread and frightening increase in marriage break-up, we are really only repeating the conditions that existed in Corinth when this letter was written. Divorce was rather rare in Jewish communities then but in the Greek cities, like Athens and Corinth, divorce was frequent. Even women could divorce their husbands and did so very easily. The apostle addresses a condition very much like that which we have in America today. Paul understands, amid the world's easy acceptance of divorce, the temptation that Christians face to take what looks like an easy way out of an unhappy or difficult marriage.

The Fundamental Position

He begins in verse 10 of chapter 7 with a word about marriage in general:

> To the married I give charge, not I but the Lord, that the wife should not separate from her husband (but if she does, let her remain single or else be reconciled to her husband)—and that the husband should not divorce his wife.

Here we have the fundamental position of Scripture on marriage: it is intended to be for life. God's desire in giving marriage to our race was that a man and a woman should live together, as the marriage vows put it, "for better or for worse" (either one), "until death do us part." Wives are *not* to leave their husbands, difficult as a marriage may become; husbands are *not* to divorce their wives even if they appear to be almost "irreconcilably incompatible," to use modern terms.

This is not a passage that needs debate as to what the apostle means. He makes it crystal clear; it is not in doubt in the least degree. Furthermore, this statement rests upon the most solid foundation. Paul says, "I charge you this," and here he uses a term he seldom employs. The full weight of apostolic authority is brought to bear on this question. "As an apostle, an appointed spokesman of the Lord himself," he says, "this is his word to us." Then he goes even further back to the Lord's own recorded words and quotes the teaching of Jesus himself on divorce, when he was here in the flesh. These words are recorded for us in the fifth and nineteenth chapters of Matthew, and in the tenth chapter of Mark. Three different times in the gospel the account is given of our Lord's words.

Now some have misunderstood what Paul is saying here. They think because Paul says, in verse 10, "I give charge, not I but the Lord," that Paul's word is at a lower level of authority than the Lord's. But the word of an apostle and the direct word of the Lord are equally authoritative for all who are Christians. An apostle only gives what the Lord himself has already given him. Apostles do not invent doctrine, nor are they free to add to what the Lord has told them or take away from it. The contrast here is not between the inspired teaching of the Lord and the uninspired teaching of an apostle, but rather between what the Lord himself uttered directly and what he has uttered indirectly through his apostle. In either case the authority is the Lord.

God never leads anyone to leave his wife! He has made very clear in both the New and the Old Testament what he thinks of divorce. In the Book of Malachi God bluntly says, "I hate divorce." He never intended divorce to interrupt marriages. But having said this, it is also necessary to say, and it is also true, that God permits divorce. "Oh," you say, "you mean God permits what God hates?" Yes, of course he does. Much of life is made up of God permitting what God hates. God hates sin, but he allows it to continue in our race and he allows people to make wrong decisions even though he hates the decisions they make. Everywhere in Scripture we are faced with what is termed the permissive will of God. The Scripture states that God is not willing that any should perish. Yet many do perish. All those who do not come to believing faith in Jesus Christ will perish—they are already perishing. Though God is not willing that any should perish, he does allow it to happen. There is a place, therefore, for divorce.

It was not Moses who permitted divorce in Israel; it was God, speaking through Moses. When the Lord was teaching on marriage and divorce he said, "Moses, because of the hardness of your hearts, permitted divorce." Many have read that as though Moses initiated the whole process, that it was Moses who thought up divorce. But Moses, a prophet, was like one of the apostles. He was a spokesman for God. Moses had no authority and no right to interpose his own desires or understanding or will over what God had said. Therefore, it was not Moses who decided to let people get divorced; it was God who spoke through Moses, and thus permitted divorce. Any realistic handling of the problem of marriage and divorce must face the fact that God does allow divorce, and under some circumstances permits it and also permits remarriage after divorce. We have to put the problem within that context to begin with.

Refusing to Listen

The Lord himself acknowledges this. He says hardness of heart creates conditions that can lead to divorce. What is "hardness of heart"? It really means a stubborn willfulness, a refusal to listen to what God has to say. A soft heart is open to instruction, willing to listen to what God is saying and willing to walk softly before God, expecting him to help fulfill what he has asked. A hardened heart is exactly the opposite. It is one partner or the other, or both, determining that he or she is not going to pay any attention to what God has said. They want their own way, and they want it now.

You see it in the case of Pharaoh of Egypt back in the days when Moses was sent to him. He hardened his heart; he determined to do it his way; he refused to give heed to the God of glory who was speaking to him and insisted on doing things according to his own desire.

A hardened heart can turn a marriage into a living hell. It can make it so unhappy and so dangerous, even, that one partner may feel that he or she must leave. Paul seems to be facing that here. He has it in view when he adds, after "the wife should not separate from her husband," the words *"but if she does. . . ."* That is a recognition that some marriages are almost impossible to live with. I have counseled wives with both eyes so black and swollen they could not see out of them, with bruises all over their bodies because their husbands had beaten them up. Now when that occurs—sometimes even to such a degree that their lives are threatened—there is no reason for a woman to live under those conditions; it is perfectly proper for her to leave for awhile. Sometimes it is the only way of bringing a husband to his senses, and the apostle seems to face that, but he adds some very strict controls. He says,

. . . if she does, let her remain single . . .

The marriage is not broken just because it has become impossible to go on with. If she leaves for a temporary separation or if it is a long continued problem—even if she gains a divorce—yet in God's sight the marriage is not broken.

Remember as Christians we are not dealing with the law; we are dealing with God and reality and what is ultimately true, regardless of what the fluctuations of the law may allow. In God's sight the marriage is not broken by separation, therefore, "let her remain single or else be reconciled to her husband." In other words, she is not to remarry because that would break the marriage, involving, in this case, some form of adultery. Therefore, while her mate lives and remains unmarried (or while his mate lives and remains unmarried, because this would apply to a man as well as a woman), neither is to remarry, for there is always the possibility that the grace of God can work to restore and reconcile that marriage.

I know of several instances in which wives (in a couple of cases, husbands) have waited patiently through years of single life with little hope that their mates would ever be changed. Yet God in grace has changed them and their marriages have been restored after years of brokenness and gone on to happiness and joy. So the apostle's word is, "There is no ground for remarriage when a divorce occurs on the basis of incompatibility of such a degree that it makes the marriage impossible. They are to remain single, with the possibility of reconciliation."

A Widely Known Exception

"Well," somebody says, "what about sexual infidelity? I understand that this breaks a marriage. Didn't Jesus say if there is adultery, sexual infidelity, that a marriage would be broken?" And the answer is, "Yes, He does say that." Three times in the Gospels it is recorded that our Lord says that divorce is wrong unless it be for adultery, for sexual infidelity. That does end a marriage. "Well," you ask, "why doesn't Paul mention that here?" I think the reason is that he has just dealt at length with the subject of sex in marriage. He has pointed out how central the sexual union is to marriage. He has even warned couples not to defraud one another, not to refuse it, not to stay away from sexual union very long, because it is central to the working out of God's purposes in marriage. Therefore, Paul does not dwell on that point because he has just referred to our Lord's teaching on marriage and divorce. I am sure he felt that this exception, which the Lord himself granted, was widely understood and known, and so he does not mention it.

It would be absolutely unthinkable that Paul would change the Lord's own teaching by deliberately ignoring the exception the Lord granted. Paul would never do that. He saw himself as bound by the word of Jesus and what Jesus said must ultimately stand.

So there is a principle in the Word of God which recognizes that infidelity destroys a marriage. But it can be repented of and it can be forgiven. I know of marriages where couples have been on the verge of a breakup because of sexual infidelity, but it has been repented of and their mate has forgiven them, and marriages have been restored and gone on to new levels of beauty and enjoyment. But if it is not repented of, or if it is a repeated pattern, then there is no question that infidelity does break a marriage. Divorce granted on that basis frees an individual to remarry because the previous marriage has been truly ended by the infidelity of the partner.

Now among Christians divorce is not permitted on any other grounds. God expects Christians, above all, to obey what he has to say along this line. Therefore, the word of the apostle clearly is, "Work out your problems within a marriage. If you cannot conceivably do so and a divorce occurs, then remain single." I think that is crystal clear.

God did not expect marriage to be beautiful and happy, necessarily, right from the very beginning. Very few marriages are. God designed marriage as a kind of locked room into which he thrusts a couple who think they know each other very well. He turns the key in the lock, throws the key away, and says, "Now get to know each other, regardless of what happens." That is what marriage is for. It is to provide an unbreakable bond, a security within which you work out the difficulties that may arise. The modern view of divorce as a kind of an ejection lever that you pull when you do not like the way things are going is absolutely contrary to the Scriptures and the teaching of God.

Valid Marriages before God

Paul has answered questions in this section about the married and the formerly married. Now he takes up what he calls "the rest," by which he means mixed marriages. These are marriages in which one partner is a Christian and one is still non-Christian—and in the case of marriages here in Corinth, probably pagan, and associated with idol worship:

To the rest I say, not the Lord, that if any brother has a wife who is an unbeliever, and she consents to live with him, he should not divorce her. If any woman has a husband who is an unbeliever, and he consents to live with her, she should not divorce him. For the unbelieving husband is consecrated (*sanctified* is the word) through his wife, and the unbelieving wife is consecrated through her husband. Otherwise, your children would be unclean, but as it is they are holy. But if the unbelieving partner desires to separate, let it be so; in such a case the brother or sister is not bound.

For God has called us to peace. Wife, how do you know whether you will save your husband? Husband, how do you know whether you will save your wife? (vv. 12–16).

Again in this section Paul is not speaking of two levels of authority. When he says, "I say this, not the Lord," he means that the Lord had not, in the days of his flesh, spoken directly to this issue, but after his resurrection and in the many appearances which he had made to the apostle Paul, he had given him counsel in this area. Therefore, what Paul says comes with equal authority as from the Lord himself. It is clear here in this passage that marriage is not just for Christians. I have had individuals say, "I got married before I became a Christian. Now I have become a Christian, and I do not think that first marriage was 'in the Lord'; therefore, I think I ought to be able to get a divorce." They imply that marriage is really given only for Christians. But marriage was given to the race. Non-Christians get married as well as Christians, and God recognizes these as valid marriages. Paul's argument is that, becoming a Christian after you have been married does not change your marriage at all; it is still a valid marriage.

I think the problem had arisen because of Paul's teaching, reflected in chapter 6, about their bodies being members of Christ, and how wrong it was to take the physical body that belongs to Jesus Christ, and to involve it with the temple prostitutes of Corinth. That was a defiling act, and perhaps many had inferred from this that any kind of sexual union with an unbeliever was a defiling act. In a marriage where one is a Christian and the other is not, the Christian is saying, "Do my sexual practices in marriage mean that I am taking the members of Christ and defiling them with an unbeliever?" Paul's assurance is, "No, you are not." The marriage remains undefiled.

In fact, the apostle says, a wonderful thing occurs. Instead of defiling it is the other way around; it is the believing mate who in a sense sanctifies the unbeliever. Now that does not mean "saves" them or "regenerates" them. That is always an individual matter, left up to individual faith. What it means is that no defilement is involved when sexual union occurs in such a marriage, but rather it sets the unbeliever apart for a special treatment by the Lord. There is a strong exposure to a loving witness that is difficult for him or her to resist, and it may well ultimately lead the unbelieving mate to the Lord.

Now what if the unbeliever does not like that? What if he (or she) resents the fact that his mate will not go along with his/her standards? What if he is angry and upset all the time because of the new-found faith, or the growing faith, of his mate, and he decides not to stay in that marriage any longer? Well, the apostle says, "let the unbeliever depart." It may cause much heartache; these things are so close to us they can hardly be carried out sometimes without heartache. But, "let him depart," Paul says. In such a case the brother or sister is not *bound*.

I have carefully checked all the commentaries available to me on this passage and have found that almost all the commentators agree that the phrase, "not bound," means that the marriage has ended, and that remarriage is permitted the Christian involved in that kind of a liaison. The reason the apostle gives is that "God has called us to peace." Continual antagonism between two people of different faiths resulting in a constant chafing of one or the other in the marriage is not good. If the unbeliever takes the initiative (this is the qualification that must always be present), and wants to leave, then do not saddle him with legal restrictions or economic barriers that prevent him from doing so.

That is supported by verse 16. Paul says,

> Wife, how do you know whether you will save your husband? Husband, how do you know whether you will save your wife?

I once held the idea that this meant to hang onto the marriage at all costs. Do not let him (or her) go, because there is still the possibility you might reach him and he will be saved. But, taken in its proper context, it is a reference to "Let him depart," and it is an argument in support of it. What the apostle is saying is, "Do not try to force him into regeneration. You cannot know that you are going to save him if he stays in the marriage. You cannot know that he is going to believe if you hold onto him legally, regardless of his desire to leave." So his argument is: God has called us to peace, rather than to continual bickering and quarreling in this area, and in the particular case of a mixed marriage, if the unbeliever desires to depart, let him depart.

The final paragraphs teach us how to handle difficult conditions in marriage or any other realm of life.

> Only let every one lead the life which the Lord has assigned to him, and in which God has called him. This is my rule in all the churches (v. 17).

This is not something peculiar to Corinth. This is a rule that should apply to Christians anywhere, both in every place and in all of time. Therefore, it is as applicable for us today as it was in Corinth.

Your Assigned Place

Where you are is not an accident. God put you where you are. You may not even yet be a Christian, but that does not mean God has not been at work in your life. Paul said that he discovered after he came to Christ he had been "separated unto Christ from his mother's womb." But he never realized that until he was on the Damascus road and found Jesus there. Yet through everything that was happening in his life, though he was a wild radical, a revolutionary anti-Christian, breathing out threatenings and slaughter, God was at work to bring him to the place and the time when his conversion would occur.

That is true of you too. God has assigned you a place in life, and you have made many choices along the line to get there. God has worked through your choices, not to control you so that you had to do something, but to allow you free choice and yet work it out. Therefore, you are where God wants you to be. "Do not fight it," Paul says. "Stay in the place where God has assigned you; he has called you there." Called you to what? This very letter tells you. It opens with the word in chapter 1, verse 9: "God is faithful, by whom you were called. . . ." Into what? ". . . into the fellowship of his Son, Jesus Christ our Lord."

That is our calling, and that inner fellowship is the means by which strength may be obtained to live in difficult or disturbing circumstances.

He does not mean by this, however, necessarily to keep on doing whatever you were doing when you became a Christian. You may have been a madam in a house of prostitution. You may have been a professional gambler, or a bootlegger, or a bank robber, and God is not saying, "Now that you are a Christian, keep on being a Christian bank robber." He does not mean that. He is not talking about occupation; he is talking about relationships, and he goes on to show you what he means.

Was any one at the time of his call already circumcised? (i.e., "Was he a Jew?") Let him not seek to remove the marks of circumcision.

That is what some of them felt they had to do. In James Michener's book, *The Source*, he tells about a young man who was a Jew and who wanted to become like the Greeks, so he went through a painful surgical operation to remove the marks of circumcision. This was common in the Greek games where the athletes competed naked. Paul says you do not have to remove those marks.

Was any one at the time of his call uncircumcised? Let him not seek circumcision.

Bodily marks that indicate a former commitment you made are insignificant; they do not have to be removed. I know Christian men who are embarrassed to take their shirts off in public because they are tattooed. They probably had it done when they were young, in the Navy, and drunk! Now they see how foolish it was and they wish they could get rid of it. Paul says that is neither here nor there. Circumcision, uncircumcision, tattooed, untattooed—it does not make any difference. The key to your life is not your outward looks, but what is going on in your heart between you and the Lord and the relationship you have to him.

> For neither circumcision counts for anything nor uncircumcision, but keeping the commandments of God. (By trust in the power and the life of God.) Every one should remain in the state in which he was called. Were you a slave when called? Never mind. But if you can gain your freedom, avail yourself of the opportunity. For he who was called in the Lord as a slave is a freedman of the Lord. Likewise he who was free when called is a slave of Christ. You were bought with a price; do not become slaves of men (vv. 19–23).

This is a very insightful passage. Paul is dealing here with the common problem of slavery in that day, and what he says is, "To be a slave or to be free is not the overriding consideration of life; it is what you are inside that counts." In the novel, *Roots*, and in the television portrayal of the book, it was evident that some of the slaves who were believers in Christ were nobler, more loving, more compassionate, more understanding, and demonstrated more integrity than their "free" masters.

Now Paul is not denying the possibility God may so arrange things that an opportunity for freedom is given. If so, "Take it," he says. Basically, it is a gift of God. Christianity, though it is revolutionary, is not a violent overthrow of systems of the past. In practice, it is designed to free one from within. So if you are in a situation that is difficult to handle and hard to bear, remember it is only external; it is only temporary and passing, and you can be free in Christ in a most beautiful, effective and influential way.

Paul says, "Do not become slaves of men." How do you become slaves of men? When you conform to the world around, when you let the opinions of secular writers shape your judgments about marriage, or whether you ought to get a divorce or not, you are becoming a slave to men instead of to the Lord. When you follow after teachers in the church and think of one as being preferable to the other, you are becoming a slave of men. When you give way to the secular pressures to sexual infidelity you are becoming a slave of men.

Paul closes with these words (v. 24):

So, brethren, in whatever state each was called, there let him remain with God.

These are key words: "with God"—regardless of what your situation may be, even if you cannot change it, even if it is a so-called "difficult" marriage, remember that God is able to meet you right where you are and to fill your life with love and joy and peace despite the struggles. The struggles themselves will help you do it if you understand them as God's choice for you.

12

Alone But Not Lonely

The section before us now is addressed to the unmarried and sets forth both the advantages and the pressures of single life. Paul begins with an explanatory word that looks over the whole subject.

Now concerning the unmarried, I have no command of the Lord, but I give my opinion as one who by the Lord's mercy is trustworthy (or faithful) (v. 25).

He means by this that the matter of single life does not have a moral issue connected with it as do the matters of marital sex and divorce. The Lord has not spoken to this, either publicly during his ministry or in private in the revelations he gave to the apostle. Therefore, Paul says, he does not speak with a command of the Lord. But he suggests that this subject ought to be settled by apostolic guidance; he understands all the great issues that touch upon a question like this. So speaking as one who, by the Lord's mercy, has been found faithful he gives an apostolic word of counsel on this matter of single life.

In verse 26 through 28 we have the first advantage that he sees in single life:

I think that in view of the impending (or present) distress it is well for a person to remain as he is. Are you bound to a wife? Do not seek to be free. Are you free from a wife? Do not seek marriage. But if you marry, you do not sin, and if a girl marries she does not sin. Yet those who marry will have worldly troubles, and I would spare you that.

That does sound as though Paul had been married, doesn't it? Here he is clearly stating for us what he sees to be a great advantage in unmarried life; it helps to handle the pressures that may come in a time of crisis. Everything in that paragraph hangs upon the statement in verse 26, "I think that in view of the present distress . . . ." He is not talking about life in general, but about times of crisis, and evidently these Corinthians were facing such a time.

The commentators are at odds as to what this crisis was. Some of them suggest that there was a local crisis in Corinth to which he is referring—perhaps some financial pressures, or a famine, or an economic situation of some kind. Others see in this a reference to Paul's hope of the coming of the Lord. Some have suggested that perhaps he is referring to the approaching crisis, when, in A.D. 70, as we now know, the Roman armies would come into Judea and quell a terrible disturbance among the Jews. This resulted in the capture of the city of Jerusalem, the overthrow of the Temple, and the dispersing of the Jewish population throughout all the nations of the earth. This Corinthian letter was written about A.D. 57, just ten or twelve years before that crisis would come, and perhaps it was beginning to develop already.

Cycles of Trouble

My own view is that because the apostle is aware that he is writing Scripture—it is for all Christians in all times, as he implies in some of his letters—he is not talking about any particular immediate crisis. He is referring to the returning crises that every generation of Christians have to face. In 2 Timothy the apostle says to his son in the faith, "In the last days there will come times of stress" (2 Tim. 3:1). It is a mistake to read that as though he meant "in *the* last days" as a reference only to the time preceding the return of Christ. Actually the church is always living in "the last days." Those stretch from the first coming of Christ to his second return, as Hebrews 1 makes clear where it says, "In many and various ways God spoke of old to our fathers by the prophets; *but in these last days* he has spoken to us by a Son . . ." (Heb. 1:1,2). Therefore, this is a reference to what Paul thinks of as continuing, returning cycles of trouble.

You can look back through history and see how true that is. Every generation of Christians has faced a time when they thought the Lord was about to return, when events were so terrible, in their view, that they were leading up to the crisis of the Great Tribulation which would precipitate the end times and bring the second coming of Christ.

We are no exception. We are facing this kind of crisis right in our own time, in our own day. Many today are saying, "Surely these are the days in which our Lord will return." But I believe God intended every generation of Christians to feel that. In fact, I think the Lord could have returned at any of those times of crisis of the past, as he could return now, but as Jesus himself said, no one knows for sure. No one knows the day nor the hour of his return.

This, then, is a word that has application to Christians no matter when they have lived. It surely has application to us today as we face the terrible crisis of our own day and time; and it is a terrible time. Perhaps this condition has been true clear back through all of human history, back to the very beginning. Somebody has suggested that when Adam and Eve left the Garden of Eden, he turned to her and said, "My dear, we must understand that we live in a time of transition." That has been true ever since. Once when I was in Washington, D.C., one of the speakers who was addressing us about the state of the nation and of the world, responded to his introduction with these words, "Mr. Chairman, and fellow passengers aboard the *Titanic*. . . ."

Now in times of crisis, Paul says, single life has an advantage: you can be more flexible. You can adapt more quickly to sudden, catastrophic events; you can pick up and move if necessary. There is less concern for handling the affairs of others for whom married people may be responsible. Paul is simply listing the advantages. He is not trying to put down marriage throughout this section. He is trying to lift up singleness as a perfectly proper way of life, and those who choose it are not second class citizens. They are exercising a degree of wisdom that is, perhaps, superior to those who have simply gone along and married without weighing the advantages or disadvantages involved. He makes clear, of course, that there is nothing wrong with being married in a time of crisis either. It may be unwise, he says, but it is not a sin, and if anyone marries he is not committing any kind of terrible misjudgment.

Then Paul adds this statement ". . . those who marry will have worldly troubles, and I would spare you that." This is a practical recognition that marriage increases responsibility. I remember a cartoon in the paper recently of two men who were discussing marriage. One of them said, "Well, I'm still single, thanks to Marriage Anonymous." The other man said, "What's that?" "Well," said the first, "when you get to feeling that you want to get married you call this number and they send over an ugly woman in cold cream and curlers and she nags you until the feeling disappears!" Paul may have had something like that in mind, though I doubt it! It seems more likely he was thinking of more mundane matters such as taxes, in-laws, children, schooling, flimsy things in the bathroom, and other problems that marriage presents. At any rate he is saying that those who get married take on greater responsibility. That is a wise, practical word. Anyone who lives in a time of crisis ought to weigh those advantages and disadvantages carefully before marriage.

The General Brevity of Life

Paul gives us a second advantage of remaining single, beginning with verse 29:

> I mean, brethren, the appointed time has grown very short; from now on, let those who have wives live as though they had none, and those who mourn as though they were not mourning, and those who rejoice as though they were not rejoicing, and those who buy as though they had no goods, and those who deal with the world as though they had no dealings with it. (the King James Version puts it better: "And they that use this world as not abusing it"). For the form of this world is passing away (vv. 29–31).

Paul is saying there that single life makes it easier to maintain the proper priorities of life. These priorities apply to all, whether you are married or single, if you are Christian. You ought to face life differently as a Christian than you would as a non-Christian. You ought to see things differently; you ought to have different values. Whether you are married or single that should be true, simply because you are a Christian.

But there is the clear implication here that it is easier to do this if you remain single. Once again Paul hangs this on a phrase marking the tensions of life: "the appointed time," he says, "has grown very short." Here again many of the commentators disagree. Some say this is a reference to the second coming of Christ—that Paul expected the Lord to return soon. It is true he did look forward to that event occurring in his lifetime, and some think this is what he means here. But I tend to reject that because nowhere else do I find the Scriptures exhorting us to evasion of life's duties because the Lord is coming. We are exhorted to faithfulness and to soberness, but not necessarily to less activity because the Lord is coming.

I would rather view this as a reference to the general brevity of life. Paul is thinking, perhaps, of the patriarchs. You read in Genesis that they lived as long as 900 years. You can take a very leisurely lunch if you know that you have 750 more years before you have to leave this earth! Life undoubtedly was very slow and sedate during the time of the patriarchs. Moses lived 120 years and he did not even start his major work until he was 80 years old. But when you get to the Psalms you find that David sings of human life as consisting of 70 years at the most, or 80 if perchance you are very strong. It is remarkable that in the 3,000 years since David's day man has never increased, or seldom even come up to, this length of life. I read the other day that the average length of life for a man in this country today is 62 years. (It's a little longer for women, because they do not wear neckties!)

But time goes by very rapidly. I am increasingly aware of the shortness of time and how few years we have on earth to do the things that God desires, to live the exciting adventures he sets before us. How one would want to pursue them more and more! The longer we live the more we are aware of how time seems to fly. As someone has said, "About the time your face clears up, your mind begins to go!" This is the way life seems to be.

But you don't have to be a Christian to see that; non-Christians see it as well. They speak of the shortness of time, and their reaction to it is, "Well, if we've only got this short a time, then let's grab all we can get of it." Their philosophy seems to be: "If you are going to be a passenger on the *Titanic*, you might as well go first class." But that is not to be the philosophy of the Christian, as Paul brings out.

Clearly the Christian is to use this short time for eternal purposes. Be sure that the aim and center of your life is not just making a living, but making a life. That is why he says, ". . . let those who have wives live as though they had none. . . ." He is not encouraging you to neglect your wife and not fulfill your responsibilities to your children and your home. What he is saying, of course, is that we are to keep things in proper focus. Do not let maintaining your home be the major reason for your existence. Do not give all your time to enjoying this present life. There are higher demands and higher challenges to life than that. Marriages are only for this life. They are not for eternity. Therefore, even marriage, God-given as it is, beautiful as it is, is not necessarily the highest choice an individual can make.

If some people choose not to get married in order that they might pursue other standards, especially greater dimensions of spiritual involvement, then they ought to be honored for this, the apostle is suggesting. They are making a choice that is proper and no one should put them down because of it. So his word to us is, "Do not let all these things the world around lives for become the center of your life." Joys and sorrows are going to be seen quite differently from the viewpoint of eternity. Success in business is not the greatest aim of life and should never be allowed to be for a believer, for all in the world is passing away, even its fame and its glory.

A few years ago I was in Norfolk, Virginia, speaking to a luncheon group. I noticed a building with a little dome on it that looked somewhat like a church, and I asked my companion what it was. He told me it was the tomb of General Douglas MacArthur. I was immediately interested because I had been an admirer of General MacArthur, having lived during the era when he was the great American hero. I admired his military prowess and his conduct as the virtual ruler of Japan. I remembered the welcome he received here in San Francisco when he finally returned to these shores after World War II, and the ticker tape parades in his honor both here and in New York.

I went over to the tomb and wandered around by myself. I saw the cabinets with his medals and his memorabilia, the letters he had written at various stages of his life, and some of the uniforms he had worn, and various things that were associated with him. They were all gathering dust, and even the paint was beginning to peel from the ceiling of the building. As I wandered around I suddenly had a deep sense of the fading glory of earth. I began to compare it mentally with what the Scriptures say is awaiting the believer in Jesus Christ. Paul speaks of an "exceeding weight of glory" which is beyond all comparison. It is something so fantastic that nothing we know of on earth can be remotely compared to what's waiting for those who have found God's purposes and realized God's fullness in this life. How tawdry all this seemed to me in this tomb; the glory of MacArthur was as nothing compared with the glory of the simplest believer in Christ. How important, therefore, it is to pursue that kind of glory rather than the empty baubles which would gather dust in the museums of the world. This is what Paul is talking about here, "For the form of this world is passing away."

When I was a new Christian one of the most powerful influences on me was the life and ministry of D. L. Moody. I remember reading that his favorite verses were found in 1 John 2·15–17,

Love not the world, neither the things that are in the world. If any man love the world, the love of the Father is not in him. For all that is in the world, the lust of the flesh, and the lust of the eyes, and the pride of life, is not of the Father, but is of the world. And the world passeth away, and the lust thereof; but he that doeth the will of God abideth forever (kjv).

This is what Paul is calling us to. What are you living for? Surely it has to be for more than to have a pleasant home and a retirement plan and to cram your sunset years with a few activities you were unable to get in before. Christians are not to live that way, because they have opportunity for fulfillment far beyond this life. If you do not have time to get in all the pleasures and enjoyments here, you will have lots of time beyond. What awaits us is so exceedingly fantastic and beyond description that to give oneself fully to the pursuit of the things of God here is a much wiser choice than to waste one's whole existence on secondary levels of activity and involvement. It is easier, Paul suggests, to do this if you remain single, and many people have made that choice.

Single for the Lord's Sake

There is still a third advantage here and it is set forth in verses 32 through 35:

I want you to be free from anxieties. The unmarried man is anxious about the affairs of the Lord, how to please the Lord; but the married man is anxious about worldly affairs, how to please his wife, and his interests are divided. And the unmarried woman or girl is anxious about the affairs of the Lord, how to be holy in body and spirit; but the married woman is anxious about worldly affairs, how to please her husband. I say this for your own benefit, not to lay any restraint upon you, but to promote good order and to secure your undivided devotion to the Lord.

That is the climax of what Paul has to say about the single life. He says it makes possible a degree of dedication and devotion, of commitment to the work of Christ, that married life does not allow. Now he does not mean there is anything wrong with a husband trying to please his wife, or a wife trying to please her husband. God has said elsewhere that this is what marriage is for. What Paul is saying here is that if you have the gift of celibacy, of singleness, then for you it is better not to be married. For others it is better to be married, but for you it is not. Your highest fulfillment with respect to the things of God can be discovered if you remain single instead.

How much the world owes to men and women who have chosen

to remain single for the Lord's sake rather than to be married. I think of men like John R. W. Stott. I never hear that great English preacher without rejoicing at the godliness, the sheer saintliness of his life. When he describes, as I have heard him state, that he spends two or three hours every morning in Bible study and prayer and worship of the Lord, you can see where much of his godly spirit comes from.

I find this very difficult to do as a married man. Certain demands, certain requirements and responsibilities of the household make it difficult to fulfill that kind of a schedule. I frankly do not do it, but I am grateful that there are men like Stott who can and do. How he has enriched the entire evangelical world by his writing and his preaching. His ministry has a deep spiritual element to it that grows out of the time he can give to the pursuit of the things of God.

I think of Henrietta Mears, that remarkable woman for so long on the staff of the Hollywood Presbyterian Church. Scores, if not hundreds, of young men are in the ministry today because she captured their imaginations and taught them the Scriptures. She chose never to be married so that she might have the time to give to the study and the teaching of the Word of God with such remarkable power and effect.

I think of C. S. Lewis who never married until he was in his 60s. He gave to the world a brilliant array of philosophic probing of the depths of Christian truth for which all ought to be eternally grateful.

If you look further back in history you see men like Robert Murray McCheyne of Scotland, the saintly young man who shook the British Isles by his godliness. Even though he died at around the age of 30 he was a remarkable influence, and still is, in many areas of the church today, because of his saintliness.

Another example is Margaret Clarkson, a prolific hymn writer, a single woman whose hymns have been a tremendous blessing to me. (One of my favorites is her hymn, "We Come, O Christ, to Thee.") She wrote an article entitled, "Single But Not Alone," and this is her opening paragraph:

> To know God, to know beyond the shadow of a doubt that he is sovereign and that my life is in his care: this is the unshakeable foundation on which I stay my soul. Such knowledge has deep significance for the single Christian.

Then she goes on to tell of her struggles, how she did not accept singleness for a long time. But she finally came to understand that this was God's choice for her. How grateful she ultimately became that he led her along these lines and how profound was her experience of discovering he could meet the loneliness of her life. She would never be alone because of his presence.

Paul himself is an example of this. We owe the herculean labors of this mighty apostle to the fact that he was free of the encumbrances of marriage. He was able to travel up and down the length and breadth of the Roman Empire. Out of that dedication of spirit and devotion of heart he lived in complete moral purity, and by the grace and power of God there come these remarkable letters which have changed the history of the world. All he is saying, of course, is that the single life is okay. If anyone desires to choose it, it is a high and a holy calling and one that is perfectly appropriate.

The Possibility of Control

He now turns to the pressures of singleness. Paul is a realist, and he knows it is not easy to be single. One of the pressures every single person faces is sexual pressure, and Paul brings that up:

> If anyone thinks that he is not behaving properly toward his betrothed, if his passions are strong, and it has to be, let him do as he wishes; let them marry—it is no sin. But whoever is firmly established in his heart, being under no necessity but having his desire under control, and has determined this in his heart, to keep her as his betrothed, he will do well. So that he who marries his betrothed does well; and he who refrains from marriage will do better (vv. 36–38).

It is somewhat difficult to understand just who the apostle is referring to here when he talks about someone and his "betrothed." Some commentators feel he is referring to a father and his virgin daughter, because in the culture of that day it was up to the father to arrange the marriage. Others feel, as this and other versions seem to indicate, that he is talking about an engaged couple, a betrothed couple. He says, in effect, if they find it difficult to keep their passions under control, if they tend toward the dangerous area of giving way to sexual immorality, then it is far better for them to marry: ". . . let them marry—it is no sin," he says. But if they have the gift of continence, though their passions are strong, if nevertheless they keep them under control and they decide they desire to pursue the other advantages that he has already listed, then, he says, it is better for them not to marry. In fact, it would be a weakness for them to do so.

Paul suggests that it is very possible to control these sexual drives. The key is this phrase, "whoever is firmly established in his heart."

What he is talking about is someone who has learned to be secure in his identity as being one with the Lord. He has learned the secret of strength, and that is the affirmation of significance and meaning which he must have in order to function; he knows who he is before God. He draws deeply upon the love and strength and affirmation of Christ himself, and therefore, he is able to handle even the pressures of sex. Now if that is the case, Paul says, then he will do well not to marry because there are doors of opportunity he can enter into that marriage would not permit.

Finally Paul takes up the matter of emotional pressure:

> A wife is bound to her husband as long as he lives. If the husband dies, she is free to be married to whom she wishes, only in the Lord. But in my judgment she is happier if she remains as she is. And I think that I have the Spirit of God (vv. 39,40).

He is obviously thinking of an older woman, a widow whose husband has died, who is left alone and facing the declining years of her life. She misses the companionship, the fellowship of her mate, and in the emptiness of her life she is tempted to plunge back into marriage just for companionship alone. Now Paul says, "Be careful there." That is an emotional pressure and many succumb to it without any thought about what the alternatives might be. But he says if she does succumb it is all right; it is not a sin to remarry as long as it is to a Christian, someone "in the Lord" whom she can share her faith and life with— "But in my judgment she is happier if she remains unmarried."

Notice the ground he chooses. Her own happiness is involved in this. Why? Because she has learned a lot of secrets about life and now has an opportunity to put them into practice in a way she never had when she was married. Now may be the golden opportunity of her life and she may find a sense of adventure and excitement that she has never felt before. So, "In my judgment," Paul says, "and I think that I have the Spirit of God" (which is probably the understatement of the century), "I think she would be happier if she remained unmarried."

The thrust of this whole passage is against those who tend to look down upon and make jokes about single people. They look upon them as odd, or strange, or even perverted, and make disparaging remarks about when they are going to get married, and what is wrong with them that no one has chosen them.

We Christians ought, above all others, to face the facts as Paul lays them out here and see that singleness is a perfectly appropriate style of life. We ought to approve of it and encourage it if some desire to choose that. What a wholesome view of life this is, whether married or single. The great thing is that we keep our priorities in focus. We live not for this passing world scene but for that greater life which lies waiting for us in the unbelievable world of opportunity beyond.

13

Liberty and Limits

The eighth chapter of 1 Corinthians deals with the second question these Corinthians had asked the apostle Paul in the letter they wrote to him. It has to do with a problem common in Christian lives today: "How much should I let other people's views control my actions?" That is, "Must I limit my liberty by the narrower, more restricted views of other Christians?"

The query was put to Paul in terms of a problem they faced in Corinth that we do not wrestle with much today: whether one ought to eat meat offered to idols. Have you struggled with that lately? There are still places in the world where you might. If you were working as a teacher or a preacher on a mission field this could still be a problem.

The answer the apostle gives is a principle that applies to many situations we do face today. He states the problem and two possible ways of handling it in verses 1 through 6:

> Now concerning food offered to idols: we know that "all of us possess knowledge." "Knowledge" puffs up, but love builds up. If any one imagines that he knows something, he does not yet know as he ought to know. But if one loves God, one is known by him. Hence, as to the eating of food offered to idols, we know that "an idol has no real existence," and that "there is no God but one." For although there may be so-called gods in heaven or on earth—as indeed there are many "gods" and many "lords"— yet for us there is one God, the Father, from whom are all things and for whom we exist, and one Lord, Jesus Christ, through whom are all things and through whom we exist.

162

The best place to buy a good roast or steak in Corinth was right next to the idol temple. In these pagan temples they did as the Jews did in Old Testament days—they offered living animals as sacrifice. And, like the Jews, they reserved some of the meat for the benefit of the priests and for public sale. Everyone in town knew that if you ate this meat you were eating meat which had been offered to an idol. So the question arose among the Christians: "If a Christian eats meat offered to an idol is he not participating in some way in the worship of that idol?"

There was a group within the Corinthian church that said, "Yes, that is exactly what he is doing. When these pagans here in the city see a known Christian sitting down in the public restaurant next to the temple, and enjoying a steak that had been offered to the idol, they will think that that person is going along with the pagan worship of the idol. As a consequence, such a Christian is giving a false testimony; he is not clearly declaring that Christ has superseded all idols everywhere. Furthermore, he is causing weak Christians, who might easily be led back into the worship of an idol, to stumble."

But there was another party who said, "No, this is not true. There is nothing to an idol—it is just a piece of wood or stone. How can you worship something that really does not exist? How can we deliver these pagans from their idolatrous ways if we act as though there is something to this? It is better that we simply proceed according to that knowledge of reality that God has brought to us in Christ. Let us enjoy our freedom and eat this meat without any question. It is perfectly good meat, and it would be wrong not to use it." Thus, there was a division within the church.

Actually, we are not as far removed from this issue as some might think. I heard some people arguing not long ago as to whether it was right for a Christian to repeat a mantra, a pagan word, in meditation. Some felt it was perfectly all right, while others said, "No, what you are repeating is the name of a heathen god. Repeating that word, even though you do not understand what it means, is in some way going along with the worship of that god." Thus some are going along with some of the ideas that are abroad today without realizing that they may, in some way, be identified with pagan worship.

On the other hand, there are Christians who will not have a Christmas tree in their homes because that custom originated with the pagans of Northern Germany who decorated a tree at the winter solstice. There are others who will not use Easter eggs because they originated in pagan spring festivals when the egg, the symbol of fertility, was offered to a pagan goddess. Clearly, the problem of Corinth is still with us.

Everybody Knows

But notice how Paul handles this. He recognizes the two groups that were present, There was the "Freedom Party" that boasted in their knowledge. Notice the quotation marks around the words in verse 1, "all of us possess knowledge." The apostle is simply repeating what the Freedom Party was saying: "Everybody knows that an idol is nothing." An amplification of this is in verse 4 where quotes are around the words, "an idol has no real existence," and "there is no God but one." That is what they were arguing to support their claim that everybody has knowledge. "There are not any 'real' idols. They are just pieces of wood and stone. They are a symbol of the mental projections of men and merely their ideas and superstitions." There is no reason, therefore, why one should not eat the meat. Christians know there is only one God, one true God, and they worship him. When they are eating this meat they are not worshiping these pagan deities for they do not even exist. They were basing their actions upon their knowledge of facts.

Paul recognizes that such knowledge is right. "For us there is indeed one God, the Father, from whom are all things and for whom we exist, and one Lord, Jesus Christ, through whom are all things and through whom we exist." Many have asked why Paul did not here include the full name of the Trinity, including the Holy Spirit, "by whom" are all things, and "in whom" we exist? But Paul is not trying to teach the doctrine of God here. He is simply answering the claims of those who are disturbed about idol worship, and he is doing it within the framework of their culture.

In the Roman Empire the deities were called gods, but Caesar was called Lord. Many struggles of the early church were over the question of whether Caesar or Jesus was Lord. Paul is making an apparent distinction here. He is pointing out that the father is the true God. Not that he is all of God; we know from other passages that our God exists as three Persons in one: Father, Son and Spirit. But here Paul accommodates, in a sense, to the pagan view of gods by pointing out that the Father represents the wholeness of God, and Jesus is Lord—he who became a man and came among us, as distinct from Caesar who was the Lord of the Roman world. Jesus is the One in charge of events; he is the One through whom all things come, and through whom we exist.

As we continue with Paul's argument, let us bring this issue into our own time. Although we do not have a meat-eating problem today, we do have similar problems: Some Christians are disturbed about the matter of drinking wine and liquors. Should a Christian take alcohol in any form—wine, beer, cocktails, whatever—or is all that proscribed to us? Some raise a question about smoking, or about public dancing. David "danced before the Lord"; does that justify discotheque dancing? These are the issues of today. What about movies? What about television? Should we keep Sunday as the Lord's day? There is a long list of issues that divide Christians.

A Superiority Complex

How shall we settle them? It is interesting to hear these being debated today and to realize that almost all of them are being settled on the basis of some "new fact" that has been discovered. Christian liberty is often defended from the point of view of knowledge. Paul points out that the "knowledge" of the Corinthians was correct, but knowledge has certain problems about it. First, "knowledge puffs up"; knowledge creates pride; it makes one feel superior. It does not make any difference which side you are on, (the liberty side or the restricted side), knowledge tends to create a sense of pride.

Some people say, "Look at those worldly Christians. I would not do some of the things they do. How can a true Christian take a drink? What a terrible thing." They are truly offended by that. They look down on those who feel liberty to do so, and point their finger at them.

On the other hand, listen to the talk of those who feel the freedom to drink. They say, "Oh, those legalistic blue noses. Why don't they realize that Christians are free of these kinds of restrictions?" The result is an all-around put-down, a failure to recognize that others hold their convictions sincerely. Knowledge does create pride. There is no doubt about it. It puffs us up and makes us feel superior to those who hold different views.

The apostle adds there is also something else wrong with knowledge: It is incomplete. "If any one imagines that he knows something, he does not yet know as he ought to know." Whenever we feel that some attitude, action, or freedom that others exercise is wrong, we are usually seeing things only from our point of view. We are not giving any weight to the other person's point of view. We judge only from our perspective, and even then we do not see all the factors involved. There may be decisive factors in our convictions of which we have no knowledge, but God does, and we will learn about them only as we go on with him.

For instance, think of the Scripture passages which suggest that Christians are being watched, not only by the world but by angels as well. Angels are watching the way we behave and thus learning from us. What effect do our actions have upon the principalities and powers that are observing us? We do not know anything about it, do we? But God does. He tells us that the angels are learning from us. What, precisely, do they learn by our actions, either of freedom or restriction? Paul simply declares that he who thinks he knows something does not see it very plainly even yet; therefore, he ought to be very careful about sitting in judgment on someone who feels differently and who has freedom to act in a different way.

All this is building up to Paul's argument that something else besides knowledge is needed to settle these kinds of problems. Knowledge alone is not enough; doctrine alone is insufficient. We also need love! Knowledge puffs up, but love builds up. Love looks at someone else's situation, not always at one's own. Knowledge is self-centered, but love reaches out to include another. Love tends to build up and edify. Furthermore, love increases the sense of intimacy with God; "if one loves God, one is known by him."

I do not know what your reaction was when you read that in the text, but my first reaction was that it was a *non sequitur;* it did not seem to follow the argument. Why should Paul suddenly shift from talking about our relationship to one another and start talking about loving God and being known by him? If he had said, "But if one loves God he shall know him," it would have made a little better sense. But what he says is, "If any one loves God, one is known *by* him"—God knows you!

As I pondered that I began to see the reason for it. This great apostle understands human behavior, because he has learned it from the Scriptures. He knows that it is difficult to get a person to think about anyone but himself. You can wag your finger at him and threaten him, warn him and exhort him all you like, but that will not get him to do anything. Then what will? Showing him how well God knows and loves him.

If you love God it is because you are responding to the love of God for you. Do not try to force yourself to love somebody else. Give yourself to responding to what God has already done for you. Think of the thousand times a day he has manifested love, concern and faithfulness to you. It will make you feel humbly grateful. You will then find yourself recognizing that other people need to be treated as God treats you. You will become more understanding of their point of view. The key to carrying out an exhortation to love one another is to love God because he has first loved you.

Someone has expressed this well in the following verse:

> Isn't it odd
> That a being like God
> Who sees the façade,
> Still loves the clod
> He made out of sod?
> Now, isn't that odd?

Start thinking about that and you will see yourself and all other persons in a different light. You will see that God has been infinitely patient with you and brought you along when you were mixed up in knowledge and arrogant in attitude. He did not wipe you out; he did not ignore what you believed; he patiently led you along and waited for you. When you see that, you will then begin to extend that love to someone else who is struggling where you are now free.

Love Individualizes

In verses 7 through 13 the apostle applies all this to the local problem in Corinth:

> However, not all possess this knowledge. But some, through being hitherto accustomed to idols, eat food as really offered to an idol; and their conscience, being weak, is defiled. Food will not commend us to God. We are no worse off if we do not eat, and no better off if we do. [Let all the food faddists take note of that.] Only take care lest this liberty of yours somehow become a stumbling block to the weak. For if any one sees you, a man of knowledge, at table in an idol's temple, might he not be encouraged, if his conscience is weak, to eat food offered to idols? And so by your knowledge this weak man is destroyed [*injured* is the word], the brother for whom Christ died. Thus, sinning against your brethren and wounding their conscience when it is weak, you sin against Christ. Therefore, if food is a cause of my brother's falling, I will never eat meat, lest I cause my brother to fall.

The apostle here sets forth three distinct advantages of love over mere knowledge alone. First, knowledge, as he admits in verse 1, tends to generalize. All of us possess knowledge. "Everybody knows," we often say, "that such-and-such is true." We base our decisions on an assumed idea that everybody understands the reason for what we are doing. But love does not do that. Love individualizes. Love says, "Not all possess this knowledge. Not everyone will act out of the understanding that I have come to. They may not see things the way I do."

The apostle admits right away that such a reaction is weakness. Their conscience is weak, he says. It needs instruction; it needs development. The Word of God acknowledges that those who lack freedom to do certain things are weak. If you do not feel free to participate in drinking wine, beer or cocktails, Paul would say that represents a "weak" view because it does not acknowledge the example that our Lord and the apostles themselves gave. Many Christians struggle at that point. Some even try to say that what the Lord and the apostles drank was unfermented grape juice and not wine. That, of course, ignores the fact that in a warm country like Palestine it is impossible to keep grape juice from fermenting without refrigeration.

But the point is, what does one do with weakness? Do you kick it in the face? Do you trample on it? Do you flaunt your strength and show off your freedom in the face of weakness? No. The Christian view toward the weak is to help them. Do not put them down; do not make them feel rejected. Reach out to them; meet them where they are and help them along. Paul reminds us that love helps those who are struggling in these areas.

The second advantage that love has over knowledge is that love evaluates clearly. In verses 8 through 12, Paul is distinguishing between two value points. The struggle is, "Shall I indulge in what I feel free to do or not?" Paul suggests by inference that whether one drinks wine or whether one feels free to smoke or dance, such momentary indulgence is a trivial thing; it can and should be set aside if there is good reason to do so. In comparison, a brother's spiritual growth is very important. To restrain yourself, therefore, for the sake of another is a gracious, godly, Christian thing to do. That is the clearsighted evaluation that love brings into the picture. We are to consider our influence upon others and weigh the fact that what we wish to do may not be very important at all compared with the possible danger to another's spiritual life. This certainly has direct bearing on how we act in public, and on whether we choose to flaunt our freedom in someone else's face.

The third thing the apostle points out is that if we indulge ourselves when we know it will offend someone, we are really sinning against Christ. We are insisting upon fulfilling some momentary desire at the expense of a brother's spiritual welfare. We must quickly point out that this kind of a situation occurs only when there is a clear possibility of injuring someone spiritually. The key word here is in verse 10, "For if any one sees you, a man of knowledge, at table in an idol's temple, might he not be encouraged, *if his conscience is weak*, to eat food offered to idols?"

In many situations today when arguments arise over these matters, it is not a question of someone's conscience being weak; it is rather a case of someone's prejudices being irritated. That is quite different. People who are in no danger of losing their faith, or of not growing in the Lord, often complain against someone who is exercising freedom in one of these areas. That is not what Paul is talking about at all. Christian courtesy would demand that we never flaunt our liberty before someone whom we know disapproves of certain indulgences. If we feel free to take a glass of wine, we would only do so if we felt there was no one at the table who would feel strongly against it. It is only a momentary fleshly indulgence and can easily be passed by if someone does not like that kind of thing. But, on the other hand, if there is no question of that, we are certainly free to exercise our freedom. The possibility that people may hear about this someplace else and be offended by it is no reason not to exercise liberty; they may actually be helped by that action if they are challenged to rethink the reasons for their limitations and their conscience freed to grow in the Lord. Great damage has been done in the church by trying to accommodate the behavior of all Christians to the conscience of the weakest brother in the church. That does not help the church to grow at all.

Paul is talking here about someone who is definitely going to be damaged by seeing liberty exercised. So the third thing he says is, "Therefore, if food is a cause of my brother's falling, I will never eat meat, lest I cause my brother to fall." Love gladly exercises self-control in these areas. Paul gladly gives in to the weakness of others. He says, "When it is a case of actually offending someone ('one of these little ones who believe in me,' as Jesus said), rather than do that I would freely give up my right." Paul is perhaps thinking of those very words from Luke 17 where Jesus said, "Temptations to sin are sure to come; but woe to him through whom they come! It would be better for him if a millstone were hung round his neck and he were cast into the sea." That is, it would be better for him to be murdered rather than to hurt one of these little ones who believe in Christ.

My dear "patron saint," Dr. H. A. Ironside, once told me of an incident that illustrates this. On one occasion he was at a picnic with other Christians and a man who had been converted from Mohammedanism was there. A girl brought a basket of sandwiches up to this man and asked if he would like some. He said, "What kind do you have?" "Oh," she said, "I'm afraid all we have left are ham or pork." He said, "Don't you have any beef or lamb?" She replied, "No, they are all gone." "Well," he said, "then I won't have any." Knowing that he was a Christian, she said to him, "Well, sir, I am really surprised. Don't you know that as a Christian you are freed from all these food restrictions and that you can eat pork or ham if you like?" He said, "Yes, I know that. I know I am free to eat pork, but I am also free not to eat it. I'm still involved with my family in the Near East, and I know that when I go home once a year, the first question my father will ask me is, 'Have those infidels taught you to eat the filthy hog meat yet?' If I have to say to him, 'Yes, father,' I will be banished from that home and have no further witness in it. But if I can say, as I have always been able to say, 'No, father, no pork has ever passed my lips,' then I have continued admittance to the family circle and I am free to tell them of the joy I have found in Jesus Christ." So we are free to eat, or free not to eat, as the case may be.

That story sets this whole problem in proper perspective. We do not *have* to have our rights. We are free to give them up any time the situation warrants it. Though we *have* the rights, we also have the right not to exercise them, for the sake of love.

This raises the question, "How far must I insist on my rights?" There were people in Corinth who said, "I am not going to give up my rights as a Christian because some legalistic brother is injured or hurt by what I am doing." They said, in effect, "We are too mature, too advanced in our knowledge of Christian doctrine to make that kind of concession."

An Advanced Example

In chapter 9 the apostle uses himself as an example of this. He says:

> Am I not free? Am I not an apostle? Have I not seen Jesus our Lord? Are not you my workmanship in the Lord? If to others I am not an apostle, at least I am to you; for you are the seal of my apostleship in the Lord (vv. 1,2).

Paul is not defending his apostleship here; rather, he is asserting it to those who clearly recognize it. If knowledge is the ground of demanding one's rights, then he has an even greater basis for it than others did. If they had knowledge, how much more did he have who was an apostle, a chosen spokesman of the Lord Jesus?

This was undeniable to those at Corinth. They knew that he had seen the Lord on that dramatic occasion when, the road to Damascus, a light brighter than the sun had shone around him. The Lord Jesus had identified himself at Paul's query. "Who are you, Lord?" by replying, "I am Jesus, whom you are persecuting." But the Lord did not appear to him only on that occasion. In this very letter Paul tells us there were other occasions when the Lord appeared to him and taught him directly. We must never forget that when we read the apostle Paul we are learning the mind of Christ, for the apostle was taught by the Lord himself.

Not only that, these Christians in Corinth owed their very existence as a church to him. They were the proof that he was an apostle. He had taught them all that they knew. It was his obedience to his apostolic commission that had brought him to Corinth in the first place. His visit had changed their lives and had brought them out of darkness into the glory and beauty of truth. Their knowledge of these facts forms the basis of his argument. He is saying, "Even though I am an apostle, and have this knowledge that is greater than yours, nevertheless I do not exercise all my rights. You object to giving up some rights for the sake of others. Well, I have been doing that for you for a long time."

That is his argument; and beginning with verse 3 through verse 23 we have his commentary on it. First, he lists the rights that he possessed:

> This is my defense to those who would examine me. Do we not have the right to our food and drink? Do we not have the right to be accompanied by a wife, as the other apostles and the brothers of the Lord [James and Jude] and Cephas [that is another name for Peter]? Or is it only Barnabas and I who have no right to refrain from working for a living? (vv. 3–6).

Here is the answer to the question many people raise about the ministry. "Should ministers be supported by a congregation?" Many people have been convinced that men become preachers in order to be parasites, to make a living off others, and they see no justification for it.

But Paul's argument is very forceful. First, he says, "We have a right to have food and drink supplied to us in our ministry—a right to eat, a right to be taken care of, a right to have everything we need, materially, furnished to us." (Notice that he does not describe a right to steak and champagne.) Further, he says, "We have the right to marry and to have our wife supported and to have her travel with us, as Peter and some of the other apostles and even the brothers of the Lord himself did." Third, Paul says, "We have a right not to have to work for our living."

Many people think that no one in the ministry really works. I have had people say to me, "Oh, you have an easy life. You only work one day a week. What do you do from Monday to Saturday anyway?" They see no labor of any sort in the ministry. But Paul does not mean that there is no work involved in the ministry. He is talking about doing secular work in order to earn a living. He says, "We have a right to be set aside and supported so that we can give our full time to study, to prayer, and to the preaching of the Word." He then proceeds to give the basis for that right:

> Who serves as a soldier at his own expense? Who plants a vineyard without eating any of its fruit? Who tends a flock without getting some of the milk?

He argues that no one labors in these three occupations without being supported for his efforts. Soldiers do not work at a trade, or craft, or a profession, but they are supported nevertheless. Anyone who works in a vineyard is at least allowed to partake of the fruit while he is working. Even someone who takes care of a flock of goats is permitted to drink of the milk. Custom supports the idea that it is perfectly proper for those who benefit from a ministry to share in supplying the material needs of that individual.

In Hope of a Share

Second, the law of Moses says the same:

> Do I say this on human authority? Does not the law say the same? For it is written in the law of Moses, "You shall not muzzle an ox when it is treading out the grain." Is it for oxen that God is concerned? (vv. 8,9).

God *is* concerned about oxen. He does not want animals abused, beaten and mistreated, and that is why he said this in the first place. But the apostle goes on:

> Does he not speak entirely for our sake? It was written for our sake, because the plowman should plow in hope and the thresher thresh in hope of a share in the crop (v.10).

Paul insists, "God said this in the beginning because of his concern for oxen, but he wrote it down for our sakes and passed it on through the Scripture to teach us the same principle." This declares the principle that runs all through life: if you reap the benefit of someone's ministry you ought to have a part in it, in a material way. That is why we take offerings, and why finances are an important part of the life of a church; it makes the ministry possible. Here is a beautiful lesson on how to use the Old Testament. Even these common rules and regulations about animal care were written down to instruct us about our relationships with one another. That is the way God teaches us from the past.

But there is also a certain logical fairness about this, as Paul goes on to argue:

> If we have sown spiritual good among you, is it too much if we reap your material benefits? If others share this rightful claim upon you, do not we still more? Nevertheless, we have not made use of this right, but we endure anything rather than put an obstacle in the way of the gospel of Christ (vv. 11,12).

This becomes, then, a principle that ought to be universally recognized. When you are blessed and helped by someone, simple gratitude would dictate that you do something in return to show your gratitude. If you have been blessed and helped in your spiritual life, and your family changed and your whole life enriched, how much more, Paul says, should you not therefore support with material benefits those who helped you in this way?

A young man in the Christian ministry told me of an incident that happened in the state of Washington, where he ministered to a couple who were older, partly retired, but still engage in a business that was making them quite a bit of money. This couple had a difficulty between them that was longstanding, and it was ruining their relationship. This young man was able to pray with them, teach them truth about themselves, and lead them to a place where they forgave one another. The relationship was healed, and over the course of several days it was evident that a total change of atmosphere had come into that household. As he was about to leave, they called him into the living room and said to him, "We are so grateful to you for helping us that we want to express our gratitude to you. You told us how you are trying to buy a motorhome to take your family with you on your ministry, and we want to have a part in that." Without solicitation from him, they handed him a check for $16,000! That was the value they set on his ministry to them. It is quite in line with the principle discussed here. Paul adds one final support for his argument, in verses 13 and 14:

> Do you not know that those who are employed in the temple service get their food from the temple, and those who serve at the altar share in the sacrificial offerings?

He is referring, of course, to the care of the Levites in the Old Testament days, when the sacrifices were divided up among them. They actually ate of the meat and of the meal offerings, and they used the wine and oil that was brought to the temple. This was all commanded by the Lord. Now Paul says,

> In the same way, the Lord commanded that those who proclaim the gospel should get their living by the gospel.

That ought forever to answer all the arguments of those who say that ministers are parasites who live on other people. Unfortunately there are ministers who have given a bad name to the ministry because of their laziness and self-indulgence. But the apostle argues powerfully that the Lord himself has commanded that this is a principle by which his ministry should be carried on.

Ministry First

At this point it is very necessary to add something else. In Paul's case, as it should be in the case of anyone wanting support, the ministry came first and then the support—not the other way around. In the New Testament you never read of anyone trying to raise support to launch a ministry. The demonstration of having a ministry is the basis for the raising of support, and we ought to apply this frequently today. Young people have often come to us asking to be supported in order to go out to a foreign field. They have been challenged and see an opportunity and they sincerely want to respond, for which may God bless them. They are willing to give up the advantages of living in the United States and are willing to deprive themselves and their families to go out to difficult places. That is a marvelous thing. But what they ought also to understand is that there is need to demonstrate *before they go* that they can do something in a ministry. It does not always have to be teaching. Sometimes just showing a helpful spirit, a willingness to help clean up some older person's backyard or to help them with some difficulty, indicates a capacity to minister and not to be ministered to. That forms the basis, then, for asking for support.

But now Paul comes to his point. He has proven that he had the right to be supported, but when he came to Corinth he had deliberately chosen not to exercise that right:

> But I have made no use of any of these rights, nor am I writing this to secure any such provision. For I would rather die than have any one deprive me of my ground for boasting (v. 15).

He feels strongly about this. He says to these people, "Look, I would rather die than have you take away my right to give up my rights. That is a right I insist on having." That is the greatest right a Christian has. Some may ask, "Why did he feel so strongly about it?" The answer is in verses 16 through 17:

> For if I preach the gospel, that gives me no ground for boasting. For necessity is laid upon me. Woe to me if I do not preach the gospel! For if I do this of my own will, I have a reward; but if not of my own will, I am [still] entrusted with a commission.

What the apostle is saying, basically, is that he had no right to pride of achievement because he faithfully preached the gospel. On the contrary, he says, he really has no choice about preaching the gospel, ". . . necessity is laid upon me." In other words, "If I do not preach I am perfectly miserable. I would much rather preach than experience the lash of my conscience, the sense of failure in what God has appointed me to do. I cannot live with that. But, he says, "if I do it willingly I gain a reward." (He will tell us in a moment what that reward is.) He implies, "If I accept this commission from God, and joyfully do what he tells me to do, it is to my great advantage. I feel fulfilled. But whether I like it or not, I have to do it."

A friend was telling me not long ago about a missionary doctor who worked among leprosy patients in Africa. On a visit to his friends in England he was telling them about the unpleasant conditions he had to work in. The patients would come in with running sores that were so putrid and foul that he could barely stand to be around them. He lived under the most trying and primitive conditions, and these people were often totally ungrateful for what the doctor tried to do. One of the ladies listening to him said, "You must love these people tremendously to go out and serve them the way you do." He said, "No, I don't. I find it very difficult to love somebody who reeks with a horrible odor. I would much rather walk away and leave them there to die in their filth. It is not love."

"Well," she said, "what is it, then?"

"Duty," he replied.

There is nothing wrong with a sense of duty. There is nothing wrong with feeling that God has given you a job to do, and you must do it whether you like it or not. Many of us are uneasy with that kind of motivation, but Paul felt it. He said, "There is no choice for me in the matter of preaching. Whether I like it or not I have a commission to fulfill, and if I want my life to be worth anything at all, I had better do it." That sense of duty which is really a form of love to his Lord is what drives him out to preach.

But that, he says, is not the reason why he preaches without charge. What is the reason? He tells us in verse 18:

> What then is my reward? Just this: that in my preaching I may make the gospel free of charge, not making full use of my right in the gospel.

He did make use of his right sometimes, but not in Corinth. There he desired to make the gospel free of charge. The thing that motivated him to work late hours at night making tents so he would not have to be supported by anybody in the church at Corinth was the sheer delight it gave him to bless and enrich someone else without taking a penny in return. It was the joy of giving that Paul was experiencing.

Something for Nothing

I too have had that joy. A few years ago I was invited by some missionaries to go to the south of France to hold a Bible conference with them. They needed to be refreshed from the Word of God, but they told me when they called, "We cannot afford to give you an honorarium." I said, "That is all right with me. I will come anyway. Can you meet the expenses of the trip?" They said, "Well, we will certainly try," and I knew that they would do so out of very meager salaries.

So I went to France. The conference ground was an old Roman Catholic convent along the Rhone River, south of Lyon. We had a great three or four days together feasting on the riches of the Word of God. I saw their spirits uplifted, changed and blessed, as they applied the truth of the Word in their lives and hearts. At the close of the conference they said, "We have put together a check from all of our contributions here. We do not know if it is enough, but it is all we have got, so here it is." It was not enough; it hardly covered half of my expenses. But I had the exquisite pleasure of turning the check over and endorsing it and handing it back to them, saying, "Use this to establish a fund to bring other speakers in to minister to you in the future." To see the joy and surprise in their faces was all the reward I needed. I went away, richly repaid for that ministry.

That is what Paul is talking about here. It was his joy to go about the Roman Empire and give people something for nothing. He saw them come to a dawning awareness that what he had given them was the greatest thing they had ever had in their lives, enriching them beyond their wildest dreams, freeing them, helping them, healing them and making them whole. To do so without asking a single penny from them in return, Paul says, was sheer delight.

What form did this take in other places? He goes on to describe it. Here we have the famous passage touching on his relationship to all men:

> For though I am free from all men, I have made myself a slave to all, that I might win the more (v. 19).

"I am free," he says, "I am an apostle. I have knowledge beyond anything you have. But that does not mean that I demand my rights. No, I am glad to give them up, freely, willingly, that I might win the more."

> To the Jews I became as a Jew, in order to win Jews . . .

He was willing to go back under the old limitations of ritual and ceremony and outlook in order to move in alongside his Jewish brethren and be understood by them. He was willing to live again as a Jew when he was with them.

> to those under the law I became as one under the law—though not being myself under the law—that I might win those under the law (v. 20).

To those who were still under dietary restrictions and various other limitations on their activity, Paul says he was willing to do the same, though, he says, he was not himself under the law.

> To those outside the law [i.e., the Gentile world] I became as one outside the law—

"When I was with the Gentiles I ate their food, even food offered to idols. It did not bother me. I did not feel any restrictions, because I was trying to reach these people." Then, lest they misunderstand the implications of being outside the law, he adds,

> not being without law toward God but under the law of Christ—that I might win those outside the law (v. 21).

This is the law of love, the law of freedom. So, never lawless, nevertheless he became as one outside the law to those who lived that way in order that he might win them to Christ.

> To the weak I became weak,

He adjusted to the conscientious scruples of those who did not yet have liberty to do some of the things that he felt free to do. What a picture! What an example!

> I have become all things to all men, that I might by all means save some (v. 22).

That is the great verse in which the apostle affirms the spirit of selfless accommodation to reach people where they are. That is what ought to characterize a Christian approach. We should be willing to set aside our personal desires in order that we might win a hearing and open a door for a witness to our Lord. Paul never denied principle, never compromised in the realm of immorality, but nevertheless adjusted to the outlook of those whom he was with. Then once again he states his reason, in verse 23:

> I do it all for the sake of the gospel, that I may share in its blessings.

The gospel—the good news that God has given us apart from any merit of ours. In line with the character of the gospel Paul says he enjoys the pleasure of giving without thought of return.

For many years, as our family was growing up, we would have a Christmas tree at Christmas with all the presents around it. Everybody in the family would look forward to that time. The presents kept growing in number as we waited for Christmas Eve, when we would gather to open the gifts. When the magic moment came we sat in the living room, and after reading the Christmas story together we would let the children open their gifts. My wife and I would also have gifts in that pile, but we would leave them until the others were opened. Often we would almost forget to open them ourselves. It was not the gifts that we were looking for—those were of minor significance—what we wanted to see, our full reward, was the joy on the faces of our children when they opened their gifts. Every Christmas I felt amply rewarded for whatever the gifts may have cost in terms of money or struggle. I saw the joy and happiness light up my children's faces when they found they were getting something they had long wanted and did not know they were going to get.

That is the reward Paul is describing. What a joy it was to go about and give people things for which he did not demand anything in return. That is the true Christian spirit.

14

—

Disqualified!

In this section, Paul reveals a second reason to exercise self-control in the Christian life. As we have just seen, there is the need for self-restraint in order not to injure others. But now a new danger looms. By giving in to the love of indulgence and luxury in our lives we may find ourselves trapped into something so spiritually injurious that we could end up "disqualified."

> Do you not know that in a race all the runners compete, but only one receives the prize? So run that you may obtain it. Every athlete exercises self-control in all things. They do it to receive a perishable wreath, but we an imperishable. Well, I do not run aimlessly, I do not box as one beating the air; but I pommel my body and subdue it, lest after preaching to others I myself should be disqualified (vv. 24–27).

This admonition employs the figure of an athletic contest familiar to these believers in Corinth—a race. Every three years the Isthmian Games were held right outside the City. Even today one can still see the areas where the races were run. The starting blocks, where the runners began, are still embedded in the stones. To Paul, life was a race like that, and every contestant needed to learn self-discipline. These Corinthians knew that any athlete who participated in the Isthmian races had to take an oath to train for ten months. They must give up certain delightful foods in their diet to enable them to endure the race. They must subject themselves to rigorous discipline in order to win. All they would win was a fading pine wreath, but in the race

179

of life which we are running, the prize, the wreath, is an imperishable one, enduring for eternity.

A Pleasing Instrument

The aim of life, as Paul understood it, is that we run the race in such a way as to be a useful and a pleasing instrument of God, to be used whenever and wherever he desires. That is the objective of the race. When Paul woke up in the morning that was first in his thoughts; that is what set the tone of his day. He was ready to give up certain indulgences if they interfered with his objective to be what God wanted him to be. For him the great objective was to win the prize, and that prize would be his final awareness that he had pleased God.

I wonder how many of us have that objective? Sooner or later each of us has to ask the question, "What am I here for anyhow? Through the normal, natural processes of procreation, why did I appear on the earth, in this particular part of the world, at this time in history?" The answer from the Bible is that God intends to use you. He wants you. He made you. He designed you, with all the peculiar abilities you have and the unique talents and gifts he has given you, that you might be useful and pleasing to him.

The figure of a race, which Paul uses, makes it obvious that one cannot win the prize if there is no self-discipline. There is always something about life which tends to derail you if you let it. There are temptations to turn aside, to give up, to rest on your laurels, to sit back and let life go on, enjoying youself. But that will often sabotage your Christian effectiveness.

Dr. Martin Lloyd-Jones, speaking on the passage in the Sermon on the Mount where Jesus says we are to "hunger and thirst after righteousness," says:

People who really want something always give some evidence of that fact. People who really desire something with the whole of their being do not sit down passively waiting for it to come. And that applies to us in this matter. There are certain things in this life that are patently opposed to God and his righteousness. There is no question about that at all. We know they are bad; we know they are harmful; we know they are sinful. I say that to hunger and thirst after righteousness means avoiding such things just as we would avoid the very plague itself. If we know there is an infection in a house, we avoid the house. We segregate the patient who has a fever because it is infectious, and obviously we avoid such persons. The same is true in the spiritual realm.

But it does not stop at that. I suggest that if we are truly hungering and thirsting after righteousness, we shall even avoid things that tend to dull or take the edge off our spiritual appetites. There are so many things like that, things that are quite harmless in themselves and which are perfectly legitimate. Yet if you find that you are spending too much of your time with them and that you desire the things of God less, you must avoid them. That is a common sense argument.*

That, basically, is what Paul is saying here. In his own life he did that; he refused to give way to intemperance or laziness. He gave himself to what God wanted him to do. He worked at it and took time to plan and act in order to accomplish it.

Gas and Spark

I have found that the Christian life is much like running a car. When I was in high school I learned to drive an old Model T Ford— "Tin Lizzie" they called them then. Once in a while the car would not start, and when that happened there were always two things you did. The first thing you did was check the spark. You would take a screwdriver and put it up against the spark plug while someone turned the engine over. If you felt a jolt that took the top of your head off, you knew the spark was all right. Then you checked the gas. If the gas was OK and the spark was OK, then it was only a matter of time for you to get the car running.

There are two things necessary in the Christian life: discipline and dependence. Some people try to run on only one. Some are so concerned about discipline they seek to regulate everything in their lives. They go overboard, setting themselves rigid schedules: getting up early in the morning, so many hours spent in prayer, so many verses memorized each week—all with the hope that they will thus be useful and effective as Christians. Those people usually end up disillusioned, discouraged, and often totally defeated in their lives, because Christian living takes more than discipline. It requires dependence as well! It is necessary to understand that God is prepared to do it with you. You labor, but he produces the results. You plant, another waters, but God gives the increase.

---

* *Studies in the Sermon on the Mount* (Grand Rapids: Eerdmans), pp. 89, 90.

So other people say that dependence is the great objective. They go into a kind of "automatic pilot" where they expect God is going to do everything; they are all spark and no gas. Those people also end up disillusioned, fruitless, ineffective. Nothing ever happens in their lives, because it takes both dependence *and* discipline. Here at Corinth they were going in for the dependence, waiting for God to do it all. But Paul says, "You will never win that way. If you are not willing to give up certain things and press toward the mark, to focus your life on a single objective, you will never win. You will find yourself ultimately disqualified." He says, "It can even happen to me. I preach all this to others, but if I do not do it, I, too, can end up disqualified."

Many have been troubled by the word *disqualified*, because in the King James Version it is translated "cast away." This sounds like the loss of salvation, but Paul is not talking about that; it never was in question with him. He understood that the new birth brought in a new life style and was an introduction into a new kingdom, and it cannot be reversed—you do not lose salvation, once it is entered into. What he was afraid of and what motivated him to keep pressing on every day was the fear that he might be set aside—lose his ministry, lose his opportunity to serve.

This great apostle, who understood life so clearly, lived in the constant awareness that a day is coming when the sons of God will be revealed, when all the world will see the reality of life. All the universe will then bow before the Lord Jesus and every tongue proclaim him as Lord. The entire population of the earth through all its ages will be there, and all Christians will be thinking back through their life, asking, "What did I do that would count toward the glory of God?" That is the only thing that will be of value then. All self-indulgences, all the times of giving way to laziness and so on, will be looked upon with shame at that moment. Everyone will want to see how much of your life was given over to the usefulness for which God created you. Paul is thinking of that day, and he is afraid that too much self-indulgence in the "good life" will trap him so that he will fall into some temptation to live for himself and end up on the shelf, "disqualified," no longer used for God's glory to the extent that might have been possible.

Ritual of Futility

This was happening in three different ways to people in the Bible and to people today. It is possible to be a disqualified Christian. In the first stage, God will turn off the power in your ministry. There are many who still go through a mechanical process, but it has lost its power. That is what Paul feared above everything else. I know men in the pastorate who, years ago, were used greatly by God, but for many years now the power has been absent. They are going through a kind of performance, a ritual of futility, a charade, in which nothing ever happens. There is no longer any power, because somewhere along the line they were disqualified. Something happened—they refused to deny themselves, to exercise discipline or self-control, or perhaps their dependence faltered, and the power was gone.

Another form of this is actually to be taken out of the ministry so that all performance ceases. There is a young man I know who was one of the most popular Christian writers of our present day. His schedule was full of meetings and he was in demand everywhere. Now this man sits in an apartment with absolutely nothing to do all day long. In the course of his ministry he fell into temptation and gave way to adultery, and was disqualified. Because I love him, I am praying that it will only be a temporary disqualification, for God can restore him.

This passage goes on to tell us that the third form of disqualification can even mean the ending of your life. God chastens us at times and seeks to bring to our attention what is happening to us. If we ignore his chastening the time may come, as Paul will later say happened to these Corinthians, when God will simply say, "Come on home. I cannot trust you there any longer," and take us away. We do not lose our salvation, but we lose all opportunity to serve him here, and our lives are wasted.

Paul has an example to give us, taken from Scripture itself.

> I want you to know, brethren, that our fathers were all under the cloud, and all passed through the sea, and all were baptized into Moses in the cloud and in the sea, and all ate the same supernatural food and all drank the same supernatural drink. For they drank from the supernatural Rock which followed them, and the Rock was Christ. Nevertheless with most of them God was not pleased; for they were overthrown in the wilderness (vv. 1–5).

What a remarkable example! Notice the repetition through that account of the word *all*. When they came out of Egypt *all* the Israelites were enjoying tremendous blessing from God; they all had certain advantages without exceptions—the weakest of them, the youngest of them, the oldest of them, the feeblest among them. Paul lists the advantages for us. First, they were "*all* under the cloud, and *all* passed through the sea." Now the "cloud" is a reference to the Shekinah cloud, the glory that hovered over the camp of Israel, shining by day to guide them, and becoming a pillar of fire at night. It was a symbol of God's protection of his people, and of the guidance that he gives them. The "sea," of course, is the Red Sea that they all passed through safely and thus left the bondage and curse of Egypt. This is a reference to the protecting, guiding, and delivering power of God that they had *all* experienced. Now see the parallel: every Christian is also in this position. We have all been delivered from Egypt, if we are Christians at all. We have been transferred from the kingdom of darkness to the kingdom of light. We are now part of a new spiritual realm, Paul says. Furthermore, we are protected. God is always watching over us and guarding us. We are guided. We have all experienced the guidance of God as he leads us into places he wants us to be. So we all share this divine oversight, like those of old.

The second thing Paul says of them is they "*all were baptized into Moses* in the cloud and in the sea." What does that mean? That is a strange phrase, "baptized into Moses," but it is parallel to what Scripture says of us, for we are all baptized into Christ. Just as we have been placed into Christ and so identified with him, these Israelites of old were likewise identified with Moses. Moses was the great mediator of the Old Testament. He stood between God and man; he was the representative of the people to God, and the spokesman of God to the people. He alone had intimate access to God, but in Moses these people all had that same access to God. This, of course, is true of us, through our position in Christ. Paul argues this in Romans 5, "Through him (Christ) we have obtained *access to this grace* in which we stand."

The third advantage the Corinthians had was that they were all strengthened and refreshed by Christ, for "all ate the same supernatural food and all drank the same supernatural drink." The food, of course, was the manna that came from heaven, and the drink was the water that flowed from the rock when Moses smote it. The Rock which followed them, Paul says, was actually Christ.

Now do not ever say that the Old Testament saints knew nothing of Christ, because they did. They saw him in these symbols and figures that were used in the Old Testament times. They were related to him just as we are related to him, and just as he fed them and refreshed them then, so we are fed and refreshed by the Spirit of God flowing out of Christ. When it says the Rock "followed them" do not imagine a great rock rolling along behind the camp. It means that wherever the symbol of a rock appears in the Old Testament, (and it does frequently) it was a reference to and a picture of Christ. The Rock from which the water flowed; the Rock of refuge into which they ran when the summer storms broke upon the landscape—these were references to Christ. Samuel erected a rock, a stone which he called Ebenezer, "the stone of help"—that was a reference to the help Christ was giving them at that time.

Yet, with all this opportunity and advantage, the amazing thing is that "God was not pleased with most of them." Is that not sobering? How many left Egypt? According to the record in Numbers, over 600,000 men alone: counting women and children that comes to almost 2,000,000 people. Of those 2,000,000 how many entered into the land? Two men: Caleb and Joshua! They were the only ones, for the rest all died in the wilderness, disqualified—no longer able to serve and function in the way God intended them to do. Paul states in verse 6, "these things are a warning for us, not to desire evil as they did."

Such things are happening to people today. I know a young man who has a girlfriend who is also a Christian. When they are together, she keeps urging him to indulge in immorality with her. He says to her, "But we're Christians, we can't do that." But she says, "Well, what is the difference? We can be forgiven afterward. Why not?" Now that is the kind of subtle lie that leads people into activities for which they will find themselves disqualified. That is what Paul feared, and what he resolutely resisted with both self-discipline and dependence upon the grace and help of God.

Danger Points

He goes on now to give us four danger points to watch. These are just as pertinent today as they were when they were written. First,

> Do not be idolaters as some of them were; as it is written, "The people sat down to eat and drink and rose up to dance" (v. 7).

This was the scene at the foot of Mount Sinai while the law was being given to Moses, who had gone up to commune with God. He was gone for forty days and forty nights, and after a while the people grew tired of waiting so they had a big feast. There is nothing wrong with that, in itself. But then someone suggested they dance. There is nothing wrong with that, either. Israel often danced before the Lord, and God is the God of the dance as well as other expressions of worship. But in their dancing, in their indulgence, they got "carried away," we would say, and they began to dance in a way that was lascivious and lewd. Finally they found themselves bowing down and worshiping a golden calf which Aaron claimed came out of the fire when he threw in some gold. What a remarkable fire! Thus they ended up in idolatry.

That is what Paul cautions against—the ease with which otherwise good things can so capture our attention and become so important to us that we feel we cannot live without them. That becomes idolatry. I am amazed at how many Christians worship their cars, their children, some sports figure, some rock-and-roll artist, or some movie star. I am amazed at how many Christians worship the United States and bow down to it. Their main purpose in life is to pursue some political activity which will enhance the prestige of the U.S. All these things are right, but they become idols when they take on supreme significance to us. That is one way to be disqualified.

Then, second, there is fornication:

> We must not indulge in immorality as some of them did, and twenty-three thousand fell in a single day (v. 8).

That is referring to the account in Numbers 25 when some of the Israelites objected to God's restraints, and the women of Moab and Midian came and tempted them and they fell into fornication with them. A plague broke out in the camp which was not arrested until Phinehas, the grandson of Aaron, took a spear and actually speared to death a couple engaged in fornication. We read these accounts and we say, "Oh! how brutal, how bloody." But it is God's way of saying, "Look, what you are getting into is far more destructive than that. Death is kindness compared with what will happen to you if you keep on doing what you are doing." Phinehas warned them faithfully, and thus the plague was arrested.

Then, third, there was a presumptuous spirit:

> We must not put the Lord to the test, as some of them did and were destroyed by serpents (v. 9).

That refers to the story in Numbers 21 of how Israel presumed to charge God with unfaithfulness. They said, "You brought us out of Egypt, and we are going to die in this wilderness. It is your fault. Why did you bring us out here?" Did you ever say anything like that to God? "What did you put me here for? It is your fault I got into this." Now that is "putting God to the test," and it is a dangerous thing to do because, long continued, it can lead to disqualification. Poisonous serpents came among them and were stopped, remember, only by Moses' lifting up a bronze serpent on a pole.

Then, the fourth danger point is murmuring, grumbling:

> nor grumble, as some of them did and were destroyed by the Destroyer (v. 10).

This refers to the story of Korah, Dathan, and Abiram, those three young men who began to grumble at the authority of Moses. They said, "We are just as good as Moses. Why can't we exercise the same kind of authority he does? He doesn't have anything over us." They began to create revolt and spread unrest in the camp of Israel, and God called them to task and said he would show them which one he had chosen. The ground opened up under Korah, Dathan, and Abiram and swallowed them alive. They were gone, destroyed by the Destroyer. It is a most sobering account, highlighting the danger of murmuring.

Paul's admonition to us follows:

> Now these things happened to them as a warning (literally, "as a type"), but they were written down for our instruction, upon whom the end of the ages has come. (We are in the terminal age of history). Therefore let any one who thinks that he stands take heed lest he fall (vv. 11, 12).

These accounts are given in the Old Testament as types, pictures. When you read these Old Testament stories, put yourself there. The enemies they faced are paralleled by the enemies we face; those principalities and powers of darkness are seeking to overcome us, assault us, discourage and defeat us, just as Israel was defeated and discouraged by their human enemies. When you see how they trusted in God, held on to his promises, renewed their strength by faith, and then set about to do what God gave them to do, you see a picture recorded for us that we may know how to overcome in the struggles and battles that we face in life.

They were types, but according to verse 12, they were also targets. So are we. We too are under attack. We are not living in a beautiful, pleasant world designed for our enjoyment, and the quicker we get over that idea the better. We are living on a battlefield, under attack. We are running a race that must be won. We are fighting a battle with a ruthless enemy, and we must never forget it, for his devices are clever, and his strategies are subtle, and we can easily be deceived and fall.

I have recently been reading the stories of the Reformation, and I am amazed again at how easily the greatest and mightiest names of the past have all, at times, succumbed to the wiles of the devil. Calvin, with his great, clear, theological mind could be austere, cold, cruel, and legalistic. Martin Luther, with his robust faith and his great courage which enabled him to stand before emperors and kings without faltering, could be vulgar, angry, and carnal in his rage against his enemies, even his brothers in Christ. Do not think that you have conquered once for all and you are not going to fall. You are up against a tough, ruthless enemy. He can trip you and trap you and, if you are not alert, it may result in your being set aside, unable to be used.

Common Trials, Controlled Pressures

That is not where Paul ends, and that is not where I wish to end either.

> No temptation has overtaken you that is not common to man. God is faithful, and he will not let you be tempted beyond your strength, but with the temptation will also provide the way of escape, that you may be able to endure it (v. 13).

What an encouragement that is! It is written that we might understand three specific things about our testings: first, they are common to all. I do not know anything more difficult to believe, when you are under testing, than that. We all think, "Why doesn't this happen to others? They deserve it as much as me. Why is it happening to me?" Well, it is just your turn, that is all. Everybody goes through it. You are not permitted to witness their martyrdom, but you will not be allowed to miss yours. You do not see what they have to go through, but no one is left out. Trials are common to all. Those others' time is coming, if it has not already come, so do not allow yourself to think that what is happening to you is unique. It is not at all. It is very common, and the minute you start inquiring around, you will find a dozen who have gone through it too.

There will be common trials—but also controlled pressures. God is faithful and will not allow you to be tempted above your strength. Again, that is hard to believe, is it not? We say, "Well, it has already happened. I am already beyond my strength." No, you are not. You merely think you are. God knows your strength better than you do. He knows how much you can handle, and how much you cannot.

One of the basic principles of training for an athlete is to develop himself to do things he does not think he can do right now. He must put more pressure on than he can handle, and thus he develops the strength to handle it. This is what God does with us. He puts pressure on, but it is controlled pressure. It will never be more than you can handle, if you will observe the third thing here, the conquering grace that he provides. "The way of escape" is always present, without fail. What is this way of escape? It is what we have been talking about—dependence. Discipline is necessary, but so is dependence!

In the Old Testament the heroes and heroines of faith have taught us that in the hour of testing God is always enough. "God is our refuge and our strength, a very present help in time of trouble," but we will never discover that until everything else has been taken away. Then we discover that God can hold us steady. He himself is the way of escape, and that is why he puts us through pressures and testing till we see how true that is.

15

The Focused Life

One of the most dramatic statements Jesus ever made to his disciples was, "Behold, I send you forth as sheep in the midst of wolves." Though I come from Montana where there are a lot of sheep, I must say I have never heard of a sheepherder who did that. But this Shepherd does, and, of course, this immediately raises the question, "How will sheep survive under those circumstances?"

The answer to that question is presented in the second half of chapter 10. The last section closed with these words from verse 13:

> No temptation has overtaken you that is not common to man. God is faithful, and he will not let you be tempted beyond your strength, but with the temptation will also provide the way of escape, that you may be able to endure it.

But the apostle goes right on in verse 14 to say:

> Therefore, my beloved, shun the worship of idols.

It is clear from this that the temptation the apostle had in mind when he wrote, "no temptation has overtaken you that is not common to man," was the temptation to idolatry.

> Therefore, my beloved, shun the worship of idols. I speak as to sensible men; judge for yourselves what I say (vv. 14, 15).

There were, of course, idol temples in Corinth. In addition to the temple of Aphrodite, within the city itself were scattered many temples whose ruins are still visible today. These Christians had once been idol worshipers, but I do not think that the apostle is really concerned that they might go back to bowing down to an idol. That is not what he means when he says, "Flee idolatry." (Literally, "Shun the worship of idols" is "Flee idolatry.") What he has in mind is not bowing and scraping before an image, but succumbing to the temptation to enjoy again the atmosphere found at the idol temple. There were many fun things going on in connection with idolatry that some of the Corinthians were hoping to be able to hang onto. If you had lived in Corinth in that first century you would have recognized that the Roman and Greek citizenry of the city regarded the temple as the most exciting place in town. There you could get the best food, served up in the open-air restaurant. There they had the wildest music and all the seductive pleasures of wine, women and song. If you wanted to enjoy yourself in Corinth you went to the temple.

More Important Than God

The apostle is doubtless concerned lest these Corinthians, in seeking to enjoy the normal pleasures of life, would ultimately find themselves lured back into belief in these idols and their power. Idolatry is not merely something you do outwardly with your body. Idolatry occurs whenever anyone or anything becomes more important to you than the living God. Even in the twentieth century this is the greatest temptation anyone faces. When something or someone becomes of greater importance to us and more controlling in our life than God himself, we have succumbed to idolatry.

This word of the apostle's, filled with affection and affirmation, is still relevant to us. "Therefore, my beloved ones" ("the ones I love," is not a light term with Paul), "flee idolatry. I speak as to sensible men; judge for yourselves what I say." He is not being ironic when he says, "I speak as to sensible men." He is acknowledging that these are sensible, thoughtful Christians, frequently exposed to the Word of God. They are able, therefore, to judge what is right and what is wrong if they refer it to the revelation of Scripture, and he is encouraging them to do this very thing. Paul is saying that there are certain situations you can get into as a Christian in which, though you are not outwardly bowing down to an idol, you are being captured by the atmosphere. It can become so strong that the only advice he can give is, "get up and leave"; "flee"; "shun idolatry."

He is urging them to avoid the mentality associated with some of these things, not the people. "Avoid the temple," he is saying, "but do not avoid the pagans who go there." It is wise and balanced truth which the apostle has given us here. You can recognize how easily this kind of idolatry can happen to us today. One can get wrapped up in sports, for instance, so as to live for them; they take over one's life. We are beginning to make national jokes about families which are split up by football, because people cannot take their eyes away from the TV when the games are on.

When something begins to possess you to that degree you are on the verge of idolatry. When what you own begins to own you, then it takes the place of God in your life. When you begin to worship great sports figures; when you learn all you can about them and spend your time pursuing contact with them, you are being drawn into a form of idolatry. Perhaps it is the atmosphere of the cocktail lounge that you enjoy, and you find yourself wanting to go there. Be careful! You may be assaulted by temptation to fall again into idolatry. Being there is not necessarily wrong, but if you succumb to the atmosphere, and it begins to possess you, you are in trouble; it is idolatry.

That is how subtle some of these pressures can be. When disco dancing becomes more than recreation but something you look forward to with such devotion that other things suffer because of it, it becomes idolatry. Skiing can do the same thing! Gambling, when it becomes a fever, is a form of idolatry that takes over a life. Fishing can keep you away from ministry. Television can rob you of Bible study. When you feel yourself growing weak over the mention of the name of some rock-and-roll artist, you are falling into idolatry. Gourmet eating that demands all your attention and your money is a form of idolatry. Some of these things are not wrong in themselves, but it is easy to fall prey to them. They lure one on into more and more involvement until, before you know it, you have a new god, a new love, and a new master.

The apostle goes on to outline three reasons why such idolatry is so dangerous. The first is suggested to us in verses 16 through 21 where he says, in effect, that any form of idolatry will displace your love for Christ:

> The cup of blessing which we bless, is it not a participation in the blood of Christ? The bread which we break, is it not a participation in the body of Christ? Because there is one bread, we who are many are one body, for we all partake of the one bread. Consider the practice of Israel; are not those who eat the sacrifices partners in the altar? What do I imply then? That food offered to idols is anything, or that an idol is anything?

No, I imply that what pagans sacrifice they offer to demons and not to God. I do not want you to be partners with demons. You cannot drink the cup of the Lord and the cup of demons. You cannot partake of the table of the Lord and the table of demons.

Clearly there are some things in life that are mutually antagonistic, and one of them has to do with worship. As Jesus put it, "No man can serve two masters: for either he will hate the one, and love the other; or else he will hold to the one, and despise the other." One of the great and continuing problems of the Christian life is that we want to make a deep, sincere, wholehearted commitment to Christ, expressed in the Lord's Table, and at the same time, fully enjoy everything that is in the world. This, the Lord says, you cannot do. John declares the same thing: "If any one loves the world, love for the Father is not in him. For all that is in the world, the lust of the flesh and the lust of the eyes and the pride of life, is not of the Father but is of the world" (1 John 2:15,16). We must deal with this problem on the basis of who we basically are; that is why the apostle begins with the table of the Lord, for it is the central act of Christian worship.

Our Basic Nature

What do we do when we celebrate the Lord's Table; when we pass the cup and break the bread? According to this passage and other scriptures, we are reminding ourselves, and anyone else observing, of who we basically are. What we are saying is that we too died with Christ. When Christ shed his blood something died within us as well, and that something was the old life that wants to be the center of attention. We resigned our self-appointed commission as Lord of the universe when we died with Christ. When we pass the bread and take of it and eat together, we are saying that we have found a new source of strength. We no longer live by self-esteem, but by the approval of God, the righteousness granted and given to us by God. We feed on the truth that God unfolds to us in his Word. We feed on the strength that Christ gives us, to love even the unlovely. We draw on it. We eat it. We take it in, moment by moment and day by day. That is, then, who we are. We basically and fundamentally belong to God. As we do this we are sharing together and declaring that we all partake of the same life. That means we are one body, united in one family. That is what the Lord's Table means. To take it in any other way is to be mechanical and ritualistic and fundamentally shallow in our Christianity.

Paul says you can see the same principle at work even in the Jewish sacrifices. "Consider the practice of Israel; are not those who eat the sacrifices partners in the altar?" What they eat is telling others who they are. That is what we do too, he says, in partaking of the Lord's Table. He has in view, of course, eating the meat offered as sacrifices, as well as eating the bread and the wine of the Lord's Table. These are symbolic manifestations by which we are saying, "We take this into ourselves; we live by this, and therefore that is who we are."

But this goes beyond the mere physical act of eating something. You can "eat" things other than food. You are always taking in things, living by them, needing them to exist and function. That is the danger of the atmosphere and lure of much of these otherwise innocent activities. You begin to live by them; you must always have them or you cannot be comfortable. This is the problem with someone who constantly has to have something new in his life to remain happy. It is the problem with the teenager who must have a transistor radio going all the time. He cannot *be* anybody, without that music blaring at him. It is a form of idolatry. It is "eating" something which is telling the world who the person basically is.

Behind the Lure

The apostle goes on to say some really revealing things here. He asks, "Am I simply trying to argue that idols are nothing? No, I imply that what pagans sacrifice they offer to demons and not to God. I do not want you to be partners with demons. You cannot drink the cup of the Lord and the cup of demons. You cannot partake of the table of the Lord and the table of demons." What is behind the lure of otherwise innocent things? The apostle's answer is, demonic control! We have to face this as literally and realistically true. Paul speaks in other places of principalities and powers, the invisible spirits who obey the god of this world. Is that not a remarkably revealing statement? The god who is behind the organization of secular life is the devil, and subject to his control is a host of wicked, evil spirits engaged in a process that is properly called by no other term than "mind control." They are controlling the thinking, the attitudes, the desires, the habits of thousands and millions of people. Why? Because their objective is death!

A vivid demonstration of this is the terrible tragedy in 1978 of the mass suicide at Jonestown, Guyana. Everywhere people were asking, "Why do otherwise innocent people get drawn into this kind of thing? How can they be trapped so that they no longer have the ability to resist a sentence of death that is levied upon them? How can 900 people voluntarily take their own lives and the lives of their children?" The answer is, demonic control. Jesus said the devil is a liar and a murderer. What he is after is no less than the physical destruction of human life. If the devil had his way we would all be wiped out before tomorrow morning. That is why we ought to give thanks for the protection of God every day, that we have not been destroyed by the malevolent, evil spirit who is in charge of this world. Every now and then he succeeds in accomplishing his objective. How does he do it? By deceiving. He is a liar. He deceives people into thinking they are going to get something great, they are going to achieve their dreams and fulfill the hungers of their life.

Paul indicates that worship is an absolute thing; it is total. You cannot serve two masters. Either you will show that you belong to Christ or you will show that you belong to the god of this age, the god of this world. You cannot mix the two.

A Proper Jealousy

Then Paul tells us the second reason to flee idolatry. Not only is love for Christ threatened by idolatry, but, as he says in verse 22,

Shall we provoke the Lord to jealousy? Are we stronger than he?

Any form of idolatry awakens the jealousy of God. All through the Old Testament we are told that God is a jealous God. What is meant by that? Is God subject to capricious whims, getting angry if anyone looks at anyone else? No. God's jealousy is a proper jealousy; it is a love so intense for the object of his love that he is angry when something threatens it, and he will act. He will not stand idly by and let you drift away into some idolatrous preoccupation with the world. He will strike at it; he will destroy it. And if your affections are deeply entwined with it you are going to get hurt in the process; you will find yourself crushed and hurt and crying out to God, "Why do you do this to me?" But it is an act of love from a jealous God who will not allow you to drift into that kind of harmful preoccupation.

The third thing the apostle says is that any form of idolatry becomes a stumbling block to our brothers and sisters:

> "All things are lawful," but not all things are helpful. "All things are lawful," but not all things build up. Let no one seek his own good, but the good of his neighbor (v. 23).

We cannot be like Cain who asked the Lord, "Am I my brother's keeper?" Yes, we are our brothers' keepers. We have a responsibility not to harm or injure the spiritual growth of another brother or sister. These words are lovingly warning us that when we find ourselves wanting something so much that it interferes with our love and desire for the things of God we are in danger; we had better watch carefully lest we awaken his jealousy and find ourselves subject to the ruthless discipline of a God who loves us.

That is the danger of idolatry. Let me summarize it. Idolatry, of any form, denies our commitment to Christ, provokes and awakens the jealousy of God, and injures our brother or sister who is trying to work out his or her problems as well. Yet what the apostle is saying is to be carefully understood. At this point many Christians, knowing the dangers in the world and the things of the world, immediately jump to the conclusion that the way to defend against the world is to stay completely away from certain things which are strongly tempting. Many Christians cut off all communication with their neighbors and their friends who are not Christians. They will not have anything to do with them. They build themselves a "Bible city" where they can escape all the dangers of being assaulted by worldly temptation. When that happens they run right into another form of worldliness. Christians who live that way end up carnal, worldly minded, filled with a pride and self-righteousness that turns off thousands from the Christian message. What Paul is saying is, "Your only defense is to keep your commitment to the Lord Jesus at a white-hot pitch, and then you are safe in the world."

Paul now turns to certain practical guidelines that are very helpful, because he wants to enable people to live in the midst of life the way it is. So, still facing the problem of eating meat offered to idols, he says:

> Eat whatever is sold in the meat market without raising any question on the ground of conscience. For "the earth is the Lord's, and everything in it" (v. 25).

Translated into terms of our idolatry, what Paul is saying is, "Do not run away from life. Live right out in the midst of it. Do not avoid being normal, natural people enjoying the normal, natural things of life around you. You will never escape by trying to get away from the temptations. They will pursue you wherever you go. So enjoy life, and do not raise overscrupulous questions, always trying to examine everything with a microscope as to whether it is going to be dangerous or hurtful to you. Relax. God knows where you are. He has put you there and provided a world for you to enjoy, so remember who you are, enter into it and live in it to the full."

Fellowship and Friendship

But what about when you are invited to the home of a non-Christian? Paul continues,

> If one of the unbelievers invites you to dinner and you are disposed to go, eat whatever is set before you without raising any question on the ground of conscience (v. 26).

I am glad he put that here. It is clear that separation to Christ does not mean isolation from non-Christians. Our *fellowship* is to be with Christ; our *friendship* is to be given to the non-Christians around us. That is important. Christians who refuse to do that are only deceiving themselves. They are disobeying the command of their Lord to "go forth as sheep in the midst of wolves." We are to go and enjoy ourselves, without asking questions. Paul says, "If somebody asks you, then go." Now no one is going to ask you to dinner if you are an uptight, self-righteous, legalistic Christian. Do not worry; you will not get any invitations into non-Christian homes. You will only get them if you are an openhearted, friendly, outgoing person who understands that people are struggling and in need, and you see through the veneer and the façade of their lives to the empty, lonely, hurting hearts behind. Then you will get an invitation to a home, and if you do, Paul says, "Go, and enjoy it, but remember your basic commitment is to Christ. Nothing must compromise that."

> (But if some one says to you, "This has been offered in sacrifice," then out of consideration for the man who informed you, and for conscience sake—I mean his conscience, not yours—do not eat it.) For why should my liberty be determined by another man's scruples? If I partake with thankfulness, why am I denounced because of that for which I give thanks? (vv. 28–30).

If someone makes an issue over the matter then refuse to go along. If someone makes it obvious that you are being tested to see whether you are willing to go the whole way with the world or whether you really belong to Christ, then make the issue crystal clear right away. Do not go along with what they want you to do because they are making a test out of it. Their own conscience may be troubled by your actions. For their sakes do not do it. Your conscience may be clear, but theirs is not.

The latter part of verse 29 and verse 30 is often taken to be contradictory to what we have just said, but what it really means is, "Why should I exercise my liberty to eat or drink or whatever, and thus arouse condemnation from others? Why should I expose myself that way?" Paul is encouraging a refusal to go along with something dubious, lest you expose yourself to condemnation from someone with a troubled conscience. This is also what Paul is saying in Romans 14:16, "So do not let what is good to you be spoken of as evil."

He closes with a rule of thumb for all occasions:

> So, whether you eat or drink, or whatever you do, do all to the glory of God. Give no offense to Jews or to Greeks or to the church of God, just as I try to please all men in everything I do, not seeking my own advantage, but that of many, that they may be saved. Be imitators of me, even as I am of Christ (vv. 31–11:1).

What a wonderful, powerful life the apostle Paul had! The effect of it is still changing the history of the world twenty centuries later. Why? Because he had a focused life. There was one thing he wanted to accomplish, and that was the glory of God. He says he had the highest of motives: "whether you eat or drink, or whatever you do, do all to the glory of God." And do it God's way and for his reasons. The practical guideline is, "Do not deliberately offend anybody." You cannot help it at times because you have to be faithful to Christ, but whenever possible do not offend them. Try not to offend the Jew, or the Gentile, or the Christian. Finally, you have a wonderful example both in the Lord himself and in his apostles. They gave themselves to help others; they put the good of others before their own desires and thus made an impact on their generation and the world ever since.

16

Essential Traditions

Chapter 11 of 1 Corinthians has become a battlefield of the twentieth century. It is a very complex chapter that deals with the question, "Are women fully human, or are they only humans j.g. (junior grade)?" This study will deal with the question of male headship and female subjection and other burning issues of today. Years ago the focus of the chapter was on the question, "Should women wear hats in church?" but that is now a long-past issue. It has now become the question, not of whether women should wear hats in church, but of whether they will wear the pants at home! We shall examine these issues that are now part of the swirl of controversy which has escalated into the feminist movement of our day.

The apostle introduces the subject with these words:

> I commend you because you remember me in everything and maintain the traditions even as I have delivered them to you (v. 2).

Not all traditions are bad. We have seen in this letter that Christianity includes not only the revelation of what Paul calls "the mysteries of God," which are undiscoverable by the natural mind, but it also includes certain important and essential traditions, practices that have been handed down from generation to generation. In chapter 11 there are two traditions the apostle considers: the tradition of male headship which dates from the creation of mankind itself, and the tradition of the Lord's Supper, instituted in the Upper Room.

First the apostle examines the great tradition of headship as a principle to govern the people of God for all time. Then in the following verses (4–16), he sets forth how this principle was to be practiced in Corinth and the world of the first century. Here is the principle:

> But I want you to understand that the head of every man is Christ, the head of a woman is her husband, and the head of Christ is God (v. 3).

The apostle's word for "head" is the usual, ordinary word for the hairy knob that sits on top of the neck, which contains the brain, and the eyes, ears, nose and mouth, and which, even in the ancient world, was understood to be the control center of the body. There are some today who argue that the ancients did not understand that, but I think they did, because four of our five senses are located in the head. They well knew that to remove the head from the body ended the life and activity of that body. Thus Herodias, the wife of Herod, ordered the head of John the Baptist brought to her on a platter because she knew that would slow John down to a point where she could handle him.

The Direction Setter

Now when "head" is used metaphorically, as it is here, it refers to priority in function. That is what the head of our body does; it is the direction-setter of the body. Used metaphorically, therefore, the word *head* means primarily leadership, and it is so used in this passage. This is clear from the threefold use of it that the apostle makes here. The use in controversy is the second one, "the head of the woman is her husband," but he brackets this with two other examples of headship so that we might understand from them what the middle one means.

The first one is, "the head of every man is Christ." That is a declaration of Christ's right to lead the whole human race. He is the leader of the race in the mind and thinking of God, and ultimately, as Scripture tells us, all humanity will bow the knee and confess that Jesus Christ is Lord. So whether men know it or not, Christ is their head and they are responsible to follow him. That is the true objective of life for any man who wishes to fulfill his manhood. Of course, that is seen in practice only in the believer and then only to a limited degree, but it is stated positively here. The Book of Hebrews declares that Christ is "the pioneer of our salvation," the one who goes before, the one who opens the way. This is the sense here of this metaphorical use of the word *head*. Christ is the leader of the race, the determiner of every man's destiny, the One to be followed.

Now move down to the third level of headship mentioned here, "the head of Christ is God." Here we have a manifestation of headship demonstrated for us in history. Jesus, the Son of God, is equal to the Father in his deity. Nevertheless when he assumes humanity he submits himself to the leadership of the Father. Everywhere Jesus went he stated this. "I do always those things which please my Father." On one occasion he said, "My meat is to do my Father's will, and to please him who sent me." On another occasion he said, "I and my Father are one," that is, we work together. He adds on still another occasion, "My Father is greater than I." That does not challenge the equality of the members of the Godhead, but when Christ became a man he voluntarily consented to take a lower position than the Father. It is in that sense he says, "My Father is greater than I."

Those two headships help us to understand the meaning of the central one, "the head of the woman is the man." The RSV says, "the head of the woman is her husband" but that is interpretation. (The word used is *aner*, the male.) Though the subsequent passage has in view a married woman, this general statement of the principle of headship has in view men and women in the way they function in society. But it must be remembered that headship never means domination. Submission is a voluntary commitment, carried out in practice from a conviction that God's will is best achieved by this means. It is to be most visible in marriage where a woman voluntarily undertakes a role of support when she marries a man. He is to be leader and she assumes a support role to help him fulfill the objectives of their life together, as Christ, his head, makes clear.

Now if she does not want to do this she is perfectly free not to undertake that role. No woman should get married if she does not wish to. If she wants to give herself to the pursuit of a career for her own objectives she has every right to do so. But then she ought not to get married, because marriage means that she desires to help advance the objectives and goals of her husband. When she marries he becomes the leader of the two. Now that is the principle of headship, and the apostle has stated it as clearly and as objectively as it can be stated. It does not involve the idea of origin so much as it does direction. This is the way headship is used in other parts of the Scripture as well. In Ephesians we are told that "Christ is the head of the church which is his body," which means he is its leader and has the right to set the ultimate direction of the relationship.

The First Century

Beginning in verse 4, the apostle applies this principle to the practice of the church, especially as it lived within the Eastern culture of that first-century world.

> Any man who prays or prophesies with his head covered dishonors his head, but any woman who prays or prophesies, with her head unveiled dishonors her head—it is the same as if her head were shaven. For if a woman will not veil herself, then she should cut off her hair; but if it is disgraceful for a woman to be shorn or shaven, let her wear a veil (vv. 4–6).

Two things are important to notice in that paragraph. One: the center of Paul's concern is the public ministry of the Word of God. He is talking here about Christians, about the church, the gathering of believers together in a public assembly. To properly function in such an assembly a woman should wear a veil. But the second thing to note is that the man should not. The veil comes in as the symbol of the acceptance and understanding of the principle of headship which he has just declared. Where public ministry is involved it is just as important that man should not be covered as that a woman should. This was the application of headship in the culture and custom of that day and time.

It is significant to note that both men and women were free to exercise ministry. Both could pray and prophesy. As is seen in other passages of Scripture (and we will come to see most clearly in chapter 14), prophesying is what today we call preaching. It is expounding the Word of God, taking the Scriptures and making them shine so as to illuminate life. Either a woman or a man could do that, but it was important how they did it. That is the emphasis this passage makes. They must do it in two different ways, the male as a man, the female as a woman. That is the central emphasis of this text.

If the man does not pray or prophesy as a man should in that culture (bareheaded) then he dishonors his head. It is remarkable that Paul would say that a man ministering in public should *not* have anything on his head, for the practice among the Jews was for men to wear a head covering when they ministered. Today, we still can see Jewish men wearing the yarmulke (a beanie, we would call it) on their heads. It is the prescribed covering for the head, and no orthodox male Jew would ever think of reading the Scripture or ministering in public without it. But Paul the apostle, raised in Judaism, says that if a Christian man does that he is dishonoring Christ, his head.

On the other hand, if a woman does not have a covering (in this first-century Christian setting) she dishonors her head, her husband. The reason for that was dramatically obvious in Corinth. In this city, the most licentious city of the times, the only women who did not wear veils were the temple prostitutes. Any woman, therefore, who appeared on the public streets without a veil was opening herself up to the suspicion that she was available to any man who wanted to pay her price. It was indeed disgraceful, shameful, for a woman to appear in public, and especially to minister the Word in a Christian assembly, without that sign of acknowledgment of the principle of headship in her life.

Notice that Paul says, "if it is disgraceful for a woman to be shorn or shaven, let her wear a veil." Mark the "if." In some cultures it would not be disgraceful for a woman to be uncovered. It is not today. It is no longer shameful that a woman does not wear a hat in church. It is only where it is disgraceful, where that is the usual interpretation put upon being uncovered, that this applies. If it is not disgraceful then it is another matter. But where it is disgraceful, as in Corinth, Paul says if she does not want to wear the sign of a relationship under headship, then she ought to go the whole way and shave her head like a prostitute because that is what she is proclaiming herself to be by her refusal to wear the veil and submit to custom.

Back to Creation

Now immediately the apostle follows this with an explanation. Here we come to the heart of the passage. He tells us *why* all this is true,

> For a man ought not to cover his head, since he is the image and glory of God; but woman is the glory of man. (For man was not made from woman, but woman from man. Neither was man created for woman, but woman for man) (vv. 7–9).

That is a crucial paragraph, and one that we must understand fully. You will notice the apostle does not base his reasons on any local custom. He goes back to creation to establish this. The principle of headship is something true from the beginning of mankind. Paul does just as Jesus did on the subject of divorce. He does not bother with the interpretations and amendments that came by the law of Moses, but he goes back to God's original created order. He says that in the beginning man was made in the image and glory of God. An image is the full manifestation of something. In this case it is God himself. Man was made in God's image in order that any creature, looking at a man, would see the likeness, the very nature of God. That is the true dignity of humanity.

What we must bear clearly in mind is that Genesis states that man was made in the image of God before the two sexes were separated. Adam was created first, and it was said of Adam, before Eve was separated from him, that man is the image and glory of God. This means that the woman shares the image and the glory of God equally with the man. They are both included when it is said that man was made in the image and the glory of God. That is why, in Genesis 5 (not Genesis 1 now, but Genesis 5) it says that God created them in the beginning male and female and he named *them* Man. Therefore, the female bears equally with the male the image and glory of God. The male, however, is called upon to manifest a different aspect of the glory of God from the woman. We shall understand that better when we understand the meaning of glory.

What is glory? As it is used here, the word refers to something in which one takes delight. We have often sung the hymn, "In the Cross of Christ I Glory." What do we mean by that? We mean the cross is something in which we find supreme delight. It is that principle of life by which we see ourselves cut off from the old Adamic life and freed from the control of sin and death—thus set free to be the men and women God intended us to be. Paul could write to the Thessalonians and say, "Who is our crown of rejoicing? Are you not our *glory* and our joy?" So used, this verse tells us that when man was created he was made to reflect the nature of God and in that God takes great delight. He delights in mankind and this is what the male is to represent. That glory of God is to be publicly and openly manifested and this is why the man must not wear a veil. He is not to cover God's creative glory. He is to be unveiled so that the glory of God in creation should be visibly manifest to everyone.

You see this beautifully in the life of Jesus. Everywhere he went he demonstrated the love of God for mankind. Even though the race had turned aside and was far from what it ought to be, everywhere in the ministry of Jesus you see him pouring forth the love of God for man. That is what drew people by great multitudes to hear his words. In him they caught a glimpse of the glory and delight that God takes in humanity and they longed to find the way back to the enjoyment of that delight. Thus in the opening words of John's Gospel it says, "the Word became flesh and dwelt among us *and we beheld his glory.*" This is the glory that a man, a male, is called upon to manifest in the ministry of the Word. He is not to be veiled because he is proclaiming that open delight which God takes in the creation of mankind.

A Private Glory

But woman is the glory of the man. It is in the woman that the man finds his delight. If you do not believe that, just watch a couple of teenagers in love. Woman is the delight of man. The apostle is now dealing with the woman as having been separated from the man. The distinction which obtained when God took Adam's rib and made of it a woman and brought her to man now comes into focus. It involves a private, intimate glory—that intimacy which a man finds in his wife, the intimacy of sexual relationship and of shared love. It is something hidden and private; therefore it is to be symbolized by a veil. It marks something protected, something marked out for a single individual's use. Thus the veil is not a mark of subjection, as many of the commentators say of this passage. It is a mark of intimacy, of privacy, voluntarily assumed by the woman. She is not forced to give herself to the man, she deliberately chooses to do so, but from then on she is marked out as belonging to him. The nearest equivalent of this in our day is the wedding ring. A wedding ring marks a woman as belonging to another, already claimed. She has given herself freely and voluntarily to a man and she is his, not in a mechanical or merely legal sense, but because she has already surrendered her right to herself to him.

That is always the meaning of the veil in the Eastern world. It still is today. A veiled woman walks down a street of an Oriental city today and she is telling the whole world "I am not for sale; I do not belong to anyone but my husband; I am his." In wearing a veil a woman also gives testimony to the existence of another aspect of the glory of God, the intimacy of delight that is achieved only through redemption. When we enter, by faith in Jesus Christ, into the new birth, we discover a glory of God beyond creation. It is redemptive glory. We all have experienced it if we are Christians. We know the ecstasy of fellowship with God, of worship, of experiencing the beautiful and intimate love relationship of a bride with her bridegroom, described in that marvelous passage in Ephesians 5. That is what a woman manifests in her public ministry when she wears a veil. She is symbolizing, that intimate delight which God has in a redeemed mankind. This is surely why Paul goes on to point out the unique purpose for the creation of woman.

> For man was not made from woman, but woman from man. Neither was man created for woman, but woman for man (vv. 8, 9).

Woman was taken *from* man that she might share fully his nature. Man and woman are not two different kinds of beings. They do not represent two species of human life. They have differences, but they are of the same basic nature. This is what is meant by woman being taken from man. But, in addition, she is brought *to* man. She was brought to him that she might be ("for") him. This, I think, is the key thought involved in headship. She is *for* her husband; she is behind him, backing him up; she is supportive of him; she wants him to succeed and she is deeply involved in the process. She is undergirding him in every way she can, and finding delight in doing so, that together they might achieve the objectives which his head, Christ, has set before them.

Now that is God's ideal of marriage. In turn, the male is to discover the secrets God has put into his wife and seek to develop her so that she will be all that she is capable of being. In doing so he is but advancing his own objectives. This is the argument of Ephesians 5. They are one and no man hates his own flesh. If he hurts his wife he hurts himself; if he ignores her, he is ignoring half of his own life. There is no way he can achieve the fullness of his manhood in marriage apart from working at developing and encouraging his wife to utilize all the gifts and abilities God has put in her.

The reciprocal relationship so frequently appearing in Scripture is what creates the beauty of every wedding. The marriage ceremony has for centuries recognized that she is giving herself to him, and he promises to treat that gift with kindness, tenderness and loving care. He is also giving himself to her; but primarily she is giving herself to him. He is responsible to cherish that gift as the most valuable gift any human has ever given him, and to protect it and guard it. She is basically saying to him those beautiful words in the Book of Ruth, "Where you go I will go. Where you live I will live. Your people shall be my people and your God, my God." Now if a man or a woman is not willing to assume his or her proper role in marriage then they should by all means stay single, but when marriage occurs that is what God has designed.

Authority on Her Head

Paul goes on to add two more important words here from the argument of creation: first, *authority (to minister)*

That is why a woman ought to have a veil on her head, because of the angels (v. 10).

What does he mean by that? Unfortunately the RSV editors have obscured this by translating the word Paul uses as "veil." But here he changes the word, and uses the word *authority*. "That is why a woman ought to have *authority* on her head, because of the angels." Authority to do what? Surely it is what he has already mentioned, what the whole passage is about: a woman ministering the Word in public. The authority for her to do so is her recognition of the principle of headship. She is to declare that she does not pray or preach apart from her husband and thus she is to wear a veil which, in that culture, was the sign of such a voluntary partnership.

She is to do so, Paul says, "because of the angels." Now that is somewhat obscure and difficult to interpret, but in a culture where unveiled women were regarded as idolators and prostitutes it would be an offense to the angels present in a Christian service for a woman to openly flaunt custom and deny the principle of headship. Angels, we are told, are ministering spirits, sent forth to minister to those who are heirs of salvation. They were present at creation and thus understand the principle of headship. Isaiah 6 indicates they veil their faces when they worship before the throne of God, and so are concerned to preserve the worship of humans from any practice that would deny the distinctives which the sexes are to manifest.

In the next two verses Paul balances all this with a strong statement of the equality of men and women in marriage,

(Nevertheless, in the Lord woman is not independent of man nor man of woman; for as woman was made from man, so man is now born of woman. And all things are from God) (vv. 11, 12).

Here is a positive statement of the full equality (as persons) of men and women. There is no inferiority involved. No matter what distortions may have crept in to reduce woman to an inferior status, nevertheless, *in the Lord,* the original intent of God is restored. Paul carefully declares that man and woman cannot exist without each other. They are equal as persons, distinct as sexes, functioning in a divinely given order which is to be freely accepted by the woman, to demonstrate to all the delight of God in his creation and redemption of mankind. If we will carefully think that through we will find it is a very powerful argument for equality of persons and yet distinctiveness of roles.

Now let us quickly handle the problem of hair:

> Judge for yourselves; is it proper for a woman to pray to God with her head uncovered? Does not nature itself teach you that for a man to wear long hair is degrading to him, but if a woman has long hair, it is her pride? For her hair is given to her for a covering (vv. 13–15).

This is really a second argument the apostle gives to support the rightness of wearing a veil. He argues now from nature. Not only does God's intent in creation sustain the principle of headship, but nature also illustrates it. Many have struggled over this passage. I have, myself, for many years. What is there about nature that indicates that a man with long hair dishonors himself while a woman with long hair is honored? It is not mere intuition, as some suggest, for such an intuition is not universal. But there is a principle that science has come to recognize as true, and it has been true from the very beginning of the race, as far as we can tell. That is the factor of baldness. Geneticists tell us that it takes two genes in a woman to produce baldness but only one in a man. Some women do get bald, but it is very rare. Here is a natural factor that has been functioning since the race began which does, indeed, display the very thing that Paul declares. Did you ever see a bald old man with long hair? It is a disgrace! Long hair is usually stringy when it is sparse and with his shining dome sticking up above it makes him look ridiculous. Almost all men, as they grow older, tend to show some degree of baldness, and the older they grow the more ridiculous long hair looks. A young man can get away with long hair, but an older man cannot. Thus there is a factor in nature which demonstrates what Paul claims. Tradition tells us that Paul himself was bald and perhaps this statement comes out of his own experience.

But a woman is a different story. Nature demonstrates that a woman has been given more beautiful hair than men in order that she might more easily manifest the principle of headship. It is remarkable that this was written after all Paul's insistence about wearing a veil in Corinth. Now Paul says that her hair was given to her for a covering. Here is the beauty of the Scripture. This was not written just for Corinth or even for the first century, but for any and every age. In a culture where the wearing of veils is *not* a custom, then a woman's long hair (longer than her husband's) is an adequate expression of the principle of headship. Surely this will help us today when the wearing of veils has lost all its original significance. But because in the Roman world veil-wearing was still the custom, he concludes the passage with these words.

> If any one is disposed to be contentious, we recognize no other practice, nor do the churches of God (v. 16).

There is no need to argue the point, he says. The universal custom in the Roman world was for the woman to declare this principle of headship by wearing a veil; therefore there is no point in arguing about it. It was such a widespread custom among the churches that anyone not doing so was immediately open to disapprobation. Yet where that was not the case then the woman's hair, longer than her husband's, was adequate testimony to the principle of headship.

Now what does this passage say to us? It says, first: Men, by all means take your responsibility as spiritual leaders in the home. You have a responsibility to your head (Christ) to know the Word of God and to see that it shapes and molds the atmosphere, the climate of your home. That is your responsibility. Women, your responsibility is to follow your husband in these matters and to support him and encourage him. If you are unwilling to do that, do not get married, but if you marry, support your husband's efforts toward a godly family. Back him up when he moves in those directions. Let him know you are behind him, for him, and supportive of him. That is the way you will find fulfillment in marriage. Consider this remarkable testimony from a well-known author. In a recent interview of Taylor Caldwell by *Family Weekly*, she was asked if the nine-hour TV production of her book, *Captains and the Kings*, would bring her solid satisfaction. Her answer was,

> There is no solid satisfaction in any career for a woman like myself. There is no home, no true freedom, no hope, no joy, no expectation for tomorrow, no contentment. I would rather cook a meal for a man and bring him his slippers and feel myself in the protection of his arms than have all the citations and awards and honors I have received worldwide, including the Ribbon of Legion of Honor and my property and my bank accounts. They mean nothing to me. And I am only one among the millions of sad women like myself.

Third, when women minister the Word in a public place let them do so with humility and respect for the leadership of the church. That is what is involved in the principle of headship.

A Second Tradition

The apostle Paul deals now, at some length with the institution of the Lord's Supper. What is the main thing in the Christian life? Clearly, all through the Scriptures, both Old and New Testament, the main thing is what the person and work of Jesus Christ really mean to you. I do not mean what you say he means to you when you are talking about your faith, or what you sing about when you sing the hymns of the church. I mean what Jesus really means to you when the hour comes for you to make a decision for right against wrong, or for good against evil, and what he means to you when you are under pressure and tempted to explode with anger, or succumb to lust, or whatever.

A Mirror Held Up

It is fitting that Paul ends this long section where he has been dealing with the troubles going on at Corinth by holding up a mirror, in effect, before these people and allowing them to see how they were behaving at the Lord's Table. Nothing is more revealing than to see what your attitude is when you come to this central act of Christian worship, and this is what Paul is doing.

In this section, beginning with verse 17, he is showing them that they were approaching the Lord's Table with a totally wrong spirit. There were two things, he says, that were wrong. First, they were dividing up into very destructive divisions, cliques, within the church:

> But in the following instructions I do not commend you, because when you come together it is not for the better but for the worse. For, in the first place, when you assemble as a church, I hear that there are divisions among you; and I partly believe it, [*Actually that should be translated: "I believe it, in part"*] for there must be factions among you in order that those who are genuine among you may be recognized (vv. 17–19).

When Paul speaks of the church "coming together," or "assembling as a church," he is not primarily talking about a Sunday morning church service. He has in view the *agape*, the feast of love and of sharing. This grew out of that atmosphere in the early church (described in the Book of Acts) where no one counted anything as belonging to himself alone but shared with others the resources and riches that God had provided so that no one was left out. This rapidly grew into a common meal which they all shared together. We would call it a "pot luck" supper. (I do not like that term because I do not believe in luck and I am sensitive to the word *pot!* I prefer "multiple-choice dinners." They are wonderful occasions where everyone brings something, and all share together.) This is what the early church was doing, too. It was a perfectly proper and beautiful thing to do, but unfortunately, here in Corinth it was being spoiled by cliques, by divisions among them. The cliques and divisions that Paul mentions earlier in this letter had ruined the gathering of the church together, so that he could say, as he does here, "It is not for the better that you come together, but for the worse." "You are actually injuring one another and destroying the character of the church by the way you are conducting yourselves at these love feasts which terminate in the celebration of the Lord's table together."

In verses 18 and 19 Paul reminds them that it is not wrong to have differences in a church: "There must indeed be factions (really the word is *heresies*) among you." He is not surprised at that. Everyone does not have the same point of view, or the same background; everyone has not had the same training and upbringing, and so there are bound to be points of view that are different, and that is normal, Paul says. In fact, it is healthy for it allows those who are approved, who are mature, to become manifest.

About a year ago I was speaking to a group of youth leaders in the state of Missouri. We had an open question-and-answer session, and one of the things they asked me about was our Body Life service. I had told them that we encourage people to share freely, that anyone who wants to can stand up and speak on any subject. Now some of them were rather threatened by that, and someone asked me, "Are you not afraid that somebody will say something that is false, and heresies will spread in the church?" I told him that we do not see it this way. Then I quoted this verse, "There must indeed be heresies among you." "We like heresies," I said. "We encourage them to be expressed because they are great teaching opportunities. How are you going to know who in your congregation is able to handle heresies unless they have some heresies to work on?"

That is what the apostle is recognizing here. There is nothing wrong with differences of opinion. They ought to be freely aired, because that gives the opportunity for those who are instructed in the things of God and the Word of God, and who understand the mind of God through the teaching of the Word, to answer these and help people with these struggles. Paul says he understands that, but unfortunately in Corinth it had gone much further. No one had answered these heresies; no one had controlled these utterances, so they had broken into harmful divisions in their love feasts and were creating chaos within the church.

Hurting the Cause of Christ

Paul goes on to describe the disorderly practices that came from this:

> When you meet together, it is not the Lord's supper that you eat. For in eating, each one goes ahead with his own meal, and one is hungry and another is drunk. What! Do you not have houses to eat and drink in? Or do you despise the church of God and humiliate those who have nothing? What shall I say to you? Shall I commend you in this? No, I will not (vv. 20–22).

Clearly he describes here the harm and the danger that was coming from these divisions among them. In effect, he says, "When you get together for your love feasts you cannot call that the Lord's Supper even though it terminates in the familiar ritual that we now call the Lord's Table. The Lord's Supper is an expression of the unity of the church, and what you are doing is a far cry from that. You are acting selfishly with one another."

Paul goes on to detail this. Some were bringing a lot of food and gathering in their own little family group to eat it, while others who had hardly anything, or nothing at all, were left hungry. Paul says, "That's an absolute parody of what the church ought to be. Instead of caring for one another you are excluding one another. Even worse, some of you are eating and drinking so much that, unfortunately, you are actually coming to the Lord's Table intoxicated."

This is hard for us to visualize, but that is what was happening. (I remember Dr. Donald Grey Barnhouse being asked on one occasion, "Don't you believe that the wine the early Christians drank was really grape juice?" In his brusque way he said, "Well, they got drunk on it at Corinth.") But even worse, in the eyes of the apostle, some of them seemed to shrug off any rebuke along this line. They were indifferent; they exhibited a careless defiance of the need to minister to one another.

When Paul asks, "Do you not have houses to eat and drink in?" he is not saying it is wrong to have church suppers (multiple-choice dinners) together. What he means is, "If all you are coming together for is to eat and drink you can do that at home. If you are not going to manifest a concern and care for hungry people among you, then you might just as well stay home and eat and drink there. When you come together you ought to be concerned about the needs and the hungers of all." Thus, fragmented, selfish, uncaring, indifferent to human needs, the church was hurting the cause of Christ rather than helping it.

By sharp contrast, the apostle now goes on to remind them of what he had taught them about the Lord's Table:

> For I received from the Lord what I also delivered to you, that the Lord Jesus on the night when he was betrayed took bread, and when he had given thanks, he broke it, and said, "This is my body which is for you. Do this in remembrance of me." In the same way also the cup, after supper, saying, "This cup is the new covenant in my blood. Do this, as often as you drink it, in remembrance of me." For as often as you eat this bread and drink the cup, you proclaim the Lord's death until he comes (vv. 23–26).

Paul makes an amazing claim in verse 23 when he says, "I received from the Lord what I also delivered to you." By these words the apostle clearly means that the One who told him what went on in the Upper Room on that dark betrayal night was Jesus himself.

In the letter to the Galatians Paul states that he did not learn what he knew of Christ and Christianity from any man. No apostle taught it to him. He had never read the Gospels of Matthew, Mark, Luke or John. They had not even been written yet. And Paul had never been told what went on in the Upper Room by any of the other disciples either. In fact, he uses here the same language he uses later in chapter 15 where he says that he delivered unto them *the gospel* which he also received from the Lord, which in Galatians he says clearly he did not receive from any other man. Therefore, we have here what amounts to the earliest description of the Lord's Table when it was instituted in the Upper Room, coming from none other than the lips of Jesus himself.

What the apostle passes on to them, and to us, is our Lord's emphasis upon two remarkable symbols, the bread and the cup. Deliberately, after the Passover feast, Jesus took the bread, and when he had broken it in order to make it available to all the eleven disciples (Judas having gone out), he said to them, "This is my body." Now unfortunately some have taken that to mean that he was teaching that the bread becomes his body, but I think it is very clear, as you look at the story of the Upper Room, that he meant it in a symbolic sense. If it was literal then there were two bodies of Christ present in the Upper

Room, the one in which he lived and by which he held the bread, and the bread itself. But clearly our Lord means this as a symbol. "This represents my body which is *for* you." Not "broken for you," as the Authorized Version has it. That is not an accurate rendering. It is not broken for us. In fact, the Scriptures tell us that not a bone of his body was broken. Rather it is intended for us to *live* on; that is the symbolism. Thus when we gather and take the bread of the Lord's Table, break it and pass it among ourselves, we are reminding ourselves that Jesus is our life; he is the One by whom we live. As Paul says, in Galatians 2, "I am crucified with Christ: nevertheless I live; yet not I, but Christ liveth in me: and the life which I now live in the flesh I live by the faith of the Son of God, who loved me, and gave himself for me."

This is what the bread symbolizes: that he is to be our power by which we obey the demands of the Word of God to love one another, to forgive one another, to be tender and merciful, kind and courteous to one another, to not return evil for evil but to pray for those who persecute us and mistrust us and misuse us. His life in us enables us to be what God asks us to be. We live by means of Christ. Jesus said it himself in John 6, "so he that eats me, even he shall live by means of me."

Some time ago, one of our teenagers wrote a song, and these verses are part of it:

> You brought me back to yourself,
> I had tried to go my own way,
> Thinking I didn't need your love,
> But you showed me the light of day.
>
> I need you to keep me strong,
> I need you to keep me from falling,
> I want to keep growing closer to you,
> I want always to hear you calling.

That captures very accurately what the bread symbolizes to us.

The End of a Life

Following that, our Lord took the cup. The wine of the cup symbolizes his blood which he said is the blood of the new covenant, the new arrangement for living that God has made, by which the old life is ended. That is what blood always means; blood marks the end of a life. The old life in which we were dependent upon ourselves and lived for ourselves and wanted only to be the center of attention is over. That is what the cup means. We agree to that; we are no longer to live for ourselves. Therefore, when we take the cup and drink it, we are publicly proclaiming we agree with that sentence of death upon our old life and believe the Christian life is a continual experience of *life* coming *out* of death.

Power with God only comes when we die to the wisdom and the power of man. We give up one in order that the other may be manifest within us. "God cannot be glorified," we are saying, "as long as we insist on being glorified." Thus we are surrendering our right to take credit for things, surrendering our right to have people praise us and affirm us, so that God, who is working in us, may have that glory and that praise.

The cup is a beautiful picture of what Jesus said of himself, "Except a corn of wheat fall into the ground and die, it abides alone." I do not think anything is more descriptive of the emptiness of life than that phrase "abides alone"—lonely, restless, bored, miserable, unhappy. This is the life which tries to live for itself and its own needs and its own rights, but the Christian life is one in which that is freely and voluntarily surrendered. And if the corn of wheat falls into the ground and dies, Jesus says, it will bring forth much fruit.

Thus, every celebration of the Lord's Table tells us the old, old story all over again: we are consenting to follow our Lord, to go to death as he went to death that we might rise again in the new life of the spirit. And this, as Paul tells us, is to go on through the whole age, from the first coming until he comes again. This is a constantly repeated feast by which we, in symbol, tell over and over the heart of our Christian faith: the old life dies that the new life might live.

In the last paragraph of this section Paul makes very clear how seriously God himself regards the Lord's Table:

> Whoever, therefore, eats the bread or drinks the cup of the Lord in an unworthy manner will be guilty of profaning the body and blood of the Lord. Let a man examine himself, and so eat of the bread and drink of the cup. For any one who eats and drinks without discerning the body eats and drinks judgment upon himself (vv. 27–29).

These are sobering words; they indicate that God himself guards the Table from unworthy partaking. Now that is, of course, the very reason why Paul has just been rebuking these Christians at Corinth. They were partaking in an unworthy manner because they were careless, selfish, and indifferent to the needs of others. They were coming to the Lord's Table in a kind of empty ritual, just going through it in a mechanical, ceremonial way. That, Paul says, is a dangerous practice, because it is acting as though the death and life of Jesus mean nothing to us. We become sharers of the guilt of those who put the Lord to death when we participate without true heart-interest and heart-concern in the Lord's Table. Therefore, according to the apostle, a proper participation involves careful self-examination. That is why he says "let a man examine himself (or herself) earnestly and so let him eat of the bread and drink of the cup."

The word *examine* means literally, "to qualify" oneself. In chapter 10 Paul said he buffeted his body and pummeled it so that, having preached to others, he himself would not be "disqualified," set aside. Now that is the negative of this term; therefore, someone who examines himself is *qualifying* himself to eat the Table of the Lord. How do you do that? Well, it does not mean to live an absolutely flawless, perfect life, because no one can do that. Even with all the help the Spirit of God gives us, there are failures and weaknesses, times of frustration and outright, sometimes deliberate, evil.

What it means, of course, is that you must handle your sin honestly. Do not try to cover it over; do not try to persuade yourself that it is not there. Admit it; call it what God calls it and repent—that is, change your mind about it. Bring it to God and let him cleanse you. David writes in Psalm 51, "The sacrifices of God are a broken spirit: a broken and a contrite heart, O God, thou wilt not despise." When you look at the things that are wrong and say, "Lord, I'm sorry. Those things are wrong. I must not act that way any more," then you have qualified yourself to participate in the Table of the Lord. That is what he says. You have proved yourself in the right way, and, Paul adds, "so let him eat."

Some people even then refuse to eat, passing by the elements in what is basically a cop-out. They think that God will bring some subsequent judgment only if they eat. But God pays no attention to surface things. He reads the hearts, and what he is after is a heart which does not lie to itself, that is honest about its misdeeds and is willing to put away a wrong spirit. As Paul says to the Ephesians, "Let all bitterness, and wrath, and anger, and clamour, and evil speaking, be put away from you." Attitudes of lust and of selfishness, and misdeeds of dishonesty and lying are what we face when we come to the Lord's Table. We acknowledge them and thank God for his cleansing grace and then partake, forgiven by the grace of God. That is why Paul goes on to add in verse 29, "For any one who eats and drinks without discerning the body eats and drinks judgment upon himself."

"Discerning the body" means two things. First, it means understanding the meaning of the symbols. The body of Christ is involved—his death on the cross was for us, and his life is made available to us. But then it means also our concern and care for others who are members with us in this body. We are members one of another, and we are to recognize those ties. The Corinthians were forgetting this when they ignored the hungry among them.

Stop and Think

In the next two verses the apostle indicates that God guards this Table by using physical judgment.

> That is why many of you are weak and ill, and some have died. But if we judged ourselves truly, we should not be judged. But when we are judged by the Lord, we are chastened so that we may not be condemned along with the world (vv. 30–32).

God knows that pain often makes us stop and think. Have you found that to be true? Many of us have suddenly become aware that we have been drifting away from our closeness with Christ because we have been laid aside for a time, maybe with nothing more than a bad cold, but it gives us a chance to think and to review our lives. That is God's hand. That is what was happening at Corinth. Some were weak, some were sickly, because God was enabling them to take a look at themselves. It was a red flag of warning saying, "Watch out now. You are going too fast. You are being tripped up by the world around you. You are reflecting its attitudes and its reactions and adopting some of its ways. Watch out. Slow down. Think it through." And, as Paul says, some of them had even died; that is, they had rejected God's tender, loving warnings; they had persisted in their evil to the point where they were "disqualified" as we saw in chapter 10. This still happens today. God is no different. Some among us, perhaps, are weak and sickly because we need time to think through what is happening in our lives. And if we refuse to do so, God may take us home.

Not all sickness comes from the disciplinary hand of God. Sometimes it can be a ministry which God deliberately gives us to open up a door that nothing else would open. Do not think that every time you are sick it may be the judging hand of God, but it is always a time to ask yourself, "Is God trying to slow me down? In his loving concern for me does he see me drifting into something dangerous that I ought to stop and rethink—my relationships with others, my attitudes about life, habits that I am forming? Are these wrong or right?" The apostle tells us if we truly judged ourselves God would not have to judge us. Therefore, when sickness or an accident occurs, take a good look, a careful look. Be honest with yourself. You can avoid the chastening of God by honestly dealing with yourself, because God will always give you a chance to change. But if those chances are passed by then God must judge you further to make clear what is happening to you. If he does, do not see it as something terrible and evil that God has sent into your life to punish you. Oh, no; Hebrews tells us, "whom the Lord loves he chastens." A loving Father is simply putting up some barriers and saying, "Look, you are getting into trouble. Now stop and take a look." It is his love that has brought this into your life.

The apostle implies by this that if you, as a professed Christian, can go on week after week and month after month doing something wrong—living in a relationship or holding an attitude that you know is wrong—and nothing ever happens to you in the way of judgment, then it is likely you are not a Christian at all. You may well be headed for that final condemnation which the whole world will ultimately face. But, Paul says, when judgment comes it is the loving hand of your heavenly Father stopping you and telling you, "Look, you are mine. I will not have you involved in that condemnation with the world. You need to straighten up some things in your life, and this is your opportunity to do so."

The last two verses simply indicate God's concern that this be done in such a way as to bring out acts of love and courtesy for one another:

> So then, my brethren, when you come together to eat, wait for one another—if any one is hungry, let him eat at home—lest you come together to be condemned. About the other things I will give directions when I come (vv. 33, 34).

God's purpose in any form of judgment of his children is that they might begin to act differently and be more thoughtful and courteous toward one another, especially in their immediate families. That is where this has to begin—not with your friends but with your family. When he says, "wait for one another," he does not necessarily mean at the Lord's Table, though that is a good thing to do. What he means is, "Be aware of the needs and the problems of others and do something to meet them, to help in that area, so that when you come together your meetings are not a curse but a blessing, a delight to everyone who comes. Your attitudes and your reactions with one another are right, and love prevails within the assembly."

Then Paul says, "That is the central thing. There are some other little things that I will set right when I come, but those can wait. The important thing is that you begin to act out of the central meaning of the Christian life. The old selfish ways are ended, the new life which thinks of others is to be expressed. It is these truths that the bread and wine reflect."

17
—
The Spirit's Point

Chapter 12 of 1 Corinthians begins a new major division in this letter. Perhaps it would be helpful to briefly survey the letter, and thus remind ourselves of what we have covered. It is an easy letter to remember because it has only four divisions. First, there is an introduction of nine verses, which contains the key verse of 1 Corinthians. In fact, it is the key to the whole Christian life. The apostle says right at the beginning,

God is faithful, by whom you were called into the fellowship of his Son, Jesus Christ our Lord (1:9).

The purpose of the Christian life is to learn to walk day by day, moment by moment, in the fellowship of the Son of God. That is where strength comes and where godliness arises; that is where love, grace, peace and joy are released to us. After that introduction, the apostle immediately begins to deal with *the carnalities:* the things that threaten and hinder fellowship with Jesus Christ. There are many of these in this Corinthian church, but they can be gathered under three main headings. First, the apostle deals with *pride and its consequences*— the spirit of self-reliance that wants to leave God on the periphery of life and handle everything itself. That is the deadly enemy of Christian faith, and yet many an individual is afflicted by this terrible pride of self-sufficiency.

Then Paul deals with a second major area, that is, *lust and its problems.* Here we saw his practical, faithful dealing with immorality and sexual license—a very forthright passage and an extremely helpful section. Third, he deals with _life and its dangers_, and here we learned that life is to be lived in the midst of danger; that we are not to hide ourselves from it, but are to learn how to handle the dangers in a way that will enable us to resist temptation and to glorify God.

That brings us to our present chapter, in which the apostle turns from _the carnalities_ to what he himself calls _the spiritualities_.

> Now concerning spiritual gifts, brethren [_actually, the word is spiritualities, or spiritual matters_], I do not want you to be uninformed (v. 1).

Beginning here through chapter 15, we find the apostle's teaching concerning the great positive forces of the Spirit which help us handle the carnalities and thus correct the wrong things that hinder fellowship with Jesus Christ. Chapter 12 will deal with the first of these spiritualities, i.e., the _gifts of the Spirit_ to the body of Christ. Then chapter 13 (the great love chapter) deals with the _fruit of the Spirit_, while chapter 14 deals with _order by the Spirit_ in the Christian assembly. Chapter 15, the resurrection chapter, deals with _glory by the Spirit_. So all this has to do with life in the Spirit, the spiritualities _(pneumatikoi)_.

The closing section of the letter takes up what I call _the practicalities_, matters such as the collection, how to relate to leadership, and so on. That is the whole sweep of the letter in four major sections.

Let us begin with _the spiritualities_ in chapter 12. This is an area which is of great interest to many today. You will recognize that when we start talking about spiritual gifts and the functioning of the body of Christ, we get into areas that are subject to much controversy and disagreement—especially concerning the gift of tongues, which will come before us here. It is amazing to me how quickly interest is aroused when you introduce a discussion on the gift of tongues. You can hardly discuss some Christian leader today before eyebrows begin to go up and people say to themselves, "Does he, or doesn't he?" Well, we will come to the gift of tongues in due course, for it is one of many spiritual gifts that Paul calls the "charismata." But before he comes to that there are three verses which are extremely important to understanding this section. Much argument on the charismata would be saved if people would give heed to these first three verses of the chapter. They deal with the unmistakable mark of religious error, as opposed to the unmistakable mark of religious truth.

When a religious group uses Christian terminology and upholds the Bible as the great Word of divine wisdom, seeming to be Christian in every way, how can you tell whether or not it is a cult that might end up in some tragic Jonestown? Here is the answer! Paul invites these Corinthians to look back and remember their life before they were Christian, and he says to them,

> You know that when you were heathen, you were led astray to dumb idols, however you may have been moved (v. 2).

In that day, the cultural norms of Corinth involved the actual worship of images. It was widespread in the first-century world and was the normal path that idolatry would take. Today, the images are gone but the idolatry remains, and such idolatry is still the mark of religious error. We have already seen in the study of this letter that idolatry is any concept or thing that begins to possess us, that exercises control over us. Thus, a perfectly proper thing can become an idol to us if it begins to possess us. But human beings were made to be possessed only by God, and that alone is a proper possession. Anything that replaces God becomes idolatry.

The Influence of Other Spirits

Notice that the apostle says that idolatry involves a process of being "led astray," which suggests a control factor. We have already learned in this letter that behind idolatry is a form of mind control exercised by demons. Any view of life which does not involve the recognition of wicked spirits is a quite different view than that of Jesus and the apostles. Because of these wicked spirits, all forms of idolatry (including those which we think of today as rather harmless ones), become destructive of human life.

This demonic activity is evident in what are frequently regarded as harmless things. It is the cause of emptiness, loneliness, the boredom of materialism or of hedonism, the mindless pursuit of pleasure. One of the revealing statistics in this regard is that suicides increase rapidly in number at Christmas. This happens because people, hoping to satisfy the aching of their hearts, a strong desire for something fulfilling, go on a binge of materialism. They find sooner or later that it is all empty. Perhaps we have all felt this. How lonely one can be with a host of Christmas gifts that mean nothing! How cold and boring life can become! Now that is a form of death, and it comes from the mind control exercised by demonic beings who are affecting the thinking of men and women all over the world. From such emptiness, Paul says, these Corinthian believers were delivered by faith in Christ. They came to life, love, peace, joy, warmth and beauty once again. He now invites them to think back to see how every path they were on led to that kind of death and to that kind of mind control. We must remind ourselves of the same.

It is the universal testimony of Scripture that man is subject to the influence of other spirits besides the Spirit of God, and Paul is giving us a way to recognize them. They can use religious jargon, they can employ biblical terminology and practices, but they will always lead eventually to some form of idolatry.

Here are the marks of idolatry, and therefore, the marks of a cult. First, some personality is always central. Some leader lifts himself up as the focus of interest and attention, and people, following him, find themselves having to worship him (or her). Second, some degree of regimentation and control is involved. To enforce the personality cult, certain demands must be made, certain limitations imposed, and certain rights must be given up. The power of the personality in charge is such that he or she enables people voluntarily to consent to give up their rightful liberties. That is always true of religious error. Third, there comes certain claims of special and unique powers. Every group must feel that they have a unique mission; a special authority has been committed to them that marks them out as different from others. Together with that, invariably there comes (fourth) a stress on money and finances as the central power of a group. Money is seen in terms of power as providing opportunities to fulfill desires and goals, and nothing can be done without it.

In the true Christian church money plays a part, but it is not the central emphasis. Anytime even a Christian group begins to talk about needing money before they can do something for God, you can know they are being influenced by demonic concepts. You do not need money to do something for God. Anyone can start wherever he is and, using the gifts of God and the power of God working through him, money will flow in when it is needed. But it is never the central thing.

The final and fifth mark of religious idolatry is that it creates unending jealousy and strife. Cults are constantly afflicted with internal dissensions, infighting, arguing, struggling for control, and cutting down of one another, thus demonstrating a total absence of all we seek to uphold in a Christian assembly: love and affection for one another.

To Exalt Jesus Christ

Now in contrast to that, the apostle helps us to recognize the true mark of the Spirit of God at work. People are asking everywhere today: "How do you know that the Spirit of God is really behind some of the manifestations that we're running into? Is the true Spirit of God behind the great healing meetings of today, or the demonstrations of tongues, or some of the other claims of religious leaders today?" Well, the apostle gives us the sign of true spirituality:

> Therefore, I want you to understand that no one speaking by the Spirit of God ever says, "Jesus be cursed!" and no one can say "Jesus is Lord" except by the Holy Spirit (v. 3).

That is how you can recognize the Spirit of God at work. He came into this world to do one thing—to exalt Jesus Christ. That is all he ever does. Everything the Spirit does aims at that goal and that point.

Paul puts it both negatively and positively here. First, negatively: no one who speaks by the Spirit of God ever demeans or in any way diminishes the centrality of Christ in the Christian life or in the Christian faith. The Person and the work of Jesus are always the central thing. I am sure that few people today would ever say the words, "Jesus be cursed." Perhaps there are groups that would say that; some of the Satanist groups might. But I am equally sure that in the first century it was common, especially in the synagogues and in Jewish organizations where Christ was seen as a threat to Judaism. It may be that Paul is referring to that time when he was a young, zealous rabbi, and may have forced Christians to say these words. In his defense before Agrippa, recorded in the Book of Acts, he says he "forced many among them to blaspheme," and it may be that he tried to get Christians to say, "Jesus be cursed."

But you do not have to say the words to fulfill what Paul is describing here. Anyone, for instance, who says that Jesus Christ is nothing but a man is virtually saying, "Jesus be cursed," because according to the teaching of the Bible the whole human race is cursed; the curse of Adam's evil has come upon us all and twisted our inner life to make us totally self-centered—that is the curse. Everyone is born with an inner drive to be the center of attention and to have the universe revolve around him. Thus when you say that Jesus was nothing but a man, a great teacher perhaps, a moral leader, you are saying that he, too, is part of this cursed race, that he was not free from its taint, although in the biblical record it is the Virgin Birth that preserved him from the curse of sin. He was thus *not* under the curse of Adam; that is why he could be our Deliverer from it. Therefore, all teaching that demeans Jesus, that denies his Deity, that says he is not our Redeemer but only a great teacher, is, in effect, saying "Jesus be cursed."

But Paul also puts it positively. When the Spirit is at work he always seeks to exalt and magnify Christ the Lord. "Jesus is Lord" was the basic creed of the early church. The Romans tried to exalt Caesar as Lord, and in the early persecutions they forced Christians to choose between saying, "Caesar is Lord," for which they could be delivered and set free, or, "Jesus is Lord," for which they would meet the lions or be burned at the stake. To the credit of most of the early Christians, they held fast and chose to give up their lives rather than deny that Jesus is Lord.

Lord means, "in charge of all human events." We Christians often-times subconsciously live less-than-Christian lives in this regard. We think Jesus will be Lord only when he comes back again and reigns in triumph over the earth. But the truth that Scripture sets forth, and the truth which the Holy Spirit always supports, is that Jesus is Lord now; he is in charge of all human events now; he is the One who holds the controls of history, and everything that is reported in our papers today is moving at his will to a single point in the future which he controls. This is what Peter declared to the assembled multitudes on the Day of Pentecost: "Him, whom you crucified, God has made both Lord and Christ." This concept was what made the early Christians fearless: "Jesus is Lord; he is in charge of these people who are giving us trouble, and he will determine how far they go and what they do with us; therefore we need not be afraid. Jesus is Lord." This is what the Holy Spirit everywhere testifies to.

Today you hear many voices denying that. Some say, "Science is lord"; science is the true hope and savior of the race. Only the wisdom of men of science can ever hope to work out the knotty problems we wrestle with on this small planet. Other voices say, "Sex is lord," "Pleasure is lord," "Feeling is lord," "Money is lord." All of them in one way or another are saying, "Man is lord; he is in charge of his own destiny." As the poem has it,

> It matters not how straight the gate,
> How charged with punishment the scroll:
> I am the master of my fate,
> I am the captain of my soul.

Those sound like brave words, but in the light of the revelation of the Word of God they are ignorant idolatry, worshiping man in the place of the Lord Jesus Christ, whom God has made to be both Lord and Christ.

Where the Spirit is at work, Christ will be glorified. This is the point of the passage. Jesus said, "When he (the Spirit) is come he will not speak of himself; he will take the things of mine and make them known unto you." A group that makes much of the Spirit is not emphasizing Christian truth. The group that makes much of Jesus and exalts him, seeing everything as focused and centered on him, is the group that will manifest the power of the Spirit of God.

To show how true this is, in the next two verses the apostle declares that everything the church possesses comes from the Lord himself:

> Now there are varieties of gifts [charismata], but the same Spirit; and there are varieties of service [or ministries], but the same Lord; and there are varieties of working, but it is the same God who inspires them all in every one (vv. 4–6).

Notice the combination of variety with sameness—that is the sign of God at work. God himself is a Triune God; there is one God, but he exists in three Persons. That means diversity in unity, and whenever you find God at work you will always find that mark—diversity in unity. When the church is fulfilling its function and is what it ought to be, you will find this mark—one body, many gifts; many distinctions, many ministries within—but only one body in Christ. This is Paul's argument here: everything in the church flows out of the nature of God himself.

At the Foot of the Tree

Let us look more closely at what he says: first, the Spirit gives gifts—that is the Holy Spirit's task. He comes to every believer and gives to everyone, without exception, a gift or gifts of the Spirit, which Paul will describe more in detail later. These gifts are capacities to serve; they are abilities which are given to us by God himself. At Christmastime we all look forward to the gifts waiting for us under the tree, but the amazing thing to me is that God, at infinite cost, has given gifts to his people without exception—no one is left out, everybody has one—and yet people can live for years and *never* ask themselves, "I wonder what my gift is?" Yet, a gift of the Spirit is what turns life into an adventure and gives it a great sense of fulfillment and meaning. It is amazing how many Christians are content to live on year after year, barely struggling along as Christians, and never enjoying life to the full, never getting excited, never getting turned on and aglow with the adventure of Christian living, because they have never tried to discover what gift God has given them. But there are the gifts, waiting for us at the cross, at the foot of the tree.

Note that it is the Lord Jesus who assigns ministries, according to this passage. The word is *diakonia*, the word from which we get "deacon," and it refers to the opportunities to use your gift. The Spirit gives the gifts; the Lord Jesus opens the opportunities to use them. The trouble is, we think opportunities must come through the church, or through the leadership; that someone is going to call you up and ask you to do something. No, perhaps no one will. But God will open a door for you. It may be in your neighborhood, or it may be at work; it may be while you are riding in the car; it may be with children or with older people. It will be some opportunity that will come right to your doorstep for you to use a gift of teaching perhaps, or helps, or encouragement, or ministry, or whatever it is that God has given you. These are opportunities that the Lord Jesus himself has given you. As he said to Peter after the resurrection, "Feed my sheep," so he might say to you, "Feed my lambs," or "Encourage my sheep," or, "Evangelize in the world." Whatever it may be, the Lord in the midst of his church provides these opportunities.

Then it is the Father, according to this passage, who is in charge of the energizings, the workings. Here we are dealing with results. What is going to happen when you exercise your gift? Who knows? It may grow into a worldwide ministry; it has with some. It may be limited or obscure. But one thing is sure: it will be exciting; it will never be dull. It may be dangerous; it certainly will be demanding. But it will never be boring—you can count on that because God is an innovative God, alive, electrifying, at work, and moving in these days.

18

Gifts for the Body

In chapter 12 the apostle gives us the blueprint for the operation of the body of Christ. I know I am mixing metaphors when I speak of blueprints in connection with bodies, but I am in good company, because Paul does the same thing in the letter to the Ephesians. He speaks of the church as a "building" which "grows" into a holy habitation for the Lord. Buildings do not grow, bodies do, but I will join the apostolic company in using mixed metaphors here because they picture accurately the miracle of the church.

The church is both a building and a body. The thing that buildings and bodies have in common is that they are both places to live in. The glory of the church is that it is the building in which God lives *and* the body through which he works. If you want to find God in the world today, his address is "the church." He is at work through his body. I do not mean only when the church is assembled on Sunday morning, but wherever members of the body are, there the church is at work. We are made to be members of that body by the Spirit. This is the theme of chapter 12.

Paul began this chapter by showing us how the body of Christ flows out of the unity and diversity of the Trinity. The Spirit, he said, gives gifts, capacities for service, to every member of the body, gifts which the members did not have before they became Christians. The Son, the Lord Jesus, assigns ministries, i.e., opportunities for service. In verse 6 Paul says there are varieties of workings which are given by the Father, and here he is speaking of power for service.

One of the fundamental declarations of the Scripture is that power belongs to God. God never gives one a package of power and says, "Go ahead and use it for whatever you like." He always holds the reins of power in his hands. You can use God's power if you use it for his purposes, but if you use it for your own he simply shuts it off and you are left to run on what the Bible calls "the flesh," which is destructive and counterproductive.

When Anyone Believes

If you were a visitor from another planet and visited churches across this country today, you would probably draw the conclusion that the church operates to run meetings on Sunday morning. Everything is aimed toward that; all the work of leadership is directed toward that, and when it is over, it starts all over again. But that is a far cry from God's concept of the church. The church consists of all those who have truly been born of the Spirit and are thereby a living body, growing and developing within the world (not apart from it), to touch the hurt and death of the world with the life and love of God.

Foundation for Work

Those born of the Spirit are members of the church. The Spirit of God has come to dwell in each one and to give to each a pattern of gifts which Paul calls here "the manifestation of the Spirit."

> To each is given the manifestation of the Spirit for the common good (v. 7).

There follows a relatively long list of various gifts of the Spirit, and these form the foundation of the work of the church in the world. God does not start by forming an organization, but by equipping his people with gifts. That is basic, and he wants us to center our thinking on that point. What is your gift? What has God the Spirit given you with which to function within the body of Christ?

Notice three things that the apostle underlines in this verse for us. First: *"To each"* is given a manifestation of the Spirit. You find that again in verse 11: "All these are inspired by one and the same Spirit, who apportions *to each one* individually as he wills." No one is left out. If you are a Christian you can never say that you were behind the door when the gifts were given out. You have one (at least one), probably more, because God has an infinite variety of combinations of gifts to give. He chooses one combination just right for you. He puts you where he wants you to use your gifts, not only in the church among other believers, but out in the world as well. The use of gifts is basically what the work of the church is, and no one is left out.

I do not know what you think of when you hear that term, "the work of the church." For many, it describes ushering and singing in the choir, pastoring and teaching Sunday school class, or perhaps heading a few committees and doing some janitorial work. But that is not what God has in mind at all. The work of the church is to heal the broken-hearted, to bring deliverance to the poor, to open the doors to the captives, setting free those who are bound in prisons of doubt, fear, anxiety and selfishness, and leading them out into liberty, freedom and power. That is what God has called us to do, and it takes every one of us to do it. We are all in the ministry, and each is given a gift for that purpose.

Notice, second, that gifts are called "the manifestation of the Spirit." They are not normal, natural abilities; they are a supernatural function. We hear much today about "the charismatic movement" as dealing with the gifts of the Spirit, but the problem with that term is that it is used to describe only gifts of tongues, or perhaps healings, or miracles. But every single gift mentioned in this list and in other lists of Scripture is a *charisma*, a spiritual gift. It is supernatural—beyond normal, natural functioning. Therefore, the gifts of the Spirit do not refer to natural abilities or talents. Most of us have natural abilities. Some have marvelous musical ability. Some have athletic ability; some have an ability to paint or to draw, and others have ability to excel in various functions of life. Those abilities are given to people all over the world, whether they are believers or not. Like the rain, they come upon the just and the unjust alike. But spiritual gifts are given only to Christians. They are something you never had before you became a Christian. They are abilities to function in the realm of the spirit, not the body, so that the health of the spirit is improved and strengthened. The result is what we usually term "blessing." When you are "blessed" you feel spiritually healthier. That is the function of spiritual gifts—to make the human spirit free and strong, and able to function as it was intended.

Of course, natural abilities and spiritual gifts both come from the same God and therefore blend together nicely. Someone who has a fine voice and sings in church may also have a spiritual gift of encouragement, of comfort, and thus by his or her music can arouse and awaken a sense of worship. Sometimes, though, one hears singers who do not use a spiritual gift. Their singing may be technically excellent but it is spiritually profitless, and one is often left feeling flat.

The third thing the apostle says is that these spiritual gifts are given for "the common good." They are not intended for our own enjoyment or blessing, though we will enjoy using them. Spiritual gifts are delightful; they are fulfilling to use, and there is nothing wrong with enjoying the use of a spiritual gift, but its true purpose is to serve others. It has been given to you only to build up and edify others. It is for the "common good." You are going to need others' spiritual gifts as they are going to need yours. Spiritual gifts create havoc when used in the power of the flesh, as they were doing here at Corinth. But spiritual gifts used to benefit others awaken and release the power of God. The result will be life, joy, harmony, and beautiful expressions of love. Then the world will see that we are truly Christians. That is why we find this section tied immediately, in chapter 13, to the apostle's great passage on love.

Dr. John R. W. Stott has gathered up the work of the church in a quotation I would like to share with you. He says:

> Our motive must be concern for the glory of God, not the glory of the church or our own glory.
> Our message must be the gospel of God as given by Christ and his apostles, not the traditions of men or our own opinions.
> Our manpower must be the whole church of God, every member of it, not a privileged few who want to retain evangelism as their prerogative.
> Our dynamic must be the Spirit of God, not the power of human personality, organization, or eloquence. Without these priorities we shall be silent when we ought to be vocal.*

The apostle now goes on to list the variety of "manifestations of the Spirit," the spiritual gifts. He gives us a representative list. It is not complete, as there are only nine gifts listed here. There is another group in Romans 12; another reference in 1 Peter 4; and still another brief list in Ephesians 4. Taken altogether, depending upon how you identify certain gifts, there are from 18 to 20 different spiritual gifts.

The apostle begins here with two beautiful gifts:

> To one is given through the Spirit the utterance of wisdom, and to another the utterance of knowledge . . . (v. 8).

---

* Our Guilty Silence (Grand Rapids: Eerdmans).

Here are the twin gifts of wisdom and knowledge. The apostle Peter, in 1 Peter 4, suggested the gifts are divided into two major divisions: speaking gifts and serving gifts—those that involve the proclamation of the Word, and those that involve helping and ministering to people. Those two divisions are very helpful in understanding gifts. Now here are two speaking gifts, "the utterance of knowledge," and "the utterance of wisdom," literally the "word" of knowledge and the "word" of wisdom (*logos* is the term). What does this refer to? Remember, these are supernatural abilities; they are given by the Spirit of God. They do not flash and make a lot of noise or call attention to themselves; they operate quietly, but they are beyond natural powers. The word of knowledge is the ability, given to many, to go through the Word of God and to see what is there and to set forth, in a systematic way, what God wants man to know.

"The word of wisdom" is the application of that knowledge to specific problems. That too is a spiritual gift—the ability to take the revelation of the way things really are and apply it to some problem you are wrestling with in your home, in your marriage, in the church, in business, or in the general concerns of the world at large. It is to have insight into the way problems can be solved by the knowledge of Scripture. That is a marvelous gift. We have all been in meetings, perhaps, where we were wrestling with some problem, and no one could see a way out. Then someone says, "Well it seems to me that this word, or this passage, applies here, and if we will do this and this and this, it will work out." And everyone says, "Of course! Why didn't we see that?" That is the utterance of wisdom.

An Increased Expression

Then the apostle mentions one of the serving gifts:

> . . . to another faith by the same Spirit (v. 9).

Here is a gift of faith. Are not all Christians to have faith? Of course! You cannot live as a Christian without faith. Faith is believing God, believing he means what he says, and acting on it. This marks a characteristic of all the gifts of the Spirit: they are an increased expression, in an unusual way, of what everyone is expected to do. We are all to have faith, but there is a gift of faith. We all can help each other, but there is a gift of helps. We all can give money, but there is a gift of giving as well. We are all to teach each other, but there is a gift of teaching. It is very much like a baseball team—people play various positions. They are especially chosen because of the special skills they have in the positions they play. Yet they all take their turn at bat. Now everyone knows that pitchers cannot bat, but they are always put up to bat because that is part of the game. Thus in the church anyone can help; anyone can give; anyone can have faith; but there are special skills above and beyond the ordinary which represent the gifts of the Spirit. The gift of faith is what I would call "vision." It is seeing him who is invisible, and acting on the basis of his invisible resources supplied to faith.

There are many throughout the church who have the gift of vision. Start talking about some problem and soon they will come up and say, "Well, I believe God wants us to do so and so," and they are ready to do it. I think of Cameron Townsend, that remarkable founder of Wycliffe Translators, who has a marvelous gift of faith. A few years ago he learned there are many tribes in Russia that have never had the Bible in their language, so he decided to see what he could do. Everybody said, "Oh! You can't do that. Russia is closed. You can't get permission to translate the Scriptures into their languages." But he has the gift of faith, so he went over and did it. Right now half a dozen Russian atheist linguists are helping translate the Gospel of John! They are translating it because one man has the gift of faith.

Then Paul mentions the "gift of healings":

to another gifts of healings [it should be in the plural] by the one Spirit (v. 9).

What are the "gifts of healings?" I believe that is the gift of restoring health, and it is in the plural because there are three levels of life where we need to be restored—physical, social or psychological, and spiritual. This gift can be given at any of those levels. In the early church it was frequently given at the level of the physical. The apostles seem to have had the gift of physical healing, the ability to lay hands on sick people who were made well instantly. I do not know anyone today who has the gift of physical healing, but I believe that healings still occur. We have had the joy of seeing the Lord touch people in our membership in answer to the prayers of the elders as they laid hands on them. God does heal, but that is not the exercise of the gift of healing. That is something beyond. This gift may be given today; I would not say it is not, but I have not seen it. Nevertheless, it is a marvelous gift.

The gift of healing can be given at the emotional level also. Some in our congregation have had the ability to know how to talk to people and restore them to emotional and spiritual health. It may be given at this level frequently today.

Then there is mentioned the "gift of miracles":

> to another the working of miracles [literally, "the energizing of powers"] (v. 10).

That means the ability to release the power of God in a unique and supernatural way, as Jesus did when he turned the water into wine, or walked on the water, or raised Lazarus from the dead. It is the release of unique power. It is rarely given today. Any of these gifts can be given at any age, at any time, as the Spirit sees a purpose for it, but I do not know of anyone who has the gift of working miracles today.

The Most Important Gift

The next gift, however, is a common and important one. In fact, it is the most important of all the gifts. Paul devotes nearly a whole chapter to it in chapter 14. It is the gift of prophesying. It is usually identified as being able to tell what will happen in the future, but that is not the biblical gift of prophesying. In the Bible the gift of prophesying is the ability to speak forth the mind of God. It does include, at times, an element of prediction, but it is essentially the ability to see what God is doing in the world, and set it forth in such a clear way that people understand where and how God is working today. That is the gift of prophesying. What a helpful gift it is in these troubled days.

Then there is listed the "gift of discerning between spirits":

> to another the ability to distinguish between spirits (v. 10).

That is the ability to spot a phony, to detect false doctrine. It is the ability to sense that behind orthodox words and orthodox actions is a phony, fleshly, even demonic spirit. It is the ability to say so before everyone else sees it from the results. Watch the TV ads in which a man talks to a pat of margarine which insists that it is really butter and you will sense that something phony is going on. Something like that can occur within the church as well. Certain people are gifted to detect counterfeit Christianity and expose it to all.

Never Mentioned in the Gospels

The last gift mentioned here is a double gift:

> to another various kinds of tongues, to another the interpretation of tongues (v. 10).

Here we come to a matter of great controversy in the church today. We shall cover it more thoroughly in 1 Corinthians 14 where Paul compares the gift of tongues to the gift of prophesying. Biblically, the gift of tongues is the ability to speak a language that one has never learned. It is not the ability to learn a language quickly. Some people who are not Christians at all have that ability. This is the ability to speak a language one has never studied, or, in the case of interpretation, to interpret a language that one has never learned.

This is the gift that is made much of today. Despite its prominence now, it is helpful to remember that it is never mentioned in the Gospels at all. That foundational section of the New Testament never mentions the gift of tongues except in the closing section of Mark's Gospel, which is under great doubt as to its authenticity. It is only mentioned three times in the Book of Acts, on the three historic occasions when it was used, and the only other mention in all the Epistles of the New Testament is here in 1 Corinthians. Even here it is only discussed once. Therefore it did not occupy in the early church the prominence given to it today.

It is helpful to understand right from the beginning that the biblical gift of tongues never occurs in private. Like all the gifts of the Spirit it is designed "for the common good." It is a public gift, and every instance of its appearance in the Bible is a public occasion, where many are present. It occurred first on the Day of Pentecost where we have a clear description of the nature of the gift. It consisted of the apostles speaking various languages—sixteen languages are mentioned—that were widely known and widely spoken not far from where these people were gathered. They were languages spoken in the world of that day, and yet they had never been learned by the apostles.

This gift had a definite sign character to it on the Day of Pentecost, and Paul says in chapter 14 that to be a sign is the primary purpose of this gift. It is to be "a sign to unbelievers." It can occur today but it must always be compared to the biblical standard. The question we need to ask today when we are exposed to any manifestation that is called the gift of tongues is, "Is this the same thing as described in the Bible?" Much confusion has arisen in the church today by the failure to ask that question and answer it. Most people assume that what they hear today is the biblical gift of tongues, but it is not. There is much fraudulent tongues-speaking around, and therefore it is important not to uncritically assume that a certain manifestation is the biblical gift, but to ask oneself, "Does it measure up to the biblical standard?" We shall see more of this when we examine chapter 14.

Once again, in verse 11, we see the trademark of God: diversity arising out of unity:

> All these are inspired by one and the same Spirit, who apportions to each one individually as he wills.

There are many gifts, many different approaches to service and speaking—not all the same by any means—but behind them only one Spirit. That is what has kept the church from breaking into hundreds of splinter groups, all claiming to have the true manifestation of the Spirit. No, Paul says, no matter what the nature of the gift or the way it varies from others, behind them all is the same Spirit. It is he who decides what gifts are given to whom.

The Spirit Chooses

Do not get out your pencil now and start making a list of the gifts you would like to have, for the apostle tells us it is the Spirit who chooses; he "apportions to each one individually *as he wills*." Many people are asking today, "Why don't we have miracles like they did in the New Testament days? Why don't we have great healings, and tremendous demonstrations of the power of God?" The answer is, the Spirit has not given those gifts today. And it is not because the church is so carnal. It is carnal, but so was Corinth. The most carnal church in the New Testament had all the gifts abounding. The true answer is, the Spirit has not chosen to give those gifts as widely today. If he so desired, he would give them regardless of how spiritual or carnal we are, as he did at Corinth. These all are given by the Spirit, "as he wills."

This is not a matter to be taken lightly. The Spirit of God has distributed gifts to every member of Christ's body, and to take a unique supernatural ability which God has given you and to use it under the leadership and authority of the Lord Jesus, using the opportunities that come to you by the power supplied by God himself (resurrection power, which does not make a big noise of open display, but quietly, persistently and resistlessly does its work) is to open a door of possibility and excitement beyond anything that you have ever dreamed of. When you get a whole church functioning that way, can you imagine what will happen to the community around? When they see people really demonstrating the life of God in family groups, in small backyard meetings, in homes, at work, in carpools, can you imagine what will happen? That is where the work of the church occurs, and that is how God expects the church to change the world. One of the most incredible things to me is to see how we have set aside this amazing program of God as though it were useless, and instead repeat endlessly old and tired ways of doing things that have never worked, and think it is an improvement on what God has said. As the apostle Paul said to Timothy, his young son in the faith: "Stir up the gift of God, which is in you." Stir up the gift which was given to you by the Holy Spirit! Then you will see God at work.

Now, beginning at verse 12, we come to a passage that answers a question frequently asked today. What do you say when someone asks you, "Have you been baptized with the Holy Spirit?"

That is a difficult question to answer because there are so many conflicting viewpoints as to what the baptism of the Holy Spirit is. This passage is the only place in the entire Bible where the baptism of the Holy Spirit is explained to us, although it is referred to in a number of places. Therefore, this is an extremely significant passage:

> For just as the body is one and has many members, and all the members of the body, though many, are one body, so it is with Christ. For by one Spirit, we were all baptized into one body—Jews or Greeks, slaves or free— and all were made to drink of one Spirit (vv. 12, 13).

The apostle here uses the analogy of a human body to draw lessons on how the body of Christ functions. It is more than a mere figure of speech to say that the church is the body of Christ. God seems to take that figure seriously. It is so truly his body by which he works today that he has given us a visual aid to live in and walk around in to help us think through the meaning of the church as the body of Christ.

So Paul begins. "Just as the body is one and yet has many members," he says, "so also it is with Christ." Notice it is not "so also it is with the church," because it is the church and Jesus which constitutes the body of Christ. If you stand in front of a mirror and look at your body you will be struck by the fact that it is divided into two major sections—the head and the torso. The head is the control center of the body, while the torso is the biggest part of it, and the part to which the members (the arms and the legs) are attached. This is all designed to help us understand how the church is to function, for the whole body, including the head, constitutes the body of Christ.

The amazing statement which Paul makes here is that we are thus part of Christ. We are the means by which Christ functions within the world. The church is a body with many members, and yet it is only one body. It is not many bodies, many denominations. All are tied together by sharing the same life, and all are connected to the Head as his means of expressing his life in this world.

Paul then answers the question, "How did we get into that body?" We were not added to it when we were born as infants; the body of Christ does not consist of everyone in the world, only certain ones. His answer is clear, "For by one Spirit we were all baptized into one body." That is the baptism with the Holy Spirit predicted by John the Baptist and referred to by Jesus himself, fulfilled for the first time on the Day of Pentecost, and continually fulfilled ever since whenever anyone believes in Jesus. At that time they are baptized by the Spirit into the body of Christ and made part of the living Christ who has been working in the world through all these twenty centuries.

That indicates, of course, that all Christians who are born again have been baptized by the Spirit, so that when someone asks you, "Have you been baptized by the Holy Spirit?" the answer, if you are a Christian, is "Yes." You could not have become a Christian without having been baptized by the Holy Spirit. You are made part of his body by that process. It is not always accompanied by tongues, or healings, or fire, or even a chill down your spine. You are made to be a part of the body of Christ without necessarily feeling that you are. Remember, "we were all baptized into one body."

Then Paul declares it does not make any difference what your national origin is (whether Jew or Greek, slave or free), "all were made to drink of one Spirit." Notice that the word all occurs twice in this one verse. We "all" were baptized; we "all" were made to drink, or to be indwelt by one Spirit. When you drink a glass of water you take the water into yourself; thus, when you drink of the Spirit you take the Spirit into yourself, and are thus indwelt by him. This passage clearly establishes for us that all believers are both "baptized by" and "indwelt by" the Holy Spirit.

This passage beautifully parallels something very profound that Jesus said to his disciples in the Upper Room, recorded in John's Gospel. There he taught them about the coming of the Holy Spirit. He said his function would be that of a strengthener, an encourager, a comforter, a teacher and a guide into all truth. But above all other things, the Holy Spirit was sent to take the things of Jesus and reveal them to us—to make Jesus himself real to every believer. This is what keeps Christians Christian. If we did not have the fellowship of a living Lord, day by day and week by week throughout all our Christian life, we would never remain Christians. It is not intellectual conviction that keeps us Christian. It is the warmth and joy and fellowship of Christ that does so. That is the work of the Holy Spirit, and that is why he came. He makes us permanently a part of Christ. We are united with him—baptized into Christ.

Jesus put that in a beautiful little formula. The relationship we would have with him would be: "You in me and I in you." That is what is accomplished by the Holy Spirit. When the Spirit baptizes us into the body of Christ he puts us into Christ, "you in me." He joins our life with his, and Christ becomes our source of existence and strength; we are part of him. Then we have all been made to "drink of one Spirit," and thus our Lord's words, "I in you" are fulfilled. That is the power by which we are to live. It is this dual ministry of the Holy Spirit (baptizing us into the body and filling us with the Spirit, so that we are both "in Christ" and he is "in us"), that constitutes the mystery and the marvel of the church.

No Insignificant Members

The apostle goes on in the next few verses to make everything crystal clear by explaining just how it works. He is answering two major problems, to mental attitudes, that one often runs up against in the church. The first one is a feeling of insignificance. Many have said to themselves at some time, "I love to come to church but I don't feel there is anything I can do. I can't contribute to the work of the church because I don't have any abilities. Others know so much more than I." Paul now addresses that very attitude:

> For the body does not consist of one member but of many. If the foot should say, "Because I am not a hand, I do not belong to the body," that would not make it any less a part of the body. And if the ear should say, "Because I am not an eye, I do not belong to the body," that would not make it any less a part of the body (vv. 14,15).

It would be ridiculous if your foot said, "Well, I can't do all the things a hand does. It's so flexible. It is hooked onto that long arm, and it is used all the time. I can't wiggle my toes like the hand can wiggle the fingers; I just can't do what the hand can do, therefore I really don't belong in this body." The foot is deceiving itself. If the ear says, "Because I can't see like an eye, I am not part of the body," the ear is deceiving itself. It *is* part of the body, whether it realizes it or not.

The apostle is saying that if you think of yourself as a member of the church, the body of Christ, and you say to yourself, "Because I can't stand up and preach, or teach, or lead a meeting, there is really nothing I can do in the body of Christ," you are deceiving yourself. You have not changed the reality any. You are still a part of the body, but you have shut your eyes to truth. You need to open them to see the part God has given you. There are no insignificant members of the body. The work of the church is not confined to church meetings. We go to meetings to get ready to do the work of the church in the world. If you have that in mind, then there is definitely a ministry for every member, without exception. You are only kidding yourself if you say that because you cannot lead, teach, or preach, you are not a part of the body and do not have a function within it. In fact Paul goes on to say:

> If the whole body were an eye, where would be the hearing? If the whole body were an ear, where would be the sense of smell? (v. 17).

What a ridiculous body it would be if everyone did the same thing, or if the work of the church only consisted of a handful of things that people did on Sunday morning. Our high school pastor once was attempting to teach the young people truth about the body. One day he painted a football white and then painted an eyeball, with iris and pupil on it. He wrapped the "eye" in a blanket, cradled it on his arm, and went into the high school group meeting. As he walked around he would say to the kids, "How do you like my baby?" They would look and see this big "eye" staring at them, and they would say, "Oh gross! That's terrible." Then he said to them, "What if your girlfriend was nothing but a big eye and you took her out for a milkshake and propped her up in the booth opposite you and tried to carry on a conversation and all she would do was stare at you with this one big unblinking eye?" They got the point and began to take seriously their part in the body of Christ.

We have been so brainwashed with the conventional idea of church that we need to be dynamited out of that concept. We need to capture again the glorious excitement of Jesus Christ walking through the hurt

of this world and touching it with a healing hand, but the instrumental-
ity of his people healing the blind eyes, the lame legs, the infirm
bodies and the destroyed lives all around. That is the work of the
church. It is Christ at work in the world.

Paul then goes on,

> But as it is, God arranged the organs in the body, each one of them, as
> he chose (v. 18).

That means that wherever you live—and the people with whom you
live—is the very place God wants you to exercise the gift he has given
you. He arranged the organs of the body wherever he chose. All are
necessary and each is in the right place. So Paul concludes,

> If all were a single organ, where would the body be? As it is, there are
> many parts, yet one body (vv. 19, 20).

I hope this is clear, because that should forever settle the question
of insignificance. You cannot say to yourself, "There is no place for
me," for there definitely is.

More like Golfers

Now let us take the second problem that surfaces in a church, an
independent spirit:

> The eye cannot say to the hand, "I have no need of you," nor again the
> head to the feet, "I have no need of you" (v. 21).

In many congregations people get the idea that they do not need
the rest of the body; they can function on their own. They have their
abilities and their own ministry, and they can do things quite apart
from others. This always creates a sense of competitiveness, of rivalry.
On one occasion I was in Palm Springs, speaking to a group of Christian
pro golfers. I was struck again by the fact that golfers are by nature
independent. A golf tournament is a struggle of independent egos
pitted against each other. The golfers all rely on their own abilities
to try to beat out the other man. That is the nature of golf. It is
not like football, where each one plays his own role but works with
the other team members to accomplish something. I am afraid many
congregations become much like golfers. But, as Paul points out, in
your own physical body you would be in a terrible state if your members
did that. What would happen if the eye said, "I don't need the rest
of the body. I'll just roll around seeing things on my own and let

the rest of the body go"? You would instantly go blind, and the rest of the body would bump into everything. No, we all need one another.

So Paul argues:

> On the contrary, the parts of the body which seem to be weaker are indispensable, and those parts of the body which we think less honorable we invest with the greater honor, and our unpresentable parts are treated with greater modesty, which our more presentable parts do not require (vv. 22–24).

He is still talking about the physical body. He says we must remember that the parts which seem to be weaker are actually indispensable. I was preaching in a certain place in the East once and a doctor came up to me afterward and said, "You may be interested to know that there is a certain part of your body that is absolutely essential to you as a preacher. You probably do not even think about it when you are preaching, and yet without it you could not do the work you are doing. Do you know what it is?" I said, "No. Is it my tongue, or my brain?" "No," he said, "those are obvious. It's your big toe. Did you know that if you didn't have a great toe on each foot you could not even stand up to preach? It is the toe that has the ability to sense when your body begins to lean, or shift, or get out of balance, and it immediately strengthens you so that you can stand up and speak." I have been guarding my great toes very carefully ever since, because I need them. They are an essential part of my ministry.

Paul is saying here that this is also true in the body of Christ. We see people with the gift of helps—people who seem to be able to see what is needed to be done, and promptly do it. Food needs to be served, chairs need to be set up, a house needs to be cleaned, some ministry needs to be helped. Such people are able to do it, and they enjoy doing it. We tend to think, "Oh, they're nice to have around, but how important are they in the work of the church? After all, they do not teach, or preach, or sing, or anything like that." Do you know what would happen in any congregation if people ceased using the gift of helps? The pastors would soon be unable to preach or teach. They would run into each other and stumble over each other and nothing would get done right.

Paul says, "Those parts of the body which we think less honorable we invest with the greater honor, and our unpresentable parts are treated with greater modesty." Have you ever noticed that people with knobby knees are always careful to choose clothing that hides their knees? If we think our shoulders are not broad enough we tend to buy clothing that emphasizes shoulders. There is an inbuilt tendency in human life to augment or disguise those parts that are less honorable. Notice how the apostle describes them, "parts we think less honorable." They are not really, it is just our idea of them that makes them appear that way, but how carefully we take account of that and try to present them to our advantage.

Paul is doubtless referring to what used to be called our "private parts" when he says "our unpresentable parts." (They are not so private anymore.) We treat these with great modesty. Paul draws the analogy with the body of Christ. He says there are hidden, secret functions within the body, never mentioned in public, that are nevertheless exceedingly important. Take the ministry of prayer, for instance, and those people who consistently pray for others. No one knows about them. There is a lady I know who spends hours each day praying for the staff and members of our church. She counts it her ministry. You seldom see her at meetings; she has difficulty getting out, but how she upholds us in prayer! What a mighty, valuable ministry that is. That is what the apostle is referring to when he says:

> But God has so adjusted the body, giving the greater honor to the inferior part, that there may be no discord in the body, but that the members may have the same care for one another (vv. 24,25).

When you begin to understand what the church is, as God sees it, this will be the result. You will have the same care for one another. You will stop saying that teachers are all-important, or a certain line of preaching or doctrine is the great and important thing. You will see that God works the whole body together in a beautifully coordinated way.

Angels and Computers

The human body is the most beautifully balanced and delicately articulated instrument the world has ever seen. All the computers in the world, put together, cannot do what a single human body can do, and does with exquisite grace when it is functioning right. In the same way there is nothing more beautiful and more balanced than the church of Jesus Christ. Spiritually, it is the most marvelous organism in the whole universe. The angels long to look into the functioning of the body of Christ in the world today. God has put it together; therefore, we ought to have great care for one another. So Paul says,

> If one member suffers, all suffer together; if one member is honored, all rejoice together (v. 26).

Notice that he does not say all "should" suffer together, or all "should" be honored together. He says they actually do. If one person falls into evil and loses his ministry, all who meet him or hear of him see the whole body of Christ less honorably than they did before. They will look upon me, as a Christian, less honorably than they did before because of his action. You do not have to be aware of the suffering or dishonor of another brother or sister to be affected by it. You *are* affected by it.

But it is true the other way around also. If one is honored, all are honored with him. If some member of the body does an outstanding piece of work that opens the door for the deliverance of hundreds of people, or even a few people, and ministers the grace and the love of Christ, everyone touched by that will be blessed by it. They will regard the church of Christ with greater honor than before. The responsibility for the reputation of the body rests with every one of us. How we act is going to govern how other people see the body of Christ at work in the world today. We belong together and we suffer together.

Some years ago I had a badly injured wrist. It swelled up and became very sore. The rest of my body was so concerned that it sat up all night with it to keep it company! That is what we are to do in the body of Christ also.

The closing paragraph of this chapter is simply a beautiful gathering up by the apostle of all these themes, highlighting the divine stamp upon the church:

> Now you are the body of Christ and individually members of it (v. 27).

There is that remarkable unity in diversity. The two combined mark the work of God.

> And God has appointed in the church first apostles, second prophets, third teachers (v. 28).

This is not in order of rank. This is in order of historic appearance; it is a chronological order. First there came the apostles; these were followed by the prophets; then the teachers began to appear in the church,

> then workers of miracles, then healers, helpers, administrators, speakers in various kinds of tongues (v. 29).

All that diversity is necessary, Paul says, to the functioning of the church in its work in the world.

> Are all apostles? Are all prophets? Are all teachers? Do all work miracles? Do all possess gifts of healing? Do all speak with tongues? Do all interpret? (vv. 29,30).

The answer obviously is, "No." No one has all the gifts. No one can do all the work of the church. We need each other; that is the point he is making. These gifts, when they are being exercised, grow into offices. Notice how that which is listed as a gift in the beginning of the chapter has become an office in the church at the end of it. Instead of having "gifts of healing" he speaks of "healers," and instead of "gifts of administrations" it has become "administrators." One grows into the other. The gift, when consistently exercised, ultimately becomes an office.

Paul then concludes with this wonderful sentence:

> But earnestly desire the higher gifts (v. 31).

That, by the way, is addressed to a congregation. It is in the plural; it is not addressed to individuals. As we have already seen, your gifts are chosen for you by the Holy Spirit, and no matter what gift you desire you are not going to get it unless the Holy Spirit has already chosen it for you. But as a congregation we can earnestly desire that the higher gifts be manifested among us. The higher ones, of course, are those that edify and help others. That is the purpose of the gifts.

Then he adds these words:

> And I will show you a still more excellent way (v. 31).

That is the introduction to the great "love" chapter which follows. Love is the essence of the fruit of the Spirit. There is a big difference between the gifts of the Spirit and the fruit of the Spirit. The fruit is what God is after. It is the character of Christ coming through. The gifts are given to enable us to achieve, in increasing degree and by mutual exercise, the fruit of the Spirit. But the fruit is what God is looking for, and every congregation should be infinitely more concerned with the fruit of the Spirit than they are with the gifts of the Spirit.

19

The Way of Love

We come now to the most beautiful chapter in the New Testament, 1 Corinthians 13. The chapter is justly famous, not only for its majestic language, but for the lofty idealism of its subject matter and the practical behavior it describes.

> If I speak in the tongues of men and of angels, but have not love, I am a noisy gong or a clanging cymbal. And if I have prophetic powers, and understand all mysteries and all knowledge, and if I have all faith, so as to remove mountains, but have not love, I am nothing. If I give away all I have, and if I deliver my body to be burned, but have not love, I gain nothing (vv. 1–3).

Analyzing those words is like tearing apart a beautiful flower. But some analysis is necessary that we might fully grasp what the apostle Paul is saying in this great hymn to love. There are three aspects of love which he considers: first, the *preeminence of love*, then the *practice of love*, and then the *permanence of love*—its enduring quality.

Let us remember that this chapter on love, though often read separately, really fits beautifully with what the apostle has been talking about in the previous section. In chapter 12 he introduced the subject of "the spiritualities," the matters pertaining to the Spirit of God. There Paul talked about the gifts of the Spirit, but now he turns to the fruit of the Spirit. The apostle has introduced it with a hint that the fruit of the Spirit is far more important than the gifts of the

Spirit. That we should become loving people is far more important
than whether we are active, busy people. Both are necessary, but one
is greater than the other. Paul has said so: "I will show you a still
more excellent way." That is the way of love.   ·

It is proper to call love "the fruit of the Spirit" because in the
letter to the Galatians, the apostle details for us what the fruit of
the Spirit consists of. It is love, joy, peace, patience, kindness, goodness,
faithfulness, gentleness and self-control. It has been pointed out that
all of those qualities are really manifestations of love; joy is love enjoying
itself; peace is love resting; patience is love waiting; kindness is love
reacting; goodness is love choosing; faithfulness is love keeping its word;
gentleness is love empathizing; and self-control is love resisting temptation.

Love is the key; love is the main thing. This chapter is setting
forth that quality of love which is the work of the Spirit of God within
us, reproducing the character of Christ. Once you have love all these
other qualities that are part of the fruit of the Spirit are possible to
you. If we have the love of God in our hearts then we can be patient;
we can be peaceful; we can be good, loving, faithful, gentle and kind.
But without love, all we can do is imitate these qualities and produce
a phony love. One of the most deadly enemies of the Christian cause
is phony love. In Romans 12 Paul says, "Let love be genuine." When
you come into the church, especially among the people of God, love
must be genuine. If it is not, it is sheer hypocrisy. If it is put on
only for the moment, and it disappears as soon as the situation changes,
it spreads death within the community. Genuine love, however, will
enfold and produce all these qualities.

Addressed to the Will

The word *love* here is not the Greek word *eros*. That word is used
to describe erotic love, sensual love; the kind you feel when you "fall
in love," a passionate attraction to another person. That kind of love
is not even mentioned in the Word of God, though it was a common
form of love then and today. Also the word here is not *philia*, which
means affection, friendship, a feeling of warmth toward someone else.
This, too, is a universally distributed love. But here Paul uses the term
agape, which is a commitment of the will to cherish and uphold another
person. It is the word that is always used for the love of God. It is a
word addressed to the will. It entails a decision that you make and a

commitment that you have launched upon to treat another person with concern, and care, and thoughtfulness, and to work for his or her best interests.

Now this kind of love is possible only to those who first love God. I do not hesitate to say that. Any attempt to exercise love like this without having first loved God will result in phony love, a fleshly kind of love. The Scripture tells us there are two great commandments. The first is, "Thou shalt love the Lord thy God with all thy heart, and with all thy soul, and with all thy mind, and with all thy strength." The second one, Jesus said, is, "Thou shalt love thy neighbor as thyself." We try to turn these around. Many of us are trying to love our neighbor (whoever he may be, in our family or anywhere else), without having loved God, but it is impossible to do that. It is "the love of God shed abroad in our hearts by the Holy Spirit," as Romans 5 puts it, that fulfills the definition given in this chapter, and only that love. You cannot truly love other people until you first love God.

Loving God is not difficult; all you need to do is be aware of how much he has loved you—in creation, in the supply of your need, in leading you and putting you in various places with various persons. But above all else he has loved you in having given his Son for you, having redeemed you, having forgiven you and healed your inner hurt. By these means God has called you to himself and given you a standing before him as a child within his family. To remember all that is to be stirred with love for God. When you love God you awaken your capacity to love people.

It is important that we understand, in reading this passage, that love is a supernatural quality. God alone can awaken in us this kind of love. God alone can lead us to make a choice to love somebody who does not appeal to us, who does not awaken anything within us. Yet that is what God's love is. That is what is so desperately needed in the world and so beautifully described in this passage. It can only come as we love God with a love awakened within us by the Holy Spirit.

This chapter comes after Paul has stated that all believers are baptized with the Holy Spirit and made a part of the body of Christ. Because of that baptism we all have the capacity to act in love. All that Paul is saying in this passage is, "If you have that capacity, then do it. Love one another!"

To encourage this he shows us the qualities of love. Number one, of course, is the preeminent value of love. What makes life worth living? Love! Paul contrasts love here with certain things that were highly regarded in Corinth and are still highly regarded in the world today. The first is the ability to communicate. These Corinthians valued communication. They enjoyed eloquence and admired oratory. They were especially entranced by the gift of tongues, which, by the power of the Spirit, enabled a person to pray and praise God. They were making much of this gift as many are today, so Paul begins on that note. He says,

> If I speak in the tongues of men and of angels, but have not love, I am a noisy gong or a clanging cymbal.

Without love the gift of tongues is only a big noisemaker, that is all. There is no suggestion in this that the gift of "glossolalia" (speaking in tongues), is identical to what Paul refers to as "the tongues of angels." Certain people today claim that the gift of tongues enables you to speak with the tongues of angels, but Paul does not say that at all. Angels do communicate, but we do not know how; nothing is said about it in the Bible. This is the only reference in all the Scriptures to the tongues of angels. All Paul is saying is that to be a loving person is more important than to be able to speak in all the languages of earth or heaven. Therefore, it is essential to learn to love. Communication without love is a useless thing.

Then he compares love to two other qualities that were admired both in Corinth and in our age as well: knowledge and power.

> And if I have prophetic powers, and understand all mysteries and all knowledge, and if I have all faith, so as to remove mountains, but have not love, I am nothing.

Paul is thinking of theologians particularly, men and women with great ability to understand the mysteries of the Scriptures, to unscrew the inscrutable, and to answer all biblical questions, riddles, and paradoxes. Paul says, "If I could explain all the mysterious movements of God and still were not a loving person—if I were difficult, cantankerous, hard to get along with—even though I could move mountains by faith, it is all nothing." Knowledge and power are worthless without love.

Finally, he takes up the matter of sacrificial zeal:

> If I give away all I have, and if I deliver my body to be burned, but have not love, I gain nothing.

There are many reasons why people give away things. Sometimes they give because they are deeply concerned about a certain cause or a need. But sometimes people give for very selfish reasons, although it appears to be a generous gift. I have known people who gave great sums of money to a cause they actually had no more use for than a hog has for hip pockets, and still they gave their money. Why? Because they had a selfish interest in it. You can impress people with your tremendous willingness to sacrifice, even, as some have done, by pouring gasoline over their bodies and setting themselves on fire, to call attention to a certain cause. That is a supreme sacrifice, and surely bears eloquent testimony to the fact that those who do so believe in the cause they are espousing. But to do that, Paul says, without having learned to love will gain nothing. At the judgment seat of Christ it will be regarded as wasted effort. Love is the all-important thing. We are put here to learn to love, and to live without learning to love is to have wasted our time, no matter how impressive our achievements in other ways may be.

Measurements of Life

In the next section the apostle shows us that a love must be practical. Love is not an ethereal thing; it is not merely an ideal to talk about. It is something that takes on shoeleather and gets right out into the normal, ordinary pursuits and aspects of life. Nothing is more helpful, in reading a chapter like this, than to ask yourself the question, "Am I growing in love? Looking back over a year, am I easier to live with now? Am I able to handle people more graciously, more courteously? Am I more compassionate, more patient?" These are the measurements of love. There is no use holding up any other quality we possess, if we lack this one. It is the paramount goal of every human life.

To help us the apostle gives us some practical ways of testing love. He says,

> Love is patient and kind; love is not jealous or boastful; it is not arrogant or rude. Love does not insist on its own way; it is not irritable or resentful; it does not rejoice at wrong, but rejoices in the right (vv. 4–6).

Notice in that paragraph there are only three positives; all the rest are negatives. Love is really only three simple things, basically. It is patient, it is kind, and it rejoices in the right (the word really is *truth*, it rejoices in the truth; that is, it is honest). The quality of love we are talking about is that which produces patience, kindness and honesty. The negatives that are given here are associated with love, in the apostle's thought, because these are the things we must set aside in order to let the love of God, which is patient and kind and honest, manifest itself. We do not have to produce this love in the Christian life. We only have to get the things that are hindering it out of the way.

All progress in the Christian life comes by first experiencing the cross and then the resurrection. These two events are a symbolic picture of all we repeatedly go through as Christians. To give up the pleasure which these negative expressions give us is to experience something of dying to self. That is the cross. But it always results in a resurrection— a release of the power of God to reach out in patience, in kindness, and in honesty.

The word for patience is always used with regard to people, not circumstances. Being patient with people means that you do not immediately wipe them out, or turn them off, but you are understanding, you wait quietly and let them work things out. The word actually means "a great suffering"—enduring suffering in order to let people have a chance to work out their problems. Kindness means to be gracious, to be pleasant to people. It entails an unfailing courtesy.

Finally, there is honesty, or truth. It is difficult to combine truth and love. There is a passage in the letter to the Ephesians that constitutes the simplest, briefest, and yet the most profound definition of Christian maturity that I know anything about. I seek to measure myself against this, and I measure others as to whether they are mature or not, by the degree to which they manifest this quality: it is Paul's *attitude* exhortation to "speak the truth in love." Now it is easy to speak the truth sometimes—to be blunt and caustic and even bitter. You can speak truth in that way but there is no love in it. Or you can be "loving" and refuse to hurt another by telling him anything that is unpleasant or distasteful. But that really reveals a lack of courage; it is a form of unloving deception. It is the man or woman who can speak the truth in love who is growing up in Christ.

Perverse Pleasure

Many people admire this chapter on love but they do not understand how to produce this kind of love. The reason the apostle does not tell us here is because that is what he has been telling us all along through the whole book. God is ready to love through us if we are ready to renounce the false, the negative expression that we enjoy experiencing. I do not have to argue with you about that. We all know the perverse pleasure we get out of some of these negative reactions. We do not want to give them up. It is too much fun to rip people apart, to give them a piece of your mind, to make them suffer for all the injuries they have done to you—to freeze them out or let them stew a little in their own juice. You know how delightful that is. We want to love, but first we want the flesh. That is why we do not experience the love of God. We are given these negative qualities here to help us understand what we must renounce.

First on Paul's list is jealousy. We are often not patient or kind because we are jealous. We are spiteful and short with people because we see them enjoying something we want. They have a relationship that we envy; they have a quality about themselves that we do not have and we are angry about it, so we are short and spiteful. That is one reason why we are often not patient and kind.

Next is boastfulness: "Love is not jealous or boastful." Oftentimes we are not patient because we cannot wait to listen to others. We are anxious to brag about ourselves so they can begin to admire us. But boastfulness must be surrendered for love to appear.

Then Paul says, love is "not arrogant." Arrogance is disdain, lack of respect for another person, ignoring how he will feel and asserting yourself, regardless of the results. Nor is love "rude," Paul says. This is to ignore another's rights; literally, the term is, "to be puffed up." It means to be haughty or cutting. One of the major expressions of rudeness is sarcasm.

Also "love does not insist on its way." It is not stubborn, insisting that everybody else adjust. It is willing to find a way, to look from a different angle. When we get stubborn and refuse to talk about a matter, we are choosing to exercise the self-centeredness of the flesh. Therefore, we cannot expect the love and patience of God to appear in that situation.

Next love "is not irritable or resentful." Nothing destroys human relationships more than that. Henry Drummond, in his great message on this passage, *The Greatest Thing in the World*, writes:

> No form of vice, not worldliness, nor greed of gold, nor drunkenness itself, does more to unChristianize society than evil temper. For embittering life, for breaking up communities, for destroying the most sacred relationships; for devastating homes, for withering up men and women, for taking the bloom off childhood; in short, for sheer gratuitous misery-producing power, this influence stands alone.*

Finally, love "does not rejoice at wrong, but rejoices in the right." Love does not gloat over other people's miseries. If someone tells you

---

* *The Greatest Thing in the World* and Other Addresses (Old Tappan, N.J.), p. 18.

he is sick and you say, "Well, I hope it is nothing trivial," you may be clever but you are not exercising love. Love does not gloat over another's misfortune, but rejoices in honesty, in the truth, when it is brought out. Love is even willing to hear the truth about oneself. It is not so concerned about being protected from hurt or injury as it is in knowing what is really happening—what reality is. This is a great quality of true love.

Love Covers

Paul now gathers it all up with this beautiful expression,

> Love bears all things, believes all things, hopes all things, endures all things (v. 7).

"Bears all things" is literally "covers everything." Love covers. When it does learn something unpleasant about another it does not run and scatter it all over the neighborhood. It does not take delight in the misdeeds of others. Love covers it over, keeps it silent. Not that it will not do something about it, but it does not spread it about for others to hear.

Love "believes all things." That does not mean love is gullible. When Jesus was kissed by Judas in the garden he did not say to him, "Oh, Judas, what a beautiful kiss. I'm so glad you have changed your mind and are greeting me with love." No, he understood that this was a traitorous action. He said to Judas, "Would you betray the Son of man with a kiss?" He was not gullible. Nevertheless, love is ready to believe anything until it knows it is wrong. What this phrase means is that love is ready to trust someone anew. It does not assume the attitude, "Well you've been wrong three times before so I'm not going to trust you anymore." If someone sincerely wants another chance, love grants it.

Then, third, love "hopes all things." No cause, no situation, no person, is ever regarded as totally hopeless. There is always a place to begin again. Love will find it; it never gives up hope. Thus Paul adds the final word in this section: love "endures all things." Love never quits; it never gives up on anyone.

It has been pointed out that you can take this paragraph and insert "Jesus" in place of the word "love" and you will find that it fits perfectly:

> Jesus is patient and kind; Jesus is not jealous or boastful; he is not arrogant or rude; he does not insist on his own way; he is not irritable or resentful; he does not rejoice at wrong, but rejoices in the right. Jesus bears all things; he believes all things; he hopes all things; he endures all things.

When you read it that way it is clearly evident that love is the character of Christ. That is what the Holy Spirit is seeking to reproduce in us. Becoming Christlike means becoming a more loving person. That is the measure of our spiritual growth. I know Christians who do not seem to have changed in twenty years. They are just as querulous and cantankerous twenty years after they became Christians as they were at the beginning. Something is wrong in a life like that. The whole purpose and thrust of the Spirit is to teach us to be loving, patient, kind, forgiving, understanding, giving others a chance, trying again, being open to correction and instruction ourselves, and easy to be entreated. These are the qualities that make life worth the living. This is the measure of true Christian spirituality.

Like Bailing a Boat

Beginning with verse 8, Paul amplifies the persistence and the permanence of love. It is expressed in the opening words of verse 8:

Love never ends;

The various versions translate that in many ways because the apostle has employed a very unusual Greek word here, translated "ends" in the Revised Standard Version. It means, "to fall." It says love never "falls." That sounds strange to our ears, but it is meant in the sense that love never falls away or disappears, it never ceases. Love is never used up; it keeps on coming; the more you use it the more there is. If you exercise this kind of love you find yourself enabled to exercise it more all the time; the more you give it away the more you seem to have. Love is like bailing water out of a boat with a hole in it—you keep on throwing it out, but there is still more. One of my favorite hymns since I was a young Christian has been, "O Love That Wilt Not Let Me Go." That is the idea—love persists despite the rebuffs it may experience.

Some years ago I spoke at a conference in North Carolina and shared the platform with a friend, Dr. Stephen Olford, who for many years was pastor of Calvary Baptist Church in Manhattan. Stephen is an Englishman, raised on the mission field in Africa as the son of missionary parents. One morning at the conference he told us about his early boyhood. His father died when he was in Africa, and his mother took him back to England on a tramp steamer that took almost two weeks to reach London. They had not been out of port more than a few days when one of the seamen injured himself. His wound began to fester and to smell very bad, and the other seamen refused to have him in the cabin with them. They lacked adequate medicines to treat this man, and it looked as though he was going to die. He was in great pain, but the other men took him up and dumped him on the deck where he was exposed to the weather, and refused to let him come down again. They passed food to him with a long pole, for no one would touch him.

Stephen Olford's mother was a godly woman, and after about a day of this treatment she took pity on this man and went up to him. No one else would draw near because the stench was so terrible, but she took a basin of warm water, knelt beside him, and washed away the pus and the collected foul excrement of the wound. He cursed her, as he had cursed everybody who had come near him, but she patiently kept on and never said a word. She brought him his food that day, again in the evening, and again washed his wounds and took care of him. This went on for the duration of the voyage. When they arrived in London he was able to hobble off the ship. As you can well imagine, the display of love he had received broke through this man's bitter defenses. He became a Christian and a lifelong love-slave of Stephen Olford's mother.

I have remembered that story because it seems to illustrate so beautifully what Paul is describing here: love will not quit despite the obstacles that stand in its way. God's love is like that, Paul says. It will never cease, even though, for the best interest of another person it may appear temporarily to turn its back. God does with us as a mother eagle does with her young. To kick it out of the nest may look cruel, but the eagle knows that is the only way the young will learn to fly. She braves the wrath of her young to force it into maturity. God's love, true love will do that too, but even then it is hovering near, waiting and watching lest disaster strike, ready to help in time of need. That is surely what Paul is describing here.

He contrasts this quality of love with the things that will not last, the things that do cease, the things that pass away:

> Love never ends; as for prophecy, it will pass away; as for tongues, they will cease; as for knowledge, it will pass away (v. 8).

Obviously, this is still referring to spiritual gifts. It is not knowledge in general or prophecy in general; it is the "gift of knowledge," the "gift of prophecy," the "gift of tongues'" that he describes, the three favorite gifts at Corinth. Paul was telling them that, important and God-given as these gifts are, they were never intended to last. Compared to love, which never ceases, they most certainly will die. Two gifts, prophesying and knowledge, will fade away gradually, Paul suggests. That is inherent in the word he employs. They are gradually being replaced by something else, which he calls "the perfect." This is made clear in verses 9 and 10:

> For our knowledge is imperfect and our prophecy is imperfect; but when the perfect comes, the imperfect will pass away.

The question this brings up is, "What is this perfect thing which, increasing in our life, replaces our concern about gifts?" Some of the commentaries suggest that "the perfect" here is the written Word of God. They tell us that in the first century they did not have the New Testament as we have it. They relied upon the teaching of prophets, evangelists, apostles and others who spoke bits and pieces of the mind of God, but as the complete, written account of the mind of God took shape and form in the New Testament, the need for these spiritual gifts passed away. It is the claim of those who teach this that as the Word of God came into being in the written New Testament these gifts began to fade, so that the gifts of prophesying and of tongues and of knowledge have all long since ceased and we are now shut up to the written Word of God. There are elements of truth in that, but it largely ignores the context in which this word *perfect* appears. It makes no reference to a written word but speaks only of love. Others have suggested that what Paul is talking about is heaven. Heaven is the perfect place. Life is imperfect, and one of these days the wheels of earthly life will cease their turning, and we will go to heaven and then the "perfect" comes. Now there are also strong elements of truth in that. In fact, Paul will take up that theme a bit later in the paragraph. But again, that is not what the context suggests for the word *perfect* here at all.

The End Replaces the Means

If we take the passage in its full context, it is clear that the word *perfect* refers to love. Love is that "perfect" thing, which as it grows in our life, replaces our need for and concern with the gifts of the Spirit. We find ourselves growing up into that for which the gifts were designed, so when *the end* begins to be accomplished *the means* to that end are no longer required. This is confirmed by the illustration Paul employs in verse 11,

When I was a child, I spoke like a child, I thought like a child, I reasoned
like a child;

There is nothing wrong with that. Children are supposed to act like
children; everybody expects them to, and it would be wholly surprising
if they did not. Paul says he did when he was a child, but,

when I became a man, I gave up childish ways.

Why? Because he had become a man! That is the end toward which
a child moves—maturity. When it is achieved, childish things are no
longer needed. So what Paul is saying to these Corinthians (and to
us) is that the mark of maturity is the ability to love: to love the
unlovely, the selfish, the distasteful, the ungrateful. As that ability
increases in our life it will replace our childish concerns about the
gifts of the Spirit. To make much ado about gifts, as though they
were the overall important thing that God wants, is to be childish in
our attitudes.

Have you ever watched children on Christmas morning opening
their gifts? Their minds are focused on these new toys; there are so
many of them they cannot take them all in. They often seem to want
the one that someone else has. They play with one for a few moments,
cast it aside, and reach for another one—until their brother or sister
grabs the one they have just discarded. Then that one seems to assume
great importance in their eyes. They try to grab it back, and soon
there is a squabble going on over gifts.

That also happens in churches. To make much over gifts, as though
they were the important thing, is to miss the thrust of this passage.
Gifts are designed to lead us on to love. Prophesying is to teach us,
by the revelation of the mystery of God, that we have a power the
world knows nothing of: it is called "resurrection power," the power
to love as God loves. We learn that we can exercise it any time we
choose. We will not always feel it; it does not surge up to remind us
that it is there waiting. We make the decision because we ought to,
in obedience to God. But when we choose to obey and begin to do
so, the power is supplied to us. That is what prophesying teaches us.
The remarkable truth is revealed that we have a new, secret—the
power to love.

The gift of knowledge is given to help us systematize truth so that
we can instruct others in these great facts, and that, too, is the action
of love. The gift of languages (the gift of tongues), is given to arrest
the attention of unbelievers (Paul specifically says that in the next

chapter), so they will give heed to the magnificences of God, as they did on the Day of Pentecost when they heard 120 different people speaking in 16 languages, praising God. That arrested the attention of this crowd and they began to listen and give heed to the fact that God was at work. That is all designed to lead to love. To focus on gifts and forget the end to which they lead is foolish and hurtful and destructive. To squabble over gifts is the utmost folly in a church. Gifts are good, but they are passing away. What we ought to be writing books about, and issuing magazines over, and broadcasting over the radio and television, is the power to love, to reach out to the hurting and to minister to them.

I get tired of all the demands from phony Christian broadcasts today. They are often bleeding the people of God to support spectacular showmanship. They are wasting time, money and effort, instead of teaching the grassroots process of loving your neighbor as yourself.

In a meeting in Houston, Texas, a few years ago, there was a man present who had a gift of seeing through to the heart of things (it is really the gift of discerning spirits). He told about a letter he recently received from a large international radio broadcast, seeking support from Christians. The appeal of the letter was that God cannot be outgiven, and that if you give to God, he will give back to you. They announced that they needed a certain large sum of money to maintain their broadcast. They had estimated the number of their listening audience and in the letter they stated that if every person who heard their broadcasts would sent in $76 this large need would be met. Furthermore, they would guarantee, on the principle that God cannot be outgiven, that he would find a way to give that $76 back three times over!

This man in Houston said he wrote a letter back saying, "Sir, I believe what you have written; I believe it is true that God cannot be outgiven; and I believe you have a tremendous need for funds. But I would like to suggest that you send me the $76, for if God will give it back to you three times over you can get rid of your debt a lot faster that way." I believe this is the way to answer a letter like that. The essence of Christianity does not lie in its showmanship, but in its ability to love the hurting, the weak and the foolish.

Face to Face with Love

Love, then, is the "perfect" thing, which Paul says one day will be perfectly ours.

For now we see in a mirror dimly, but then face to face. Now I know in part; then I shall understand fully, even as I have been fully understood (v. 12).

Clearly he is anticipating the end of life and the dawning of a new day when every shadow will flee away, the imperfection of life will come to an end, and we will stand face to face with Love. Now, he says, it is like looking in a mirror dimly. He is describing the way we love today. Those ancient mirrors were not like the silvered glass we have today, giving a clear and beautiful image. Then, mirrors were simply highly polished metal, so that when you looked in them all you saw was a rather indistinct, blurred image. Paul says that is the way we love today.

We sometimes try to visualize the face of Jesus, but it is instructive that the Spirit of God has never given us a physical description of him. I do not like pictures of Jesus because to me they distract from what the Spirit is seeking to impart: the true beauty of his being, his life, his character. Others may be helped by pictures; I do not fault them for that. But Paul suggests our efforts to visualize the personality and the glory of Jesus are imperfect now, for we do not see him very clearly. But one of these days all those imperfect images will fade away, the mists will be dissolved, and we will suddenly find ourselves face to face with the Lord. Then we will love as we have been loved.

The disciples experienced a bit of this on the Day of Pentecost. In the Upper Room the Lord had said to them, "It is to your advantage that I go away." They looked at him with unbelieving eyes. They were surely thinking in their hearts, "How could that be? To lose you, to lose our chief treasure, is to leave life empty and meaningless, dull and dreary. We can hardly stand the thought of it. How could it be to our advantage that you go away?" But on the Day of Pentecost, when the Spirit came to reveal Christ to them, they understood what he meant, for suddenly all the questions they had been asking were answered and all the doubts they had were resolved. An inner confidence sprang up within them that Jesus was alive and was with them. They understood now what he had said; words that had puzzled them and had raised endless doubts and misconceptions in their minds were suddenly clear. That was just a foretaste of what will happen on the day when we stand in the presence of Jesus. "We shall be like him, for we shall see him as he is."

Paul suggests that that will happen with our knowledge as well. Now we try to grasp the way God works in history, to understand what he is doing in the events that fill our newspapers. We ask ourselves why God allows certain events to happen. We find ourselves able to see only dimly, only getting blurred and incomplete images of what God is doing. But one of these days, Paul says, we shall understand; we shall know him as fully as he now knows us. All our questions will be answered; all our problems will be resolved.

Throughout Eternity

So, in his final summary, Paul gathers it all up in the things that continually abide:

So faith, hope, love abide, these three; but the greatest of these is love (v. 13).

Faith abides, because faith is a human response to a divine provision. Faith is doing something with what God has given you, and that will go on through all eternity. We lack everything, we human beings have nothing in ourselves. We are constantly taking wisdom, power, instruction and ability from the hand of God. Everyone is, whether he knows it or not. We have no ability to function as a human being without receiving a gift of God first. Faith is a simple, deliberate response to such provision of God; therefore it abides, because we will go on doing that throughout eternity.

Hope abides, because hope is the expectation of yet more to come. There is a phrase earlier in this letter where Paul speaks of "the things God has prepared for those who love him." We are beginning to dabble in the shallows of that now; we have found a few of those things already, but there is an infinite number of such things and finiteness can never encompass infinity. God is going to keep on opening our eyes to new vistas, new adventures of faith forever. It will never grow old; it will never get less, because he is infinite. Hope, therefore, abides. But love abides too, and the reason it abides and is the greatest is because God is love. God is not faith; God is not hope; but God *is* love. To learn to love is to achieve the paramount value of the entire universe: to become like God. That is what life is all about, isn't it? The lie of the devil in the Garden of Eden was that if you disobey God you will be like God; you will learn how to have a godlike life. That lie and its sad results are visible all around us, in our own lives and everywhere in the world today. But the Word of God tells us to trust him, to follow him. To use what he gives you is one day to discover that the clouds pass away, the mists melt and the morning breaks, and all the shadows flee away. You are face to face with him—and you will be like him. When we see him we shall be like him; for we shall see him as he is. Therefore, "the greatest of these is love," for to learn to love is to learn to be godlike.

Paul concludes this section with the opening words of chapter 14.

Make love your aim.

The word is "pursue" it; set your heart on it; make it your chief goal. To become a loving, compassionate, patient, kind, truthful person is the reason we exist. Everything else must minister to that end or be regarded as useless and wasted time. May God help us to hold this clearly in our minds and understand the reality of these words, "the greatest of these is love."

20
—

Speaking of Tongues

Surely the subject of tongues is one of the most controversial issues in the church today. Practically the whole of chapter 14 is devoted to a comparison of the gifts of tongues and of prophesying. Both of these gifts were featured and focused upon in the church of Corinth, so the apostle gives some helpful insights on these gifts and how they contrast one with another.

The most important verse in the whole chapter is verse 1:

Make love your aim, and earnestly desire the spiritual gifts, especially that you may prophesy.

That verse ties back to the love chapter. It is good to remind ourselves that love is to be the basic, biblical reason for exercising a spiritual gift. To that end, the apostle says, "desire spiritual gifts" in order that they may be the means to help others and thus display love. This is not addressed to an individual but to a congregation. They all are to desire that the higher spiritual gifts will be exercised among them, to help them grow in spiritual power, effectiveness and influence in the city. Clearly, the one spiritual gift that is most effective in that direction is prophesying. Thus Paul says, "Make love your aim and earnestly desire the spiritual gifts, [but] especially that you may prophesy."

We have already seen that the gift of prophesying is not primarily predictive. It is basically explaining the present in the light of the revelation of God. the closest term we would use today is "expository preaching," the unfolding of the mind of God and applying it to the daily struggles of life. That, Paul says, is the gift to desire above all others.

Verses 2 through 5 are a little section that compares these two gifts in their value to the church. Paul begins with the gift of tongues:

> For one who speaks in a tongue speaks not to men but to God; for no one understands him, but he utters mysteries in the Spirit.

That is an important verse to help understand much of the controversy raging on this subject today. There are several things we need to learn from this. First, the word *tongue* is a reference to a real language. It is the common Greek word for language, and it is also the word for the member of the body that is used in speaking—the organ called the tongue. Metaphorically, it means a language spoken by that member of the body. There are numerous instances in Scripture where it is translated "language"; thus we have a clear hint at the beginning that the gift of tongues is the supernatural gift of speaking languages never learned, just as it was on the Day of Pentecost.

Then the apostle tells us that the language so spoken is not addressed to men but to God. Sometimes today, when interpretations of tongues are made, the content makes clear that the message is a kind of exhortation to the audience. That is not the true gift of tongues, for according to the Word of God tongues are never addressed to men.

The true gift of tongues consists of praise, prayer, thanksgiving and singing unto God. This is confirmed in verses 14 through 17. Here Paul is describing his own practice in this regard. He says (v. 15), "I will *pray* with the spirit," (that is, in tongues), "and I will pray with the mind" (in normal prayer); also, "I will *sing* with the spirit." Then he says in verse 16, "if you *bless* with the spirit . . ." (bless God); again, in verse 16, "your *thanksgiving,*" and in verse 17, "you may *give thanks* well enough. . . ." Obviously, the content of tongues is a message of praise and prayer, addressed to God himself, thanking him for his mercy and blessing.

Paul also declares that anyone who speaks in tongues is not understood in the congregation because "he speaks mysteries in the Spirit." This does not mean he was speaking things no one had ever heard before; it meant that he was simply speaking in a language they did not understand. It would, therefore, appear to be something mysterious. In the church at Corinth people were standing up and speaking in tongues which, perhaps, were recognizable as languages used somewhere nearby (as on the Day of Pentecost), but the people in the church did not understand the language and so they could not know what the speaker was saying. He was uttering "mysteries [to them] in the Spirit."

One further thing needs to be said before leaving this section. The verse clearly makes apparent that it is the true, Spirit-given, biblical gift of tongues that is being discussed in this chapter. Some commentators today tell us that what Paul is discussing here is a carry-over from the pagan practices around. In the pagan mystery religions there was a kind of ecstatic utterance, a purely psychological phenomenon (which I will comment on later) that was induced by religious excitement. It consisted of babble, an incoherent stammering made up of various syllables and sounds. Because this was practiced in the mystery religions of Corinth, some expositors tell us that this was also the problem in the church at Corinth.

I cannot agree with that because all through this chapter the apostle interjects references to his own practice of the gift of tongues. He makes no distinction whatsoever between the way he spoke in tongues and the way these Corinthians were speaking in tongues. He does not put their gift down. In fact in this very verse he declares it is "in the Spirit" and it is addressed to God. He himself spoke in tongues, as he tells us plainly in this chapter. Therefore, it could not be the pagan practice that is referred to here; it was the true, biblical gift of tongues as it was manifested also on the Day of Pentecost.

Explaining Revelation

In contrast, Paul now describes the gift of prophesying:

> On the other hand, he who prophesies speaks to men for their upbuilding and encouragement and consolation (v. 3).

Prophesying, as we have already said, is basically the explaining and expounding of the mind of God. Calvin called it "the peculiar gift of explaining revelation." It is to apply the world view of Scripture to the circumstances of men, so that men can see what is happening in their lives in terms of how God understands it to be, and as different from the illusions, fantasies, and mistaken concepts of the world around them. It is a needed gift in our day as well as in the first century because it has, as Paul says, a threefold effect. First, it builds people up; the word is *oikodomen*. In the Greek, *oiko* means "house," and *domen* means "to build." To build a house on a solid foundation is the concept; so the gift of prophesying gives people a solid foundation of truth upon which to build their lives.

One of the major problems among Christians today is the struggle to achieve a true identity. Many people are emotionally torn because they do not understand the revelation of the Word of God that they are new creatures in Christ Jesus; they are no longer what they once were. Because they still feel like what they once were, they believe those feelings and they react accordingly. There follows an up-and-down experience that they can never get away from. But prophesying corrects that. It teaches us who we truly are in Christ. That is why it is so needed in our day, as it was needed in Corinth.

The second thing prophesying does is to strengthen people. This is the Greek word from which we get the word *Paraclete*, one of the titles of the Holy Spirit. He is the Strengthener of God's people. The word means to support and encourage; it is literally "one called alongside," to support, steady, and strengthen.

The third ministry of prophesying is that of comforting. The Greek word used here is *paramuthian* which means to "empathize, to put oneself in the place of others, to feel the pressures they are under." It means to be able to identify with them and thus to comfort them with the fact that you too have been there, but to assure them God is working it out with them as he worked it out with you. That is what the word of prophesying is intended to do. We have all had the experience of listening to the text of Scripture expounded so as to speak right to our basic problem. That is the gift of prophesying. It is easy to see how useful and important it is to have this gift exercised in a church.

The apostle now goes on:

> He who speaks in a tongue edifies himself, but he who prophesies edifies the church (v. 4).

There is some personal benefit to the individual who is praising God in a language he has never learned and does not even understand himself. His spirit is praising God and, therefore, it is blessed, and he himself feels refreshed. There is benefit to him, but he is the only one helped; therefore, tongues without interpretation is self-centered; it ignores the needs of others. It is denying the apostle's appeal to act in love, and to "make love your aim," which is to build up, bless, and strengthen others around you. But prophesying, as Paul says, "edifies the church," and, therefore, fulfills the demands of love. So he continues:

> Now I want you all to speak in tongues, but even more to prophesy. He who prophesies is greater than he who speaks in tongues, unless some one interprets, so that the church may be edified (v.5).

That is his thrust throughout the rest of this chapter. The church must be fed, and tongues by itself will not do it, unless they are interpreted.

In the next section (v. 6 through v. 12) he is simply developing this need a little more. To understand this we must put ourselves back into that first-century world where people were glorying in these supernatural manifestations of being able to do what no natural man could do—speak a language they had never learned. They were encouraging this sort of thing rather than encouraging people to really expound and explain the mind of God. That is why Paul spends time with this.

Profitable Things

In this section he describes the effect of uninterpreted tongues in the church. First, he declares it is not profitable:

> Now, brethren, if I come to you speaking in tongues, how shall I benefit you unless I bring you some revelation or knowledge or prophecy or teaching? (v. 6).

Paul uses himself as an example. He says, in effect, "If I come to you and all I do is stand up and praise God in an unlearned language I am perhaps blessed by that, but you are not profited at all. What I could do that would profit you would be these four: First, I might bring you a revelation." This was his special privilege as an apostle. Christ had taught him truth others did not know. The writings of the New Testament are apostolic revelation. For him to do this at Corinth would have blessed them tremendously.

Or, he could have exercised the gift of knowledge. He is referring to his vast knowledge of the Old Testament. He could have shared an Old Testament account and taught them from it. That too would have been a great blessing to them. Or, he could have prophesied. He could have illuminated their present situation by an insight from the mind of God. That would have strengthened them. He could have simply taught them, explaining in detail certain doctrinal matters that would have made them understand more of the range and spectrum of divine instruction. But to simply stand up and speak in tongues was of no benefit at all unless someone explained what he had said. He thus sets tongues aside as a ministry that would not benefit the church.

As an illustration, he gives two pictures which would parallel the use of tongues without interpretation. One is in the realm of music:

> If even lifeless instruments, such as the flute or the harp, do not give distinct notes, how will any one know what is played? And if the bugle gives an indistinct sound, who will get ready for battle? (vv. 7, 8).

If I were appointed to be a bugler in a military camp, and it was my responsibility to blow reveille or retreat, the whole place would soon be in chaos. No one would know whether to get up, or go to a meal, or what, because I do not know how to play a bugle. So Paul suggests, "If you are going to blow a bugle you had better blow it so everybody understands." He draws the conclusion:

> So with yourselves; if you in a tongue utter speech that is not intelligible [in a language that no one understands], how will any one know what is said? For you will be speaking into the air (v. 9).

He follows this with an illustration from the realm of communication:

> There are doubtless many different languages in the world, and none is without meaning; but if I do not know the meaning of the language, I shall be a foreigner to the speaker and the speaker a foreigner to me. So with yourselves; since you are eager for manifestations of the Spirit, strive to excel in building up the church (vv. 10–12).

That is very plain, is it not? There are many languages (here again is a confirmation that the gift of tongues is a gift of languages), and Paul says those languages all have meanings. But you cannot get at the meaning if you do not know the language. Someone must interpret it for you, or it is all a waste of time.

Therefore, in verses 13 through 19, he suggests how to make the true, biblical gift of tongues (languages) of benefit to the congregation. First, he says,

> Therefore, he who speaks in a tongue should pray for the power to interpret (v. 13).

This suggests that when God gives the gift of tongues (as he obviously did in the first-century world), he also gives a gift of interpretation. But there must be a deliberate attempt made to exercise that gift.

So Paul urges them that if they can exercise the gift of tongues they ought to pray to exercise the gift of interpretation. The one is useless in the church without the other.

Then he brings in his own practice again:

> For if I pray in a tongue, my spirit prays but my mind is unfruitful (v. 14).

There is the testimony of a man whom we love and trust, telling us what the effect of this gift is upon the one who exercises it. His spirit, the deep, central essence of his humanity, is worshiping God, but it is not articulated into words. He himself, in his own mind, does not understand. He senses that he is worshiping, but he does not know how. He does not understand the language he is speaking and, therefore, he does not know specifically what he is praising God about. So Paul says, "If I pray in a tongue my spirit prays but my mind is unfruitful."

What am I to do?

Well, the answer is obvious. He has just told us. He should pray for the power to interpret. That is what he does.

> I will pray with the spirit and I will pray with the mind also (v. 15).

"If I am going to speak in tongues in a church," he says, "I will never do it unless I also interpret what I say. I will pray with the mind also."

> I will sing with the spirit and I will sing with the mind also. ["I will never do one without the other."] Otherwise, if you bless with the spirit, how can any one in the position of an outsider say the "Amen" to your thanksgiving when he does not know what you are saying? For you may give thanks well enough, but the other man is not edified (vv. 15–17).

Here again it is clear that the exercise of tongues without interpretation in a public assembly is a self-centered procedure that does not allow the participation of others even to say "Amen." Nothing must be done in church that does not edify all.

Impressive to the Jews

Again speaking of himself, Paul adds a biographical section:

> I thank God that I speak in tongues more than you all; nevertheless, in church I would rather speak five words with my mind, in order to instruct others, than ten thousand words in a tongue (vv. 18, 19).

That is a strong emphasis, and it raises the question, "When did the apostle Paul speak in tongues?" He obviously does not intend to do it in church, for there he would much rather exercise the gift of prophesying. When then did he do it? Modern charismatics and Pentecostals tell us, "This proves that the gift of tongues is for private use, to be used at home as a prayer language." I know that sounds logical at this point, but I do not think it is true, for nowhere in the Word of God is the exercise of the gift of tongues ever referred to as a private practice. Every manifestation of tongues in the New Testament, without exception, is a public demonstration. That was true on the Day of Pentecost; in the home of Cornelius, where many were assembled; and in the synagogue at Ephesus, referred to in Acts 19. These were the only places where the gift of tongues was recorded as exercised, beside the manifestations at Corinth, and they were public manifestations, occurring in the church assembly. Then when and where did Paul speak in tongues? The only situation that fulfills all the biblical requirements for the use of the gift of tongues would be those occasions when Paul went into the Jewish synagogues. There provision was made for visitors to praise God publicly. Such praise, in a language never learned, would be most impressive to the Jewish people present, especially if it were a Gentile tongue. It would fulfill Isaiah's prophecy, "By men of strange tongues and by the lips of foreigners will I speak to this people."

To confirm this explanation, the apostle goes on to describe, in a brief paragraph, what the intended purpose of the gift of tongues was. He opens with a word of caution:

> Brethren, do not be children in your thinking; be babes in evil, but in thinking be mature (v. 20).

Why does he insert that exhortation here? Because in the mystery religions there was a kind of babbling, ecstatic sound that could sound much like a language. To an uninitiated person it would be hard to tell the difference. So he warns these Corinthians: "Now investigate such matters. Do not be naïve, like children, and assume that everything you might hear is the true gift of tongues. Obvious evil you do not have to investigate. When you know something is evil stay away from it; you do not need to delve into it or probe it for you already know it is evil. But when it comes to spiritual gifts, be mature in your thinking and investigate."

Then Paul gives them the basis upon which they were to judge. He quotes from the Book of Isaiah in the Old Testament. It is the only prediction of tongues in the Old Testament and is, therefore, to be the basis for their decision: does the manifestation you are hearing fulfill the predicted purpose for the gift of tongues?

In the law it is written, "By men of strange tongues and by the lips of foreigners will I speak to this people, and even then they will not listen to me, says the Lord." Thus, tongues are a sign not for believers but for unbelievers, while prophesying is not for unbelievers but for believers (vv. 21, 22).

You could hardly ask for plainer language than that. The gift of tongues is a *sign gift*. A sign to whom? The quotation from Isaiah 28 makes it clear. Isaiah was speaking to the whole nation of Israel at a time when the Assyrians were knocking at the doors of Jerusalem, threatening to capture it. Through the prophet God is warning the nation that if they do not repent and turn from their evil and idolatrous ways they will hear foreigners talking in the streets of the Holy City; they will hear Gentile tongues spoken throughout the city. It was a warning to Israel to clear up their relationship with God lest he turn from them to the Gentile world.

That was the setting for Isaiah's words. One hundred years later they were completely fulfilled when the Babylonians came in and the streets of Jerusalem were filled with foreigners speaking strange tongues. Read the account of the Day of Pentecost in that light and you will see how fully it accords with this prediction. On that day, when the streets of Jerusalem were filled with thousands of people, mostly Jews, who had come from many of the nations around, they heard the disciples speaking strange, Gentile languages which they had never learned. It was a sign to the unbelieving Jews that God was about to end Israel's favored position and turn to the Gentile world. On that day Peter stood up and warned the Jews that they were facing the judgment of God. Being convicted in their hearts, they said, "Men and brethren, what must we do?" and 3000 of them turned to God while the rest of the city, the mass of the population, remained in unbelief.

That is what Isaiah said would happen: "By men of strange tongues and by the lips of foreigners will I speak to this people, and even then they will not listen to me, says the Lord." So, Paul says, that is the purpose of the gift of tongues; that is why he used it in synagogues wherever he went. It would be a sign of warning to unbelieving Jews that God was turning to the Gentiles.

Not for the Church

Now many have been confused by the next two verses, which appear to be a reversal of that position.

If, therefore, the whole church assembles and all speak in tongues, and outsiders or believers enter, will they not say that you are mad? But if all prophesy, and an unbeliever or outsider enters, he is convicted by all, he is called to account by all, the secrets of his heart are disclosed; and so, falling on his face, he will worship God and declare that God is really among you (vv. 23, 24).

Many say, "That sounds like the opposite of what Paul has just said." He said, "Tongues are a sign for unbelievers," and yet he goes on to say that if people speak in tongues in the church and a nonbeliever comes in he will not be at all impressed by that sign. He will say, "They are all mad; they are crazy; they all speak in languages I cannot understand." But if they all prophesy, Paul says, the unbeliever will hear the Word of God and be convicted. He will fall on his face and say that God is among them. In fact, verse 23 seems to be so much the reverse of what Paul has just said in verse 22 that J. B. Phillips actually dares to change the two verses around. In his translation he makes Paul say exactly the opposite of what he says here. That is why you cannot always trust paraphrases, because they take liberties with the text.

What does Paul mean? He is going back to what has been his thesis all through this passage: that the gift of tongues is not really intended for the church. It is "not for believers"; it is "for unbelievers." If it is exercised in a church, especially by several people who stand up and speak and no one interprets, any unbelievers who happen to be there will not understand it as a sign gift because it is not apparently addressed to them. They will see it as an attempt to minister to the people present, even though no one understands the tongues. So the visitors will think that everybody is mad. I have seen this actually happen in meetings today where what is claimed to be the gift of tongues is exercised.

But if prophesying occurs and unbelievers hear the Spirit of God speaking the mind of God, they are often convicted. I have known hundreds of people who came to Christ while I was teaching the Christians. They hear the truth, the Spirit brings it home to their hearts, and they are converted. That is what Paul said would happen. Thus, when the gift of tongues was properly exercised it was addressed to unbelieving Jews in some public meeting place. Now that means that it could properly be exercised today. Once again the nation Israel has come back into prominence, and there are many unbelieving Jews being reached today. This gift could reappear in our day, but if it does, it will have all the marks of the biblical gift of tongues.

That raises a final question: "Is what we are hearing around us today the biblical gift of tongues?" My judgment is, "No, it is not." I have heard hundreds of manifestations of what is called "tongues" today, and I am alarmed by the fact that hardly anyone ever asks, "Is this a true language, or not?" William Samarin, professor of linguistics at the University of Toronto, says,

> Over a period of five years I have taken part in meetings in Italy, Holland, Jamaica, Canada and the United States. I have observed old-fashioned Pentecostals and neo-Pentecostals. I have been in small meetings in private homes as well as in mammoth public meetings. I have seen such different cultural settings as are found among Puerto Ricans of the Bronx, the snake handlers of the Appalachians and the Russian Molakans of Los Angeles. . . . I have interviewed tongue speakers, and tape recorded and analyzed countless samples of tongues. In every case, glossolalia turns out to be linguistic nonsense. In spite of superficial similarities, glossolalia is fundamentally not language.

The present manifestation is not a language, and it is usually not addressed to God. It is more often addressed to the people present, so again it does not fit the qualifications of the biblical gift. It is primarily exercised privately today, whereas, as we have seen, there is no indication of the private use of tongues in the New Testament. Finally, it is not a sign to unbelievers today; therefore, we must judge that the phenomenon which we see and hear today is not the biblical gift of tongues. Many people are being misled, oftentimes quite earnestly and sincerely, into identifying a purely psychological phenomenon as the biblical gift of tongues. Many temperaments are capable of this kind of self-induced hypnosis which results in a repetition of sounds and syllables that have no meaning in themselves. In itself the phenomenon is relatively harmless. It was common throughout the ancient world. Plato discussed it in several of his discourses, and it was practiced commonly in the mystery religions of that day. It is often, throughout the history of the church, associated with religious excitement and is practiced by cults and non-Christian religions as well. But this is what is being identified today as the gift of tongues.

Now if the true gift is present, Paul says, ". . . forbid not to speak with tongues." But when that which is not the biblical gift, but is mistakenly called such, is being exercised, we have every right to discourage its use and even forbid it as a divisive activity within the church.

Paul now brings the discussion into the arena of general behavior at the regular meetings of the Church at Corinth. It is hard to define a local church in the New Testament concept. It is almost like nailing jello to the wall! Every time you think you have grasped it, it slips between your fingers. But one thing is clear from the biblical accounts, and that is, the early church frequently met together. From the earliest times, Christians felt the urge to meet and share together with brothers and sisters in the family of God. What they did when they met was largely to worship and to minister to one another. They shared their spiritual gifts, exercising what God had given them for each other's benefit.

Verse 26 describes that procedure:

> What then, brethren? When you come together each one has a hymn, a lesson, a revelation, a tongue, or an interpretation. Let all things be done for edification.

We do not know how large the church at Corinth was. Perhaps by this time, several years after it had begun, it was of considerable size—possibly several hundred people had been converted and were meeting together. If so, it would have been difficult always to allow everyone to have a part. We know that shortly after Pentecost the early church in Jerusalem consisted of as many as 10,000 members. Obviously, they would have had great difficulty in finding a place to meet together with a church that large, and certainly it would be impossible to let *everyone* have "a hymn, a lesson, a revelation, etc." The meetings would probably still be going on, knowing how Christians tend to run on at times. This verse probably describes a smaller, home-type meeting where it was possible to have this kind of intimacy of sharing and this universality of participation. But in either type of meeting, one thing was clearly evident; there was but one aim in getting together. Paul says, "Let all things be done for edification."

"Edification" means more than simply teaching, or instruction of the mind; the word is larger than that. It means to build people up. When you come to church you expect to be built up, edified, instructed, encouraged, comforted, uplifted. It does something for you to gather together. It starts the week out right. It cleanses away the cobwebs that have been gathering through the previous week. That is what the apostle describes here. When Christians get together it ought to be the aim of the meeting that everything done contributes to the understanding of the mind, the uplifting of the spirit, and the encouraging of the heart. That is the edifying process, involving growth, understanding, worship, and exhortation to activity on the basis that God is going to be with you and working through you all week. That was the reason for the church meeting in the first century, and it still ought to be today.

In the next section, beginning with verse 27 and through to the end of the chapter, the apostle will deal with three problem areas in the church: the exercise of three gifts which create, or tend to create, certain problems. The first is the exercise of the gift of tongues. Then the matter of prophesying. As excellent a gift as prophesying was, it could be misused, and Paul is concerned about that. Third, there was the question of the freedom of women to minister in the church. All these issues gave rise to debate, division and dissension, and that created problems in the church at Corinth.

Fundamental Rules

To avoid these problems, Paul suggests certain rules. "Oh," you say, "I don't like rules. They always lay restrictions on people." Well, I do not like rules either. I basically resist rules, but I learned many years ago that you cannot function as a corporate body without some rules. You cannot play a game of football without rules; the rules make the game possible. You cannot play a game of chess without rules; you cannot drive through traffic without rules.

So certain fundamental rules are necessary, and the apostle turns first to rules about tongues:

> If any speak in a tongue, let there be only two or at most three, and each in turn; and let one interpret. But if there is no one to interpret, let each of them keep silence in church and speak to himself and to God (vv. 27, 28).

Three simple limits govern the exercise of the biblical gift of tongues. First, only one or two should speak—at the very most the limit would be three. Why? Because tongues-speaking was an emotional experience, and too much emotion in a meeting is destructive. Too little is destructive, too, but the apostle is trying to regulate it so it will not be too much of a good thing. Therefore, he limits it to one or two, and they must speak in order. There is to be no duplication or multiplicity of people speaking all at once, so that everyone may enjoy the ministry of praise to God.

Second, he seems to imply that one of those who spoke in these unlearned languages must have the gift of interpretation. He says, "Let there be only two or at most three, and each in turn; and let

one interpret." Third, if no one is able to interpret, then no one is
to speak in tongues in the church because tongues *must* be interpreted,
for edification. Paul seems to imply that one who speaks in a language
ought to find out whether anyone has the ability to interpret before
he speaks. If there is no one to interpret, then, Paul says, "let him
speak to himself." That means to praise God in his spirit, in his
thoughts, but not in words. Anyone can do that without disturbing a
meeting. Paul then turns to rules concerning prophesying.

> Let two or three prophets speak, and let the others weigh what is said. If
> a revelation is made to another sitting by, let the first be silent. For you
> can all prophesy one by one, so that all may learn and all be encouraged;
> and the spirits of prophets are subject to prophets. For God is not a God
> of confusion but of peace (vv. 29–33).

Once again, there are three simple controls. Remember, Paul has in
view a small home-type meeting where there were probably no more
than twenty people present, so they could each take turns prophesying.
But at any one meeting it was to be limited to two, or three at the
most. This was in order to prevent lengthy meetings. When one prophe-
sies one tends to take a little longer time; that is because one is explaining things. Preachers are notorious for being long-winded. Some seem
to have no terminal facilities, so it is necessary to control them by
artificial means. The apostle seems well aware of the truth of the
saying, "The mind can absorb only what the seat can endure."

Then the second rule was that prophesying should be evaluated:
"Let the others weigh what is said." Prophesying is an attempt to
expound and explain the mind of God. It is not guaranteed by inspira-
tion. Everything a prophet says is not necessarily true; therefore, it is
subject to the judgment and comment of others. In these small meetings
in Corinth it was expected that anyone who spoke as a prophet would
be subject to the confirmation and correction, if necessary, of the
others present.

The third limit was to let prophesying be one by one: "If a revelation
is made to another sitting by, let the first be silent." In other words,
no one was to take over the meeting. That was for two reasons. First,
because "the spirit of the prophet is subject to the prophet." Someone
might have insisted, "I can't help what I say. The Spirit of God is
in me and he is speaking through me, therefore, everything I say is
of God." Paul would say, "Rubbish! The spirit of the prophet is subject
to the prophet. You can control yourself; you need not claim that
you have to say these things." Someone has said there are always two

kinds of speakers—those who have something to say, and those who
have to say something. The apostle wants to limit the latter. The
second reason is that the Spirit of God never creates confusion or
disorder. No one is to dominate a meeting, because God does not
work that way. Let the meeting be orderly so as to give room for
others to speak and to share in the ministry. Remember, if there is
strife, jealousy, confusion, argument and that kind of thing, it is not
a meeting led by the Spirit of God. Some other spirit is at work.

Getting Carried Away

That brings Paul to the third major area of difficulty in the church,
and that is the ministry of women. Verse 33 is properly divided here
in the RSV.

> As in all the churches of the saints, the women should keep silence in
> the churches. For they are not permitted to speak, but should be subordinate,
> as even the law says. If there is anything they desire to know, let them
> ask their husbands at home. For it is shameful for a woman to speak in
> church (vv. 33–35).

This passage has caused many today to write off the apostle Paul as
a bitter old bachelor who hated women and who was threatened by
the exercise of any gifts by women. But, of course, that is a total
travesty on the character of the apostle. It ignores many other detailings
of his relationship with women in the Scriptures. It is clear from several
accounts that there were certain women who traveled in a mixed group
of men and women together, to help him in many ways in his ministry.
The apostle speaks of these individual women with respect and love,
showing warmth and praise for their work in the ministry. To regard
Paul as a woman-hating bachelor is to misread the Scriptures. In fact,
in chapter 11 of this same letter, Paul strongly defends the right of
women to pray and prophesy in the church meeting. The only problem,
he says, is that they must demonstrate in some way that they recognize
God's moral order of leadership, the principle of headship. Paul dealt
with that at length in that chapter.

No, the problem here is not whether a woman should minister in
the church at all. That was done at Corinth, despite the traditional
interpretation of these verses during the last two centuries. The problem
was still, as the context makes clear, one of disorder and confusion.
It was a problem which grew out of the very freedom that women
did have to minister in the church at Corinth. Both the Jewish community, and to a large degree the Greek community, put down the ministry

of women. Certainly the Jews did; they did not allow it at all, but here in a Christian church women were permitted to minister under the recognition of the principle of headship. As a consequence, some of them undoubtedly went too far. This is a normal human tendency within all of us. They ran away with freedom. Some were evidently asking questions and entering into debates, thus turning the church meetings into a discussion group. Some, as Paul indicated earlier, had abandoned the head covering which in the city of Corinth was a sign that they recognized the leadership order that God had instituted. They were thus creating not only dissension, but as he indicates here, a "shameful" situation. Non-Christians in the city were disregarding the word of Christians because of this.

That this is what the apostle was concerned about is confirmed by his choice of words here. Notice that he does not say it is forbidden for women to minister in the church. He does not say that women may not prophesy or pray or teach. Women are forbidden, he says, to speak—"the women should keep silence . . . they are not permitted to speak." The word for "speak" is *laleo*, which is the most common word for conversation. We could well use the word *chatter*. Women were entering into discussions and often were carried away so that they turned the meeting into a free discussion session.

It is well known that garrulousness is more frequently found in women than in men. Men can be loose-tongued and run off at the mouth, too, but women more often have this problem. There is a story of a woman who was rebuked for talking too much. She said, "But how can I know what I think till I've heard what I have to say?" But Paul says the place for extensive discussion about these matters is the home—"let her ask her husband at home." If you come to my house when my wife and I are involved in a theological discussion, you will know exactly what the apostle means. It goes on for hours, upstairs and downstairs. Then it is broken off for a while and we pick it up again at the table. My wife has a keen, theological mind, which I greatly appreciate, and we have some interesting discussions on theological matters. Paul says that is where these lengthy discussions and debates ought to take place, not in the church meeting.

Recognize the Authority

In verses 36 through 38 the apostle anticipates the reaction of many:

What! Did the word of God originate with you, or are you the only ones it has reached?

That is clearly satire. He is recognizing there was a tendency among some in Corinth to think they had unique revelation, and were free to do what others could not. There are people who assume they have direct authority from God, and they will even set aside the Scripture to sustain that. So Paul says:

If any one thinks that he is a prophet, or spiritual, he should acknowledge that what I am writing to you is a command of the Lord.

Truly spiritual people always recognize the authority of the Scripture. This is important in these days when people are claiming to be specially led of the Spirit. When you point out from the Scripture that something they say or do is contrary to it, they still insist that their feeling, or experience, or understanding is superior to the Word of God. Paul declares this is not true. The Spirit of God never operates contrary to the written Word. Anyone who is truly Spirit-minded and Spirit-filled will recognize the authority of the Word of God.

The third thing he says to them follows in verse 38:

If any one does not recognize this, he is not recognized.

Literally, "If any one be ignorant, let him be ignored." In other words, do not pay attention to him; do not needlessly exalt him or her by getting engaged in a lengthy debate about it. If they will not listen to the authority of the Word, then do not give them a platform from which to speak. Ignore them.

He closes with a statement which gathers up the whole matter of disorder.

So, my brethren, earnestly desire to prophesy, and do not forbid speaking in tongues; but all things should be done decently and in order.

That has been his thrust in the whole passage. Encourage prophesying, he says, it will build people up—it will comfort, strengthen, and edify them. That is to be the supreme ministry when the church comes together. But do not forbid speaking in tongues, he says. No one knows whether there will come in an unbeliever for whom a message in tongues may be a sign. God is sovereign, and he has the right to give gifts as he pleases, so do not forbid their exercise. But if it is the true, biblical gift of tongues it will have the effect of being a sign to unbelievers. In all things, Paul says, let everything be done decently and in order for God is a God of order.

21

The Foundation of Faith

The fifteenth chapter of 1 Corinthians is undoubtedly the climax of all that Paul has been saying in this letter. One of the most relevant questions of our day is, "What happens after death?" A dozen books have come off the presses recently dealing with this theme. Many are speculating about it; many testimonies are being given of the experiences of those who supposedly have died and then come back to life again. The apostle is dealing with that theme in this chapter. He brings us face to face with a great reality of life, one that is even more certain than taxes, and that is death. You may evade paying your taxes, but you will not avoid growing old and ultimately dying. Many try to avoid it. I know people who are working hard at trying to cover up the evidences of age and decay. But we must face the fact that there is an irresistible and inevitable process going on in every one of us right now. No matter how old or how young we may be, this process is slowly stealing the bloom from our cheeks, taking the spring from our steps, reducing the sharpness of our senses, decreasing our sexual powers, and in many ways depriving us of what we think to be the joy of living.

Now, in one of the most wonderful passages in all literature, the apostle Paul faces this ultimate enemy of mankind with the declaration that Jesus is victor in this area as in others. Paul shows us in the opening verses that the resurrection of the body is part of the foundation of the Christian faith—an essential part of the good news of the gospel.

279

> Now I would remind you, brethren, in what terms I preached to you the gospel, which you received, in which you stand, by which you are saved, if you hold it fast—unless you believed in vain. For I delivered to you as of first importance what I also received, that Christ died for our sins in accordance with the scriptures, that he was buried, that he was raised on the third day in accordance with the scriptures . . . (vv. 1–3).

There the apostle sets forth in forthright, simple language the good news about Jesus.

There are two simple and obvious divisions of what he says. He talks about what the gospel *does*, and what the gospel *is*, in that order. We shall look first at what the gospel is, because many people really do not understand it. You ask someone, "What is the gospel?" and he may say, "Jesus died and rose again." But that is not the gospel, and that is not what Paul says is the gospel. We must learn precisely what the gospel is. Let us look at that first and then come back to what the apostle says the gospel does.

There are three elements of the gospel, according to Paul. First, "I delivered to you as of first importance (that which is foundational, fundamental to our understanding) what I also received." From whom did he receive it? In other places he tells us that it was from the Lord Jesus himself who appeared to him and taught him the gospel. He did not learn it from the other apostles. Read the opening words of Paul's letter to the Galatians. There Paul says, "I did not learn it from men, nor was I taught it by man." The Lord himself delivered it to him, and what he thus received from the lips of Jesus he passed on to these Corinthians. They received it, they believed it, they accepted the One of whom it spoke, and thus they became Christians.

Starting with His Death

Paul now declares what that word is. He reminds them what he had preached to them. First: "Christ died for our sins in accordance with the scriptures." That is the first element. It is amazing that he does not mention a word about the life of Jesus. He passes over the marvelous birth in a cave in Bethlehem, omits the silent years at Nazareth and the journeying up and down the hillsides of Judea and Galilee, even the marvel of his teaching and his miracles, and comes quickly and immediately to his death. There, Paul says, is the first element of the gospel.

That is rather startling, but that is where the gospel begins. Even here he does not simply say, "Christ died." Everyone believes that

Jesus died. Go to any of the modern presentations of the life of Jesus, such as *Jesus Christ Superstar,* and you will find they all end at the death of Jesus. Every humanistic philosophy today accepts the fact that Jesus died. But there is no good news in that. The good news is that Christ died *for our sins according to the Scriptures.* That is good news, that his death accomplished something for us. It changed us, it delivered us, it set us free. That death had great significance in the mind and heart of God. That is the good news. As Peter puts it, "He himself bore our sins in his body on the tree." Or, to use the words of Isaiah, "He was wounded *for our transgressions,* he was bruised *for our iniquities:* the chastisement of our peace was upon him; and with his stripes *we are healed."*

That is the good news. God did something for us in that marvelous event of the cross. As we contemplate the cross and the dying of Jesus in our place, we learn that the good news is that God takes it seriously and he is prepared to treat us in an entirely different way than we deserve on the basis of the death of Jesus on our behalf. There on the cross, we are told, he dealt with our failures, our rebellion, our sinful, guilty lives. Our besmirched past need no longer trouble us. It has been set aside by the death of Jesus. By that fact we enter into hope and freedom.

Apart from that fact life is really hopeless. The philosophy many have is that God is a judge, weighing the good and the evil of life, and if the good outweighs the evil you get in and if it doesn't you go to hell. That view is not only unbiblical but it is illogical. How could a God of holiness, justice and purity ever accept evil at all? His demands are for perfection and never anything less. He himself is perfect, and he says to us, "Be ye perfect for I am perfect." What are we going to do with a guilty past in the light of that? The answer, of course, is the good news of the cross. In the cross of Jesus God has dealt with our sinful past. He offers to us freely the forgiveness of our sins, and full acceptance before him.

The second element of the gospel, according to Paul, is that Jesus not only "died for our sins in accordance with the scriptures," but he was also buried. I am always startled when I read that. Why does Paul include the burial of Jesus as part of the gospel? Is it not enough that Jesus died and rose again? Would that not be good news? Surely the reason for this is that when his disciples came and took the body of Jesus down from the cross, his burial marked their acceptance of the fact of his death.

It was hard for them to accept the fact that he had died. They did not want to believe when he himself told them that he was about to die. They refused it, they shut their minds to it. When it actually happened they went away stunned and unbelieving, unwilling to see that all the hopes and dreams which they had built up in those marvelous years with him should come crashing down and end in ashes at their feet. But after the cross some realist among them faced up to it and said, "We have got to go and get his body and bury him." Joseph of Arimathea came forward and offered a tomb, and with loving hands they took his body down from the tree. They wrapped it in graveclothes and bound it tightly, wrapping his head in a separate cloth. They embalmed him with spices and then placed him in a tomb where he lay for at least two long nights. There is no question that the disciples believed he was actually dead. They could never have accepted the idea of some today that he had merely fainted on the cross or was in a coma, for they themsleves had performed the burial service. That burial testifies to all succeeding generations that Jesus of Nazareth was thoroughly and positively dead.

The third element of the gospel is, "he was raised on the third day in accordance with the scriptures." Once again he fulfilled the predictions. It was long anticipated that he would die; it was equally anticipated that he would rise again from the dead. The Old Testament had said so. On the third day, to the amazement of the disciples, he fulfilled all the predictions. He was not resuscitated (that is, returning to the life he had before), he was resurrected. That means he came back to a life he had never lived before as a man, a real life, a glorified life, a different life. Yet, in the amazing mystery of the resurrection, it was the same Jesus, with wounds in his body that men could touch and feel and see for themselves.

That is the complete gospel—three basic facts. These are not mere doctrines; these are not philosophies, nor ideas that men have had about what God should be like. These are simple, hard-nosed facts which occurred in history and cannot be eliminated or evaded. There they are. These facts have changed the history of the world, and they are the permanent foundation for our faith.

A Pattern for Us

That is the gospel as Paul gave it to the Corinthians. But implied in this is another level of meaning which I want to mention before we look at what the gospel does. Not only did this happen to Jesus, but subsequently everywhere in the Word of God we learn that in some way it happened also to us. That is part of the gospel too. There is a sense in which these facts about Jesus—his death, his burial and his resurrection—are a foreview of what happens to us when we become Christians. They are a pattern, a picture, of how God works with us.

Something in us must die when we become Christians. Something in us can no longer go on living; it must end. Many passages of Scripture set this out for us. We are to "put off the old man" because it "died with Christ." We learn that the old man is this selfish self, this god which is me, this insistence on running my own life and making my own decisions. This is what has to go. Jesus himself said so. "If any man will come after me, let him deny himself and *take up his cross, daily,* and follow me."

Something has to die, and that hurts; we do not like it. It disturbs our ego and undermines our self-confidence. Yet it keeps happening to us all the time. Every Christian must learn this. You are involved in a continuing process in which something in you has been put to death and you have to give it up.

Ah, but when it dies then it has to be buried! We must accept the fact that what dies within us must remain dead. That is part of the gospel too. We must not try to revive it again for we cannot do so. If that thing is the selfish self, the hunger for ego-expression and self-fulfillment, then we must agree to let it remain dead. We must bury it. That is not easy to do. We like to assert ourselves. But a part of the gospel is this: we must bury that which is dead. This is what Paul means when he says, "put off the old man which was crucified." Put it away. Do not try to hang onto it and cling to fancied prerogatives.

The third element is that when we bury the "old man," we experience a surprising recovery. Suddenly we find that beyond the humiliation and hurt of death something has happened. A resurrection occurs and tragedy turns into triumph. What we thought to be an end becomes a new beginning, and with it comes peace, love and joy. We discover there was meaning and purpose in our being put through the painful experience that brought us to death. The reason for it is that we might come into newness of life again and again. That is the gospel as it finds expression in our daily experience.

Paul adds a condition here which we must not miss. Notice how he puts it: "if you hold it fast—unless you believed in vain." It is clearly possible to believe in vain. Faith in Christ can be of such a superficial nature that though one accepts the hope of the gospel as a kind of insurance policy against going to hell, it does not really change anything. That is what Paul calls "believing in vain." It happens all around us. There can be a mechanical acceptance of Christianity which never truly trusts in Christ but rests on Christian activities such as Bible study, prayer, and church attendance. That is believing in vain. Jesus said this will not hold up in the tests of life. When a crisis comes it collapses and fails. He said of certain ones, "Many will say to me, 'Did we not do many mighty works in your name?' " But he will say, "I never knew you; depart from me."

The test of true faith, of course, is that it cannot quit. It can falter at times, but it cannot really quit. Some years ago a young man phoned me and said, "I'm tired of being a Christian. I'm fed up with it. I've tried my best and nothing seems to work so I'm going to quit. I just wanted to let you know." I said, "I think it's a good idea." He said, "What do you mean?" "Well," I replied, "You said you were going to quit, and I think it's a good idea. Why don't you stop trying to be a Christian and go ahead and live the way you like? Pay no attention to the Bible or the church or the gospel and just enjoy yourself." He said, "You know I can't do that." I said, "Yes, I do, and I think it is about time you knew it too." No, the test of true faith is that it will never quit.

Let us look now at what the gospel does for us. There are two simple divisions, Paul suggests. First, it makes us stand. Notice, "the gospel, which you received, by which you stand." That means we have a sure foundation, a security to which we can resort at any time of pressure; we can stand steady, no matter what force comes against us. When you believe that God has forgiven your sins for Christ's sake; that God loves you and has made you his child; and that he is working in you by the power of his resurrected life, you have a place to stand that is secure. You know that he will also enable you to love and to live as you ought. He will give you power to say no when you need to say no. In the gospel you have a place to stand from which you can handle anything that comes. Because of the gospel these Corinthians were loved by God; therefore, they had a place of emotional security. That is the first thing the gospel does for us.

In a dangerous and slippery world it is a tremendous thing to have a place where you can find immediate love, acceptance, understanding and support. That is what the gospel gives. How do you feel when you pick up the newspaper and read that the Middle East is aflame and in turmoil; that wars are breaking out in the African states; that the South American countries are restless and filled with violence and threat of revolution? What does it do to you, to live in a world like that? Warfare may break out at any time and nuclear bombs may shortly scream across our country. In the face of such an uncertain future, it is the gospel which gives us a sense of certainty and security. It reminds us that there is One who is above all principalities and authorities and powers; he is in charge of all human events. When you fail and slide away, the gospel invites you to come back again, though sick of soul and hungry of heart, and find forgiveness and healing for your hurting heart. That is the gospel—the fact that God loves you despite your failure and your weakness. He is always ready to pick you up again and wash the hurt away, to start you out anew and teach you to walk in his strength and by his grace. That is forever a place to stand.

Three Tenses of Salvation

Second, Paul goes on to say that the gospel is the means "by which you are *being* saved." He puts it in the present tense; it is not "by which you *were* saved," past tense; or "by which you *will be* saved," future tense. It is that by which you are now "being saved." He is thinking about our present, earthly experience. There are three tenses of salvation simply because there are three parts of our humanity. There is the spirit, which is the essential "you." That is who we really are. As spirits, we are living in these various, multicolored, multishaped bodies. Some bodies are nice looking, some are a little loose and flabby, but our spirits live in these bodies. We cannot see the spirit. You have never seen me; I have never seen you, for we are spirits. When you came to Christ your spirit was regenerated; it was made alive; it was indwelt by the Holy Spirit and thus was linked to Jesus himself so that you and he are one spirit. That is salvation in its past tense.

Then there is salvation in the future; you *will be* saved. Paul will be talking about the salvation of the body in this great resurrection chapter. The body too has a part in God's plan. God will not throw it away. You can grind it up, or burn it and scatter it to the winds, but God can gather it together again. We shall see how and why he does it in this very chapter. God has a purpose for the body. He will resurrect it and restore it and it will be useful to you throughout eternity. That is salvation yet to come.

But here Paul is talking about the soul, about your life lived from day to day. You are "being saved" progressively as you rest on God at work in you, and allow yourself to be the instrument of his grace. Salvation now is buying you back from wasting your life. It is telling us that as we walk with God what we do becomes eternally profitable, not only for this present time, but in eternity. You can use your money for eternal profit; you can use your time for eternal profit; you can now lay up treasures in heaven and not upon earth. It is determined by the way you use your moments and your days, whether you live them in the strength of God or from the energy of the flesh. Thus you determine what is going to be good or bad at the judgment seat of Christ, when "everyone shall receive the things done in his body, whether they be good or bad."

Now those two points define the effect of the gospel. The gospel gives us stability, an immovable foundation, a place of recovery, of healing and of wholeness; and it redeems our present existence so that what we do has eternal meaning as we live day by day.

Now we come to the apostle's basis for believing the gospel: "they saw him alive." There is a chorus of voices from the first century that say loudly and clearly, "Yes, Jesus did rise from the dead. We saw him; we talked with him; we handled him [John says that in his letter]. We ate and drank with him. It was unmistakably Jesus. We recognized him by the marks of crucifixion still in his body. Our encounters with him were so frequent and so satisfying that we have never been the same since. When he rose from the dead it completely changed our lives." Christianity has always rested on the powerful evidence of eyewitnesses who saw him alive from the dead.

Perhaps you have seen on television the film on "Big Foot," the strange, apelike creature that supposedly lives in the forests of Northern California, Oregon and Washington. The film examines the question, "Is there such a creature?" and the answer it gives is, "Yes, there is, and here are the people who have seen him." It presents various individuals and groups who have actually seen some of these creatures and bear earnest witness to what they have seen.

This is the same kind of evidence that the resurrection rests on. If we believe that Jesus rose from the dead on the basis of the accounts of eyewitnesses who saw him and talked about him, it is difficult to escape the logic that we must also believe in the existence of "Big Foot." These people who saw and encountered these animals were the same kind of people as the witnesses of the resurrection—artless, simple people, who are not trying to put something over and have no axe to grind, but are bearing witness to an encounter they had experienced. I am not trying to equate the importance of believing in "Big Foot" with the importance of the resurrection of Christ. There is a remarkable and important difference between the level of evidence for believing in "Big Foot" and that for believing in the resurrection. At the end of this section I want to point out what that difference is, if you have not caught it yourself before then. But I do want to stress the point that the resurrection of Jesus is supported by the most powerful line of evidence that we can have: direct, eyewitness evidence, the kind that is employed in every courtroom in America.

This is what the apostle says:

> . . . and that he appeared to Cephas, [another name for the apostle Peter] then to the twelve. Then he appeared to more than five hundred brethren at one time, most of whom are still alive, though some have fallen asleep. Then he appeared to James, then to all the apostles. Last of all, as to one untimely born, he appeared also to me (vv. 5–8).

According to the Gospel records the actual first appearance of our Lord was not to Peter but to Mary Magdalene. John's gospel tells us she was first at the tomb and mistook Jesus for the gardener. It was only when he spoke to her that she realized he was the Lord, and she held him by the feet and worshiped him. Then he sent her away to find the disciples. But in the chauvinistic mentality of that first century, a woman's testimony did not count. Paul is conceding a point here to the age in which he lived by listing the apostle Peter as the one who first saw the risen Lord.

The Most Hurting Apostle

We do not know when and where our Lord appeared to Peter. Peter was surely the apostle who was hurting the most at that particular time. He had denied his Lord in that black night before the crucifixion. Three times he had professed that he did not even know him, and had emphasized it with curses and oaths. When he realized what he had done he went out into the night and wept bitterly. You can imagine how Peter must have been feeling all through this terrible time after the crucifixion of Jesus. Undoubtedly it is for that reason that Jesus sought him out first. How like him that is! He found Peter in his brokenness and forgave him. Later, in Galilee, Jesus restored him to his public office again.

I have always wished I could have been watching nearby when our Lord appeared to Peter. What a moving scene that must have been. I know how Peter must have felt, for the Lord has done this with me on numerous occasions when I felt I had done things for which I had no hope to be forgiven at all, and still he forgave me. The

Gospels confirm this appearance of Jesus to Peter without describing the event. Paul lists this time as the first of the appearances of our Lord to his apostles.

Then the second appearance was to all the apostles, "to the twelve," Paul says. Here the apostle undoubtedly is grouping together several appearances that our Lord made to the apostles. One of these was on the Emmaus road that Sunday afternoon after his resurrection when he appeared as a stranger and then later was recognized by them as they were sitting at bread together. That same evening he appeared suddenly in the midst of ten of the apostles. (Judas, of course, was dead, and Thomas was absent.) He revealed himself to them and showed them he was truly the risen Lord, for he actually ate with them on that occasion. Then, one week later when Thomas was present, Jesus appeared again. This time he invited Thomas to come and put his finger in the wounds in his hands, to feel his side, and to establish to his own satisfaction that Jesus was indeed risen from the dead.

There are other appearances to the disciples that are gathered up in a phrase or two in the Scriptures which suggest that Jesus repeatedly appeared to them during the whole forty-day period and that he taught them many things during that time. We are not given the details, but Paul summarizes it in these words, "He appeared . . . . then to the twelve." Paul's third reference is to an event of which we have no full account in the Scriptures, although we do have a brief reference to it:

> Then he appeared to more than five hundred brethren at one time, most of whom are still alive, though some have fallen asleep (v. 6).

For twenty centuries the theory has been propounded that Jesus really did not rise from the dead physically, that the disciples were so caught up in the wonder of his personality and so wanted him back that they hallucinated and imagined they saw him. But this event, of course, clearly denies that theory, for here there were over five hundred individuals who saw him at one time. It is hard enough to get one person to hallucinate, but to get five hundred people, from various backgrounds and temperaments, to do so together, is simple incredible.

This event occurred on a mountainside in Galilee, for even before his crucifixion the Lord had said that he would meet his disciples in Galilee after the resurrection. The first message he sent by the women who were at the tomb was, ". . . go and tell my brethren to go to Galilee, and there they will see me." Surely word of that spread rapidly throughout the believing community and everyone who could get away headed for Galilee. No one would have wanted to miss that most exciting of all Christian meetings. It is no wonder there were five hundred or more waiting for him on the mountainside when he appeared.

The brief reference to this is found in the closing words of Matthew's Gospel where we are told that our Lord appeared in Galilee and there he gave the disciples the Great Commission: "All authority in heaven and on earth has been given to me. Go therefore and make disciples of all nations, baptizing them in the name of the Father and of the Son and of the Holy Spirit, teaching them to observe all that I have commanded you." With those words Jesus sent them, and every generation of Christians since, out to the farthest reaches of the earth.

Now Paul says to these Corinthians, "most of these people are still alive." When he wrote this letter it was at least twenty-five years after the crucifixion, and most of the witnesses were still alive. Some had fallen asleep, as he said, but if the Corinthians wanted to check, there were still hundreds of people who had seen Jesus and could bear testimony of it.

Paul's fourth reference is to an appearance that is not reported in the gospels:

Then he appeared to James. . . .

This James is undoubtedly the half-brother of Jesus, the oldest remaining son of the family that grew up in Nazareth. John tells us in his Gospel that his brothers did not believe that Jesus was the Messiah. You can understand why. It would have been difficult to believe that someone you made mud pies with, someone you ran through the fields with, and went skinny-dipping with, and did all the things that kids do, was the Son of God, the Creator of the universe. So his brothers did not believe in him until after the resurrection.

It was that phenomenal event, that magnificent recovery, that finally convinced James that his brother, Jesus, was the Son of God. We do not know when Jesus appeared to him. Again it would have been fascinating to have been there and heard what Jesus said when he revealed himself to his brother. It is this James who wrote the Epistle of James in our New Testament. If you read through that letter you will see how reverently he refers to Jesus. He calls him twice, "the Lord Jesus Christ," and once "the Lord of Glory," so it is apparent that James was solidly and firmly convinced that Jesus had risen from the dead.

The fifth in Paul's list of Jesus' appearances is:

Then [he appeared] to all the apostles.

This is the occasion recorded in the first chapter of Acts when our Lord led his disciples out to the Mount of Olives. There, looking over the city of Jerusalem, he began to teach them. While he was speaking, the account says, they noticed his body rising from the ground. To their amazement, he ascended into the heavens until a cloud received him, and he disappeared out of sight. They stood there, gazing into the sky, until two strange men, who they afterward realized were angels, said to them, "You men of Galilee, why do you stand gazing up into heaven? This same Jesus, which is taken up from you into heaven, shall so come in like manner as you have seen him go into heaven." With that event our Lord disappeared bodily from earth. This ended the postresurrection appearances, *except*, as Paul goes on to say:

Last of all, as to one untimely born, he appeared also to me (v. 8).

This refers to that remarkable scene on the Damascus road that forever changed Paul's life. He could never forget his burning hatred of Christians. It explains the phrase he uses here about himself, "one untimely born." He means that he did not come to spiritual birth in the usual, ordinary way. The word he employs really means "miscarriage." He saw himself as a miscarriage, or, as some that translated it, an "abortion." Had Paul written his spiritual biography, the title would not have been *Born Again*—it would have been *The Miscarriage*, or *The Abortion*. This is what he thought of himself because of the way he came to birth. He is thinking of the twelve apostles as having been born in the normal way. When they heard the word of the Lord they believed it. Gradually it took root in their minds and hearts until they came to the place where they acted on it. In this way their spiritual birth followed a normal "pregnancy" that could be observed developing.

But Paul's experience was not like that; his new birth was very precipitous and unexpected. That may account for the fact that Paul had a difficult time in his early Christian life. When someone is prematurely born he does not handle life like a normal baby. He is specially cared for; he is nurtured and protected from exposure to danger and disease. It is a long time before he begins to function normally. This was the case with Paul. He was born again on the Damascus road, but it was such a sudden, precipitous thing that it took a long time for him to adjust his thinking to this fantastic event. He spent three years in Damascus and Arabia, and another seven years in his hometown of Tarsus before he got it all together and was ready to begin his great ministry of teaching and preaching around the world. The Spirit of God sent Barnabas to Tarsus to find him ten years after he had left Jerusalem, and only then did Paul begin his great worldwide ministry.

Grace Uses Us

In verses 9 and 10 Paul gives us his evaluation of that ministry.

> For I am the least of the apostles, unfit to be called an apostle, because I persecuted the church of God. But by the grace of God I am what I am, and his grace toward me was not in vain. On the contrary, I worked harder than any of them, though it was not I, but the grace of God which is with me.

It is astonishing to hear people sometimes accuse the apostle Paul of being conceited. They have never really listened to what Paul has to say about himself. Here he declares what he thought were his natural qualifications for his work as an apostle and they turn out to be zero, and less than that! "I am the least of the apostles," he says, "because I persecuted the church." Not only had he not believed in Jesus, but he had arrogantly and defiantly opposed God. He saw himself as having forfeited every possible right to be an apostle. His natural qualifications were nil, but his spiritual qualifications proved sufficient. "Nevertheless, by the grace of God, I am what I am."

He knew what he was. By this time he was a well-known apostle, in many ways the chief of the apostolic band, to whom the other apostles looked for support and guidance. He was the most remarkable missionary who has ever appeared on the earth. He had already spent years preaching the Word of God in the most difficult places. Now, he seems to ask, how could someone with no natural qualifications achieve something like that? His answer is three times stated, "the grace of God." He is referring to what he regarded, without doubt, as the greatest element in the gospel. It is the fact that the risen, ascended Lord promised to come himself and live in a human heart, and to reproduce his character and reveal his life through the ordinary, natural things that a human being does. That is what he means by the grace of God. It sets aside natural folly and weakness, and uses men in simple but effective ways, wherever they are. That is Paul's explanation of his ministry.

I hope that encourages many hearts, for many feel, like Paul, that we have lost every right to be used of God. We have so fouled up our lives and hurt ourselves and others that we say, how can God use us? Well, Paul is our great encouragement. He had been the persecutor of the church and the most ardent enemy of the faith, but now he was the greatest apostle of all, and God was using him throughout the world. Wherever this great apostle went he found whole cities blanketed with despair. Then he would begin, in simple ways, through the normal contacts he had, to tell them about Jesus. As people believed, one by one, a redeemed community would spring up. Their lives would be so different, so glowing, so loving, that word would spread throughout the city and many others would come to hear. Gradually a whole city would be stirred and changed. City after city began to respond like that until, within a few decades of the first century, the Roman world was drastically affected by the power of a risen Lord.

No wonder Paul gloried in the resurrection of Jesus. We too should glory in it. We are not sent out as Christians to mobilize our best human resources and do what we can for God. We too are filled with a risen Lord who is ready to release through us, old or young alike, his quiet power to transform humanity from within. That is what will bring about fantastic changes in society and the social structures as the gospel does its work.

Paul now sums this up in verse 11:

> Whether then it was I or they, [that is, I or the other apostles] so we preach and so you believed.

It did not make any difference which apostle preached the gospel. There is no difference between Paul's gospel and Peter's gospel. Peter preached to the Jews while Paul went to the Gentiles, but the gospel was the same and it had everywhere the same effects.

This, then, is the difference between believing the eyewitnesses concerning the resurrection of Jesus and believing eyewitnesses about any other human event, including the existence of a "Big Foot." Do you see what the difference is? When you believe eyewitnesses concerning "Big Foot" you are convinced there is such an animal, but that belief does not give you contact with it. You still have not seen a Big Foot, you cannot lay hold of the power and strength or cunning of such a creature by your belief. But when you believe in Jesus something remarkable happens. He makes himself known to you; you "receive" him. That is the great difference. That is what made the change in these Corinthian believers. Paul says he preached the gospel, but they received it. And when you receive the gospel you receive Jesus, and changes begin to occur. John tells us, "But as many as received him, to them gave he power to become the sons of God." That fundamental change occurs when you believe the gospel.

It has been more than fifty years since, as a boy of eleven, I knelt at a Methodist altar in a rough camp meeting in North Dakota and received Jesus as Lord. I still remember clearly how I felt at the moment and the changes which occurred in my life immediately following that event. They began to fade after a while, for without adequate nurture I drifted back into a way of life such that many would have thought nothing had happened to me. But I knew that something had, and I could never really be the same again. In my early twenties, when I returned to Christ and began to walk anew with the Lord, I found that the risen Lord was still present with me and making changes in me. He still had power to alter my affections and my desires, and to supply me with strength and grace to say and do what I ought to do, and to stop me from doing things that I should not do.

That has grown more evident through the years since, and I can bear testimony today that Jesus Christ is real. He is not a distant God, far-off in space, watching us poor, struggling mortals down here. He is real. He is alive. He has borne witness to his resurrection by imparting to my heart (and to thousands like me) eternal life. That becomes the ultimate testimony of the reality of his resurrection. The existence of the church through these twenty centuries could never have been achieved had he not risen from the dead.

22

What If . . . ?

What do you do when doubt attacks and you feel that Christianity is all wrong; that it is all a psychological trick which you have been playing on yourself? What do you do when you suddenly feel that the Scripture is merely a collection of ancient myths and legends, as we are frequently told, and that there is no life after death, no God, and no judgment? Every Christian feels that way at times. Those are normal attacks upon our faith, for we live in a day when faith is under attack.

When we feel that way the temptation is always to think, "Then I'd better get all I can now." These were the feelings that were widespread in Corinth. The Corinthians were concerned about getting the most out of life now. They were not denying the resurrection of Jesus, for there was too much evidence for that. But they were denying that the bodies of Christians would be resurrected. They had surrendered to the thinking of the Greek philosophers who taught that the human body is essentially evil; that it is a kind of prison we have to live in now. When the day comes that we can escape the body we will be free, for the body will have served its purpose. That will be the end of it—it will no longer be needed.

Many of the new cults that are springing up today—especially those that reflect an Eastern or Oriental thinking—are based upon that philosophy. The natural result of such philosophy is to feel that if you are ever going to enjoy the delights of the body, now is the time to do so. Thus there had arisen in Corinth, as throughout the whole Greek world, a philosophy expressed in the well-known phrase, "Eat, drink, and be merry, for tomorrow we must die." Paul examines this attitude briefly in the section now before us.

> Now if Christ is preached as raised from the dead, how can some of you say that there is no resurrection of the dead? But if there is no resurrection of the dead, then Christ has not been raised (vv. 12, 13).

Paul is pointing out an inconsistency in their beliefs. If they truly believe what he had preached to them, that Christ had been raised from the dead, then how could they accept the philosophical teaching that there was no such thing as bodily resurrection? If that philosophy is true, then Christ, was not resurrected. They can't have it both ways. But if Christ was raised, then there is no need for the philosophy, "Eat, drink, and be merry."

Enjoyment Unlimited

The practical conclusion, then, is that bodily pleasures are not limited to this life. If, for some reason, you cannot partake of bodily pleasure in this life, do not feel that you have been cheated; there is still the greatest opportunity for the body yet to come. The full enjoyment of the body lies ahead for believers in Christ.

I do not have to convince anybody that our human bodies give us great enjoyment. There is nothing like sitting down to a good, well cooked meal, with a great variety of food, following by a great dessert. It is hard to pass by the taste of a good cup of coffee in the morning, or a cool drink on a hot day. These are bodily pleasures that God delights to give us. There is the joy of seeing the glorious beauty of springtime flowers. There are the delights of great music and of good conversation. There are the pleasures of tactile sense, of touching things, and the joys of sex. All these are pleasures of the body, and God has intended them for us.

But the question arises, "Do we lose all these forever when we die? Is there to be no more of such sensuous delights?" If the body is not raised, it would make sense to "eat, drink, and be merry" for this life would be the only chance we will ever have to enjoy the delights of the flesh. But the Christian answer is, "No, we do not lose such delights forever. We shall enjoy them in a fuller way than every before when the body is raised from the dead. God has a future purpose for the body, as well as for the spirit and the soul. Our bodies will be transformed and enriched. All they are able to do now will be experienced to greater degree than ever in the life to come.

"Oh," you say, "that may be true for some of these pleasures, but how about sex? The Lord said that there is no marriage or giving in marriage in heaven." Many people are tremendously frightened at that thought. There is much pressure on them to experience the joys of sex now, while they still have a body capable of this kind of relationship. But they fail to see why God gives us physical pleasures now. The things experienced now are but a taste of the possibilities that lie beyond. Even the pleasure of sex in marriage is given to us now to teach us the exquisite ecstasy of intimate relationship with another person. Though it is true that it will not be expressed physically in heaven—that seems to be the implication of Scripture—it nevertheless pictures a far greater delight and joy we will experience in heaven from relating to other people and especially to God himself. To sit and talk with someone in heaven will be a bliss beyond imagining. We will experience a delightful sense of union with that person, and the nearest thing on earth that can picture it is sexual orgasm. To worship God in a resurrection body will be to find your whole being suffused with a glory that orgasm only faintly pictures now, and certainly can never surpass.

C. S. Lewis has a message called *Weight of Glory*, which is one of his greatest works. In it he examines some of the possibilities of resurrected life:

> It may be possible for each to think too much of his own potential glory hereafter, it is hardly possible for him to think too often or too deeply about that of his neighbor. The load, or weight, or burden, of my neighbor's glory should be laid daily on my back, a load so heavy that only humility can carry it, and the backs of the proud will be broken.

Then he further declares:

> It is a serious thing to live in a society of possible gods and goddesses; to remember that the dullest and most uninteresting person you talk to may one day be a creature which, if you saw it now, you would strongly be tempted to worship; or else a horror and a corruption such as you now meet, if at all, only in a nightmare. All day long we are, in some degree, helping each other to one or the other of the destinations. It is in the light of these overwhelming possibilities, it is with the awe and circumspection proper to them, that we should conduct all our dealings with one

another, all friendships, all loves, all play, all politics. There are no ordinary people. You have never talked to a mere mortal!*

Those are biblical concepts. But beyond the doctrines that we are so familiar with (until they have become commonplace) are great truths which these teachings are seeking to convey. We do not need to fear if circumstances do not permit the satisfaction of all present bodily desires. Nothing is permanently lost, for a greater glory awaits us. That is the great hope which the truth of the resurrection of the body seeks to convey to us. Sometimes I can hardly wait for it all to come to pass. People often ask me, "Do you find it disturbing to grow old?" I answer, "No, I don't. I find it very exciting. I have no desire to go back." The hope I have for ultimate fulfillment lies in the future more than in the present or the past. What lies ahead is so entrancing, so remarkable, I can hardly wait for it to come.

The Stone Unmoved

In verses 14 through 19, the apostle faces the vexing question, "What if?" What would the world be like if Jesus had not been raised? What if the women who went to the tomb on that resurrection morning had found the stone still in front and the guards still pacing up and down? What if nothing had changed; if there were no escape from their memory of those dead eyes and the cold body of Jesus when they had taken him down from the cross and laid him in the tomb? What would the world be like today if, as Matthew Arnold once put it,

> Now he is dead,
> Henceforth he lies
>   in some lone Syrian town,
> And on his grave
>   with shining eyes,
> The Syrian stars look down.

Here is Paul's answer:

. . . if Christ has not been raised, then our preaching is in vain and your faith is in vain. We are even found to be misrepresenting God, because we testified of God that he raised Christ, whom he did not raise if it is

---

* *Weight of Glory* (Grand Rapids: Eerdmann, 1965).

true that the dead are not raised. For if the dead are not raised, then Christ has not been raised. If Christ has not been raised, your faith is futile and you are still in your sins. Then those also who have fallen asleep in Christ have perished. If in this life only we have hoped in Christ, we are of all men most to be pitied (vv. 14–19).

There are six history-changing facts Paul mentions that would have followed if Jesus had not risen from the dead. First, without the resurrection all Christian preaching would have been a waste of time. All sermons, all messages you have ever heard or read, all the Christian books you have read, all tapes, and radio and television broadcasts of the gospel you have ever listened to, would have been a total waste of time had Jesus not risen from the dead.

"But," someone says, "there is still a lot left to Christianity when you take away the resurrection. There are all those wonderful teachings of Jesus, crystallized in the Sermon on the Mount. We would still have those. And there is the death of Jesus, the crucifixion. He would still have died for our sins. We would still have that, even though we gave up the resurrection."

Of course, that is true. We would have all these things. But the point the apostle makes is that without the resurrection not one of those things would do us the least bit of good. Apart from the resurrection of Jesus there would be no power available for us to obey his Word. The teachings of Jesus would only condemn us more. They would only reveal how much farther away we are from the mind and heart of God than we ever thought. The death of Jesus would but hold out to us an empty promise that could never be realized. Without the resurrection all preaching would be in vain.

Second, without the resurrection, all Christian faith, Paul says, would be useless. What would be the point of going to church every Sunday, or to a Bible study, or reading the Scriptures, or even believing that God exists? All that would be worthless, useless. It would be only a kind of religious game. Life would be reduced to grim, stark realities, with no hope now or later, for death would bring everything to a hopeless and final end.

Sir Bertrand Russell (1872–1970) was a man who had no faith in the Bible or God. He describes in eloquent terms the natural outcome of a life from which all faith in the resurrection of Christ is removed:

> The life of Man is a long march through the night, surrounded by invisible foes, tortured by weariness and pain, towards a goal that few can hope to reach and where none can tarry long. One by one, as they march, our

comrades vanish from our sight, seized by the silent orders of omnipotent Death.

Brief and powerless is Man's life; on his and all his race the slow, sure doom falls, pitiless and dark. Blind to good and evil, reckless of destruction, omnipotent matter rolls on its relentless way. For Man, condemned today to lose his dearest, tomorrow himself to pass through the gates of darkness, it remains only to cherish, ere yet the blow falls, the lofty thoughts that ennoble his little day.

What pessimism! What despair! What darkness! But that is what is left when the resurrection of Jesus is taken away.

Then, third, if the resurrection is untrue, Paul says the apostles are the world's greatest liars: "We are even found to be misrepresenting God, because we testified of God that he raised Christ, whom he did not raise if it is true that the dead are not raised." If there is no resurrection the apostles of Christ deserve to be treated as arch-deceivers rather than as honored men of integrity and truth. They are hypocrites, and worse, they are deliberate deceivers who have led many into gross darkness and error. You cannot avoid that conclusion if there is no resurrection, because the apostles staked their reputation on the fact that Jesus had risen from the dead.

Then a fourth point. If Christ was not raised, then all our past sins are still with us; we are yet in our sins. This means that if there is a God, then we must stand at last before him and give an account of all we have done. There is no way to escape the justice with which God would deal with our sins. There is no hiding place, no hope for mercy, no loving Christ to say, "I've paid the penalty on your behalf; I've taken your place; I've loved you and given myself for you." When we stand before God we will get everything we deserve, for every evil action or thought that we have had.

The fifth thing, Paul says, is, ". . . those also who have fallen asleep in Christ have perished." All those loved ones whom we thought to have gone on to be with the Lord, whom we hoped to meet again, we shall never see again. Our children, our parents, our friends—those who have been taken suddenly, those to whom we bade a weeping farewell with the hope that one day we would see them again in glory, are all gone forever from our sight. A terrible silence has fallen; they are gone for good.

Finally, the sixth fact: "If in this life only we have hoped in Christ, we are of all men most to be pitied." Even the present is changed, if there is no resurrection. We must give up our beautiful dreams and go back to coldness, selfishness, drabness, grimness, and darkness.

It is all made worse by the fact that we once thought we had escaped; we once thought we had hold of something beautiful and marvelous, so that it gave us great joy and peace and blessing. But if there is no resurrection, all this crumbles and is taken away from us; our darkness is all the darker for it. "We are of all men most to be pitied."

That is quite a list. Let me go through it again:

Our preaching is vain;
Our faith is empty;
The apostles are made to be liars;
Our sin still remains unatoned for;
Death has triumphed over our loved ones;
Life itself is made utterly miserable.

Would you like to live like that? Millions do today. Every one who does not know the reality of a risen Lord must live every day of his life on that basis. That is why the world seeks so desperately to find some anesthetic that will dull the pain of an empty, aching heart. That is why people are caught up in a continual round of noise and action that will not let them think about life. They cannot stand life without a hope beyond the grave.

Let us, then, thank God for verse 20:

But *in fact* Christ has been raised from the dead. . . .

What a transformation that verse makes! It means that the most fundamental fact of life, of history, of the world, is the resurrection of Jesus. It is the darkness and the grimness and the death which are unnecessary. Those who live that way live in a delusion, for the great, striking reality of all history and life is: Jesus Christ has risen from the dead.

Sample Resurrection

At verse 20, we come to a section where the apostle's thoughts sweep across the centuries and declare the ultimate effects in history of the resurrection of Jesus. There are three remarkable effects of the resurrection. The first is to guarantee the resurrection of the bodies of all who believe in Jesus; our resurrection is tied in with his.

But in fact Christ has been raised from the dead, the first fruits of those who have fallen asleep. For as by a man came death, by a man has come also the resurrection of the dead. For as in Adam all die, so also in Christ shall all be made alive. But each in his own order: Christ the first fruits, then at his coming those who belong to Christ (vv. 20–23).

The key to that passage is the twice-repeated words, *first fruits*. Paul is referring here to the ceremony that was given to Israel in chapter 23 of the Book of Leviticus. On the Feast of Unleavened Bread, which followed the Passover, there would occur the offering of the first fruits of the barley harvest. The Jews were commanded to bring a sheaf of grain, the first of the harvest, to the priest, who would then wave it before the Lord. The striking thing is that that was done on the morning of our Lord's resurrection. Thus in the feasts of Israel we have a prediction that the resurrection of Jesus would correspond with the offering of the first fruits of the harvest. Paul's argument is that not only did Jesus rise from the dead on the exact day foreseen in the ritual, but furthermore, his resurrection was a sample and guarantee of the coming "harvest" of resurrection, which would include ours as well.

It is important for us to understand that Jesus was the first human being ever to be resurrected from the dead. "Well," someone says, "what about Lazarus, and the Old Testament stories of people being raised from the dead?" Yes, there were others who returned from the dead, but they were not resurrected. As I mentioned earlier, the proper term for them would be "resuscitated" because they came back to the same life they left. But resurrection does not do that. Resurrection brings about a quality and dimension of life, which has never been lived before. It is not simply a return to existence as we know it now; it is a lifting to a higher, freer, more marvelous dimension of existence than we have ever known. So Jesus was the first one to be resurrected from the dead. It was the same Jesus; he came back in the same body, but he was living on a different level of life. Paul says that Jesus' resurrection is a sample of ours.

He then goes on to argue that it is absolutely certain all this will happen. Here is the way he puts it: "For as by a man came death, by a man has come also the resurrection of the dead." Death passed upon our race because of the fall of Adam, so all who are part of the new creation, the new race in Christ, will also participate in his resurrection from the dead. "For as in Adam all die so also in Christ shall all be made alive."

He is talking only about believers, those who have fallen asleep *in Christ*. In verse 18, he says, "Then those also who have fallen asleep in Christ . . . "; in verse 20 he speaks of "those who have fallen asleep"; and in verse 23, "those who belong to Christ." So when he says, "in Adam all die," he does not include the unbelieving world, although it is true that they "all die in Adam." But he is talking peculiarly about believers. Believers too die because their unresurrected bodies are still part of the race of Adam. That is why our bodies are put into graves. But as persons we are "in Christ," and those "in Christ shall all be made alive." By man (Adam) came the breakout from Eden; by man (Jesus) came also the breakthrough back into Paradise, by means of resurrection.

What Paul is saying is that resurrection is as certain as death. It is not up to you to resurrect yourself, but it will happen. The apostle puts it in the strongest terms possible. From other Scriptures we learn that even the dead apart from Christ are resurrected. There is a "resurrection of both the just and the unjust." But the "resurrection to life" involves only those who are "in Christ." The apostle makes that very clear.

At His Coming

When will it happen? Paul answers that great question in verse 23:

> But each in his own order: Christ the first fruits, then at his coming those who belong to Christ.

The answer is: "at his coming." This agrees with other passages where the apostle says there will be some who will never die. Paul describes this in 1 Thessalonians 4:16, 17:

> For the Lord himself will descend from heaven with a shout, with the voice of the archangel, and with the trump of God; and the dead in Christ shall rise first: Then we which are alive and remain shall be caught up together with them in the clouds, to meet the Lord in the air: and so shall we ever be with the Lord (KJV).

There is a generation of believers who will never die, even though death is now at work in them. For over nineteen hundred years every generation has hoped it would be the one that would yet be alive when Christ returned. That hope blazes high in many hearts today because of the things taking place in the world. The nations are gathering in what may well be the final arrangement before the Lord returns. No one can say for certain though, for it may all flow back again into other configurations. For nineteen hundred years all those who have expected to escape death by the return of Christ have been disappointed. They have all died in faith and been cremated or buried in a normal fashion.

Well, what about them? When will they be resurrected? The answer again is: "at his coming." "The dead in Christ shall rise first" (1 Thess. 4:16). Because of this many have felt that those who die before the coming of the Lord either lie asleep in the grave until he comes, or they wait for the resurrection in a disembodied state. (Some have even suggested that perhaps God gives them a kind of temporary body, a sort of heavenly bathrobe to wait in, until their good clothes get back from the cleaners.) But this is to misread what the Scriptures are saying.

It is my understanding that there is a radical difference between time in which we now live, and eternity, which is a different kind of existence. Eternity has no past or future as time does. If we understand that difference then we can understand that when a believer lays down his life here and steps out of time into eternity, the first event to await him is the coming of the Lord for his own. It will be, for him, the resurrection of his body. So there is no waiting for those who go to be with the Lord. If you want further explanation of that, I would suggest the chapter, "Time and Eternity," in the book I have written, *Authentic Christianity*, which goes into this more at length. But I believe this theory is the explanation of many baffling and difficult passages in the Scriptures. The view has given me great hope and anticipation of that moment when I shall step out of time into eternity, and the first event I shall experience is that wonderful moment when "the Lord himself shall descend from heaven with a shout"—and I shall join with the saints of all ages who are just arriving, as I am, in the courts of glory.

He Reigns Now

At verse 24 the apostle moves on to view the final scene, the time when Christ has returned into time and reigned already for 1,000 years of peace and righteousness on the earth. He will have completed his work, subdued his enemies, cast the devil and death and Hades into the lake of fire (as we read in the Book of Revelation), and delivered the kingdom back to the Father. That is what Paul now describes:

> Then comes the end, when he delivers the kingdom to God the Father after destroying every rule and every authority and power. For he must reign until he has put all his enemies under his feet. The last enemy to be destroyed is death (vv. 24, 25).

Notice something important: the reign of Christ does not begin after he subdues his enemies, although we often think of it that way. There is a great hymn by Isaac Watts that states:

> Jesus shall reign where 'er the sun
> Does his successive journeys run,
> His kingdom spread from shore to shore,
> 'Til moons shall wax and wane no more.

That is all couched in the future tense, Jesus *shall* reign. But the biblical truth is that he *does* reign, and will continue to reign "*until* he has put all his enemies under his feet.*" I do not know anything that has more power to steady us in times of pressure, and undergird us in times of discouragement and defeat, than the realization that Jesus *now* reigns. He is in control *now*. When we run up against oppressive governments and severe limitations to our freedom, or even outright, violent persecution of our Christian faith, we are to remember that all this takes place under the overall authority of Jesus Christ who said, when he rose from the dead. "*All power* is given unto me in heaven and in earth." He permits opposition in order to accomplish his purposes, just as in the Old Testament God raised up the Babylonians and Assyrians and brought them against Israel. He allowed Jerusalem to be taken; he allowed the Israelites to be taken into captivity— not because that was the end he ultimately desired for earth, but because it was necessary to teach his people the lessons they needed to know. God brings these things to pass "for our sake," and it is the authority of Christ that allows them to happen. This is a very important truth that we often forget.

The apostle says, "The last enemy to be destroyed is death." This is true in both an individual and a universal sense. Universally, death will never disappear from this earth until we come to that moment described in the Book of Revelation when a new heaven and a new earth come into existence. In this present heaven and earth, death reigns, and will continue to do so even during the millennium, during the time when Christ personally rules on earth, when peace and righteousness shall prevail all over the earth. Nevertheless, even then death is present. The prophet Isaiah says, "the child shall die a hundred years old." He means that death will then be an unusual experience, for someone one hundred years old will still be regarded as a mere child. But death is still present, and it is not until the end, when our Lord subdues his enemies, that death is finally destroyed and cast into the lake of fire. Thus, the last enemy to be destroyed is death.

But there is a sense in which this is individually true of us now. What is going on in your life and mine now? We are engaged in a great battle in which we are assaulted continually with temptations to yield and experience death. Yet, despite those times of failure, by the grace of God's forgiveness we are restored. Life is handed back to us, in a sense, and we go on to walk for even a longer time without failure, until gradually we gain victory over evil habits and evil attitudes. Life is forever coming out of death; it is pain leading to joy—and that will never end as long as we are in this present life.

But a time is coming when our bodies will die, and death is then destroyed for us. "The last enemy to be destroyed is death." Once we pass through the experience of death into resurrection, like our Lord himself we shall never die again; that is the wonderful statement of Scripture. Christ having once died, Paul says in Romans, never dies again; and we share his experience. He is the first fruits of the great harvest of which we are a part.

The End of Christ's Work

In verses 27, 28 there is a description of the end of which Paul speaks, when the kingdom shall be restored to God the Father:

> "For God has put all things in subjection under his feet." But when it says, "All things are put in subjection under him," it is plain that he is excepted who put all things under him. When all things are subjected to him, then the Son himself will also be subjected to him who put all things under him, that God may be everything to every one.

This describes the end of Christ's work as a mediator between God and man. During this present time our Lord Jesus is singled out, as it were, from the persons of the Godhead to be the supreme object of worship. We are invited to worship him and give honor to him. Paul tells us in Philippians 2 that because of our Lord's faithfulness unto death,

> God has highly exalted him and bestowed on him the name which is above every name, that at the name of Jesus every knee should bow . . . and every tongue confess that Jesus Christ is Lord, to the glory of God the Father (vv. 9–11).

To worship Christ honors God. In that great scene in Revelation 5 John sees the whole universe gathering about the throne, worshiping the Lamb that was slain, and crying, "Worthy is the Lamb that was slain, to receive power, and riches, and wisdom, and strength, and honor, and glory, and blessing." Everyone is expected to worship the Son.

But there is coming a time, Paul says here, when the work of the Son in subduing a lost creation will be finished. When the full results of the atonement of the cross have been completed, and all the harvest of the earth is gathered, then, according to this account, the Lord Jesus will return the kingdom to the Father, in order that "God [the threefold God: Father, Son, and Spirit] may be everything to every one."

Then, for the first time in our experience, we will understand the mystery of the Trinity. We now know that the Bible teaches there are three persons in the Godhead; that they are equal in glory and honor; and that they somehow coalesce so there are three persons but only one God. Intellectually we can grasp that; emotionally I do not think anyone does. But in that day we will thoroughly understand, even emotionally, the makeup of God. We shall understand the great truth which God has been seeking to teach us throughout this earthly experience, that he is all we need, that he is everything to every one.

I often talk with those who are having struggles in their Christian lives, and almost always I find their struggles come from an unwillingness to believe that God can actually supply what they need. They feel that somehow they must lean upon human resources. They feel that they must look to other human beings to get what they need, and that if they are denied what they need, life is hardly worth the living. But God continually labors to show us that this is not true. He is all we need. He knows that we need bread and food and shelter. That is our Lord's argument in the Sermon on the Mount, "Your Father knows that you have need of all these things." Do you think he is unable to supply them to you? If he can feed the birds of the air and clothe the lilies of the field, do you think he cannot find some way to meet your need as well? It is a constant rebuke to our little faith that we do not trust God more and believe that when we obey him and walk with him he will give us all we need. This is the struggle of faith. But the mark of maturity, the sign that indicates we have grown up and are fulfilling God's purpose, is when we understand with all our heart and mind and soul that "God is everything to every one." When that truly occurs the mediation of our Lord is no longer required. God, the Triune God, is everything to every one.

There is a third remarkable characteristic of the resurrection, brought out in the next section, in verses 29 to 34. The apostle reveals the motivating power of the resurrection. He starts in verse 29 with a puzzling statement—

> Otherwise, what do people mean by being baptized on behalf of the dead? If the dead are not raised at all, why are people baptized on their behalf?

The Mormon church bases a major part of its religious activity on this one verse. Non-Mormons are not permitted to enter one of their temples, and this makes people ask; what goes on in them? One of the things they are doing is being baptized on behalf of the dead. The Mormons believe that they can go back through history and be baptized for all their ancestors. That is why they put great reliance upon genealogical tables and spend a lot of time tracing their ancestry. They believe they can be baptized on their behalf, and thus save them. I met a woman once who said that she had been baptized for many thousands of people! Some Mormons pick out well-known figures of history and are baptized for them, as for instance, Julius Caesar, Alexander the Great, Napoleon, etc. It is all based on this one verse; there is no other reference in the Bible to being baptized on behalf of the dead.

Well, what does the verse mean? I do not know. It evidently refers to some form of proxy baptism, but it is noteworthy that the apostle does not refer to it as something the Christians in Corinth practiced, because he puts it in the third person: "Otherwise what do *people* mean"—not what do "we" mean, or "you" mean by being baptized on behalf of the dead, but what do "they" mean. Literally he says, "If the dead are not raised at all, why are 'they' baptized on their behalf?" He returns to the first person in the next verse, so it is clear this is a practice that some were engaged in of which he does not necessarily approve or disapprove. He simply refers to it as a practice. It would be a shame to miss the significance of the point he is making because we do not understand what the practice was.

The point is this: some powerful belief was motivating people to take this action; something had a powerful effect upon them. They were so strongly moved by it that they actually went out of their way to be baptized on behalf of others. Presumably these "others" had become Christians by faith, but they had not had an opportunity to be baptized before they died. So some were adopting the practice of being baptized on their behalf, out of a kind of superstitious idea that the others could not enter heaven unless they were baptized. Many people still have that idea today. Whatever the practice was, the apostle is arguing that a belief in the resurrection has a profound motivating force upon people. It will make them do things to help others. Now he is not arguing this as a proof that the resurrection occurred, because many people believe in things that do not really exist, and their belief does not prove that such things exist. (You can believe in Santa Claus but that does not mean he really exists.) What he is saying is that believing in the resurrection has a great effect upon you. It will change your life. It will make you do things that you would not otherwise do. One of the things is that you will be concerned about the salvation of others, even to the extent of seeking to be baptized on their behalf.

Figurative Beasts

He states a similar effect, in verses 30 through 32, concerning himself.

> Why am I in peril every hour? I protest, brethren, by my pride in you which I have in Christ Jesus our Lord, I die every day! What do I gain if, humanly speaking, I fought with beasts at Ephesus?

That is a reference to certain persecution he endured about which we know very little. There is a verse in 2 Corinthians that probably refers to the same thing. In chapter 1, verses 8 and 9, he says:

> For we do not want you to be ignorant, brethren, of the affliction we experienced in Asia; for we were so utterly, unbearably crushed that we despaired of life itself. Why, we felt that we had received the sentence of death; but that was to make us rely not on ourselves but on God who raises the dead. . . .

To believe that God raises the dead is a tremendous encouragement to endure suffering and even physical affliction now. The fact that the apostle understood this enabled him to bear up in a time of great physical pressure. As he put it, I think figuratively, he "fought with beasts at Ephesus." His difficulty was almost like going into the arena to fight wild beasts. I do not think he actually did that, because, as a Roman citizen he could not be compelled to fight in the arena with wild beasts or gladiators. But, in a figurative way, this is what he went through. It was the hope of resurrection which strengthened him to rely on "God who raises the dead."

Are you, perhaps, wearing your life out in some obscure corner? Do you think you will never be heard of, that no one will ever know of the punishment you have had to take? Have no fear. Paul assures us that this "light affliction, which is but for a moment, is working for us a far more exceeding and eternal weight of glory." The resurrection provides ample recompense for all human suffering, no matter how bad it may be.

He closes the section with an appeal to let the hope of resurrection determine your life style:

> If the dead are not raised, "Let us eat and drink, for tomorrow we die."

That was the philosophy of Epicureanism in Corinth, and it is widespread today. But, he also says:

> Do not be deceived: "Bad company ruins good morals." Come to your right mind [that is, be realistic], and sin no more. For some have no knowledge of God. I say this to your shame (vv. 33, 34).

What was happening in Corinth is still what is happening today. Many Christians were giving way to this "live it up" philosophy, and they were keeping company with people who thought that way. Paul reminds them, quoting a proverb of that day, "Bad company ruins good morals." So he says, "Come to your right mind"; i.e., begin to face life realistically; stop kidding yourselves. Life is a battle, and we have the privilege of living in this time of history and so affecting the world of our day. Our time on earth is rapidly passing. "Make the proper use of it," he says, "for some are even professing to be Christians yet have no real knowledge of God at all, because they are living just like everyone around them."

So the apostle closes the section with this note. We are not creatures of time, we are immortal beings. When we gather at the throne of God our greatest delight will be that we had the opportunity to labor for his name's sake in this life.

23

The Victory of the Mystery

.

For many people, the key question of the great resurrection chapter is: how does resurrection occur? The apostle Paul now discusses that.

But some one will ask, "How are the dead raised? With what kind of body do they come?" (v. 35).

It is obvious that skepticism oozes from those questions. In verse 12 of this chapter Paul had recognized that some among these Corinthians were saying there was no resurrection from the dead. "We do not understand how it can happen," they were saying; "therefore, we do not believe it will happen." These questions the apostle now raises were expressions of that unbelief.

For twenty centuries skeptics of all ages have asked these same questions. Of course, they amplify them by imposing various obstacles. They say, for instance, "We can understand, perhaps, that a body which has been carefully embalmed and placed in a grave might possibly be brought back to life, but what about those that have been burned? How are you going to restore a body like that?" The skeptics also ask, "What about those that are eaten by animals or by marine life? Those animals, in turn, have died and their bodies have returned to ashes, and have even been taken up as parts of plants or other animals. How can God sort it all out?"

These questions invariably arise when unbelief faces the resurrection of the dead. The Greeks, of course, were teaching that it was a good thing, an advantage, to lose the body. The Oriental religions, on the

310

other hand, taught that bodies were needed in the process of salvation, so that one must return to earth many times. Their question would be, "Which body is raised from the dead? Is it the cow body you once had, or the gorilla body you may have had, or the one you are walking around in now?" Reincarnation would, for them, pose an entirely different question concerning the resurrection of the body.

Ample Evidence

Paul now answers these two questions. His answer to the first is found in verses 36 through 38:

> You foolish man! What you sow does not come to life unless it dies. And what you sow is not the body which is to be, but a bare kernel, perhaps of wheat or of some other grain. But God gives it a body as he has chosen, and to each kind of seed its own body.

Notice that Paul says, first, "To ask *how* this can be is a foolish question." Why does he say that? It is a normal question, one almost everybody asks, and yet Paul immediately brands it as a foolish question. It is foolish because everywhere around are examples of what happens in resurrection. He is referring to the normal process of plants growing from seeds or bulbs when they are placed in the ground. They first die and lose their consistency, but out of this death emerges another kind of body which is yet the same seed that was placed in the ground.

I do not think it is any accident at all that Easter comes at the height of the spring season. We do not know when our Lord was born—Christmas is a debatable date—but there is no question about the date of Easter. For centuries it has been pegged to the movements of the moon and tied to the ancient Jewish celebration of the Passover, so that everyone knows without a shadow of a doubt, that Easter is celebrated on the very day that our Lord rose from the dead. Easter always falls in the midst of the awakening of earth from its death in winter, amid the coming to life again of things that once were dead. Paul points out that we have ample evidence, in the processes of nature itself, to believe in a resurrection of the body.

Nature teaches us two obvious lessons: death is necessary to the process. Far from being an obstacle to resurrection, death is essential to it. You can put that in the form of an axiom: Nothing that has never died shall ever be raised from the dead! Obviously, if it is to be raised from the dead it has first to die. So death is not an obstacle to resurrection but it is an ingredient of it and necessary to it. The fact that people die and that their bodies lose their ability to function ought never to be a hindrance to believing that life will emerge from death. The body must die just as the seed must die, and nature repeatedly confirms this.

The second lesson nature teaches us is that the body which emerges from the seed which dies is different from the one that was planted. Put a grain of wheat or a kernel of corn into the ground and what comes up? Another grain of wheat or another kernel? No. What comes up is a green stem which does not look at all like what you put into the ground. Nevertheless it is linked to it; it is continuous from it; it has an identity with it. It is the same without being similar. Now if you had never seen that process before, would you believe it if someone said it would happen? You would look at him as though he were mad! You can put almost anything else into the ground and that will not happen. It is one of those miracles of nature so familiar to us that we miss the miraculous part of it. But Paul says it happens so frequently there should be no struggle in believing in the resurrection of the dead.

On one occasion, reported in the Book of Acts, Paul is defending himself before King Agrippa. He says to the king, "Why should it be thought a thing incredible that God should raise the dead?" And why should it, when we have the testimony of nature continually that this kind of thing can and does happen? If it was not incredible in the first century how much more should it be believable today, when by the discoveries of science we know a great deal more about the processes of transferring energy and of retaining life? We are now acquainted with a process called "cloning." Scientists say it is possible to take a single cell of the human body—any cell, it does not have to be a sex cell—and by a process now known in theory, though not yet in practice, to restore that body completely as a human being. Why then should it be thought incredible that God can do it; that all he needs is a single cell from a body to restore the body exactly as it was? Man can do it; surely God will catch up with man one of these days! Thus Paul answers the question: how are the dead raised?

Lessons of Nature

He now faces the skeptics' second question, "With what kind of body do they come?" "All right, supposing there is a resurrection," they say, "what is the resurrection body like? How will it differ from the one we have now?" Paul's answer is found in verses 39 through

49. He takes it in three movements. First, he goes back again to the lessons which are visible in nature itself; then he draws a parallel with the reality of resurrection; and finally, in a great theological argument, he establishes the absolute certainty that this is going to happen.

First, the lesson from nature:

> For not all flesh is alike, but there is one kind for men, another for animals, another for birds, and another for fish. There are celestial bodies and there are terrestrial bodies; but the glory of the celestial is one, and the glory of the terrestrial is another. There is one glory of the sun, and another of the moon, and another glory of the stars; for star differs from star in glory (vv. 39–41).

Paul is still dealing with the world of observable phenomena, which is designed to teach men spiritual lessons. Here is the first truth he brings out: all bodies are not alike! If you do not believe that, you are going to have difficulty when you go to a restaurant, for you could order beef and they would serve you fish and you would never know the difference. But there is such a difference that a trained scientist can tell whether a single cell comes from a human, an animal, a bird, or a fish. Truly, "not all flesh is alike."

The second part of verse 38 suggests that this difference is a result of the inner difference of nature, or personality, that these plants or animals have. Paul says, "to each kind of seed its own body." In other words, there is a correspondence between what the body looks like and what the entity inside is like. That is why animals have various natures. It is for this reason that animals are used in Scripture as symbols of corresponding qualities in human beings—wolves are always ferocious and dangerous; sheep are always helpless and so on. All these qualities are there because God wants to demonstrate to us truth about ourselves as we see it reflected in the natural world.

Then the second thing the apostle points out is that there are two major divisions of bodies:

> There are celestial bodies and there are terrestrial bodies; but the glory of the celestial is one, and the glory of the terrestrial is another.

"Celestial bodies" are heavenly bodies. Paul goes on to list them—the sun, the moon, the stars. There are also "terrestrial bodies," which are earthly bodies. He has already said what they are—men, animals, birds, and fish. The point he makes is that there is a marked and deliberate difference between heavenly bodies and earthly bodies. The function of heavenly bodies is to shine, to have a certain glory about them. Earthly bodies, however, do not shine; they function; they articulate and coordinate in various ways. That is the glory of an earthly body.

Heavenly bodies move in limitless space, which we measure in light years; but earthly bodies are more limited. They must function within a very tightly compressed time-space sphere. Heavenly bodies control and influence other things. The sun affects this planet in every way. We are completely dependent upon it. The moon affects us also. It controls the tides and the seasons and much of our life in ways we hardly understand. The stars also affect the earth. So it is the nature of heavenly bodies to control and affect; and it is the nature of an earthly body to respond, to follow, to adapt. Thus Paul points out a very important distinction which nature would teach us if we had the eyes to observe.

The third thing he says is that there is a difference in the glory of celestial bodies. There is one glory of the sun and another glory of the moon and another glory of the stars, "for star differs from star in glory." How obviously true that is! Solar power is by far the greatest power known to man, and though we have only touched a fraction of its use, all energy in life basically comes from the sun. There is a different glory of the moon, but it has a profound effect, even upon lovers. Out together on a moonlit night they will do things they would not have done otherwise. Then the stars differ in glory. Some shine brilliantly, while others are very faint and dim. Paul is saying that all this has its parallel in the resurrection. If we could only read the lessons of nature we would have a panorama of theological truth about the resurrection spread before us. Open your eyes and look, Paul suggests.

So is it with the resurrection of the dead . . .

Then he goes on to draw the parallel for us:

What is sown is perishable, what is raised is imperishable (v. 42).

What is there about me that is perishable? Well, it is my body. My body is losing its ability to function. It is perishing; it is decaying; it is gradually slowing down. Just as the seed buried in the ground becomes a beautiful plant, so an earthly body put into the ground in death, or scattered across the oceans, will become a body designed for the heavens, an imperishable body, no longer subject to decay. That is what Paul is teaching us here.

It is sown in weakness (dishonor), it is raised in power . . . (v. 43).

What is it about you and me that is dishonorable? Well, it is the body, isn't it? Let me tell you a secret about mine: it sags; it groans; it even smells. When it dies it will become foul, loathsome. When put into the ground or in any other way disposed of, the body ends its existence in dishonor. But it will be raised, Paul says, in power. It will be clean, sweet, fragrant, eternally fresh, and able to function in a marvelous way.

It is sown a physical ("soulish") body, it is raised a spiritual body (v. 44).

It is amazing how we boast about our strength as human beings, yet a tiny, nearly invisible microbe can carry us away and end it all. A gnat so small you can hardly see it can choke you to death. Human life is really very fragile and easily ended. The body you are living in now, Paul says, is suited to the soul; it is animated by the soul, kept warm and functioning by the soul.

The "soulish body" is designed to function by the control of the soul—the mind, the emotions, the will. I like to think of the body as a kind of "earth suit" designed for time, a "time suit" that I live in. It is not me. I live in it. But this "earth suit" is designed only for this life. It is not designed for anything else. It works fairly well in this life, but something could happen to this "earth suit" while I am talking or walking around. I could fall over and somebody would come along and say, "He's dead!" But it would not be so. I would not be dead. The "earth suit" would have died, but I would be as much alive as I have ever been, and already enjoying the new body, the "heaven suit," the "eternity suit." Paul's argument is, there is a body designed for the heavens, as well as one for the earth. What the apostle is saying throughout this whole chapter is that there is a definite link between the two.

You see this wonderfully illustrated in the resurrected body of Jesus. He rose from the dead, and yet upon his body were still the marks of crucifixion by which his apostles could be absolutely sure that it was the same Jesus, in the same body. Yet what a difference! His body had been glorified, transformed. It was functioning on a different dimension and level of existence. It was able to pass through doors, able to appear and disappear from the earthly scene and function also in an "eternity suit," a "heaven suit" that God had provided for him. What a marvelous truth this is!

Only Two Men

We come now to the great statement of certainty which closes the chapter, beginning in the middle of verse 44.

> If there is a physical [soulish] body [designed to be operated by the soul], there is also a spiritual body [designed to be operated by the spirit].

That is Paul's summary of the truth he has just presented. Now he goes on to prove it:

> Thus it is written, "The first man Adam became a living being"; the last Adam became a life-giving spirit. But it is not the spiritual which is first but the physical, and then the spiritual. The first man was from the earth, a man of dust; the second man is from heaven. As was the man of dust, so are those who are of the dust; and as is the man of heaven, so are those who are of heaven. Just as we have borne the image of the man of dust, we shall also bear the image of the man of heaven (vv. 45–49).

How certain that is! Paul suggests there are really only two men who have ever lived in all of history. Both of them he calls "Adam." There is the first Adam and the last Adam. Do not call Jesus "the second Adam" because that would allow for a third and fourth and a fifth. There are only two—the first Adam, and the last Adam, Jesus. The only other human being beside Adam to head up a race is Jesus.

The first Adam, Paul says, was made a living soul. He had a body made from dust, and into that body of dust God himself, a Spirit, breathed a breath, and the joining together of spirit and body produced another phenomenon called the "soul," the personality. It is the presence of a spirit in a body that creates the soul and allows a person to function as a human being with mind, emotion, and will. That is what the first Adam was. But in the fall, the Holy Spirit which dwelt in the human spirit of Adam was withdrawn, and the human spirit became as though it was lifeless and dead. Man was no longer governed by his spirit but was governed by his soul, now the highest part of his being, which can feel and touch and taste and reason, but it has no contact with anything beyond and above. Because the human spirit is "dead in trespasses and sins," the body is directed only by the soul. It is a soulish body. We were all born that way. Every human being is a son or daughter of the first Adam, by nature.

But then there came a last Adam, Jesus, "a life-giving spirit." As a spirit he indwells our human spirits when we receive him and open up our life to him. He regenerates our human spirit, and from that vantage point within us, he is beginning to impart life to the soul again; to recapture the mind, the emotions and the will and to bring them back under subjection to his lordship. So we begin to experience, right now, the joy of being once again in right relationship with the God who made us. He is a life-giving spirit. He is waiting to impart life to the "earth suit" as well, and to make it into a "heaven suit," designed for the heavens. That will be the resurrection of the body.

The order is determined by God:

> . . . it is not the spiritual which is first.

The Mormon church teaches that we were once spirit beings who then came to earth and became men, but this verse flatly contradicts that. It is not the spiritual which is first, it is the physical. We came into existence on a physical level, but beyond that is the spiritual. That is next in order, and death is but a step in that process, and necessary to it. So now we are in a state of transition, as Paul goes on to describe,

> The first man was from the earth, a man of dust [and by natural birth we share that nature from Adam] the second man is from heaven. As was the man of dust, so are those who are of the dust; and as *is* [notice the change of tense] the man of heaven, so are those who are of heaven.

Let me ask you a question: Are you "of heaven"? Having been born into this race, part of Adam's race, have you, by faith, become also a part of the kingdom of God? Have you opened your heart to him? Have you received the Lord Jesus Christ into your human spirit so that you have the hope expressed here of becoming body, soul, and spirit, a man or woman as God intended man and woman to be? That is the great question of all time. Are you one of those who are "of heaven"? For the promise is,

> Just as we have borne the image of the man of dust [we look and act and talk and think like Adam], we shall also bear the image of the man of heaven.

I love the way the apostle John puts that. He says,

> . . . it does not yet appear what we shall be [the sons of God do not look any different than anybody else]. But we know that when he appears, we shall be like him, for we shall see him as he is (1 John 3:2).

What a hope! What a difference that makes to everything in life! It transforms the way you act and the way you think. It transforms your dreams, your aspirations, and what you do with your time. Everything is changed if you are a man of heaven as well as a man of the dust.

Nothing of Value

A young man once called me and introduced himself on the phone as a young Christian and a businessman. He said he was sure that in the next few years he would probably be making about fifty million dollars, and his question was, "How can I use my money to lay up treasures in heaven and not treasures on earth?" I told him, "You do not need money for that. In fact, the biggest obstacle you will have to laying up treasures in heaven may be your money. It all depends on how you use it." Then I quoted to him the words of Jesus in Luke 16, ". . . that which is highly esteemed among men is abomination in the sight of God." Now if you are going to take that verse seriously—and remember it comes from the lips of Jesus himself— you will see that it agrees exactly with what Paul is saying in this last section of chapter 15, verse 50:

> I tell you this, brethren: flesh and blood cannot inherit the kingdom of God, nor does the perishable inherit the imperishable.

That may sound like theological doubletalk, but what it is saying is, "There is no way to achieve enduring value in God's eyes by utilizing your natural human resources." That is what "flesh and blood" means. That sounds strange, does it not? What Paul says, in effect, is, "Nothing that wins the approval or the applause of men has any value at all in the sight of God." That includes Hollywood Oscars, athletic trophies, academic degrees, Nobel prizes, or achievements of a lifetime of labor. None of these can ever impress God in the least degree. That is frightening! Flesh and blood cannot do anything of value in the kingdom of God. It cannot lay hold of it; it cannot achieve anything within it. This is what startled Nicodemus when he came to Jesus. He was a respected and highly successful leader in Israel, or so, he thought. But Jesus said to him, "You must start all over again. You must be born again." That is also what Paul is saying here. By nature (flesh and blood) you cannot inherit the kingdom of God. There must be a change from the perishable to the imperishable.

What is the answer then? How can our life become worthwhile in God's sight? How can we achieve in this life something that will enable us to survive beyond this life? Paul's answer is:

> Lo! I tell you a mystery.

That is his response. We have already come to understand that the word *mystery*, when used like this in Scripture, does not refer to something mysterious or hard to understand. What it refers to is a truth that our human senses can never discover, that no scientific investigation will ever reveal, or that no amount of research on the part of human beings will ever unravel.

Here is the mystery:

> We shall not all sleep, but we shall all be changed, in a moment, in the twinkling of an eye, at the last trumpet. For the trumpet will sound, and the dead will be raised imperishable, and we shall be changed. For this perishable nature must put on the imperishable, and this mortal nature must put on immortality (vv. 51–53).

This gathers up the apostle's argument that the change we anticipate as believers is a direct result of the resurrection of Jesus from the dead. It is in connection with "the last trump" and will be "in the twinkling of an eye."

Unable to Die

The mystery is not that "we shall not all sleep," although that is true. There is a generation of Christians that will never die. Scripture declares this. There are some who will not have to pass through the portals of death, but will instantly, while they are walking about, suddenly, without warning, be changed—"in a moment, in the twinkling of an eye." That phrase refers to the twinkle of light that occurs when you blink. It is one of the fastest speeds known to human observation, and that is how fast the change will take place.

There are others who will die. Every generation of Christians before us has died, but that too is not the important thing. Whether you live or die, Paul says, the mystery is, *"we shall all be changed."* It will be a most remarkable change. As we have already seen, it means that our bodies will take on opposite characteristics to what they now have. "This perishable must put on the imperishable." This mortal (subject to death), must become no longer so; it must become imperishable, immortal, unable to die. That is the change.

When will this be? Paul's answer is, "at the last trump." The next question, of course, is "When is the last trump?" That is what everybody wants to know. The answer of Scripture is, "at the return of Jesus." That is the great event that is coming. All this we have discussed earlier.

What the apostle is seeking to stress now is that it is a certain change. It must occur. Notice how he puts it: "This perishable nature *must* put on the imperishable, and this mortal nature *must* put on immortality." Why? Why must it? The answer is in the next verses:

When the perishable puts on the imperishable, and the mortal puts on immortality, then shall come to pass the saying that is written:

"Death is swallowed up in victory."
"O death, where is thy victory?
O death, where is thy sting?" (vv. 54, 55).

I prefer the King James rendering here, based on the Textus Receptus, which declares Paul's triumphant shout is:

O, death, where is thy sting?
O grave, [or, literally, Hades] where is thy victory?

Standing beside the grave of a Christian, I have often felt like shouting those words. There was sorrow as loved ones bade good-by to someone they had loved, nevertheless I have often sensed an electric excitement in the air and seen a radiant hope pervading a whole group. Their hearts and mine were saying, "O death, where is your sting? O Hades, where is your victory?" I have been at funeral services where the whole congregation stood and, led by a thundering organ, sang the "Hallelujah Chorus." I thought it an appropriate expression of what people were feeling at that moment.

Paul declares that this change must occur *because it is the outworking of a change that has already occurred* in the hearts of those who have faith in Jesus. There is something that has already happened, he says, and that guarantees the change he describes. What is that? He tells us, "Death is swallowed up in victory." The fear of death is gone. Every one of us in our natural life fears death. What makes us afraid of death? Paul analyzes it:

The sting of death is sin . . .

We are afraid of death because it is an unknown, over which we have no control. We cannot evade it; it is beyond us. We are in the grip of superior forces and what makes us afraid is that we are being plunged into accountability! Beyond death lies a settling for our sins, an answering for what we have done and how we have lived. That is why death is such a fearsome thing. Furthermore,

. . . the power of sin is the law.

Sin is made all the more frightening by the law which says we cannot escape the evil of our past. God cannot set it aside, nor can any man. It must be faced. There can be no deliverance from it. That is what makes us afraid of death.

But the good news, coming to us from the resurrection of Jesus, is that this power of sin is broken. We are no longer helpless against it; we are no longer unable to change. Many today are troubled by an unending struggle to be different, but they cannot find the way. I read a letter from a girl who had written to Ann Landers because she was trying to stop smoking and nothing she did could break that habit. She started lying to her husband and to others around because she could not find a way to break it. But breaking the smoking habit is a lot easier than breaking many other habits that afflict us—such as a vicious temper, or a lustful mind which turns everything into sexual fantasies, or a bitter spirit which views the actions of others in a suspicious light. How does one get free from those terrible feelings, especially the guilt that comes because of them? How can one escape from the sense of having hurt many people and yet there is nothing one can do about it, though some day it will have to be accounted for? The good news is that there is a way. Sin's power has been broken. We have been delivered from the guilt of sin by the death of Jesus, and we are freed from its power by his resurrected life within us. Even when we fail there is a way of relief so that the failure can be cleansed and no longer needs to haunt us.

No Distant Savior

That way of victory is declared in verse 57. This is really the heart of the mystery:

> But thanks be to God, who gives us the victory through our Lord Jesus Christ.

Notice that it is put in the present tense. It is not past—"Who *gave* us the victory." It is "thanks be to God who *keeps on giving* us the victory, through our Lord Jesus Christ." I do not know anything that means more to me as a Christian than the fact that every day I can lay hold afresh of the grace of Jesus Christ. He is alive, and I meet with him every day. When I find myself faltering and sinning, I come and receive from him the cleansing that he has won for me on Calvary. My sins are washed away afresh. I find a new power to say "no" to evil, and to stand firm in the afflictions and pressures of life. I know that evil is put away; it will never come back to haunt me; I will not have to face it at the judgment seat of God. I can turn instead to make up to others in as many ways as I can for the hurt I have done, and to help still others find the way of release and deliverance from heartbreak and sorrow which I myself have found. So I cry with Paul, "Thanks be to God who is giving us the victory through our Lord Jesus Christ."

He concludes with the thought of passing it on to others.

> Therefore, my beloved brethren, be steadfast, immovable, always abounding in the work of the Lord. . . .

What God weighs is how we are behaving toward others. How much do we show a loving spirit, a gracious, forgiving attitude, a willingness to return good for evil, an ability to speak a word of release to those who are prisoners of their own habits, to set free those who are oppressed by wrong, hateful attitudes, to bind up the brokenhearted and to open the eyes of the blind? That is the work of the Lord. That is why God gives us contact with others.

> Therefore, my beloved brethren, be steadfast [faithful], immovable [do not let the world's philosophy change you], always abounding in the work of the Lord, knowing that in the Lord [do it unto him, faithful at your task, radiant in your witness], your labor is not in vain.

There is coming a day when we shall all be changed. On that day what God has been working out in secret among us will become radiantly visible to all. Paul calls it "the day of the manifestation of the sons of God." Then we shall know as we are known. Then we shall learn, if not before, that our labor was not in vain.

24

Giving and Living

In the last chapter of 1 Corinthians, Paul deals with "the practicalities," practical principles to guide us in doing certain things. There are three practical matters in this chapter—how to give, how to plan and schedule, and how to work with others.

It is rather striking that after the great and lofty themes of the resurrection, where one can almost hear the sound of the "last trump" ringing in one's ears, suddenly Paul says, "And now concerning the collection." But money is not to be separated from the great spiritual entities of Christianity. It is very important how a Christian gives. This whole chapter grows out of 1 Corinthians 15:58, in which Paul exhorts us to be "always abounding in the work of the Lord." Giving is one way you can abound in the work of the Lord. The apostle begins with that:

> Now concerning the contribution for the saints: as I directed the churches of Galatia, so you also are to do. On the first day of every week, each of you is to put something aside and store it up, as he may prosper, so that contributions need not be made when I come. And when I arrive, I will send those whom you accredit by letter to carry your gift to Jerusalem. If it seems advisable that I should go also, they will accompany me (vv. 1–4).

He is speaking, of course, of the collection that was being made in many churches to send to the impoverished, discouraged, and afflicted church in Jerusalem. This was a theme close to Paul's heart. He mentions it in several of his letters. He is anxious that these Gentile churches, scattered in the Roman world, should have a part in meeting the needs of the afflicted saints in Jerusalem. As you read the Book of Acts you can see two reasons why this church in Jerusalem was having trouble. One of them was circumstantial and the other was consequential; that is, one they were not to blame for, and the other they were. The one they were not to blame for was a series of famines that had occurred. Crops had not grown adequately, and with a limited system of distribution, they were without food. This they could not help though it was very distressing.

But then there was another reason why the church was suffering, and that was their own failure to obey what the Lord had said. Before his ascension Jesus had said to this church, "Begin in Jerusalem and then go to all Judea and Samaria and then reach out to the uttermost part of the earth." Reading the record of Acts, we can see that they totally ignored those words. They were having a great time in Jerusalem. All the apostles were there, teaching them; they had all the gifts of the Spirit active in their midst; they were experiencing miracles and wonders and signs, and tremendous numbers of people were being converted at a time. No one wanted to leave. They were enjoying their privileges and clinging to them. So the Lord, in his wisdom, allowed a time of persecution. Acts tells us that at the time of the death of Stephen a great persecution against the church broke out which forced many of them to leave. In the process they lost their resources. The wealthy people were either driven away or they lost their wealth. So the church was reduced to poverty, and it became necessary for the Gentile churches, who had profited from them spiritually to minister to their material needs. Such sharing constitutes a beautiful picture of the way the church is one over all the earth. What happens to our brothers and sisters in other corners of the world is, and ought to be, of immediate concern to us as well. So Paul exhorts these churches in Corinth and other places to meet that need.

Giving is no Option

As he does this, he also gives us some wonderful principles to govern our giving. You may seldom hear a message on this, but the Word of God touches even this area of our life and gives us practical guidelines on how to give. There are seven marvelous principles in this brief paragraph.

First, you will note, giving is to be a universal practice. Paul says to the Corinthians,

> . . . as I directed the churches of Galatia, so you also are to do.

It was not something that only the Corinthians were to do. Everywhere Paul went, wherever he founded a church he taught them to give, because giving is an essential part of Christianity. It is not an option; it is something every Christian must do. Remember the words of Jesus, "freely you have received, freely give." If you have not received anything from the Lord, by all means do not give anything. But if God has blessed your life, remember that you could not have bought that for any amount of money. You have received a gift of enrichment, of forgiveness, of healing for your home or your marriage. It is given without charge to you. "Freely you have received, freely give." A young man was telling me that he was working with some new Christians. He wanted to set up financial subsidies for them so they would have certain bills paid while they were growing as Christians. His heart was right but I told him if he did that he would ruin them. The apostles never did anything like that. They taught people to give when they had hardly anything, because giving is essential for a Christian. Giving is the very essence and breath of Christianity.

The second principle Paul declares is that giving is to be done every week:

> On the first day of every week. . . .

This is one of the first indications we have in the Epistles that the Christians had begun to gather regularly to worship, pray and give on Sunday, the first day of the week. The Jewish day of worship was Saturday. (Actually it began on Friday evening.) But now these Christians had forsaken that and had begun to worship on Sunday, the day of resurrection. It is no accident that this paragraph follows the great themes of resurrection in chapter 15, for the essence of the new life in Christ is that it is a new beginning, it is life lived on a different level entirely. The Christians worshiped on that day because it was the day on which Jesus rose from the dead. So the apostle gathers up this whole matter of giving and associates it with their wonder at the resurrection of Jesus and their worship of a risen Lord. That, he suggests, is the atmosphere in which you are to give—on the first day of the week.

Then, third, giving is to be a personal act.

> . . . each [one] of you. . . .

He does not leave anyone out. Even children should be taught to give. It may be only a few pennies, a nickel or a dime, but on every Sunday there ought to be a gift from every Christian. It is not the amount that is important, it is the regularity of it, the fact that there is to be a continual reminder that you have freely received, and therefore, freely give. Each one is to do this; it is a necessity growing out of our relationship to Christ.

Fourth, Paul says, the amount of giving is to be determined beforehand.

> . . . each of you is to put something aside and store it up.

This comes out of a culture where people were paid every day. They were to go home and each day put aside (in the sugar bowl), a certain amount of money so that on Sunday they would have a larger amount to bring to the services and contribute to the needs of others. The principle is that they had determined a specific amount. They were not merely giving; they had determined to what degree they would have part in a specific need, and they were giving regularly to meet that need.

The Motive of the Heart

Then a fifth principle is revealed in the words,

> . . . as he may prosper.

That means they were to give according to the degree God had given to them. Had he poured out abundantly? Then they were to give abundantly. Are you having a hard time and barely making it? Well, then your gift may be reduced proportionately. It ought to be something, but if necessary it can be very little because God is not interested in the total amount at all. He is only interested in the motive of the heart in giving. That is why Jesus said of the widow who threw in two tiny pieces of money, "she has given more than all they who have cast into the treasury." The proportion is to be based on your awareness of how much God has given to you and how much your heart has been stirred by the gifts and grace of God.

That proportionate gift is not the tithe. "Tithe" means 10 percent, and in the Old Testament the Israelites were commanded to give a tithe. It did not make any difference whether they were poor or rich.

A tithe of 10 percent to a poor person might be very difficult to give, while 10 percent to a rich person would never be missed. In Christian circles there has been perpetuated the idea that God wants 10 percent and you can do what you like with the rest; you can indulge yourself to the full. That, of course, is entirely contrary to the principle of New Testament giving. If God has richly blessed you, then you are to increase *the percentage* of your giving so that it is 10, 20, 30, 40, or even 90 percent. There are Christians I know today whom God has richly blessed who give 90 percent of their income away. They live on the remaining 10 percent and live abundantly on that. Nowhere in the New Testament do you find tithing taught or laid upon Christians. But proportionate giving is, for God does not give us wealth in order that we may lavish it upon ourselves but that we might share it more abundantly with those who have pressing needs. If this simple principle were thoroughly grasped, all the needs of Christendom would be met by those who give as God has prospered them.

The sixth principle is very important. Paul says do this,

> so that contributions need not be made when I come.

Why would he say that? Because the apostle knew that when he was personally present he had a tremendous impact on people. He did not want their giving to be because they were moved by his preaching, or by his stories of what God had done, or in any other way to be pressured. No professional fund raisers would have been permitted in the early churches. Paul says, in effect, "Do not bring out the thermometer; do not put on a three-ring circus, with people running down the aisle bringing pledges to meet a predetermined goal. I do not want that." Your giving is to come out of a heart that has been moved by the grace of God. God does not want giving on any terms other than those. Giving must be without special pressure.

The seventh principle, that giving is to be responsibly administered, is set forth in verses 3 and 4:

> And when I arrive, I will send those whom you accredit by letter to carry our gift to Jerusalem.

Another rendering of that is a little better:

> I will accredit by letter those whom you choose to bear your gift to Jerusalem.

It is Paul who is going to write the letter. He knows the leaders in Jerusalem and he will write a letter assuring them that the ones who bring this money are trustworthy, responsible men. He will be glad to do that so that these men can be welcomed; or,

If it seems advisable that I should go also, they will accompany me.

All he is emphasizing here is that giving should be carried out responsibly and there should be a provision made to see that it gets to its recipients in the right way. He is very careful, as we see in other letters, that he does not have this responsibility alone.

Here again are the principles of New Testament giving.

a universal practice
a weekly activity
a personal act
a predetermined objective
a proportionate amount
an unpressured response
a responsible delivery.

If Christian congregations would act on these principles today, great work could be accomplished, and the gospel itself would be honored.

Gloriously Indefinite

In the next section we have a beautiful picture of how the apostle himself operated. Out of it comes great help to us in learning how to plan and schedule our activities. Do you have a problem with that? One of my biggest problems is to know what to commit myself to in the future. This is not a problem only for pastors or speakers, it is a problem for every Christian. What do you commit yourself to? How do you make arrangements? Here are some wonderful principles:

I will visit you after passing through Macedonia, for I intend to pass through Macedonia, and perhaps I will stay with you or even spend the winter, so that you may speed me on my journey, wherever I go. For I do not want to see you now just in passing; I hope to spend some time with you, if the Lord permits. But I will stay in Ephesus until Pentecost, for a wide door for effective work has opened to me, and there are many adversaries (vv. 5–9).

How gloriously indefinite that is! How unsettled the apostle is in this! This paragraph should make certain advocates of church planning tear their hair out. Hardly a month goes by that I am not asked, "What are your ten-year plans for Peninsula Bible Church?" I reply, "I haven't the slightest idea. We are committed, year after year, to follow the principles God has taught us from the Word and we plan

to keep on doing that until the Lord returns. That is our program
for the future." I believe this was also the apostle's program. He did
not know where he would go next. He tells us he had a strong desire
to go to Rome, but he had tried to go for years and had not been
able to make it. His plan was constantly changing. Thus he indicates
there must be flexibility about planning.

Notice that certain factors emerge from this concerning Paul. First,
his immediate goals are short-range ones:

> I intend to pass through Macedonia . . . I will stay with you.

If we note the length of time involved here it is probably something
less than a year that he has planned ahead. The apostle James suggests
that we should not try to plan more than a year ahead. It is all right
to think of where you ought to be, and go, and what you ought to
do, but limit it to a short-range goal that is possible to accomplish.
Do not try to project interminably into the future and make definite
plans about where you will be five or ten years from now. How do
you know where you will be? Dr. A. W Tozer says to "beware the
file-card mentality" that wants to put everything on a three-by-five
card—where you are going to be, what you are going to do, and how
you are going to function. It removes us from the surprises and innova-
tions of the Spirit of God who may lead us in unexpected ways, as
you see demonstrated all the way through the Book of Acts.

The second factor is that Paul has flexible commitments. Notice
verse 6:

> Perhaps I will stay with you . . . [and v. 7] I hope to spend some time
> with you.

These are terms that express desire, but they do not set anything in
concrete. I know many get uncomfortable with this, but there is a
good reason for it, and the apostle tells us what it is. It is contained
in these words, "if the Lord permits." Paul never forgot that he was
a servant of Christ, that he worked for a Master, and though he was
free to plan he never forgot that the Lord was also free to overrule
his plans any time he chose. Paul always allowed for that possibility.

It used to be customary among Christians to say, "The Lord willing,
I'll do this. The Lord willing, I'll do that." I know it can be run
into the ground, but I think it would be good to return to that. The
Lord may interject illnesses, accidents, a change of plans, a sudden
catastrophe, or a sudden demand upon you. You must be ready to
acknowledge that you are under authority. The apostle is not a robot,

being told to go here and go there. He is an agent, free to make plans, and he does so; but he also recognizes that God has the right to check the square that says "none of the above" and send him in a different direction.

Then there is a third factor, brought out in the latter part of verse 6. Paul says he wants to come to Corinth,

> . . . so that you may speed me on my journey wherever I go.

He believes that God will not give him all he needs before he starts out, but that he will make provision for him as he goes along. This is an important principle to remember in undertaking various projects. If we are really convinced that there is a need to do something and God has promised to supply our needs, then we do not need to have everything in hand before we start. We venture on the power and the provision of God. (If it is merely a matter of personal wants, there is no promise for those.) Many feel that they must somehow get a total amount of funds together before they undertake anything, which makes me suspicious as to whether they should be undertaking it or not! It may be simply a want and not a need. But if there is a sense, with others in strong agreement, that this is a need, then God has promised to supply it and he will make provisions as you go.

A fourth factor emerges in verse 8,

> . . . but I will stay in Ephesus [where he is writing this letter] until Pentecost.

We do not know how far in the future that would be, but there is a reason why he chose Pentecost. As you read the secular literature of that day, you discover that Pentecost (which comes fifty days after the Passover) is the time when shipping resumed in the Aegean Sea. During the winter months it was impossible for the frail little boats of that day to survive the great storms that would sweep through the Mediterranean, but by Pentecost the weather would calm and shipping would resume. Paul is simply taking this into account, and he is basing his plans on that fact. Thus he plans in line with the normal circumstances of life.

A True Opportunity

The last factor is set forth in verse 9,

> . . . for a wide door for effective work has opened to me, and there are many adversaries.

There are two reasons why he is going to stay in Ephesus. (He could have traveled by land even though the sea lanes were closed.) One, there is a "wide door for effective service open." You have only to read Acts 19 to learn what that wide door was. There we are told that Paul had been driven out of the synagogue and had to rent a hall to teach in. For six days of the week, one manuscript tells us, five hours every day, the apostle gathered people in that hall and taught them the Word of God. The effect of that phenomenal teaching was that the gospel literally exploded throughout the Roman province of Asia. Churches like Colossae, Laodicea, Sardis and Pergamum (and others mentioned in the seven letters in Revelation) were planted throughout the Lycus valley. All this because the apostle was teaching revolutionary truth that turned people on and sent them out with such a spirit of enthusiasm that they could not contain it. Churches were being started all over the place. Paul said, "I'm not going to miss this opportunity. But there are many adversaries." The nineteenth chapter of Acts also tells us what they are.

Ephesus was the second city of the Roman world. Just outside of it was the Temple of Diana, a pagan temple where idols were worshiped in disgusting and degrading sexual ways. The Christian church stood against the traffic of that temple, and yet the temple was the heartbeat of the city; it was the banking place for the merchants, and everything of note in the city occurred within it. In Ephesus also were Jewish synagogues which bitterly opposed what Paul was doing. They hated him and hounded him everywhere. Further, Ephesus was given over to superstition, magic, and occult practices. Then there was the overall authority of Rome, with its studied indifference to spiritual things. Against these many adversaries a tiny church stood, absolutely contrary to everything within the city, and yet equipped with such power that it was overturning the economic system of the city. The silversmiths were getting upset because their idol-making business was being destroyed. It was indeed an open door with many adversaries.

Paul is suggesting here that both of these factors will be present if you have a true opportunity. There will be a "wide door," but there will also be "many adversaries." Beware the wide door where there are no adversaries! That could be a trick of the devil to uplift you in pride and make you so confident in yourself that you are thereby destroyed. Beware also heavy opposition and many adversaries when there is no open door for ministry. Jesus himself told his disciples, "If they will not hear you, shake off the dust from your feet and go to the next city." Where there is no opportunity for ministry and oppression is heavy, avoid it; but where there is an open door and many adversaries, then by all means stay, because you will have one of the most exciting adventures of your life, seeing God at work in the midst of great opposition and great pressure. These are the principles for scheduling life. I hope they will help you as you plan in the days ahead.

Lions and Lambs

In the next section Paul tells how to treat fellow workers. Many years ago I preached a message at Peninsula Bible Church concerning the form of church government from Isaiah 11. There the prophet predicts that a time will come when the lion shall lie down with the lamb, the cow and the bear shall feed together, and a little child shall lead them. I suggested that was a wonderful description of our Board of Elders meeting together. We have one man who is like a lion—bold, resolute, and very commanding. Another is like a leopard—quiet, but deadly. We have one who is like a bear—very affectionate (he gives you a big hug), but he can also be surly and growly at times. And here I am—an innocent, helpless lamb in the midst of these wild animals! But when we meet together a miracle occurs under the leadership of our invisible Head. The lion lies down with the lamb, and we are brought into unanimity of viewpoint. God has led us, for more than thirty years, to follow a principle of acting only in complete agreement, when strong-minded men are brought by the Lord into unanimity of decision.

Thus also the great apostle directs the Corinthians to treat different types of people in different ways. First, he discusses the quiet, unassuming kind of person, represented here by Timothy:

> When Timothy comes, see that you put him at ease among you, for he is doing the work of the Lord, as I am. So let no one despise him. Speed him on his way in peace, that he may return to me; for I am expecting him with the brethren (vv. 10, 11).

Perhaps no other companion of Paul's is quite as well known to us as Timothy. Two of the letters of the New Testament are written to him. He was but a young boy, probably in his late teens, when he joined the apostle in Timothy's home city of Lystra. On that occasion Paul was stoned and left to die on the rubbish heap of the city, but God graciously intervened and restored him, and he resumed his ministry. This must have made a great impression on Timothy. He later joined Paul and traveled with him as his beloved and faithful son in the faith. Most commentators believe that Timothy was a timid young man, afraid to get involved, for Paul exhorts him frequently to be more aggressive. But perhaps it was not timidity so much as a quiet and unassuming temperament which did not enjoy the role of a leader.

Whenever I think of Timothy, I think of Os Guinness, that remarkable young Englishman who has a marvelous ability to analyze what is happening in our world. Os and I were sitting together on one occasion, talking about certain people who had inquired about his age. He said, "I guess I was cursed with a baby face. Everyone thinks I'm younger than I am." Because of that he is not always listened to quite as attentively as he might otherwise be. That was probably Timothy's problem. He was not a weak young man, but he was quiet, and not pushy. So Paul writes to the Corinthians. "When Timothy comes, put him at ease among you." That is, reassure him, make him welcome. Special effort needs to be made to encourage the quiet ones.

Then Paul says, "Value his work, for he is doing the work of the Lord, as I am." The work of the Lord is always redemptive. It is to break down illusions and to restore reality. It is a freeing work, bringing men and women out of bondage to evil habits, bad attitudes and wrongful practices, and setting them free. It is the work of bringing beauty from ashes, and giving the oil of joy for mourning. That is always the work of the Lord, and Timothy was an effective instrument in that. Therefore, Paul says, when you see someone with that ability, receive him and encourage him, young as he may be. Value him for his work's sake.

Paul's third point is, "Do not despise him." People despising someone of Timothy's character would probably do so because of his youth. Paul wrote to Timothy himself and said, "Let no man despise your youth." That reflects something of the culture of the day. In the twentieth century we glorify youth and hold it up as the greatest time of life. But in most cultures in the world today, and certainly in the ancient world, it was old age that was reverenced and respected. People understood that older people have had an experience of life that youth has not had.

Then, fourth, Paul suggests that they support Timothy financially; "Speed him on his way." That is, do not send him away penniless when he leaves; give him something to go on, help him out. This is in line with the continual principle of Scripture that if anyone has ministered to you spiritually, you are to support and help him physically and materially. Timothy certainly deserved that. These people shared the benefits of his labor among them, therefore he ought to have the benefit of their help.

Then, finally, do not "hassle" him. I put it that way because Paul says, "Speed him on his way *in peace.*" There is a temptation to challenge and argue with a young man, especially a young man who has been associated with the apostle Paul himself. Some who would not have dared confront or argue with Paul would grab Timothy and take him to task for certain viewpoints. Paul is warning them against this natural tendency to be overbearing toward a young man. Treat that kind of temperament and personality with kindness, encouragement, and restraint.

Respect for Apollos

In verse 12 Paul moves to more mature leaders and how to handle them. Here the representative man is Apollos.

> As for our brother Apollos, I strongly urged him to visit you with the other brethren, but it was not at all his will [The Greek does not have "God's will," but "his will"] to come now. He will come when he has opportunity.

That is a more remarkable verse, especially in view of the attitude of many today that the apostles were generals in the army of the Lord, sending people out, ordering them here or there. This verse indicates that Paul does not command Apollos at all; he has no authority over him. Rather, he urges him. In several places in the New Testament we are reminded by the apostle that he was not "lord" over anyone else.

Lording it over the brethren is, in my judgment, one of the great curses of the church today. Some men assume, for instance, that the office of pastor gives them an authority over other people. Perhaps the redefining, from the Bible, of the issue of authority will be one of the most important issues the church will face in the next decade. Paul respects the personal freedom of Apollos to be directed of the Lord, even as he himself is. He does not tell Apollos what he must do, for Apollos had said it was not his will to come, and Paul accepts that. Apollos, too, was operating under the direct control of God. This is not only true of leaders, such as Paul and Apollos, it is true of all Christians. Perhaps the clearest word on this was spoken by the Lord himself when he said, "One is your Master, all you are brothers." The church must return to that sense of being brothers with one another, working together.

Christians everywhere are found under the authority of men who seem to be dictators—much like Diotrephes, whom John mentions in one of his letters, who "loved to have the pre-eminence among them." I am becoming much more bold in speaking along this line because of the widespread nature of this problem. I tell congregations at times that no pastor has the right to tell them what they can do with their spiritual gifts. No pastor has the right to say that you cannot have a meeting in your home, or teach the Word of God to whomever will come and listen. You should listen to him as a wise brother, perhaps, who understands the nature of truth and can give you helpful suggestions. But no pastor ever, anywhere, has the right to tell you that you cannot follow the leading of the Lord as to the ministry he has given you, unless your doctrine is faulty. Paul makes that clear in this passage.

Observe how he supports Apollos in this, "Apollos will come," he says, "when he has opportunity." Remember that Paul, Apollos and Peter were three men around whom factions were gathering in this church. Perhaps Paul wanted Apollos to go to Corinth because he thought it might improve that situation. But that may be the very reason why Apollos did not want to go. As he might have seen it, his visiting Corinth might even have aggravated the tendency of the Corinthians to cluster around an individual. At any rate he did not choose to go, and the apostle supports him.

In verses 13 and 14 we have a word of exhortation on how to treat *anyone* who comes into the body:

> Be watchful, stand firm in your faith, be courageous, be strong. Let all that you do be done in love.

Here are two general rules that should govern any relationship with others: Be careful, and be loving. There is a need for carefulness. Some of you have heard of John Todd, who went to many congregations and told them amazing things about when he had been a member of a witches' coven. He had been party, he said, to the inner circle of a group he called "the Illuminati," who were working out a plan to take over and control the world. He spoke so realistically that many people believed him. Many pastors supported him. No one challenged him until a few people began to get suspicious and investigated. They found that most of what he was saying was pure fabrication.

So be careful, Paul says. There are many philosophies around that sound good when you take them by themselves. Certain approaches to mental health, such as transactional analysis or transcendental meditation sound very good, but there is a catch to them. When you get into them you find yourself hooked into something that will move you gradually farther and farther away from the truth of Jesus Christ.

Then Paul says, "Be steadfast. Stand firm in your faith." In a visit with Os Guinness, I questioned him about Oxford University, where he was then studying. Oxford was for many years the home of C. S. Lewis, that unparalleled champion of Christian faith. Os told me that the atmosphere there is very anti-Christian. We had commented earlier on how England is drifting into paganism, and the church is very weak in its testimony. I asked him, "Why is it that men like C. S. Lewis and John Stott—these great champions of faith—have not awakened a band of young men, hundreds of them, who will follow their pattern and arouse a great testimony of faith in England today? Have these men failed?" "No," he said, "they have not. There are many young men who have followed them, but the problem is, when they are exposed to the withering contempt of modern secular scholarship in a university like Oxford, with its anti-Christian bias, they wilt, they compromise, they give in to it. As a result, the university remains in darkness." What a day to stand firm in our faith! Do not be misled by these secular ideas that seize the popular mind for the moment.

With steadfastness Paul links courage: "Be strong." Strength, in Scripture, is never seen to derive from building up your own abilities or your self-confidence. It is quite the opposite. It is to be aware of your utter weakness and to rely upon the greatness of God to work within you. In the Word of God, strength always comes out of weakness. The apostle's word to those in any time of stress and danger is, "Be strong *in the Lord* and in the strength of *his* might. Put on the whole armor of God, that you may be able to stand against the wiles of the devil." So be careful, be strong—but also be loving. He says, "Let all that you do be done in love."

Nothing hurts the Christian cause more than the discourteousness that is so frequently displayed. Some time ago I listened to a man teaching some great truth, but he did it with an arrogant attitude of contempt for those of whom he was speaking that everyone went away, turned off at what he was saying. What he was saying was right, but he could have helped his cause tremendously had he been courteous.

Addicted to Hospitality

Then Paul mentions the final group, these among us who serve:

Now, brethren, you know that the household of Stephanas were the first converts in Achaia [that is an ancient name for Greece], and they have devoted themselves to the service of the saints; I urge you to be subject

to such men and to every fellow worker and laborer. I rejoice at the coming
of Stephanas and Fortunatus and Achaicus, because they made up for your
absence; for they refreshed my spirit as well as yours. Give recognition to
such men (vv. 15–18).

The three men named here were the ones who brought the letter
from Corinth that Paul is partially answering in this letter we are
studying. They had given him a report of the conditions of the church
there, and, as he says, they had encouraged him and refreshed his
spirit. By implication, he suggests that that is what we are to do with
those who have helped us. Stephanas, Paul says, was the first convert
in Greece. That means he probably was a citizen of Athens, for it
was there that Paul first began to preach in Greece. He may have
been one who was converted by that remarkable message preached
in the Areopagus that is recorded in Acts 17. At any rate, he was
the very first convert, and Paul never forgot him.

Remember also, he suggests, the love of these men. Stephanas and
his household devoted themselves to the service of the saints. Stephanas
had a problem—he was an addict. That is literally the word here.
He "addicted himself" to the service of the saints. He did it so consistently and continuously that he as like an addict—he had become
hooked on hospitality. Now we are to remember such men and give
heed to them, Paul suggests; be subject to them. That does not mean
obey them. It means listen to them; they have something to say. Their
ministry of hospitality makes them people with ideas to which you
ought to listen.

And rejoice in them, as Paul himself did at the coming of these
men, because they refreshed his spirit. Do you know people like that?
When you are with them they pick you up, they make your day,
they refresh your spirit. Well, rejoice over that, praise God for it,
thank him for it. More than that, thank them! That is the last thing
Paul tells us—give recognition to such men. Just say a warm "thank
you" to people for the way they refresh your spirit by their ministry
of hospitality to others.

That brings us to the closing greetings of the letter:

The churches of Asia send greetings. Aquila and Prisca, together with the
church in their house, send you hearty greetings in the Lord. All the brethren
send greetings. Greet one another with a holy kiss.

First, the churches greet each other. There are two kinds of churches
suggested here. Paul himself was teaching in a rented hall, the hall
of Tyrannus. Can you imagine the crowd that must have jammed

into that hall to hear this mighty apostle? It was an urban church in the heart of Ephesus, and it sent greetings, together with all the spin-off churches that had come out of that remarkable ministry, throughout the province.

There is also mentioned a house church that sent greetings—the church that met in the home of Aquila and Priscilla. Paul met this remarkable couple, who appear in several of his letters, in Corinth. They had come from Rome and after this letter they return there, for in the letter to the Romans you find them there again with another church in their house.

Then individuals send greetings. Their way of doing this, Paul says, is to greet one another with a holy kiss. Unfortunately we have gotten away from that today. We just hug each other. That at least is getting close—I am glad to see hugs coming back. In Poland, where I have ministered, they still have kisses. When I was there not long ago I was a bit embarrassed by being kissed three times—they always end up on the cheek they started with—by old men like myself. This was what was going on in the early church and should again today, in some form at least, as a warm expression of affection.

Paul closes with his own personal greeting:

I, Paul, write this greeting with my own hand. If any one has no love for the Lord, let him be accursed. Our Lord, come! The grace of the Lord Jesus be with you. My love be with you all in Christ Jesus. Amen (vv. 21–24).

This handwritten greeting is Paul's way of authenticating his letter. From the letter to the Galatians we know that he had a habit of taking the pen from the secretary and adding, in his own handwriting, a greeting to the people to whom he wrote. Since, as many feel, Paul was almost blind, he wrote with large letters scrawled across the bottom of the manuscript words like, "I, Paul, write this greeting with my own hand." If you ever travel in the Middle East and run across some old, dusty manuscripts with some large letters at the bottom, call me collect from anywhere on earth! It would undoubtedly be the most valuable document in all history.

A Test of Reality

Finally he wrote this rather strange greeting at the close: "If anyone has no love for the Lord, let him be accursed." The word is *anathema*—

literally, "Let him be damned." That seems harsh to many, but there are certain things we must understand about it. First, it was not written to non-Christians. There were many millions who did not love the Lord Jesus, but Paul is not condemning them all to hell. He is writing to those who *profess* to be Christians. He is writing to those in a church where Jesus was preached and taught, and where every day many of them had at least the opportunity for fellowship with the Lord of glory. So what he says here is a kind of test of reality. He does not even use the word *agape* when he refers to love; he uses the lower word *phileo*, affection, friendship. If someone has no affection for the Lord Jesus, then what does he have affection for? If he does not love truth and love and mercy and grace and life itself, reflected in Jesus, then he must surely love the opposite. That is what Paul is warning against—that one who had been touched by the reality of the presence of Christ in the church, but has not learned to love him is only kidding himself about his Christian testimony. He is on his way to being damned.

Paul thus closes the letter with this remarkable tribute to the centrality of Christ in Christian faith. Christianity is not merely a series of philosophies or doctrines to be taught. It is a Person to know. If anyone, knowing him, has not developed an affection for him, something is seriously wrong in his life.

Then in a kind of a play on words he adds to the word *anathema* another word from another language, the Aramaic word *maranatha*. It is translated here, "Our Lord, come." Actually, it can be translated either, "Our Lord has come," or "is coming all the time," or "shall come." That is the way with Hebrew/Aramaic words; it is difficult to tell the tense that was intended. I think the word ought to be translated, "Our Lord is at hand, he is present." Anyone who does not know him will find that he is not very far away; he is at hand. If you do not know him, you can settle it very quickly, because he is available to man. Paul himself preached on Mars Hill that God is not very far from every one of us, if we will only search after him and find him. In the Lord Jesus, that finding is always made possible.

Paul ends with a salutation which states the greatest need of Christians:

The grace of the Lord Jesus Christ be with you.

And then Paul's own personal gift.

My love be with you all in Christ Jesus, Amen.

So the great letter ends. Did you notice how it follows the pattern of the gospel? Paul began with the cross: "I am determined not to know anything among you save Jesus Christ, and him crucified," because that alone will undercut the false and phony wisdom of man. Then it moved to the burial of Jesus, the putting away of the flesh, the carnalities, the empty things that destroy Christian life. That is the content of the body of this letter. Then it closes with a great note on the resurrection—with our eyes set upon the hope that is to come, and the glory of the transformation of the body at the return of Jesus. In the light of all that truth—the cross, the refusal of all that is contrary to Jesus, and the hope of the resurrection—let us read again Paul's great word at the end of chapter 15:

> Therefore, my beloved brethren, be steadfast, immovable, always abounding in the work of the Lord, knowing that in the Lord your labor is not in vain.

Lord, we thank you for your Word. How it has blessed our hearts, enlightened our minds, instructed us, awakened our emotions, moved our wills, and changed our whole lives. Such is the power and character of your Word. Help us to continue in it in the midst of the pressures of these days, and to stand fast in our faith. We ask in the name of our Lord Jesus, and by his daily grace, Amen.

I. INTRODUCTION, 1:1–9
  A. The Implied Problems, 1–2
  B. The Universal Basis for Confidence, 3
  C. The Fullness They Enjoyed, 4–8
  D. The Fellowship They Lacked, 9
II. THE CARNALITIES, 1:10–11:34
  A. Pride and Its Consequences, 1:10–4:21
    1. Divisions, 1:10–17
    2. Boastings, 1:18–2:16
    3. Jealousy and strife, 3:1–4:7
    4. Complacency, 4:8–21
  B. Lust and Its Problems, 5:1–6:20
    1. Shameful immorality, 5:1–13
    2. Inappropriate litigation, 6:1–11
    3. Unholy prostitution, 6:12–20
  C. Life and Its Dangers, 7:1–11:34
    1. About marriage, 7:1–24
    2. About singleness, 25–40
    3. About influence on others, 8:1–13
    4. About personal rights, 9:1–23
    5. About self-discipline, 9:24–10:13
    6. About idolatry, 10:14–11:1
    7. About traditions, 11:2–34
III. THE SPIRITUALITIES, 12:1–15:58
  A. The Goal of the Spirit, 12:1–3
    1. The identifying mark of error, 1–2
    2. The identifying mark of the Spirit, 3
  B. The Gifts of the Spirit, 12:4–31
    1. Related to the triune God, 4–6
    2. Related to the redeemed community, 7
    3. Distributed by the Spirit, 8–11
    4. The functioning of the gifts, 12–26
    5. The divine strategy, 27–31
  C. The Fruit of the Spirit, 13:1–13
    1. The preeminence of love, 1–3
    2. The practice of love, 4–7
    3. The persistence of love, 8–13
  D. The Relationship of Fruit and Gifts, 14:1–40
    1. Comparison of tongues and prophesying, 1–5
    2. The difficulty with tongues in church, 6–19